Financial Liberalization and the Asian Crisis

Also by Ha-Joon Chang

THE POLITICAL ECONOMY OF INDUSTRIAL POLICY

Also by Gabriel Palma

KALDOR'S CONTRIBUTION TO POLITICAL ECONOMY (*co-editor*)

CAPITAL CONTROVERSY, POST-KEYNESIAN ECONOMICS AND THE HISTORY OF ECONOMIC THOUGHT (*co-editor*)

MARKETS, UNEMPLOYMENT AND ECONOMIC POLICY: Essays in Honour of Geoff Harcourt (*co-editor*)

Also by D. Hugh Whittaker

MANAGING INNOVATION: A Study of British and Japanese Factories

SMALL FIRMS IN THE JAPANESE ECONOMY

Financial Liberalization and the Asian Crisis

Edited by

Ha-Joon Chang
Assistant Director of Development Studies
Faculty of Economics and Politics
University of Cambridge

Gabriel Palma
Lecturer in Economics
Faculty of Economics and Politics
University of Cambridge

and

D. Hugh Whittaker
Reader in Japanese and Comparative Economic Sociology
Assistant Director of ESRC Centre for Business Research
University of Cambridge

palgrave

First published 2001 by
PALGRAVE
Houndmills, Basingstoke, Hampshire RG21 6XS and
175 Fifth Avenue, New York, N. Y. 10010
Companies and representatives throughout the world

PALGRAVE is the new global academic imprint of St. Martin's Press LLC Scholarly and Reference Division and Palgrave Publishers Ltd (formerly Macmillan Press Ltd).

ISBN 0–333–92158–5

This book is printed on paper suitable for recycling and made from fully managed and sustained forest sources.

A catalogue record for this book is available from the British Library.

Library of Congress Cataloging-in-Publication Data
Financial liberalization and the Asian crisis / edited by Ha-Joon Chang, Gabriel Palma, and D. Hugh Whittaker.
p. cm.
Includes bibliographical references and index.
ISBN 0–333–92158–5
1. Financial crises—Asia. 2. Asia—Economic conditions–
–1945– I. Chang, Ha-Joon. II. Palma, J. Gabriel. III. Whittaker, D. H. (D. Hugh)

HB3808 .F56 2001
330.95'0429—dc21

2001021884

10 9 8 7 6 5 4 3 2 1
10 09 08 07 06 05 04 03 02 01

Printed and bound in Great Britain by
Antony Rowe Ltd, Chippenham, Wiltshire

To James Briffitt, in memoriam

Contents

List of Figures and Tables

Figures

Tables

List of Contributors

Chris Baker	Freelance researcher and writer, Bangkok
A. S. Bhalla	Sidney Sussex College, Cambridge
Ha-Joon Chang	Faculty of Economics and Politics, University of Cambridge
Ronald Dore	Centre for Economic Performance, London School of Economics and INSEAD, Fontainebleau
Dieter Ernst	East-West Center, Honolulu and Center for Innovation & Technology (TIK), University of Oslo
Chalmers Johnson	Japan Policy Research Institute, Cardiff CA
Jomo K. S.	Department of Applied Economics, University of Malaya, Kuala Lumpur
J. A. Kregel	University of Bologna
Yoshitaka Kurosawa	Nihon University, Japan
John A. Mathews	Macquarie Graduate School of Management, Sydney
D. M. Nachane	Department of Economics, University of Mumbai, India
Gabriel Palma	Faculty of Economics and Politics, University of Cambridge
Hong-Jae Park	School of Oriental and African Studies, University of London
Pasuk Phongpaichit	Faculty of Economics, Chulalongkorn University, Bangkok
Jonathan Pincus	School of Oriental and African Studies, University of London
Rizal Ramli	Coordinating Minister of the Economy, Government of Indonesia
Lance Taylor	New School for Social Research, New York
Robert Wade	London School of Economics
D. Hugh Whittaker	Faculty of Oriental Studies, University of Cambridge
Chul Gyue Yoo	Korea Long-term Credit Bank Economic Research Institute, Korea

1
Introduction

Ha-Joon Chang, Gabriel Palma and D. Hugh Whittaker

The floating of the Thai baht on 2 July 1997 marked the onset of the 'Asian Crisis', which had serious repercussions for the 'miracle' economies of East Asia, for developing countries in general, and for financial markets worldwide. The Crisis – and subsequent crises in Russia and Brazil – did not result in global financial meltdown, but did generate a heated debate on fundamental issues of economics, finance and policy-making in general.

In its early stages, the debate was dominated by simplistic – and reductionist – attempts to pin the Asian Crisis on issues such as 'cronyism', which we feared would foreclose rather than stimulate serious discussion, particularly on the role of market failures in this crisis. We were, we felt, witnessing a revival of Orientalism, in which all manner of fantasies and prejudices are projected onto Asia, with no real concern for their veracity. The above-mentioned 'cronyism', for example, was becoming a modern substitute for 'Oriental despotism' or 'Asiatic absolutism'. To challenge such ideas, we invited contributions from researchers with specialist knowledge either of the countries in question, or of issues critical for an understanding of the Crisis.

Most of these papers were originally published in a Special Issue of the *Cambridge Journal of Economics*.[1] Given the wide range of issues to be covered, we placed limitations on paper length. The objective was to produce focused arguments, some based on research still in progress, rather than exhaustive accounts. The original papers have not been significantly modified because we feel that subsequent events have generally vindicated the positions taken, and because they constitute an important contribution to debates which need re-emphasizing. Although all the crisis economies in Asia except Hong Kong and Indonesia were staging a healthy comeback by the summer of 1999, questions remain about the sustainability of the recovery, given continued instability in the world economy. Many of the papers address the causes of that instability.

Three new papers, on Thailand, China and India, and the electronics industry, have been added in order to fill the gaps in coverage that we knew existed in the Special Issue. We are thus able to present here a set of papers which together provide an overview, country-specific analyses, thematic analyses and theoretical elaboration. We shall not attempt to summarize them here, but shall instead spell out some of the underlying themes and main findings.

The most contentious issue is whether the Crisis resulted primarily from institutional and structural weaknesses of the Asian economies, such as 'cronyistic' political economic structures, non-transparent corporate governance or misguided government policies, or from market failures which are characteristic of (or endogenous to) under-regulated and over-liquid international financial markets. Almost all the chapters address this issue, and by and large they come down on the side of the latter type of explanation. This is particularly significant because it has major implications for policy prescriptions.

Wade (Chapter 5) suggests that the debate about causes is less a debate than a case of paradigms ('parrot-times') talking past each other, reflecting basic beliefs about rationality and markets. Those espousing the first view above tend to stress (at least short-term) rational calculations responding to market distortions and institutional weaknesses. Those espousing the second view stress market failures and under-regulation (rather than over-regulation). Not surprisingly, perhaps, in view of the comments above about Orientalism, the rational actors are predictably international investors, and their rational behaviour is a response to market-thwarting Asian 'cronyism'.

Johnson (Chapter 2) challenges such arguments, suggesting not only that economic growth and 'cronyism' can co-exist, but that there is abundant evidence of this in the US in the 1990s, and of 'cronyism' in IMF bailouts. The catch-all nature of Asian 'cronyism' is also criticized. At the very least, a distinction should be made between North-east Asian ('ex-Confucian', 'transformative', 'developmental') states and those of South-east Asia. But distinctions should also be made, for instance, between nepotism under Suharto and Mahathir's inter-ethnic redistribution policies. Regarding those countries, both Pincus and Ramli on Indonesia (Chapter 8), and Jomo on Malaysia (Chapter 7), emphasize the process of financial liberalization as a key antecedent to the Crisis, and they highlight the political nature of the process of liberalization. Phongpaichit and Baker present a similar analysis for Thailand (Chapter 6). Indeed, the combination of liberalization and dubious policy choices is a theme that recurs in all the country analyses, including the North-east Asian states. The main thrust of Chang, Park and Yoo's thesis (Chapter 9), for instance, is that it was the dismantling of the traditional mechanisms of industrial policy and financial regulation rather than the perpetuation of the traditional regime which led to the Korean crisis. This dismantling was accelerated under the Kim Young Sam government, which undoubtedly contributed to a marked rise in corruption in the key manufacturing sectors.

Moral hazard has become another catch-all concept relating to market distortions, invoked to explain the Asian Crisis. Most contributors here assign it little explanatory power, at least in *ex ante* investment and loan decisions. Fund managers did not think they would need a bailout, and the rapidity of their exit suggests they were far from assured that one would appear. Herd investor behaviour, resulting from pressure on fund managers, who have more to lose by not going with the herd than by going with it, is more plausible, according to Taylor (Chapter 3), Whittaker and Kurosawa (Chapter 11), and Wade. Chang, Park and Yoo also deny that Korean *chaebol* over-invested because of moral hazard, pointing to examples of failed *chaebol* and their managers (who lost their jobs as a result of their poor performance). Several of the contributors do argue, however, that there is a serious potential for moral hazard in the *ex post* IMF intervention, which may well shorten the memories of traders, and increase the potential for future crises.

Palma (Chapter 15) suggests that in situations of excess liquidity and under-regulation on the one hand, and almost limitless demand for liquidity from LDCs on the other, the 'market clearing' problem is solved by loosening quantity restrictions to those countries. This explains why, for example, bankers and financiers were happy to expand their lending to East Asia hugely (as they had previously done to Latin America), and with declining spreads, precisely at a time when the 'fundamentals' of these economies were deteriorating, the stock of short-term unhedged private debt mounting, gearing ratios rising, profit margins of the real sector declining, corruption and 'cronyism' worsening (in so far as these were important), and the level of investment in some economies (particularly in speculative real estate) reaching heights which even for this part of the world were difficult to justify. In over-liquid and under-regulated financial markets both lenders and borrowers seem unable to assess and price their risks properly, and end up accumulating more risk than is privately (let alone socially) efficient. Nor was it the case that a lack of transparency hid all those risks. As several of the authors note, the key problem was the evaluation of the information available: as in most periods of financial 'mania', market operators were simply unwilling to focus on the down-side risks as the up-side was more attractive.

Taylor, too, argues that despite the central role often assigned to it, moral hazard has not been the cause of boom and bust crises in Latin America and East Asia, but rather that a more central explanatory role should be given to the government's withdrawal from regulating the real economy, the financial sector, and especially the capital account. Kregel (Chapter 4) looks at the role of derivatives in international financial markets, which are not at all transparent, and difficult to regulate. He suggests that the derivative contracts involved do not lead to the allocation of funds at their highest global returns, but are designed to provide banks with low-risk fee and commission income. Derivative contracts also go some way towards explaining the predominance of commercial banks as lenders, as well as the short-term, volatile nature of the flows. Furthermore, the way some contracts combined currency risk and market price risk amplified declines during the crisis.

As Palma argues, the market failures leading to this crisis were largely endogenous. These failings were later amplified by herd behaviour and currency attacks leading to 'overshooting' – correction became collapse (Jomo). These developments in turn had disastrous knock-on effects in the real economy, potentially turning 'showcases' into 'basket cases' (Pincus and Ramli). Although the crisis countries may have had 'crony', structural and short-term problems (exacerbated by China's devaluation in 1994), these were not the principal cause of the Asian Crisis. Thus, as Whittaker and Kurosawa suggest, the 'model causes crisis' view is misleading.

But what about the 'crisis ends model' view? Are we witnessing the decline of the various Asian models, their end hastened by the Asian Crisis, in which upheavals in financial markets diffuse throughout the rest of the economy? In particular, will Anglo-Saxon governance practices come to prevail throughout East Asia, either because they are perceived as the most rational, or because they are forced on the countries which accept IMF assistance?

The main discussion of models is, not surprisingly, confined to Japan and South Korea. Chang, Park and Yoo remind us that the Japanese and German models emerged from a period of direct US Occupation, and Occupation-led institutional and legal reforms. Even concerted attempts at institutional transfer can lead to different outcomes. Is there any reason to believe that this no longer applies? Whittaker and Kurosawa suggest that in the case of Japan the 'model(s)' are in the process of evolution, but not necessarily towards convergence with Anglo-Saxon capitalism, with corporate governance being a case in point. Dore (Chapter 13) is perhaps more equivocal in view of the 'soft power'of the US, but he also suggests that changes in the Japanese model are only partly due to the Asian Crisis, and more to do with long-term socio-economic changes such as the weakening of labour unions, declining egalitarianism and generational change. As far as Korea is concerned, Mathews (Chapter 10) argues that a new 'model' may well emerge as a direct result of the crisis. He suggests that the IMF agreements incorporated three agendas – a conventional IMF agenda, a US agenda to open Korean markets to foreign (US) investment, and a reformist agenda of the incoming Kim Dae Jung government, seeking changes it might not otherwise have been able to introduce. This is very much in the tradition of using external pressures as leverage on internal reforms, noted by Dore for Japan.

All these chapters point to evolving models, with perhaps limited convergence towards Anglo-Saxon practices, or 'global standards'. The reasons are both intrinsic and extrinsic, and here we must question the role of the IMF, whose 'rescue' packages have been strongly interventionist, with visible consequences for the lives of millions of people in the countries in which the packages have been applied. The legitimacy of intervention on this scale may be questioned, as may its efficacy. Several papers take Kregel's view that the Fund not only misdiagnosed the situation as a traditional balance of payments problem, but that its austerity packages exacerbated the real debt deflation problem. High interest rates did not reverse currency falls, and the expected export-led recovery did not materialize in the short term because of initial severe credit squeezes. Taylor also notes that the drip-feed manner in which IMF money was disbursed was also debilitating, and risked driving fundamentally healthy economies from illiquidity into insolvency.

It is ironic, indeed, that the IMF lacks the transparency or accountability it demands of financial institutions in recipient countries. (Johnson puts it bluntly: 'Is this not cronyism?') Moreover, as Palma argues, IMF packages have ensured that international financial operators (particularly the largest) have not paid for their share of responsibility in the events that led to the Crisis: that is, have not only made profits when things have gone well, but also when they have gone wrong – they operate in a market with carrots and no sticks, in direct contradiction to the neo-liberal creed. Furthermore, 'conditionalities' were totally one-sided: only LDCs had to accept adjustment and structural reforms that were supposed to make them less crisis-prone. International financial operators, especially large ones, received help without being required to make institutional and regulatory reforms which would make it more likely that in the future they would assess and price risks properly and allocate financial resources more efficiently.

As already mentioned, this process may well shorten traders' and fund managers' memories, increasing the likelihood of future crises. That likelihood is also increased by the market-opening 'medicine' prescribed. If the analyses presented here are correct, we may expect further major crises, even if financial market and capital account liberalization is carried out in an 'orderly' manner. Indeed, Palma points to the likelihood of such a crisis in a number of other countrie. After discussing the period between financial liberalization and crisis in Chile (1975–82), Mexico (1988–94) and East Asia (1988–97), he looks particularly at Brazil and concludes that (at the time of writing, in the first half of 1998) it was already highly vulnerable to a sudden collapse in confidence and withdrawal of funds. Although there were, of course, important differences in the Brazilian case, it was heading in the same direction as those other countries where experiments with rapid financial liberalization had ended up in financial crises. Events in Brazil after the Russian devaluation of mid-1998 have confirmed this view.

Meanwhile, Asian Crisis countries have to deal not only with the consequences of the Crisis, but with the severe effects of IMF medicine as well. Phongpaichit and Baker describe how IMF packages were progressively modified in the face of local economic and political realities, to produce what, if it were not for face-saving rhetoric, would be called a fundamental revision. This goes beyond a switch from deflationary stringency to a policy of mild Keynesian stimulus, to include an expansion of the state role, temporarily at least. Long-term recovery will be far from easy, however, in part because there are problems in the industrial structures of the Asian Crisis. Ernst (Chapter 12) shows how specialization in the electronics sector, which accelerated growth during the 'miracle' years, may well be complicating recovery. In addition, there are questions as to how much steam is left in the post-Asian Crisis locomotive of the world economy, the US.

The prevention of crises such as the Asian Crisis is surely preferable to trying to cure them after they have happened, especially given the nature of the medicine now on offer. Bhalla and Nachane (Chapter 14) describe the efforts of India and China to prevent the spread of the Crisis to those countries. They conclude that domestic reforms are necessary, including deregulation, but urge caution over liberalization of foreign portfolio investment and the capital account.

Taylor provides a checklist of 'dos and don'ts' in the event of crisis, so we need not repeat it here. However, better information for the regulatory authorities is necessary, and international or regional co-operation can play a role here. Short-term fund flows in particular must be monitored carefully. Some of the contributors, too, suggest reconsidering the regional approach of the Asian Monetary Fund proposal, mooted during the early days of the Asian crisis, which met an ignominious fate at the hands of the IMF and the US.

As Taylor puts it, when a crisis does happen, 'bail-ins' instead of bailouts, and rapid disbursement of money may minimize the damage. Rescue packages may require greater government intervention rather than less, at least for a time. And there is now ample evidence to show that forcing radical market-opening reforms in the middle of a crisis is frequently counterproductive.

Openness to new perspectives and empirical evidence is critical. We offer this book in the hope that it will contribute towards this end.

Note

1. Volume 22, No. 6, November 1998.

2

Economic Crisis in East Asia: The Clash of Capitalisms

Chalmers Johnson

Since mid 1997, Americans have been told that the Asian economic model is obsolete and that the meltdown in East Asia will not affect them, their jobs, or the American stockmarket. Even the continuing US trade deficits with Asia of well over $100 billion are considered good news because cheap imports will keep down inflation. But what was and still is at risk in East Asia is the real possibility of a global collapse of demand and another Great Depression. Even if that does not happen, America's system of rich satellites serving as hosts to an expeditionary force of some 100,000 US troops is virtually certain to come to an end.

Something very serious has happened in East Asia. But the causes are so complex and so few agree on them that any prudent observer should be very careful about making overly quick judgements. There are at least three caveats that must precede any discussion of the details of the so-called meltdown.

First, the Asian model does not apply evenly across East Asia. For the sake of discussion and simplification, I think of the East Asian model as consisting of Asian values on subjects such as the nature of government, priority given to the community over the individual, and government guidance of a nonetheless privately owned and managed market economy, with economic growth tied above all to exports. This contrasts with the Anglo-American emphasis on what Westerners claim are (or should be) universal values: individualism and *laissez-faire*, with economic growth tied above all to domestic demand. In terms of the countries affected by the meltdown, the Asian model really only applies to Japan and South Korea. It never existed in Thailand or Indonesia – that is one reason why they were the first to crash under the speculative pressures against their currencies. It is only incipiently relevant to mainland China or Vietnam. And although the

Malaysians talk a great deal about Asian values, they violated the tenets of the Asian economic model by allowing Japanese, European, and American banks to export their own versions of the bubble economy to Malaysia. The Asian economic model is alive and flourishing in Taiwan, the Hong Kong Special Administrative Region of the People's Republic of China, and Singapore, and it may eventually take hold, now that the Americans have finally left, in the Philippines. In the minds of most Asians, particularly the Chinese, the meltdown has, if anything, reinforced the need for the Asian model of development rather than repudiating it. Linda Weiss, in her recent book *The Myth of the Powerless State* (1998) offers the best analysis of the differences between the North-east Asian transformative states and the South-east Asian pilotless states.

The second caveat is that an explanation of the meltdown in terms of 'crony capitalism' is wildly overdrawn. I take crony capitalism to mean corruption, nepotism, excessive bureaucratic rigidity, and other forms of trust violation that can occur whenever a state tries to manipulate incentives or, in other ways, alter market outcomes. The system of tax deductions for household mortgages in the US is a standard example of this form of state guidance of the market.

Crony capitalism is said to promote many sins, including the overbuilding of real estate throughout the region and the excessive importing of consumer goods, such as luxury cars – that is, the kinds of things the Mexicans did a few years ago when foreign financial institutions poured money into their country. But foreign loans to South Korea did not go into real-estate investment, and what has been wrong in Thailand and Indonesia was precisely the lack of a pilot agency, such as Japan's Ministry of International Trade and Industry, to keep such practices under control. The most glaring instance of nepotism affecting an economy in East Asia has been under General Suharto in Indonesia, who is, we hope, the last of the Marcos-style Asian dictators that the Americans have always preferred and supported. The ultimate in crony capitalism is actually the US-dominated International Monetary Fund (the IMF) and its bailing out of Thailand, Indonesia, and South Korea; the IMF's money does not go to the people of those countries. It goes to the foreign banks that made too many shaky and imprudent loans to Thai, Indonesian, and South Korean banks and businesses in the first place.

In 1994 South Korea, in an attempt to follow the nagging of its patron, the United States, abolished the Economic Planning Board, Korea's main body for making economic policy since the early 1960s, and loosened virtually all controls over financial institutions. In return for these self-inflicted wounds, Korea was admitted to the club of rich nations, the Organization for Economic Cooperation and Development (OECD), with its headquarters in Paris. As a direct result of these 'reforms', the government failed to monitor properly the foreign borrowing activities of inexperienced merchant banks. But the situation in Korea differs greatly from that in South-east Asia. With the election of a new, anti-establishment president in South Korea, Kim Dae Jung, the country is using the meltdown to rationalize the old system while killing off the weak conglomerates. Although President Kim is having some problems with Labour, if he manages to restrain labour strife and costs, a leaner, meaner Korean industry will emerge in the future. South Korea's re-emergence as an economic powerhouse will also smooth the way for unification with the North, without interference from the US, China or Japan.

Throughout the region, the 1997 crisis was caused much more by under-regulation than by corruption or any other side effects of an overly close relationship between businesses and the government. What all these places need is neither more nor less regulation but effective, expert guidance of the sort Japan and South Korea exercised during their periods of high-speed economic growth.

Only Japan truly fits the crony capitalism description. Ever since Japan's bubble economy started to deflate in 1989 and 1990, Japan has complacently continued to protect its structurally corrupt and sometimes gangster-ridden firms and has made only gestures toward holding anyone responsible. Virtually all of its public funds to stimulate the domestic economy have gone to the politically powerful but environmentally disastrous construction industry. Japan has been able to get away with palliatives largely because of the perpetuation of Japan's cosy Cold War relationship with the United States. This means that Japan is not being forced to make the painful choices that adjusting to a global economy would require. Japan remains today essentially a protectorate of the United States, not fully in charge of its own government or destiny. When that changes, Japan will change.

In the meantime, it is well to remember that crony capitalism was not the intent but a by-product of the structural characteristics of the Asian-type economies. These structures include cartelization of the *keiretsu–chaebol* variety, bank-based systems of capital supply, mercantilism and protectionism *vis-à-vis* external economies, and rule by bureaucratic elites despite a pretence of democracy. The intent of these structures was to enrich the nations of East Asia, not to meet consumer demand, global efficiency, individual choice, or any of the other motives posited by neoclassical economics. That they succeeded so spectacularly during the historical era known as the Cold War altered the world balance of power.

Over time, crony capitalism has become a serious side effect of Japanese-type economies, but its economic costs can easily be exaggerated. The United States's strong economic performance during the 1990s coincided with the biggest outbreak of American crony capitalism since the arrival on the scene of the military-industrial complex during the 1950s. Yet no one is proposing a total restructuring of the American economy because the Lippo Bank of Jakarta tried to buy influence in Washington, or despite evidence of the sale of ambassadorships and executive pardons for big contributors who are tax evaders, or military budgets bigger than all the United States's allies and potential enemies combined. John Carlin in the *Independent* (24 May 1998) describes the United States as 'the most legally corrupt political system in the world'. If crony capitalism brought down East Asia, why has it not similarly affected the United States, where it seems to be endemic?

The third caveat about the Asian meltdown concerns the widespread criticism that foreign analysts of East Asian capitalism failed to predict it or even to perceive the shadowy side of the East Asian model. This criticism is directed particularly against the so-called 'revisionists' and their books on the Japanese economy (including writers such as James Fallows, Clyde Prestowitz, Karel van Wolferen, and myself). These writers are now routinely lumped together with the Chrysanthemum Club of Japan apologists and accused of wishful thinking about Asia. For the editorial boards of the *Wall Street Journal* and the London *Economist*, together with virtually the whole tenurocracy of professors of economics in the English-speaking countries, the news of the East Asian meltdown came as a gift from heaven. They saw it as a massive vindication of their neoclassical economic orthodoxy. But has revisionism been repudiated? I think not.

It was the so-called revisionist writers who first outlined the differences between East Asian and American capitalism. During the early 1980s, when Japan's trade surpluses with the United States set new records every month and came close to destroying vital parts of the manufacturing base of the American economy, the revisionists warned that this situation was not the result of 'invisible hands' guiding market outcomes but of 'capitalist developmental states' engineering high-speed economic growth. The revisionists advocated using the full market power of the United States – which was and still is the main market for all the East Asian economies – to force them to make international trade mutually beneficial by opening their markets.

During the Reagan, Bush, and Clinton administrations, American elites listened to the revisionists' message, but they did something else. In the Reagan era, they had become too dependent on Japan's savings to finance their combination of tax cuts and rearmament to confront Japan directly. Therefore they set out to cut the trade imbalances by manipulating the exchange rates of the US dollar and the Japanese yen. This was good neoclassical economics but abominable Japanese area studies. In order for a cheap dollar and an expensive yen to make a difference, the primary problem between the two countries would have had to have been competition on prices. But the real issue was that Japan's markets were closed to foreign investors and retailers, as well as cartels, lack of enforcement of trade agreements, sham antitrust laws, and a host of other practices that Japan had perfected over the previous 40 years.

The results of the United States pursuing an exchange-rate approach to the problem of trade with Japan were profound. They made no difference to the trade imbalance, but they stimulated Japan to undertake countermeasures to the high yen, which led to Japan's bubble economy, then to the collapse of the bubble economy, then to Japan's export of its bubble economy to South-east Asia, and finally to the economic meltdown. What Japan needed was to develop an economy that relied more on domestic demand than on exports. But Japan's answer to the high yen was wild over-investment to enlarge productive capacity in order to continue exporting to any and all markets.

This is, of course, not what the revisionists advocated. A stronger case could be made that the 1997 economic crisis threatening the entire world – it was certainly the worst such crisis since the OPEC oil price hikes of 1973 – came about because too many rich nations knew next to nothing about the nations of East Asia. The Anglo-American economies refused to heed in a timely fashion the extraordinary imbalances, dependencies, and irresponsibilities that the East Asian capitalist developmental states were creating. Western economists, unable to explain Japan's growth or, for that matter, even to read a Japanese newspaper, rejected so-called revisionism because its findings were incompatible with orthodox neoclassical economic theory. The disaster of 1997 did not refute revisionism but rather confirmed the essence of the revisionists' message – there are differences among capitalist systems that are not trivial and that under certain circumstances can blow the system apart.

But the revisionists did not get the whole story right. Above all, they did not analyse correctly the Cold War context of East Asia's enrichment. They knew that the United States's chief contribution to this enrichment had not been its wars, its military deployments or its diplomacy, but rather its markets. The Americans bought the high-quality, low-cost manufactured goods of East Asia in greater quantities than any other external market. The revisionists understood that Asia's rigged economies depended to a critical extent on access to the American market and that they would all be in trouble if and when the US ceased to play the role of market of last resort. But they did not understand how the collapse of the Soviet Union, the end of bipolarity, and the tendencies toward globalization of finance and manufacturing would expose the contradictions in the American– East Asian relationship. The revisionists, like virtually all Western analysts, were intellectually captives of the separation of economics and politics, of trade and defence, that has for so many years dominated all thinking about the role of the United States in East Asia.

The events of 1997 were the first developments that would force an end to the artificial distinction between trade and defence and cause Asians and Americans alike to begin to look with clarity at the political, military and economic relations that lie behind the Asian meltdown. Thus far in the crisis, the United States has been willing to tolerate growing trade deficits as the stricken economies of East Asia try to export their way out of their troubles. But as Japan's refusal to help by opening its own markets, and even its competing with the stricken economies in exporting to the US, become common knowledge, the pressures to protect the US market will become intense. A concomitant will be a rethinking of American military strategy in East Asia, possibly beginning to bring to an end Japan's status as the most privileged satellite of the US in the area.

The Asian economic model does not exist uniformly in East Asia and is itself only a model, not the complex economic reality of a huge and diverse area. Crony capitalism is an inadequate explanation for what has happened in East Asia. And in the debate between Anglo-American economic orthodoxy and revisionism, the meltdown has tended to confirm the results of revisionist research. Like the caveats, there are also three main contenders among explanations – all three of which may prove to be true. I call these differing views the liquidity-crunch explanation, the overcapacity explanation, and the end-of-the-Cold-War-in-East-Asia explanation.

The liquidity-crunch explanation asserts that the 1997 East Asian crisis was essentially a financial problem rather than a crisis of the 'real economy'. Given a globalized financial system overloaded with money and a lack of elementary prudence on the part of borrowers in Thailand, Indonesia, Malaysia, and South Korea, these countries, starting in about 1994, borrowed hundreds of billions of dollars from foreign lenders. They invested these funds in sometimes foolish projects, such as fancy apartment and office buildings, or in export industries that were soon crippled by overcapacity. They believed, without truly analysing the matter, that their export industries would continue to grow and remain in their countries indefinitely, even though jogging shoes – to name one example – were once made in South Korea, then Indonesia, and now China and Vietnam. Businessmen in these countries also believed that, in the context of a continuously growing economy, their governments would help out any particular bank or conglomerate that found itself running out of money to pay back the loans.

But in July 1997, starting first with Thailand, foreign lenders began to realize that some of their Asian clients could not repay their loans. This caused other foreign investors to start withdrawing huge amounts of money from both poorly managed and completely healthy enterprises. Given globalized financial markets, the instantaneous transmission of data to anyone who wants it, and a lack of effective safety-valves, the crisis rapidly spread all over Asia. It raised the possibility of runs on banks even in the world's second largest economy, which is also the richest in per capita terms and the major source of long-term capital for the world – namely, Japan. The foreign lenders, big banks such as Citicorp and J. P. Morgan, had made the loans because the four international bail-outs of Mexico since 1976 taught them that, so long as they lent money to countries that were part of the informal American empire, they could expect the American government or some surrogate of it such as the IMF to step in and make good on their so-called non-performing assets.

The crisis was exacerbated not just by gullible borrowers and complacent lenders but also by some developments among the great powers that have been largely overlooked. In the last ten years China's share of East Asia's exports to the US market has grown from 6% to 26%. Even more important, in 1994 China devalued its currency by 35%, thereby making its exports hypercompetitive with those of South Korea and South-east Asia.

Something similar to the emergence of China as a competitor occurred elsewhere in the summer of 1995. The American Treasury and the Japanese Ministry of Finance agreed on a deal intended to help re-elect President Clinton the following year and to allow Japan to grow its way out of its own, post-bubble banking crisis via the usual export drive. Robert Rubin for the Americans and Eisuke Sakakibara for the Japanese decided between themselves that they would depreciate the yen against the dollar, thereby greatly increasing Japan's export competitiveness, in return for which Japan would continue to supply capital to the United States, thereby keeping American interest rates at politically desirable low levels. The American government also agreed to end its plan to put duties on imported luxury cars from Japan, keep quiet about America's billion-dollar-a-week trade deficit with Japan, and shift the focus of the Japanese–American alliance away from economic relations and back to security issues, even though there were no threats to security in the region.

Between April 1995 and April 1997, the yen fell 60% against the dollar. That alone priced most economies of South-east Asia out of the market. Thailand still tied the exchange rate of its own currency to the now seriously overvalued dollar and was ruined as a result. Given the overcapacities that too much investment generated and the competitive challenges from China and Japan, export growth in South Korea and in the ASEAN countries fell from 30% in early 1995 to zero by mid-1996. A balance-of-payments crisis was inevitable.

When the loans started to come due in the summer of 1997, the logical, economic-textbook response of the borrowers should have been to default and declare bankruptcy. That would have seriously pained the lenders, teaching them what markets are supposed to teach – that one is responsible for the risks one assumes. The foreign bankers would have had to renegotiate their loans to the East Asian countries, spreading them out over time and also adding a few profitable points to their interest rates. The Western and Japanese banks would probably never have got all their money back. However, under this scenario, the people who lost financially would have been the investors in the G-7 democracies, not the people of Asia; and reform of the East Asian economies would have been forthcoming because of market forces, not orders from Washington. Many Asian and American bankers and politicians would have been sacked, but the people of East Asia would have accepted the need for long overdue reforms and would have implemented them much more willingly.

What was actually done turned a liquidity crisis into a full-blown economic disaster. At first the Japanese stepped forward and said that they would provide at least some of the money in order to redeem their fellow Asian's debts. They proposed a new multinational financial institution led by Japan and restricted to making loans to Asian countries. The Americans instantly objected. They correctly sensed that Japan was about to try its hand at long promised but never delivered international leadership. If the Japanese had succeeded, they would have slipped the leash of the American Cold War system. Moreover, they would have started using their surplus capital to help countries in Asia rather than continuing to send it to the world's number one debtor nation, the United States. If the Americans ever have to finance their own stupendous debts rather than depend on Japanese savers, American interest rates will soar to double-digit levels. At the 19 November 1997 meeting in Manila where the newly proposed Japanese institution was quietly put to sleep, the Americans' pointman, Deputy Treasury Secretary Lawrence Summers, declared himself pleased that the clean-up was to be entrusted to the IMF. Japan's viceminister of international finance, Eisuke Sakakibara, commented *sotto voce* that he and others still believed the IMF was not up to the task. He turned out to be right.

The IMF is an old Bretton Woods institution set up in 1944 to service the system of fixed exchange rates that lasted until the 'Nixon Shocks' of 1971. It survived its loss of mission to become, in Robert Kuttner's words, 'the premier instrument of deflation, as well as the most powerful unaccountable institution in the world' (*Boston Globe*, 4 January 1998). It is also an instrument of American power, one that allows the United States to collect money from its allies and to spend the amassed funds on various international economic operations that serve American national interests.

The IMF roared into Asia and promised to supply $17 billion to Bangkok, $40 billion to Jakarta, and $57 billion to Seoul. In return it demanded austerity budgets, high interest rates, and sales of local businesses to foreign bargain-hunters. It claimed that these measures would restore economic health to the 'Asian tigers' and turn them into orthodox Anglo-American-type capitalist economies.

There was almost no chance that the IMF's one-size-fits-all remedies would succeed. Its economic ideologues not only know nothing about East Asia, they believe there is no *need* for them to know anything.

Totally devoid of concepts of culture or of cultural differences, the IMF did not know that it was undercutting Korean housewives' investment co-ops with their millions of untaxable funds, or that the Indonesian government's subsidies went to food and fuel, not just to cronies of Suharto. Not surprisingly, Asian editorial writers started to write essays with titles like 'The Second Opium War' and to mutter about American imperialism. Meanwhile, the social chaos that Western advisers produced in post-communist Russia seemed just around the corner in Asia.

The second explanation of the meltdown, that it was caused by overcapacity, follows directly from the first but has much more ominous implications. The difference is that the first explanation stresses Asia's short-term indebtedness problems, whereas the second explanation says that, regardless of the rather obvious financial problems, the Asian economies do not rest on good fundamentals. The Asians may save a lot, keep their children in school longer than anybody else, and recruit smarter state bureaucrats than Washington does, but they are catastrophically over-invested in the wrong industries – principally cars, shipbuilding, steel, petrochemicals, and semiconductors. This explanation also explicitly includes Japan as part of the Asian problem.

Because Japanese, European, and American multinational corporations have also moved so much of their manufacturing to places where skilled workers are paid very little, these new workers cannot possibly consume what they produce. But the consumers back in the G-7 democracies also cannot buy much more because either their economies are stagnant or they have just lost their jobs. The financial difficulties that the IMF is trying to deal with are only a symptom of a more serious disease. The underlying danger is a structural collapse of demand leading to recession and ultimately to something like the Great Depression. As William Greider has put it in his *One World, Ready or Not*, 'Shipping high-wage jobs to low-wage economies has obvious, immediate economic benefits. But, roughly speaking, it also replaces high-wage consumers with low-wage ones. That exchange is debilitating for the entire system' (1997, p. 221).

It is one thing to have IMF bungling cause a recession in East Asia; it is quite another to have a huge overcapacity to manufacture things that no one wants or can afford causing a recession. If the meltdown of 1997 represents manufacturing capacity that can never recover its costs, then the world requires the direct opposite of the policies the IMF has been pursuing in East Asia. It requires the creation of new demand, not the deflation of the demand that exists at the present time.

The third explanation – the end of the Cold War in East Asia – relates to the second in that it starts by asking how so much overcapacity came to be built in East Asia in the first place. One answer is that the economies of Japan and South Korea have been rigged since early in the Cold War in order to serve the grand strategy of the United States against communism in Asia and to ensure that they did not toy with neutralism or socialism. Many other places in East Asia, including Taiwan, Hong Kong, Singapore, Thailand and the Philippines, were outposts of American capitalism, protectorates, or recently closed bases of operation for America's wars. The Cold War deal the Americans offered to keep these satellites in line was unrestricted access to the American market, toleration of their mercantilism and protectionism, and technology transfers at often concessionary prices in return for public anti-communism and basing rights. (There are still 100,000 American troops based in Japan and South Korea and the US Seventh Fleet patrols the waters of East Asia.)

The Cold War ended in Europe in 1989 when the Soviet Union allowed the people of Berlin to tear down the wall that divided their city. It is possible that what happened to the Soviet Empire in Eastern Europe in 1989 started to happen to the American empire in East Asia in 1997. The difference is that in Eastern Europe the Soviet Union's satellites wanted to end their deal with the Russians, whereas in East Asia the American satellites still want to remain in their deal with the US. As far as Japan and South Korea are concerned, they have kept their side of the bargain – the American bases are still on their soil and they are still paying for them more generously than any other American allies around the world. (In Japan's case, the bases are on Okinawan soil that the US and Japan collaborate in keeping dependent.) What the two systems of satellites have in common is that neither the Russians nor the Americans can afford them any longer. Even if he might later have regretted it, in 1989 Gorbachev decided that he could no longer afford to keep the Red Army based in East Germany, Poland and the former Czechoslovakia. The Americans have not yet acknowledged that they cannot afford their satellites in East Asia. But either because of fiscal constraints or because their currency has depreciated so badly, the Japanese and the South Koreans cannot continue to pay for the upkeep of American troops on their soil or buy the panoply of American weapons that the Pentagon wants to sell them. Already the Thai government has had to cancel its purchase of eight American-made F/A-18 fighter jets, and South Korea does not have the money to pay for the power reactors promised to North

Korea. The more the Americans succeed in forcing the Asians to revamp their economies, the more independent the Asians will become of American influence.

What is to be done? That depends on which explanation you accept. If it is the first, then the answers are fairly straightforward. Stop the IMF before it turns a problem into a disaster and implement some elementary controls on capital movements. The idea is to end the volatility of hot money. A tax on short-term loans of 2%–3% would have the same effect. Government regulations could also favour direct foreign investment over purchases of shares of stock. An appropriate regulatory regime would be one that inhibits short-term investments and discourages local businesses from accumulating big debts in foreign currencies. It is absolutely certain that China, so far relatively insulated from the meltdown by the lack of convertibility of its currency, will be experimenting with these types of control over the coming years.

If one accepts the overcapacity explanation, then the US should start using the full power of the American market to raise the wages of workers in places where multinational companies are investing, so they can purchase new products more or less on a par with employed American workers. The collapse of demand that caused the Great Depression was ultimately overcome only by war production for the Second World War. The better way is to stimulate demand among poor people by increasing their incomes.

If one accepts the third explanation, then the Americans must finally let the Cold War end. This will have the effect in East Asia of forcing economically powerful countries such as Japan and South Korea to start coming to grips with the real challenges of this new century – the unification of Korea, adjustment to the emergence of China, avoidance of ethnic and religious violence in South and South-east Asia, and mitigating environmental degradation. Failure of the United States to adjust to its status as an ordinary country will only expose it further to imperial overstretch and Soviet-style decline. Certainly, the US should continue to push for economic reform in countries like South Korea and political reform in countries like Indonesia. But these will make no difference without reform and greater independence in Japan. And no amount of foreign money or pressure will cause Japan to reform. Only cutting its apron strings to the US will energize the Japanese political system. If that happens, we are likely to see a renewed burst of growth and prosperity throughout the region. If not, global recession is a serious possibility.

References

Fallows, J. (1994) *Looking at the Sun: The Rise of the New East Asian Economic and Political System*, New York, Pantheon.

Greider, W. (1997) *One World, Ready or Not: The Manic Logic of Global Capitalism*, New York, Simon & Schuster.

Johnson, C. (1982) *MITI and the Japanese Miracle: The Rise of Industrial Policy, 1925–1975*, Stanford, CA, Stanford University Press.

Prestowitz, C. (1988) *Trading Places: How We Allowed Japan to Take the Lead*, New York, Basic Books.

Weiss, L. (1998) *The Myth of the Powerless State: Governing the Economy in a Global Era*, Cambridge, Polity Press, and Ithaca, New York, Cornell University Press.

Wolferen, K. van (1989) *The Enigma of Japanese Power*, New York, Knopf.

3

Capital Market Crises: Liberalization, Fixed Exchange Rates and Market-Driven Destabilization

*Lance Taylor**

Tolstoy was wrong (about international capital markets, at least)

Everyone knows the epigraph to *Anna Karenina*, 'Happy families are all alike; every unhappy family is unhappy in its own way'. Tolstoy may well have been right about families, but the extension of his judgement to economies hit by capital market crises distinctly fails. Their causes and unhappy consequences in Latin America and Asia over the past 20 years have many elements in common.

These boom and bust episodes were *not* caused by excessive fiscal expansion or the creation of wholesale moral hazards by market-distorting state interventions. Rather, they pivoted around the government's withdrawal from regulating the real side of the economy, the financial sector, and especially the international capital market. This premeditated laxity created strong incentives for destabilizing private sector financial behaviour, on the part of both domestic and external players. Feedbacks of their actions to the macroeconomic level upset the system.

To think about how markets can be rebuilt in more stable fashion, we have to understand why the crises happened in the first place. That is not an easy task. A plausible place to begin is with the models that economists have designed to explain events such as Latin America's 'Southern Cone' crisis around 1980, European problems with the ERM in 1992, Mexico and the 'tequila' crisis in 1994, and events in East Asia in 1997–98. We begin in Section 2 with a review of mainstream work – accounting conventions, crisis models, 'moral hazards', and other abstract niceties. We then go on to a narrative proposed by people who operate close to macro policy choices and micro financial decisions. Experience shows that the overlap between mainstream models and the reality they are supposed to describe is slight; the practitioners' framework fits history better. In Section 3, it is used as a basis for suggestions about reasonable policy lines to follow in wake of the recent disasters.

Existing theory

This section comprises a review of existing crisis theories. It begins with relatively innocuous but important accounting conventions, and goes on to present mainstream models and a more plausible alternative.

Accounting preliminaries

Table 3.1 presents a simplified but realistic set of accounts for an economy with five institutional sectors – households, business, government, a financial sector, and the rest of the world.

Table 3.1 Macroeconomic accounting relationships

Generation of savings	
Household:	$S_h = W + J_b + J_g + \xi_h - C_h - T_h - Z_h$
Business:	$S_b = \Pi - J_b - T_b - Z_b - eZ_b^*$
Government:	$S_g = T_h + T_b - C_g - J_g - Z_g - eZ_g^*$
Financial system:	$O = Z_h + Z_b + Z_g - \xi_h$
Foreign:	$S_f = e[M + Z_b^* + Z_g^* - E]$
Resource balance	
	$S_h + S_b + S_g + S_f = W + \Pi - (C_h + C_g) + e(M - E)$
Investment–saving balance	
	$(I_h - S_h) + (I_b - S_b) + (I_g - S_g) = S_f$
Accumulation	
Household:	$(I_h - S_h) = \Delta D_h - \Delta H_h$
Business:	$(I_b - S_b) = \Delta D_b + e\Delta D_b^*$
Government:	$(I_g - S_g) = \Delta D_g + e\Delta D_g^*$
Financial system:	$O = \Delta H_h - (\Delta D_h + \Delta D_b + \Delta D_g) - e\Delta R^*$
Foreign:	$O = S_f - e(\Delta D_b^* + \Delta D_g^*) + e\Delta R$
Spreads	
Interest rate:	$\Sigma_i = i - [i^* + (\Delta e/e)^E] = i - (i^* + e^{*E})$
Capital gains:	$\Sigma_Q = (\Delta Q/Q)^E - [i^* + (\Delta e/e)^E = \hat{Q}^E - (i^* + \hat{e}^E)$

How each sector's saving originates from its incomes and outlays is illustrated in the top panel. Households in the first line receive labour income W, transfers from business J_b (that is, dividends, rents, etc.) and from government J_g, and interest payments ξ_h on their assets held with the financial system. They use income for consumption C_h, to pay taxes T_h, and to pay interest Z_h to the financial system. What is left over is their saving Sh. To keep the number of symbols in Table 3.1 within reason, households are assumed to hold liabilities of the financial system only. That is, their holdings of business equity are 'small' and/or do not change, and they neither borrow nor hold assets abroad. The last two assumptions reflect a major problem with the data – it is far easier to register funds flowing into a country via the capital market than to observe money going out as capital flight by numerous less than fully legal channels. Repatriation of such household assets is implicitly treated as foreign lending to business or government in the discussion that follows.

Similar accounting statements apply to the other sectors. Business gets gross profit income Π, and has outlays for transfers to households, taxes T_b, and interest payments to the local financial system (Z_b) and the rest of the world. The latter payment, eZ_b^*, amounts to Z_b^* in foreign currency terms converted to local currency at the exchange rate e. Business saving S_b is profits net of these expenditures. It will be lower insofar as interest payments Z_b and eZ_b^* are high. Firms in Asia are often said to suffer from constricted saving possibilities because their debt/equity ratios are high. Standard stabilization programmes that drive up interest rates and currency values and thereby Z_b and eZ_b^* can easily lead to heavy business losses (negative values of S_b), culminating in waves of bankruptcy.

Government saving S_g is total tax revenue net of public consumption C_g, transfers to households, and interest payments at home (Z_g) and abroad (eZ_g^*). For simplicity, the financial system is assumed to have zero saving, so that its interest income flows from households, business, and government just cover its payments to households. Finally, 'foreign saving', S_f, in local currency terms is the exchange rate times the foreign currency values of imports (M) and interest payments less exports (E). The implication is that the rest of the world applies part of its overall saving to cover 'our' excess of spending over income.

This interpretation shows up clearly in the 'resource balance' equation or the sum of all the savings definitions. It shows that total saving results from the excesses of income from production ($W + \Pi$) over private and public consumption ($C_h + C_g$), and of imports over exports.

Or in other words S_f equals total income minus total outlays and the sum of domestic saving supplies.

Likewise, the 'investment–saving balance' shows that the sum over sectors of investment less saving must equal zero. Much of the macroeconomic drama in recent crises results from large shifts in these 'financial deficits'. They show up in each sector's accumulation of assets and liabilities in the penultimate panel of the table.

Households, for example, are assumed to finance their deficit $(I_h - S_h)$ by running up new debt ΔD_h with the financial system, partially offset by their greater holdings of the system's liabilities or the increase ΔH_h in the 'money' supply.[1] Business and government both cover their deficits by new domestic (the ΔD terms) and foreign (the ΔD^* terms) borrowing.

The accounts for the financial system and the rest of the world are slightly less transparent, but essential to the following discussion. The former's flow balances show that new money creation ΔHh is backed by increases in domestic debt owed by households, business, and government, as well as by increases in the system's foreign reserves $e\Delta R^*$. In the foreign balance, reserve increments and foreign saving are 'financed' by increases in the foreign debts of business and government $e(\Delta D^*_b + \Delta D^*_g)$.

How the 'spreads' in Table 3.1's last panel enter the analysis is taken up below. What we can do now is say something about how the public sector was supposed to be the prime culprit for 'old' financial upheavals, for example, the debt crisis of the 1980s. This assertion is far from the truth, but it is so widely accepted that we must discuss it on its own terms.

Mainstream crisis models

The first post-Second World War wave of developing economy crises in which private external financial flows played a significant role took place around 1980. The countries affected included Turkey in the late 1970s, the Southern Cone in 1980–81, Mexico and many others in 1982, and South Africa in 1985. The Southern Cone collapses attracted great attention. They teach significant lessons about how market deregulation by the public sector and private responses to it can be extremely destabilizing.

The academic models underlying the belief that the public sector fiscal expansion 'caused' the early crises are built around a regime shift (or 'transcritical bifurcation' in the jargon of elementary catastrophe theory). They emphasize how gradually evolving 'fundamentals' can alter financial returns in such a way as to provoke an abrupt change of conditions or crisis – a ball rolls smoothly over the surface of a table until it falls off.

The regime change is triggered when the profit from liquidating a 'distortion' created by the state intervention becomes large enough – investors choose their moment to punish the government for interfering in the market. Such sentiments underlie balance-of-payments crisis models of the sort proposed by Krugman (1979) and pursued by many others. They assert that expansionary policy when the economy is subject to a foreign exchange constraint can provoke a flight from the local currency.[2]

In a typical scenario, the nominal exchange rate is implicitly assumed to be fixed or have a predetermined percentage rate of devaluation $\hat{e} = \Delta e/e$. Moreover, the local interest rate i exceeds the foreign rate i^*. Under a 'credible' fixed-rate regime, the expected rate of devaluation $\hat{e}^E = (\Delta e/e)^E$ will equal zero. From the last panel of Table 3.1, the interest rate 'spread' $\Sigma_i > 0$ will favour investing in the home country.

Now suppose that the government pursues expansionary fiscal policy, increasing the fiscal deficit $I_g - S_g$. If the household and business sectors do not alter their behaviour, the investment–saving balance in Table 3.1 shows that foreign saving S_f or the external current-account deficit has to rise. A perceived 'twin deficit' problem of this sort lies at the heart of traditional IMF stabilization packages that have thrown many countries (now including those in East Asia) into recession.[3] The external imbalance can lead to crisis via several channels. We describe two.

The first is based on the recognition that the government has to issue more debt, i.e., in the 'Accumulation' panel of Table 3.1, ΔD_g or ΔD^*_g must rise when $I_g - S_g$ is increased. Assume that the government is credit-constrained in external markets so that ΔD_g expands. To maintain its own balances, the financial system can 'monetize' this new debt so that ΔH_h goes up as well. If the domestic price level P is driven up by money creation (which does not always happen), then the real value of the currency eP^*/P (where P^* is the foreign price level) will appreciate or decline in absolute value. Imports are likely to rise and exports to fall, leading to greater external imbalance. With more borrowing ruled out by assumption, foreign reserves will begin to erode.

Falling reserves suggest that the trade deficit cannot be maintained indefinitely. When they are exhausted, presumably there will have to be a discrete 'maxi'-devaluation, a regime shift which will inflicit a capital loss on external investors holding liabilities of the home country denominated in local currency. At some point, it becomes rational to expect the devaluation to occur, making $\hat{e}^E$ strongly positive and reversing the spread. A currency attack follows. The economically untenable fiscal expansion is instantly erased.

A second version of this tale is based on the assumption that the local monetary authorities raise 'deposit' interest rates to induce households to hold financial system liabilities created in response to greater public borrowing. In the financial system balance in the first panel of Table 3.1, ξ_h will increase so that interest rates on outstanding domestic debts have to go up as well.

The spread Σ_i immediately widens. Foreign players begin to shift portfolios toward home assets, so that from the foreign accumulation balance in Table 3.1 reserves begin to grow. If the monetary authorities allow the reserve increase to feed into faster growth of the money supply, we are back to the previous story. If they 'sterilize' a higher ΔR^* by cutting the growth of household (ΔD_h) or business (ΔD_b) debt, then interest rates will go up even further, drawing more foreign investment into the system. From the foreign accumulation balance, pressures will mount for the current account deficit S_f to increase, say via exchange appreciation induced by inflation or else a downward drift of the nominal rate as the authorities allow the currency to gain strength. A foreign crisis looms again.

Moral hazards

The notion of moral hazard comes from the economic theory of insurance. The basic idea is that insurance reduces incentives for prudence – the more fire insurance I hold on my house, the more arson becomes an intriguing thought. Insurance companies frustrate such temptation by allowing homeowners to insure their properties for no more than 75% or so of their market valuations.

In the finance literature, moral hazard has been picked up in diverse lines of argument. Writing in an American context, the unconventional macroeconomist Hyman Minsky (1986) saw it as arising after the 1930s as a consequence of counter-cyclical policy aimed at moderating real/financial business cycles. As is always the case, such economic engineering had unexpected consequences.

One was a move of corporations toward more financially 'fragile' positions, leading them to seek higher short-term profitability. With no fears of price and sales downswings, high-risk/high-return projects became more attractive. This shift was exemplified by increased 'short-termism' of investment activities, and the push toward merger and acquisition (M&A) activity in the 1970s and 1980s.

Second, the intermediaries financing such initiatives gained more explicit protection against risky actions by their borrowers through 'lender of last resort' (or LLR) interventions on the part of the Federal Reserve. The resulting moral hazard induced both banks and firms to seek more risky placements of resources. Banks, in particular, pursued financial innovations. Among them were the elimination of interest-rate ceilings on deposits and the consequent creation of money market funds which effectively jacked up interest rates in the 1970s, a push towards high risk/high return loans that led to the Savings and Loan (S&L) crisis of the 1980s, the appearance of investment funds and 'asset securitization' at about the same time, and the later emergence of widespread derivatives markets and hedge funds.

To an extent all these changes were driven by a gradual relaxation of restrictions on external capital movements (D'Arista, 1998). When Eurocurrency markets began to boom in the 1970s, the higher deposit rates they paid put pressure on US regulators to lift interest-rate ceilings. Meanwhile, without reserve requirements offshore banks (and offshore branches of American banks) could lend more cheaply in the domestic market, leading to further deregulation. The US took the lead in pushing for new regulatory mechanisms, e.g., the 'Basle' standards for capital adequacy adopted in 1988.

Unfortunately, these changes introduced a strong pro-cyclical bias into regulation, just the opposite of the sort of system that should be in place. In an upswing, banks typically have no problem in building up equity to satisfy adequacy requirements. In a downswing, however, unless they already have the capital they can easily be wiped out. As will be seen, such regulatory structures helped exacerbate developing-country financial crises.

So far, moral hazard looks sensible; it can be used to underpin plausible historical narratives. Extensions out of context begin to stretch verisimilitude. Deposit insurance, for example, certainly played a role in the S&L crisis in the US. In the Garn St Germain Act of 1982, depositors were allowed to have any number of fully insured $100,000 accounts with an S&L. With their prudential responsibilities removed by the Act, S&L managers were free to engage in any high-risk, high-return projects they saw fit – which they immediately proceeded to do.

However, a frequently stated extension of this observation to developing-country markets makes less sense. For example, deposit guarantees have been accused of worsening the Southern Cone crises, but in Chile they had been abolished precisely to avoid moral hazard! Similarly, for (South) Korea, Krugman's (1998) assertion that the government provided implicit guarantees for banks and industrial corporations holds no water. He argues that Korean conglomerates or *chaebol* engaged in reckless investment and had low efficiency, as proven by their low profitability. But as Chang, Park, and Yoo (1998) point out, profitability was low only *after* interest payments, not before. Moreover, over the 1980s and 1990s the government did *not* bail out any *chaebol*; in the period 1990–7 three of the 30 biggest ones went bankrupt. The government did have a history of stepping in to restructive enterprises in trouble, but that left little room for moral hazard – managers knew they would lose control over their companies if they failed to perform.

Despite such shaky empirical antecedents, moral hazard is given a central role in mainstream crisis models. In a typical example, Dooley (1997) argues that developing-country governments self-insure by accumulating international reserves to back up poorly regulated financial markets. National players feel justified in offering high returns to foreign investors, setting up a spread. Domestic liabilities are acquired by outsiders (or perhaps nationals resident in more pleasant climes or just engaging in offshore manipulations) until such point as the stock of insured claims exceeds the government's reserves. A speculative attack follows.

The leitmotif of an alert private sector chastising an inept government recurs. This time the state encourages reckless investment behaviour. All a sensible private sector can be expected to do is to make money out of such misguided public action.

A more plausible theory

A more realistic perspective is that the public and private sectors generate positive financial feedbacks between themselves first at the micro and then at the macro level, ultimately destabilizing the system. This line of analysis is pursued by Salih Neftci (1998), a market practitioner, and Roberto Frenkel (1983), a macroeconomist. Both focus on an initial situation in which the nominal exchange rate is 'credibly' fixed (setting the $\hat{e}^E$ terms equal to zero in Table 3.1's equations for spreads), and show how an unstable dynamic process can arise. A Frenkel–Neftci (or FN) cycle begins in financial markets which generate capital inflows. They spill over to the macroeconomy via the financial system and the balance of payments as the upswing gains momentum. At the peak, before a (more or less rapid) downswing, the economy-wide consequences can be overwhelming.

To trace through an example, suppose that a spread Σ_i (e.g., on Mexican government peso-denominated bonds with a high interest rate but carrying an implicit exchange risk) or Σ_Q (e.g., capital gains from booming Bangkok real estate, where $\hat{Q}$ is the growth rate of the relevant asset price) opens. A few local players take positions in the relevant assets, borrowing abroad to do so. Their exposure is risky but *small*. It may well go unnoticed by regulators; Indeed for the system as a whole the risk is negligible.

Destabilizing market competition enters in a second stage. The pioneering institutions are exploiting a spread of (say) 10%, while others are earning (say) 5% on traditional placements. Even if the risks are recognized, it is difficult for other players not to jump in. A trader or loan officer holding 5% paper will reason that the probability of losing his or her job is close to 100% *now* if he or she does not take the high-risk/high-return position. Such potentially explosive behaviour is standard market practice, as interview studies by Rude (1998) and Sharma (1998) make clear. In the former's words, 'the speculative excesses of the international investors in the Asian financial crisis were not an exception, ... but instead the result of normal business practices and thus to a certain degree inevitable.'

After some months or years of this process, the balance sheet of the local financial system will be risky overall, short on foreign currency and long on local assets.[4] Potential losses from the long position are finite – they at most amount to what the assets cost in the first place. Losses from short-selling foreign exchange are in principle unbounded – who knows how high the local currency-to-dollar exchange rate may finally have to rise?

In a typical macroeconomic paradox, individual players' risks have now been shifted to the aggregate. Any policy move that threatens the overall position – for example, cutting interest rates or pricking the property bubble – could cause a collapse of the currency and local asset prices. The authorities will use reserves and/or regulations to prevent a crash, consciously ratifying the private sector's market decisions. Unfortunately, macroeconomic factors will ultimately force their hand.

In a familiar scenario, suppose that the initial capital inflows have boosted domestic output growth. The current-account deficit S_f will widen, leading at some point to a fall in reserves as capital inflows level off and total interest payments on outstanding obligations rise. Higher interest rates will be needed to equilibrate portfolios and attract foreign capital. In turn, S_b will fall or turn negative as illiquidity and insolvency spread à la Minsky, threatening a systemic crisis. Bankruptcies of banks and firms may further contribute to reducing the credibility of the exchange rate.

A downturn becomes inevitable, since finally no local interest rate will be high enough to induce more external lending in support of what is recognized as a short foreign exchange position at the economy-wide level. Shrewd players will unwind their positions before the downswing begins (as Mexican nationals were said to have done before the December 1994 devaluation); they can even retain positive earnings over the cycle by getting out while the currency weakens visibly. But others – typically including the macroeconomic policy team – are likely to go under.

The dynamics of this narrative differ from that of standard crisis models – it does *not* involve a regime shift when a spread Σ_i or Σ_Q switches sign from positive to negative. Rather, movements in the spread itself feed back into cyclical changes within the economy that finally lead to massive instability. Reverting to catastrophe theory jargon, the standard models invoke a 'static' instability such as a buckling beam. More relevant to history are 'dynamic' or cyclical instabilities that appear when effective damping of the dynamic system vanishes. A classic engineering example is the Tacoma Narrows suspension bridge. Opened in July 1940, it soon became known as 'Galloping Gertie' because of its antics in the wind. Its canter became strong enough to make it disintegrate in a 41-mile-per-hour windstorm in November of that year. Despite their best efforts, economists have yet to design a system that fails so fast.

Finally, a *soupçon* of moral hazard enters an FN crisis, but more by way of pro-cyclical regulation than through 'promised' LLR interventions or government provision of 'insurance' in the form of international reserves. After a downswing, some players will be bailed out and others will not, but such eventualities will be subject to high discount rates while the cycle is on the way up. In that phase, traders and treasurers of finance houses are far more interested in their spreads and regulatory acquiescence in exploiting them than in what sort of safety net they may or may not fall into some time down the road.

Policy alternatives

A companion paper (Taylor, 1998) reviews experiences in the Southern Cone around 1980, Mexico in 1994–5, and Asia in 1997–8. Its principal conclusion is that financial crises are not made by an alert private sector taking advantage of the public sector's fiscal or moral hazard foolishness. They are better described as private sectors (both domestic and foreign) acting to make high short-term profits when policy and history provide the preconditions and the public sector acquiesces. Mutual feedbacks between the financial sector and the real side of the economy then lead to a crisis. By global standards, the financial flows involved in a Frenkel–Neftci conflagration are not large – \$10–20 billion of capital flows annually (around 10% of the inflow the US routinely absorbs) for a few years are more than enough to destabilize a middle income economy. The outcomes are now visible worldwide.

A number of policy issues are posed by these episodes. It is convenient to discuss them under three headings: steps which can be taken at the country level to reduce the likelihood of future conflagrations; actions both an afflicted country and the international community can take to cope with a future crisis, when and if it happens; and how the international regulatory system might be modified to enhance global economic comity and stability.

Avoiding Frenkel–Neftci cycles

Rather than a formal model, Neftci and Frenkel provide a framework which can be used to analyse crisis dynamics. There are five essential elements: (1) the nominal exchange rate is fixed or close to being predetermined; (2) there are few barriers to external capital inflows and outflows; (3) historical factors and current circumstances act together to create wide spreads of the form Σ_i and Σ_Q in Table 3.1 – these in turn generate capital movements which push the domestic financial system in the direction of being long on domestic assets and short on foreign holdings; (4) regulation of the system is lax and probably pro-cyclical; (5) macroeconomic reprercussions via the balance of payments and the financial systems' flows of funds and balance sheets set off a dynamic process that is unstable.

To a greater or lesser extent, national policy-makers can prevent these components from coming together explosively.

(1) There are often good reasons to have a pegged nominal exchange rate. It is antiinflationary, which was crucially important to Latin American stabilization packages, beginning with Mexico's in the late 1980s. It can also enhance export competitiveness, as happened when countries in South-east Asia pegged to the falling dollar after the Plaza Accord. Problems with a pegged rate arise when it contributes to big spreads and (especially) when it is over-valued. These are good arguments for a thoughtfully designed crawling nominal depreciation or (harder for developing economies with thin foreign exchange markets to manage) a 'dirty' float. An even better argument is that such an exchange rate regime can help avoid real appreciation, which in turn

can widen the trade deficit, bring in capital inflows or induce reserve losses, and kick off an unstable macro cycle.

(2) Without international assistance it is virtually impossible to prevent capital from fleeing the country in a crisis; it is much more feasible to construct obstacles to slow it down (at least) as it comes in. In the recent period, Chile and Colombia have had some success with prior deposits and taxes on inflows, especially when they are short term. In a not much more distant past, Asian economies had fairly effective restrictions on how much and how easily households and firms could borrow abroad. In non-crisis times, acquisition of foreign assets can also be monitored.

The key task is to prevent a locational mismatch in the macro balance sheet, with a preponderance of foreign liabilities (especially short term) and national assets. Local regulatory systems can certainly be configured toward this end. If imbalances are detected, the relevant authorities can direct or encourage players to unwind their positions.

(3) Under a fixed exchange rate regime, it is easy to spot a 10% differential between local and foreign short-term interest rates or a similarly sized gap between the growth rate of the local stock-market index or property prices and a foreign borrowing rate. Such yields are an open invitation to capital inflows that can be extremely destabilizing. Whether policy-makers feel they are able to reduce interest rates or deflate an asset market boom is another question, one that merits real concern.

Another source of potential spreads is through off-balance-sheet and derivative operations. Here, local regulators can be at a major disadvantage – they do not necessarily know the latest devices. Staying up to date as far as possible and inculcating a culture of probity in the local financial system are the best defences here.

(4) There is of course a serious question as to whether many developing-country regulatory systems can meet such goals, especially in the wake of liberalization episodes. Another difficulty arises with timing. It is very difficult to put a stop to capital flows *after* the financial system has a locationally unbalanced position; at such a point, interest rate increases or a discrete devaluation can easily provoke a crash. The authorities have to stifle a destabilizing cycle early in its upswing; otherwise, they may be powerless to act.

(5) Each balance-of-payments crisis is *sui generis*; to produce a set of formal descriptions one would have to write a separate model for each episode in each country. Many of the components, however, would be the same. The simplest classification is in terms of disequilibria

between stocks and flows, along with microeconomic correlates. Here are some examples:

Flow–flow. One key issue here is identifying the internal 'twin(s)' of an external deficit. In the country examples discussed in Taylor (1998), the financial deficits were in the hands of the private sector – business or households. The follow-up question is how they are being paid for. Are rising interest obligations likely to cut into savings and investment flows? Are flows cumulating to produce locational or maturity mismatches in balance sheets? Another precursor of crisis is the relationship between the volume of capital inflows and the current-account deficit. If the former exceeds the latter, reserves will be rising, perhaps lulling the authorities into a false sense of security. As in the Southern Cone crises, it will rudely vanish when interest payments on accumulating foreign debt begin to exceed the amount of capital flowing in.

Stock–flow. Have some asset or liability stocks become 'large' in relation to local flows? East Asia's short-term debt exceeding 10% of GDP in 1996 was a typical example; it was a stock with a level that could change rapidly, with sharply destabilizing repercussions. Rapid expansion of bank credit to the private sector as a share of GDP while booms were under way in the Southern Cone, Mexico, and Thailand might have served as an early warning indicator, had the authorities been looking. The causes included monetization of reserve increases and growth of loans against collateral assets such as securities and property with rapidly inflating values.

Stock–stock. Besides lopsided balance sheets in the financial sector, indicators such as debt/equity ratios and the currency composition of portfolios (including their 'dollarization' in Latin America recently) become relevant here. They can signal future problems with financing investment–saving differentials of the sort presented in Table 3.1. For example, producers of non-traded goods may borrow in dollar terms from the local banking system. In the event of a devaluation, their real incomes would fall and some might not be able to service their debts. A crisis could follow, even if banks had held their 'dollar' liabilities and assets generally in balance. It could be avoided if the central bank had ample reserves to back an LLR operation in dollars, but many countries are not so lucky.

Microeconomics. Micro-level developments go along with these macro changes. Investment coordination across firms may be breaking down, leading to 'excess competition'; property speculation and luxury consumption may be on the rise.

The problem with all such indicators is that they lag an unstable dynamic process. By the time they are visibly out of line it may be too late to attempt to prevent a crisis; its management becomes the urgent task of the day.

Moral hazard abroad?

Within countries, moral hazard did not play a central role in generating crises. On the side of the lenders, it also did not seem to be important. In the East Asian crisis, international banks were the big offenders. In 1996 there had been a net flow of capital into the five most affected economies of $93 billion. There was a net outflow of $12 billion in 1997, with the most volatile item being commercial bank credit, which shifted from an inflow of over $50 billion in 1996 to an outflow of $21 billion the following year. The overall turnaround of $105 billion was close to the five countries' total reserves of $127 billion and exceeded 10% of their combined GDP (about two percentage points higher than the impact of the 1982 debt crisis on the GDP of Latin America). It was a supply shock with sharp contractionary effects on the macroeconomy. Taking advantage of the short-term nature of their credits, the banks ran from their borrowers before they had a chance to default, making default itself, or a massive international bail-out, a self-fulfilling prophecy.

Did the banks enter heavily into Asian lending because of moral hazards from home, or did they just like the spreads? One will never know for certain. Perhaps the Americans were emboldened by the Mexican 'rescue' of 1995, which pumped tens of billions of dollars through that economy back to its creditors on Wall Street (the Mexicans themselves are now trying to cope with bad internal debt to the tune of 15% of GDP that the rescue left behind). But the same cannot be said about the Europeans and Japanese. The fact that all international players left so fast suggests that they did not place much faith in the 'implicit guarantees' that the Asian governments allegedly had offered.

Rescue attempts

Once a country enters into a payments crisis, it cannot cope on its own. International assistance has to be called in. Each situation follows its own rules, but there are a few obvious 'dos' and 'don'ts' for the actions of the rescue team. We begin with the former.

The contrast between Mexico's and Asia's 'rescues' is striking. At least for the creditors, the rescue did happen in 1995; in 1998 it did not. Very slow disbursement of funds by the International Monetary Fund may well be crippling the Asian effort permanently, pushing fundamentally healthy economies from illiquidity into insolvency. Against the $105 billion external shock that the region received in 1997, international financial institutions may disburse around $45 billion in 1998.

The first and most obvious 'do' that emerges is to disburse rescue money fast. In Helleiner's (1998) words, '[f]inance that is supplied only on the basis of negotiated conditions and which is released only the basis of compliance with them ... is *not* liquidity'. East Asian economies became highly illiquid in 1997. By mid-1998, their position had not significantly improved, despite more than six months of Fund psychotherapy accompanied by liquidity transfusions on a homeopathic scale.

In fact, the transfusions might not even have been required if the rescuers had 'bailed-in' the countries' creditors instead of bailing *them* out. By appealing to G7 regulatory authorities if need be, the IMF presumably has enough clout to prevent international creditors – especially large international banks – from closing out Asian borrowers overnight. This is a sort of 'do' that should be built into rescue protocols before the next crisis strikes.

After a crisis, countries often also have an ample load of 'bad debt', typically non-performing assets of the banking sector. Domestic refinancing via a bond issue to the non-bank private sector, an administratively enforced credit roll-over, and price inflation are three ways of dealing with the problem. The latter two would almost certainly require re-imposition of tight controls on outward capital movements, which the international community would have to abet.

Distributional questions also come to the fore. As nations, the Asians are big and visible. But what about small, poor, raw material or assembled goods exporters in sub-Saharan Africa, Central America, the Pacific, and the Caribbean? Several have been hit by rapid reversals of private capital inflows. Presumably they merit international help as much as Korea or Thailand. They are not now receiving it.

Within all afflicted countries, income generation and employment problems are critical. The authorities can repress their peoples, up to a point, but ultimately they will have to offer them a degree of social and economic support. Such an effort goes diametrically against the emphasis of Fund-type packages. As Singh (1998) puts it:

> To provide such assistance effectively and on an adequate scale will require not only considerable imagination but also a large expansion in government activity and often direct intervention in the

market processes. Such emergency safety net programs may include wider subsidies, food for work schemes, and public works projects. How to pay for these measures within the limits of fiscal prudence, let alone within IMF fiscal austerity programs, will be a major issue of political economy for these countries.

The most obvious 'don't' is *not* to liberalize the capital accounts of affected countries further. If the single most apparent cause of crisis was a door three-quarters open, the last thing one wants to do is move it the rest of the way. A similar observation applies to attempts to restructure economic institutions in depth in crisis-afflicted economies. This strategy is now being pursued by the IMF in Asia, Russia, and elsewhere, using conditionality-laden credit disbursements as bait. This effort runs directly against well-entrenched social and economic structures. It will undoubtedly fail, leaving a big store of political resentment to be paid for in the future.

Changing the global regulatory system

The foregoing observations lead naturally to five suggestions for restructuring international financial arrangements.

First, recent experiences demonstrate that the global macroeconomic/financial system is not well understood. 'Miracle economies' one month turn into incompetent bastions of 'crony capitalism' the next, and the commentators do not skip a beat. Under such circumstances, an immediate recommendation is for humility on the part of the major institutional players (Eatwell and Taylor, 1998). There is *no* reason to force all countries into the same regulatory mould; international institutions should wholeheartedly support whatever capital market, trade, and investment regimes that any nation, after due consultation, chooses to put into place.

Second, international agencies should support national regulatory initiatives. There was a lot of information available from the BIS and other sources about the gathering storm in Asia; it was not factored into either the private or public sectors' calculations. If national regulators are made more aware of what is happening in their countries, perhaps they can take prudent steps to avoid a pro-cyclical bias in their decisions.

Third, the IMF seems unlikely to receive large additional sums of money to allow it to serve as a (conditional) lender of last resort. It will therefore have to become more of a signaller to other sources of finance, for example, central banks and the BIS. That opens room for new forms of regional cooperation such as Japan's summer 1997 proposal for an Asian bail-out fund, which died after being opposed vigorously by the US government and the IMF. Such institutional innovations should be thought through seriously, and very possibly put into place.

Fourth, specific changes in international regulatory practices may make sense. One obvious modification to the Basle capital adequacy provisions is to permit 20% as opposed to 100% backing on loans to non-OECD countries for maturities of (say) only three months or less, as opposed to one year at present. Such an adjustment should substantially reduce incentives for banks to concentrate their lending to developing countries in the short term.

Finally, there is no independent external body with power to assess the IMF's actions. More transparency (especially regarding relationships between the American government and the Fund) and independent evaluations of the IMF are sorely needed in light of its largely unsuccessful economy-building enterprises in post-socialist nations and now in East Asia.

Postscript

It will take the economic historians many years to sort out the tumultous changes in Russia during the 1990s, and certainly the currency crisis of summer 1998 is not yet fully understood. Nevertheless, its key features were consistent with the framework sketched in this paper. The capital market had been open since the 'global shock' of 1992, facilitating capital flight (permitted by the trade surplus and foreign lending) to the tune of $20–30 billion per year. The exchange rate was strong, with real ruble purchasing power at least doubling between 1993 and 1996, when the nominal rate was stabilized as an anti-inflation 'anchor'. Finally, there was virtually no domestic financial regulation.

Money emission had been cut back sharply (indeed the money/GDP ratio was very low by international standards), and the government was paying high interest rates on short-term liabilities. Equity prices rose sharply, beginning in 1996. Both interest rate and capital gains spreads were large and foreign investors poured in. As the relevant intermediaries, Russian financial institutions assumed a locationally unbalanced position (long in rubles, short in dollars); in particular, banks borrowed heavily abroad to speculate on the government's short-term liabilities. They were effectively bankrupted by the devaluation in August.

The main contrast with Mexico and East Asia was that, owing to a collapse in tax collection, there was a large fiscal deficit which supported the government bill market. The other side of that coin was strict monetary policy in a Muscovite re-run of early Reagonomics. The resulting high interest rates and strong ruble were part and parcel of the débâcle.

Notes

* This paper draws heavily on the results of a project on International Capital Markets and the Future of Economic Policy, Center for Economic Policy Analysis, New School for Social Research, with support from the Ford Foundation. Comments by Alice Amsden, Jane D'Arista, Thorsten Block, Sandy Darity, Roberto Frenkel, Gerry Helleiner, and the referees are gratefully acknowledged. An expanded version of this paper will be published by the United Nations Conference on Trade and Development.

1. The 'Δ' term signifies a change over time, e.g., $\Delta H_h = H_h(t) - H_h(t-1)$ where $H_h(t)$ and $H_h(t-1)$ are money stocks at the ends of periods t and $t-1$ respectively.
2. The following discussion concentrates on 'first generation' speculative attack models because they have had the major impact on the policy debate. 'Second generation' models make the fundamentals sensitive to shifts in private expectations, thereby allowing extrinsic, random 'sunspot' shocks to generate multiple equilibria. The mathematical complications are intriguing to the academic mind but add little to attempts to understand historical crises. There are numerous surveys of these models. Nouriel Roubini's useful website, www.stern.nyu.edu/~nroubini/asia/ AsiaHomepage, contains an ample selection.
3. Pieper and Taylor (1998) present a fairly up-to-date review. In various numbers of its *World Economic Outlook*, the IMF is 'up front' about attributing crisis in both Latin America and Asia to 'incompatibilities;' between macro policies and the exchange rate regime as well as 'excessive regulation' and 'too little competition' in the financial sector.
4. For analysis in the Asian context, see Islam (1998). There may also be problems with maturity structures of claims, especially if local players borrow from abroad short term. Nervous foreign lenders may then compare a country's total external payment obligations over the next year (say) with its international reserves. Such ratios proved disastrous for Mexico in 1995 and several Asian countries in 1997. A maturity mismatch in which local players borrow short term abroad and lend long term at home may be less significant – a property developer will default on his or her loan if the property market crashes, regardless of whether it is formally of short or long duration.

References

Change, H.-J., Park, H. J. and Yoo, C. G. (1998) 'Interpreting the Korean crisis: financial liberalisation, industrial policy, and corporate governance', *Cambridge Journal of Economics*, vol. 22, no. 6.

D'Arista, J. (1998) 'Financial Regulation in a Liberalized Global Environment', Center for Economic Policy Analysis, New School for Social Research, mimeo.

Dooley, M. P. (1997) 'A Model of Crises in Emerging Markets', Department of Economics, University of California at Santa Cruz, mimeo.

Eatwell, J. and Taylor, L. (1998) 'International Capital Markets and the Future of Economic Policy', Center for Economic Policy Analysis, New School for Social Research, mimeo.

Frenkel, R. (1983) 'Mercado financiero, expectativas cambiales, y movimientos de captal', *El Trimestre Economica*, vol. 50, 2041–76.

Helleiner, G. K. (1998) *The East Asian and Other Financial Crises: Causes, Responses, and Prevention*, Geneva, United Nations Conference on Trade and Development.

Islam, A. (1998) *Dynamics of Asian Economic Crisis and Selected Policy Implications*, Bangkok, Economic and Social Commission for Asia and the Pacific.

Krugman, P. (1979) 'A model of balance-of-payments crises', *Journal of Money, Credit, and Banking*, vol. 11, 311–25.

Krugman, P. (1998) 'What Happened to Asia?', Department of Economics, Massachusetts Institute of Technology, mimeo.

Minsky, H. P. (1986) *Stabilizing an Unstable Economy*, New Haven, CT, Yale University Press.

Neftci, S. N. (1998) 'FX Short Positions, Balance Sheets, and Financial Turbulence: An Interpretation of the Asian Financial Crisis, Center for Economic Policy Analysis, New School for Social Research, mimeo.

Pieper, U., and Taylor, L. (1998) 'The revival of the liberal creed: the IMF, the World Bank, and inequality in a globalized economy', in Baker, D. Epstein, G. and Pollin, R. (eds), *Globalization and Progressive Economic Policy: What are the Real Constraints and Options*? New York, Cambridge University Press.

Rude, C. (1998) 'The 1997–98 East Asian Financial Crisis: A New York Market-informed View', New York, Department of Economic and Social Affairs, United Nations, mimeo.

Sharma, K. (1998) 'Understanding the Dynamics behind Excess Capital Inflows and Excess Capital Outflows in East Asia', New York, Department of Economic and Social Affairs, United Nations, mimeo.

Singh, A. (1998) '"Asian Capitalism" and the Financial Crisis', Center for Economic Policy Analysis, New School for Social Research, mimeo.

Taylor, L. (1998) Lax public sector, destabilizing private sector: origins of capital market crises', in United Nations Conference on Trade and Development, *International Monetary and Financial Issues for the 1990s*, vol. 10.

4

Derivatives and Global Capital Flows: Applications to Asia

J. A. Kregel

Introduction: four puzzles

There are four factors involved in the 1997 financial crisis in Asia that have caused surprise. This paper suggests that an understanding of the role of derivatives contracts in facilitating the financial flows to Asia may provide a key to understanding them.

The Latin American debt crisis of 1982 was thought to have been aggravated by the dominance of syndicated lending by commercial banks. Developing-country borrowers were thus encouraged to increase their reliance on non-bank lending, in particular private direct investment flows. The dominance of direct investment flows to a number of Asian countries was used as an example of the greater stability of such lending. Yet, the Asian crisis appears to have been precipitated by the reversal of short-term private bank lending which had come to dominate capital flows to the region.

Second, the flows of capital to Asia have been used as an example of the benefits of free international capital markets in directing resources to the most productive uses. Yet, in the aftermath of the crisis, it appears that total returns on equity investments in Asia have in fact been lower than in most other regions throughout the 1990s.

Third, it appears that in a number of Asian countries the majority of international lending was between foreign and domestic banks. It has been suggested that the major cause of the crisis is unsafe lending practices by the Asian banks, permitted by inadequate national prudential supervision. But these economies were the most advanced on the road to market liberalization. One of the cardinal principles of financial liberalization, formed in the aftermath of the Chilean crisis, is that the creation of institutional structures ensuring the stability of the financial system should precede financial market liberalization. Indeed, many of the Asian countries were following this advice. It is interesting to note that the developed-country lending banks were generally large, global banks employing highly sophisticated risk-assessment procedures. However, they appear to have continued lending well after the increased risks in the region were generally apparent. This suggests that even the most sophisticated operators in global financial markets have difficulties in assessing risk, and that their regulators were no more successful in imposing prudent limits than those in the less advanced markets.

Finally, private portfolio and direct investment flows were considered to be preferable to syndicated bank lending because they were thought to segregate the problem of foreign exchange instability from asset market instability. Syndicated lending was denominated in the currency of the lending bank, and the exchange rate risk was thus borne by the borrower. However, direct equity investors purchase foreign financial assets in foreign currency and thus bear the currency risk. It was suggested that in a crisis the foreign investor would suffer from a fall in asset prices as well as from a decline in the exchange rate, which would discourage sales of security investments, thereby reducing selling pressure in the foreign exchange market. Yet, the linkage between the collapse in exchange rates and equity markets appears to have been even closer in Asia than in other experiences of financial crisis.

One explanation of the crisis in foreign exchange markets is that a large proportion of foreign borrowing by corporates and banks was unhedged because of prevailing expectations of stable exchange rates. When these expectations were disappointed, the scramble to repay these foreign currency loans created a massive market imbalance and a collapse of the foreign exchanges. This absence of generalized hedging of foreign borrowing has been interpreted to mean that financial derivative contracts played little or no role in the crisis. This position has been reinforced by the repeated references to an IMF study which suggests that global hedge funds were not active catalysts in the Asian crisis.[1] However, the recent quarterly reports (for the 4th quarter of 1997 and 1st quarter of 1998) of US money-centre banks, reflecting the initial impact of the Asian crisis on their lending to the area, suggest that most of their initial losses have been related to derivative-based credit swap contracts. Thus, at least in the case of US banks, certain types of derivative contract appear to have played some role in the flows of funds to Asia and thus in the instability of these flows. While bank derivatives are 'tailored-to-the-client', 'over-the-counter' contracts, and as such are not generally public knowledge, the experience of such contracts in the 'Tequila' crisis earlier in this decade provides some indication of the kinds of contract that might have been involved. This short paper thus suggests ways in which bank derivative contracts may have been linked to the rise in short-term bank lending to Asia and contributed to the four puzzles noted above concerning capital flows to the region.

Structured derivatives: global allocation of capital, transparency and prudential supervision

Most people are now familiar with the standard derivative contracts used in hedging risk, such as forwards, futures and options. While foreign currency forwards remain the province of bank foreign exchange dealers, most basic futures and options contracts are standardized and traded in organized, regulated markets. Banks also offer derivative contracts to their clients in what is termed the 'over-the-counter' (OTC) market. But there is no market involved in these contracts, which may involve the stipulation of standard futures and options contracts outside the organized market on a bilateral basis with individual clients. However, the majority of OTC activity involves individually tailored, often highly complex, combinations of standard financial instruments, packaged together with derivative contracts designed to meet the particular needs of clients. These contract packages involve very little direct lending by banks to clients, and thus generate little net interest income. However, since they are often executed through special purpose vehicles (i.e., specialized investment firms that are independently capitalized), they have the advantage, under the Basle capital adequacy requirements, of requiring little or no capital, or of being classified as off-balance-sheet items, because they do not represent a direct risk exposure for the bank. In addition, they generate substantial fee and commission income. Rather than committing their own capital, the banks serve in these transactions as intermediaries whose services involve not only matching borrowers and lenders, but acting as market innovators to create investment vehicles that attract lenders and borrowers. Nonetheless, these activities often require banks to accept some of the risks associated with the derivatives created in order to produce packages with the characteristics desired by final borrowers and lenders. These derivative risks may or may not be hedged by the bank, depending on its own proprietary investment strategy.

When hedging does occur, it can be done either by physical hedging (i.e., the actual purchase of an offsetting position in the underlying financial asset), through the purchase of derivative contracts in organized markets, or by producing a package that involves risks which offset those involved in other packages (cross hedging or risk matching across clients).

The major objective of active, global financial institutions is thus no longer the maximization of profits by seeking the lowest cost funds and channelling them to the highest risk-adjusted return, but rather in maximizing the amount of funds intermediated in order to maximize fees and commissions, thereby maximizing the rate of return on bank capital. This means a shift from continuous risk assessment and risk monitoring of funded investment projects that produce recurring flows of interest payments over time to the identification of riskless 'trades' that produce large, single payments, with as much of the residual risks as possible carried by the purchasers of the package. This process has been accelerated by the introduction of risk-weighted capital requirements. As a result, banks have come to play a declining role in the process of the efficient international allocation of investment funds. Rather, they serve to facilitate this process by linking primary lenders and final borrowers. This means that the efficient allocation of funds to the highest risk-adjusted rate of return depends increasingly on assessment of risks and returns by the lender. Yet, it is the role of most derivative packages to mask the actual risk involved in an investment, and to increase the difficulty in assessing the final return on funds provided.[2] As a result, certain types of derivative may increase the difficulties faced by private capital markets in effectuating the efficient allocation of resources. By extension, if they make investment evaluation more difficult for primary lenders, they may also create difficulties for financial market regulators and supervisors.

These particular aspects can be most clearly seen by reference to structured credit derivative contracts, which expanded dramatically during the 1990s. Most US institutional investors do not face unlimited investment choices. Most are limited to investments in assets with a minimum of risk as represented by an 'investment grade' credit rating on the issue, and many are precluded from certain types of risk, such as foreign exchange risks, or foreign credit risk (these often are simply the result of the application of the investment grade restriction). This means that a large proportion of professionally managed institutional investment funds cannot invest in emerging markets or in particular asset classes such as foreign exchange. Structured derivative packages, created by global investment banks, have often provided the means to circumvent these restrictions.

Structured derivative contracts have been used for this purpose in two ways. In 1992 and 1993, in a falling interest rate environment, they provided a means to increase returns for money managers and then, when rates started to rise, to provide borrowers with below-market borrowing rates. They usually involved structured credit notes with embedded options. 'These notes only carried a higher coupon because they contained an embedded short position in interest rate options. In other words, often when an investor bought a structured note, he simultaneously sold an interest rate option ... There is no doubt that some less knowledgeable investors did not realize that by buying these securities, they were selling options or engaging in leveraged bets, because some of these features were quite cleverly concealed' (Chew, 1996, pp. 54–5). The assumption behind such contracts is that the price of the instrument underlying the contract would not change sufficiently to produce a loss that completely eliminated the premium earned from selling the option.[3]

An example closer to the present context might involve US government agency dollar-denominated structured notes with the interest payment, or the principal value, linked to an index representing some foreign asset.[4] The return to these notes would be higher than US domestic rates, but the increased yield would be accompanied by the increased risk due to foreign exchange exposure. Such an asset might be a one-year dollar-denominated note paying a guaranteed above-market interest rate, but with the amount of repayment of principal linked to an index, say the Thai baht/dollar exchange rate. Since the asset is denominated in US dollars, and the interest is guaranteed and paid in US dollars, the notes carry an investment grade credit rating and would be entered on the balance sheets of investors as the equivalent of a US Treasury or Agency security, not as a foreign investment subject to foreign exchange or country risks. Yet, the above-market interest rate on the note is generated by the sale of a put option on the Thai baht at a strike price just above the current market rate that is in fact embedded in the contract. This is equivalent to the buyer having purchased the Thai currency. If the baht exchange rate remains constant, the written put is not exercised and the option premium received is retained by the writer and is used to meet the above-market guaranteed interest rate payable on the contract.

However, if the baht were to depreciate to a value below the strike price, then the buyer of the put would exercise his right given by the option to sell baht at a price that is higher than the market price. The writer of the option would thus incur a loss determined by the difference between the strike price and the market price for baht. Since the interest rate on the instrument is guaranteed, the loss cannot be reflected in a reduction in the rate of interest. However, the augmented interest payment produced by the margin over the market interest rate, and any loss on the option position, would be recovered by means of a reduction in the principal returned to the purchaser at maturity. An investor seeking to maximize yield may be attracted by the guarantee on the interest rate, and underestimate or even ignore the risk of loss in capital value. Since the writer of an option has an unlimited exposure, a large change in the exchange rate could cause a total loss of capital invested.

Alternatively, this contract could have been constructed by lending the principal (less the discounted value of the guaranteed dollar interest payment which is invested in a one-year Treasury bill) directly to a Thai bank by buying a bank acceptance. Again, the implicit assumption is that the baht/dollar exchange rate should remain constant so that the baht interest and principal repayment can be converted at maturity to a dollar value equal to the original investment of principal. If the baht devalues relative to the dollar, then the amount available to repay the principal will be lower. The buyer thus has the entire principal at risk, only the interest is guaranteed. The contract arranged in this way would provide Thai banks with below-market rate funds, provide US investors with above-market returns (US rates were in decline from 1991 to 1993) and the banks with fees and commissions for arranging the trade, but with no commitment of capital (most US banks were emerging from the experiences of the real estate crisis of the 1980s and were seeking to rebuild capital).

It is virtually impossible for the US investor to evaluate the use of the funds made by the Thai bank, and there is little incentive for the US bank to do so, since once the structured note issue is sold, the foreign credit and foreign exchange risks are borne by the US investor. The investor is not only subverting prudential controls (on its balance sheet these assets would be classified as exposure to a US entity, with investment grade credit risk), but is in all probability evaluating the return without any adjustment for the foreign exchange risk, even if that risk is recognized as such. There is thus little economic interest or possibility for the market to assess either the risk or the returns of the investment. There is thus no incentive for market agents to act so as to ensure that capital is allocated globally to those uses providing the highest risk-adjusted rates of return.

Structured credit derivatives

Structured products have been the basis for the growing market in credit derivative contracts. These contracts usually involve credit swaps embedded in structured notes to form credit-linked notes. The objective of a credit swap is to allow counterparties to exchange the credit risks associated with an instrument, while retaining the cash-flow characteristics. Total return swaps 'enable counterparties to swap the total economic risk attached to a reference asset without actually transferring the asset itself ... Under the terms of the swap, [the first counterparty] pays [the second counterparty] the cashflows generated by the reference asset, including coupon payments and any appreciations in its capital valued calculated on a periodic mark to market basis. [The second counterparty], in exchange, pays a LIBOR-linked margin plus any depreciations in the capital value of the reference asset' (Ghose, 1997, p. 3; see also the description given in Federal Reserve System, 1998, section 4350.1, pp. 1–2). A credit swap or equity swap thus transfers the credit risk, including the impact of a credit event on the capital value of the asset.

It was the creation of the Brady bond that provided the recipe for the extension of many of these structured loans to emerging markets. A collateralized Brady bond is a variety of structured derivative in which the developing country (Mexico was the first) uses foreign exchange reserves as equity capital to create an investment company (special investment vehicle). The investment company uses the equity (i.e., the foreign exchange) to buy long-term, stripped US Treasury bonds to serve as collateral. The investment company then issues its own fixed-interest liabilities in the form of long-term bonds (which came to be called Brady bonds after the US Secretary of the Treasury who held office at the time), which carry a sovereign government guarantee, in an amount equal to the maturity value of the US Treasury discount bonds. The investment company's bonds are usually only sold in exchange for the debtor country's outstanding foreign bank debt at its current market value (in Mexico's case this represented a discount to its face value of about 35%). The principal of the bonds issued by the investment vehicle (the Brady bonds) is thus guaranteed or collateralized by the Treasury bonds held, and repayment of principal in full at maturity is riskless. Additional short-term Treasury coupon strips (which provide only payment of coupon interest, without any right to principal repayment) would also be purchased by the investment vehicle to provide a guarantee for the interest payments during the first 18 or 24 months of life of the bonds. After that, interest would have to be paid from the proceeds of the underlying loans or from other government sources. The interest is thus only partially guaranteed and only riskless for the payments backed by the US Treasury strips. Banks that exchanged their participations in syndicated loans to developing countries for 'Brady bonds' could then trade those bonds in the open market, with their values determined by changes in the issuing country's sovereign credit rating and in US interest rates which affect the current value of the underlying collateral – the Treasury bonds.

Although the maturities of the Brady bonds were usually 20 or more years, in the case of a Brady bond with a two-year rolling interest guarantee, it was identical to buying a 20-year discount zero coupon bond, a 6-month zero bond, a 12-month zero, an 18-month zero, and a 2-year zero. These streams were default-free, so they could be considered as AAA. It was only the interest payments to be paid after the second year (which could be represented as 36 zero coupon bonds with maturities running from 30 months to 20 years at six-month intervals) that carried foreign exchange and sovereign credit risk. The Brady structure thus provided complicated market valuation, and it also provided an infinite number of possibilities for rearranging the various pieces of the bond into more attractive cash-flow structures:

> An example would be transferring Brady bonds into a trust structure, rearranging the cash flows and swapping them from floating USD into fixed DEM with a bullet repayment. Investors are thus able to achieve a higher yield than a Latin American DEM Eurobond with essentially the same counter-party risk. The bank arranging the issue is left with a contingent default risk on the underlying Brady bonds. There can be a loss in the case of a default, as the residual value of the Brady bonds in the trust might not be sufficient to cover the bank's potential loss from unwinding the cross currency swap. (Watzinger, 1997, p. 49)

Thus, a company set up to buy Brady bonds could issue its own two-year bonds that would carry a AAA credit rating since the interest payments were backed by US Treasury securities, and another series of bonds with a 20-year guaranteed principal value at maturity and a lower credit rating reflecting the risk on the remaining interest payments. If this second series could be rated investment grade, the final result would be to transform high-risk, impaired, syndicated loans of banks to Latin American governments into low-risk investment-grade bonds that could be sold to institutional investors, with a profit from the price differences reflecting the credit-rating differential, as well as the associated fees and commissions. This is called credit enhancement, and investment banks quickly extended the Brady principle to other types of developing country debt. Since the first Brady issues were in Mexico (J. P. Morgan had produced a prototype of the Brady bond called the Aztec bond in 1988), this extension beyond syndicated bank loans also appears to have started in Mexico.

The problem facing investment bankers was to find structures that allowed improvement in credit ratings of the original issues at minimal cost. The first step in this process was the creation of a special investment vehicle in the form of an offshore trust that would buy a high interest rate domestic bond (say a Mexican government-issued security, such as Ajustabonos or Cetes, which carries an investment grade domestic credit rating), along with some zero coupon US Treasury bonds. These purchases would be financed through the issue of its own dollar-denominated bonds (no longer called Brady). The bonds could be divided into two classes: one class would have its principal collateralized by the Treasury discount bonds in Brady fashion, while the other class, backed by the domestic bonds, would carry no guarantee. The interest would be paid from the income generated by the peso asset. For the rating agencies, these were credit-enhanced peso bonds, and they were assigned a credit rating equal to the Mexican government rating on its peso issues in the domestic capital market. Since a government is always the benchmark, and thus the domestic risk-free rate, it is almost by definition investment grade in its own market. The enhanced bonds issued by the trust were thus given an investment-grade rating. But, as dollar-denominated bonds paying dollar interest rates, they could be sold to US institutional investors. What the investor was in fact buying was a peso-denominated Mexican government bond, and the exchange rate risk on the interest payments. However, on the balance sheet of the US investor, these instruments were represented as if they were US dollar investment-grade bonds. Again, the result was that US institutional investor funds were being invested in emerging market debt, earning above-market interest rates, without their balance sheets necessarily reflecting the actual risk involved. These structures were offered in various combinations, but it still remains true that neither the investor nor the bank intermediary has any direct interest in evaluating either the final use made of the funds, nor the risk-adjusted returns earned by the investments. For the intermediary there was no risk, unless the bank was required to guarantee that it could convert the interest payments into dollars, which only represented a risk if the foreign currency was to become inconvertible (this is not devaluation risk, but the risk that the currency could not be sold at any price).

This provides one possible explanation of why so much effort was made to prevent Mexico from suspending convertibility in 1994. Structures similar to these were used in Asia, as well as in Latin America. Thus the structured note and the credit-enhanced Brady structure provide simple examples of how funds were moved from developed to developing countries, despite the existence of prudential regulatory barriers, and why there was little effort expended in ensuring that the funds were moving to the highest risk-adjusted uses. The buyers were interested in enhancing yield in a low yield environment, while the intermediaries were interested in producing zero risk, zero capital-using vehicles that would maximize fee and commission income. Earnings on structured vehicles are estimated to have been in excess of 2% of principal.

The result of these packages is to change the credit-risk characteristics of the bonds by shifting the risks to different individuals. They thus allow access for investors whose activities are limited by the credit-risk classification of the assets they can buy:

> Emerging market borrowers use total return swaps to get access to funding, or reduce the cost of it. The borrower sells assets to a bank and enters into a total return swap. In this swap, he receives the total return on the assets sold and pays Libor plus spread. Consequently, the borrower raises funds while at the same time still being able to benefit from a price appreciation of the asset sold ... Investors use total return swaps to get access to their desired emerging market exposure. In a number of countries, severe restrictions in the cash market prevail. For instance, cumbersome settlement procedures, withholding taxes or minimum holding periods. Total return swaps can be an effective means for investors to structure a way around these restrictions. (Chew, 1996, p. 49)

Asset prices and foreign exchange market linkages

Linkage between foreign exchange markets and emerging asset markets may result from the use of some extensions of the structured and credit derivatives contracts discussed above. These extensions generally involve using hard currency exposure to fund a position in an emerging market asset denominated in an emerging market currency. They thus create both currency and emerging asset market price risk.

In an equity swap, the owner of an emerging market asset exchanges its return (i.e., interest or dividend income plus the change in capital value) for a fixed term (or until maturity or perpetuity) against a zero interest loan (which may be in foreign currency) of its current value (or the expected value of the future income stream) of the asset. This is, of course, equivalent to sale of the asset, but without actual transfer of ownership. Such a transaction avoids having to book a loss on the asset (an advantage to a bank in difficulty) or to book a tax event (an advantage to a rich businessman), while liquidating the value of the asset. There is currency risk represented by the receipt of the total return on the asset by the developed country bank, as well as market price risk, represented by the necessity to offset changes in capital value. Thus, both exchange rate risk and asset price risk are present in these contracts.

A variant of this structure is a form of total return swap that was common in the run-up to the 1994–5 peso crisis.[5] A total return swap can be made using any underlying asset as the reference rate which is swapped against the benchmark rate, usually a US dollar rate plus a margin. A US bank may agree to pay the total return (in pesos) on a Mexican government security against the payment by a Mexican bank of a dollar benchmark interest rate plus a spread. The Mexican bank is effectively borrowing dollars and investing them in Mexican securities, earning the spread between dollar and peso interest rates. The advantage in this structure (as opposed to the equity swap discussed above) is that the asset does not appear on the Mexican bank's balance sheet, while it profits from what is in effect borrowing at a cost below the domestic market interest rate without adding to its risk-adjusted capital requirement.

On the other hand, the US bank is effectively lending dollars against the collateral of an emerging market asset, and paying the total peso return on the foreign asset against receipt of a dollar interest payment. The US bank profits from the spread over market interest rates, which is substantially greater than it could have charged domestic clients. As far as the developing country bank is concerned, it faces foreign exchange risk and possible interest rate or maturity risk, as well as the price risk on the asset (the borrower must compensate the lender for any depreciation in the capital value of the asset). Risk coverage for the US bank would be arranged by buying the underlying asset (this hedges the commitment to pay the interest return on the asset plus any capital appreciation), and then financing the purchase through a repurchase agreement with another US bank; thus getting the asset off its own balance sheet. But exchange rate and convertibility risk exposure still remain on the notional amount of the swap contract. This could be hedged by issuing a floating-rate note at a guaranteed above-market interest rate for the value of the principal, with a clause permitting payment in foreign currency in the event of a suspension of currency convertibility. Thus, both the US and emerging market banks incur currency mismatches, and the profitability of the contract to each depends on movements in the exchange rate as well as the relative movements of US and emerging market interest rates, and thus on asset prices in the emerging market.

Either of these two structures may thus provide an explanation of a direct linkage between exchange rates and domestic asset markets. As already mentioned, most of these instruments were set up on the presumption of stable exchange rates. Any indication that there might be a change in the way a central bank handled exchange rate policy would create the potential for substantial losses to investors. To see this, consider the foreign bank paying dollar interest and receiving total return on the domestic asset. The domestic currency costs of the dollar payments will increase with any increase in the dollar interest rate or any devaluation of the domestic currency. While a rise in domestic interest rates will increase returns, the associated depreciation in the value of the asset will normally more than offset this, so that the financing costs of the position (the cost of carry) in domestic currency terms will increase and profitability decline. When depreciation in the currency is accompanied by rising domestic interest rates, a contract with a positive carry (i.e., a profit on the interest differential paid and received) may be quickly reversed, creating an incentive to unwind the swap or to hedge the foreign exchange risk by going long dollar assets. This creates an increase in the demand for dollars in a market that is already showing excess dollar demand. If the fall in the price of the underlying asset is large, or the devaluation is large, hedging the position may be impossible, or convertibility may be suspended and there is a default.

Further, the natural response for the US bank, recognizing the possibility of counterparty default, would be to hedge its dollar exposure represented by the loan against the foreign asset. This would be accomplished by unwinding the hedge of its total return commitment, i.e., unwinding the repo of the foreign asset, selling that asset in the foreign market and repatriating the proceeds at the best possible exchange rate. The net result is that both parties to the swap will react by selling emerging market financial assets and/or selling the domestic currency proceeds against dollars, providing levered downward pressure on both asset market prices and the foreign exchange market. Extensive use of these contracts would thus explain an increased correlation between exchange rates and asset prices.

Most global investment banks were cognizant of risks that exchange rate instability represented for such contracts. Given this type of exposure, it is perhaps not surprising that the investment banks selling these products continued publicly to express confidence in the prospects for exchange rate stability in countries to which they had large outstanding exposures. Even if they had performed appropriate risk assessment, it would not have been in their interests to inform market participants until they had succeeded in unwinding their derivative positions. It is thus also not surprising that funds continued to flow to countries showing a distinct risk of currency instability, for this is what was required in order for structured positions to be closed without substantial loss.

Since most of these structured products are expressly designed to hide risk exposure by providing credit enhancement, or by being classified as 'off-balance-sheet', it is not surprising that bank regulators in emerging economies had difficulty in discovering or controlling them. There is no reason why Asian regulators should be any more efficient than US regulators, who admit to difficulties in evaluating such instruments. Further, Asian banks were being encouraged, just as US thrifts were encouraged in the 1980s, to deregulate, liberalize and to attempt to grow their way out of weakness by investing in assets with higher returns. The regulators accepted this strategy for resolution of the difficulties facing US institutions; it would be difficult not to accept it in emerging markets if it was supported by both the government and the multilateral institutions.

Derivatives and Asian capital flows in the 1990s

Although direct information on the role of derivatives in the Asian crisis is scarce,[6] the majority of losses reported by major US money-centre banks[7] on their Asian lending has been listed as due to swaps contracts. Further, the legal suits that have been filed by J. P. Morgan and SK Securities in their payments dispute, are reported to relate to total return swaps.[8] It is also the case that the issue of capital market instruments by Asian borrowers surged in 1995 and 1996. For example, Asian issuance rose from $25.2 billion in 1995 to $43.1 billion in 1996. Not only were US banks involved, but much of the success of local investment banks, such as Hong Kong-based Peregrine Securities, was primarily in underwriting and selling debt for Asian corporations. It could only do this if it could provide reasonable guarantees for the placement for these issues. That its liquidation apparently placed a large number of Asian corporates' foreign currency hedges in jeopardy because of failure of the counterparty suggests that the investment bank Peregrine might have been a major source of the high-return Asian assets which served to form the assets of high-return, special purpose vehicles for banks in Korea and investors in the developed countries. Korean securities houses and investment banks were also apparently actively involved. The Korean Securities Supervisory Board reported that Korean institutions were operating over 100 offshore investment funds with portfolios valued at around $3 billion, two-thirds of which represented Korean assets.[9]

The lawsuits that have recently been filed by a number of Korean entities that were swap counterparties of J. P. Morgan shed some light on the nature of these transactions. For example, in one transaction Morgan engaged in a $/won currency swap with Boram Bank.[10] In a straight currency swap, the counterparties exchange principal and interest payments on the currencies, so presumably Boram gave won to Morgan in exchange for dollars, and was paying Morgan a fixed interest rate linked to the US dollar, while Morgan was paying a rate linked to won interest rates (the differential in the rates when the swap was initiated in February 1997 was about 2 to 1, suggesting a substantial profit on the interest rate differential). When the swap is unwound the principal sums are usually returned at a prearranged exchange rate, so that Boram would have had to return dollars that were worth about three times as many won as at the beginning of the swap. To cover this risk, Boram engaged in a series of swaps with SK Securities, presumably passing the dollars on to SK Securities which now carried the foreign exchange risks, but was borrowing at cheap dollar interest rates, against the won loans it was extending to its clients at domestic market rates. The exchange rate loss on the swap was thus borne by SK, who owed this sum to Boram, who in turn owed it to Morgan. The Morgan lawsuit places the value at $189 million. Given the changes in exchange rates, the original principal could have been less than $250 million.[11] This is a relatively straightforward derivative transaction, but it gives an idea of the potential losses involved, and why there was such pressure on the foreign exchange market to acquire funds to unwind swaps of this nature.

The other transactions relate to swaps between Morgan and Korean offshore investment funds operated by SK Securities and Shinsegi Investment Trust.[12] It is highly likely that these transactions involved equity swaps or total return swaps. Thus bonds issued by Korean companies, underwritten by SK, were placed in an offshore, special purpose vehicle, financed by the sale of investment shares to the Korean public or other financial institutions. The offshore trusts also invested in other Asian assets. These assets could then be used by the offshore units to generate dollar loans equal to the value of the assets, plus won interest rate and capital appreciation flows, against payment of dollar interest rates. These dollars could then be used to make further loans to Korean companies, while the won payments received from Morgan would be used to pay the local investors in the offshore vehicles.

Again, the magnitude of the change in the exchange rate witnessed after the decision to float the won would have produced capital losses on the underlying assets and thus negative won inflows, which would have been transformed into larger net dollar interest payments due to Morgan. The offshore trusts would have had to borrow to meet any fixed-interest payments, while the loss on the dollar borrowing would have decimated the capital value of the investment portfolio, irrespective of changes in stock prices. The rush to hedge such exposure thus made the fall in the exchange and asset markets that much worse. The legal cases at this stage simply involve failure of the trusts to meet periodic payments on the swaps.[13] It is reported that more than 40 of the 100 or so such trusts had engaged in similar swaps with Morgan.[14] Of its total of $3.4 billion of exposure to Korea, $2 billion are linked to derivative contracts. This perhaps explains why Morgan was at the forefront of the move to convert Korean banks' short-term debt into sovereign debt.

Another way of identifying the importance of derivatives activity in the Asian crisis is with reference to the Country Exposure Lending Survey for money-centre banks published by the US Federal Financial Institutions Examination Council (FFIEC), which reports figures for total amounts lent by country of borrower, net of derivatives, and the cross-border exposure resulting from revaluation gains on foreign exchange and derivative products after adjustments for guarantees and external borrowings. These figures are given for the amounts outstanding at the end of 1997 and the end of the first quarter of 1998 (in parentheses) (see Table 4.1). Since derivatives exposure only results when a counterparty default places the bank under a risk of having to replace the instrument at a loss to current market conditions, the figures in the second column represent the profits for US money-centre banks on their derivatives activity plus any increases in the value of their outstanding loans due to changes in exchange rates. Since US banks' exposure is primarily in dollars, the majority of these changes should be the result of changes in the valuation of derivatives contracts rather than changes in the dollar value of outstanding direct loans.

In Thailand, for example, the profits from derivatives and currency revaluations far exceed the total amounts owed for traditional lending. This suggests that a majority of the short-term bank funds that entered Thailand were linked to derivative contracts. For Korea, the profit figures are well over half the amount of total lending, leading to a similar conclusion. In Indonesia they are roughly two-thirds. Thus, in all three countries that have had to apply for IMF support, derivatives sold by US banks to domestic institutions appear to have played as large a part as traditional financing activities.[15] While these figures do not allow a calculation of the actual amount of funds that were channelled to Asia via structured derivative products, they do support the view that derivative contracts played an integral role in the rise in short-term flows to the region. This thus helps to explain the shift in the composition of lending into the region towards short-term bank flows.

Table 4.1 Country exposure of US money-centre banks: loans and derivatives (31 December 1997) (figures for 31 March 1998 in parentheses)

Country (\$ millions)	*Total amount owed by country of borrower (derivative contracts excepted)*	*Cross-border exposure from foreign exchange revaluation and derivative contracts*
Indonesia	\$3,000 (2,284)	\$2,266 (1,612)
Korea	\$9,791 (9,155)	\$4,633 (2,890)
Malaysia	\$1,543 (1,070)	\$555 (266)
Philippines	\$1,533 (1,357)	\$40 (157)
Thailand	\$1,771 (920)	\$2,509 (1,145)

Source: Federal Financial Institutions Examination Council (FFIEC), 1998, *Statistical Release, e-16: Country Exposure Lending Survey/1*, table 1, pp. 18–19, 8 April 1998 for 31 December 1997, and 8 July 1998 for 31 March 1998.

Conclusions

Clearly, as the crisis unfolds we shall learn more of the role of derivatives in facilitating the flow of short-term funds to the Asian economies. This note is not meant to argue that all the difficulties created by the volatility of capital flows to Asia were the result of the increased use of derivative instruments or of structured derivative packages. However, the characteristics of these contracts do provide an insight into the four puzzles that were raised in the introductory section. First, the increased use of over-the-counter derivatives contracts as the vehicle for lending to Asia explains the predominance of commercial banks as lenders, as well as the dominantly short-term nature of the flows. It also explains why the lending was so volatile. Second, the characteristics of the contracts that were most probably involved suggest that they are motivated by factors that are not directly related to the allocation of funds to their highest global returns. Rather, they are linked to attempts to circumvent particular prudential regulations and to provide banks with low-risk fee and commission income, rather than to profit from assessing relative risk-adjusted returns. The incentives motivating such contracts provide little support for the common belief in the self-regulating nature of private capital markets in terms of risk assessment or of their ability to allocate capital efficiently. Third, the fact that developed country banks and regulators had difficulty in foreseeing the risks involved in the derivative positions used suggests that the crisis was not completely due to the inability of emerging markets bankers and regulators to provide acceptable risk management. Finally, the way particular swap contracts and credit derivatives combine currency risk and market price risks provides an explanation of why these markets tended to move in sympathy, creating a cumulative causation that produced unexpected declines and excessive instability in both currency and asset markets during the height of the crisis. What evidence there is of derivative contracts that were actually employed in Asia tends to support these conclusions and contradicts the commonly held position that derivative contracts played no role in the evolution of the financial crisis in Asia.

Appendix

Glossary of terms[16]

Bullet – a security with a payment schedule in which the fixed periodic payments are composed only of interest on principal, with no amortization of principal, which is due in full at maturity. Used in contrast to a traditional self-amortizing mortgage contract in which each payment is comprised of amortization of principal and interest on the remaining balance.

Cost of carry, carry cost – the difference between the interest cost of borrowing funds to purchase a security and the periodic interest or dividend earned from owning the security. A positive carry position has the latter greater than the former so that the owner profits from the position without commiting any capital and irrespective of any change in the price of the asset.

Coupon payments – the fixed periodic payments of interest paid to the owner of a bond until maturity.

Coupon strips – the right to the periodic coupon interest payments that have been removed from the stripped or zero coupon bond; strips pay only periodic interest and no principal at maturity.

Credit derivatives are off-balance-sheet financial instruments that permit one party (the beneficiary) to transfer the credit risk of a reference asset, which it typically owns, to another party (the guarantor) without actually selling the asset. In other words, credit derivatives allow users to 'unbundle' credit risk from financial instruments and trade it separately.

Credit event – a change in the conditions of the issuer of an asset affecting its ability to meet its contractual obligations, leading to a change in the credit quality of the asset and usually reflected in a change in the rating assigned by a credit agency.

Credit-enhanced bonds are issued by a special purpose vehicle and have a higher credit rating than the primary assets held by the vehicle because of the inclusion of some higher quality assets or because the primary assets have a higher nominal value than the bonds issued. Brady bonds are credit-enhanced bonds.

Discount bonds – bonds that pay no coupon interest; their return is determined by the difference between their purchase price and maturity value.

Mark to market valuation – value of an asset calculated on the basis of prices recorded for recent transactions in the asset, or on the basis of firm offers to buy the asset, in difference from the price paid to aquire the asset (historic cost) or the maturity or redemption value.

Options contracts transfer the right but not the obligation to buy or sell an underlying asset, instrument, or index on or before the option's exercise date at a specified price (the strike price). A call option gives the option purchaser the right, but not the obligation, to purchase a specific quantity of the underlying asset (from the call option seller) on or before the option's exercise date at the strike price. Conversely, a put option gives the option purchaser the right, but not the obligation, to sell a specific quantity of the underlying asset (to the put option seller) on or before the option's exercise date at the strike price.

Reference asset – a derivative instrument derives its value from movements in the value of an underlying or reference security or security index.

Repurchase agreement or repo involves the sale of a security to a counterparty with an agreement to repurchase it at a fixed price on an established future date. At initiation of the transaction, the buyer pays the principal amount to the seller, and the security is transferred to the possession of the buyer. At expiration of the repo, the principal amount is returned to the initial buyer (or lender) and possession of the security reverts to the initial seller (or borrower). The security serves as collateral against the obligation of the borrower and does not actually become the property of the lender.

Stripped bonds (STRIPS) are zero-coupon securities created by the US Treasury by physically separating the principal and interest cash flows. This process of separating cash flows from standard fixed-rate Treasury securities is referred to as coupon stripping. The bonds are sold without the right to receive the periodic payment of coupon interest, thus they have 'zero' interest-rate coupons. They are equivalent to discount securities with their return determined by the difference between their purchase price and (higher) maturity value.

Structured notes are hybrid securities, possessing characteristics of straight debt instruments and derivative instruments. Rather than paying a straight fixed or floating coupon, the interest payments of these instruments are linked to the performance of a reference asset's price or interest rate or index. The derivative contracts are embedded in the security, and may not be presented explicitly as such. They pay a higher interest rate than a straight debt instrument with this differential determined by the value of the embedded option.

Total-rate-of-return swaps are credit derivative contracts in which one counterparty (Bank A) agrees to pay the total return on an underlying reference asset to its counterparty (Bank B) in exchange for a dollar interest rate plus a spread. Most often, the reference asset is a corporate or sovereign bond or a traded commercial loan.

Notes

1. This frequently cited study was not available in April 1998 when this article was drafted. The summary that appears in the IMF's *World Economic Outlook* (Part II, Box 1, 1998) suggests that hedge funds mainly attack countries whose 'macroeconomic variables are far out of line with sustainable values'. Another recent study (Brown, Goetzmann and Park, 1998) suggests that hedge funds did not take major positions against Asian currencies or financial assets and did not make abnormal returns from their operations during the last half of 1997. From this one might conclude that the hedge fund managers did not detect any unsustainable policies in these countries.
2. For example, Chew (1996, p. 57) observes the '[s]tructured notes are the epitome of how investment technology helped and continues to help money managers circumvent guidelines that were framed to protect the interest of small, unsophisticated investors ...'
3. The widely reported derivatives losses incurred by Procter and Gamble and Gibson Greeting Cards involved contracts of precisely this type. Their borrowing costs were reduced by the amount of the option premium gained from writing put options on interest rates with a highly levered pay-off profile. Such contracts provided below-market borrowing costs as long as the losses on the option positions did not exceed the premia received from selling the options contracts. However, in the winter of 1994 interest rates rose sharply, leading to net losses (cf., Chew, 1996).
4. 'The Federal Home Loan Bank (FHLB), one of the largest issuers of such products in the United States, has more than 175 indexes or index combinations against which cash flows are calculated ... Structured notes are pri-

marily issued by government-sponsored enterprises (GSEs), such as the Federal Home Loan Bank (FHLB), Federal National Mortgage Association (FNMA), Student Loan Marketing Association (SNMA), and Federal Home Loan Mortgage Corporation (FHLMC). Although the credit risk of these securities is minimal, other risks such as interest-rate risk, market (price) risk, and liquidity risk can be material. [However,] [i]nvestment banks and the section 20 subsidiaries of banks often act to underwrite structured-note issuances. They are often actively involved in making a market in secondary structured notes ... In its heyday, the structured-note market was a by-product of a unique period in financial history. In 1992 and 1993, Wall Street firms engineered debt that allowed borrowers to attain highly attractive below-market funding and that rewarded investors (in large part) as long as interest rates remained low. The incredible and at times implausible array of structure types came into being in response to the investment community's desire for higher returns during a sustained period of low interest rates. Issuers and investment dealer firms were more than willing to address this need, introducing investors to more attractive (and by definition riskier) securities whose cash flows were linked to, for example, the performance of the yen; the yen's relationship to the lira; and a host of other indexes, currencies, or benchmarks. Investors' quest for enhanced yield caused them to adopt, in many cases, very tenuous risk-reward measures with respect to potential investment choices' (Federal Reserve System, 1998, Section 4040.1, pp. 1, 5, 6).

5. The use of this particular structure by a large US investment bank is described by Partnoy (1997, ch. 9). It is important to remember that even if no assets or currency are actually exchanged, the impact on the participating banks' profit and loss position is just as if the funds had actually been lent and/or invested and in the case of leveraged contracts exceed those amounts.
6. Since they are private, over-the-counter, contracts between banks and their clients, their particulars are not revealed even in reports to shareholders. They do become public if they are subject to litigation and most of the information reported here comes from this source.
7. It is clear that German and French banks were also heavily involved in derivatives trading in the region. Andrews (1998) reports that Deutsche Bank set aside $777 million (double its loss provisions for 1996) to cover losses of as much as $100 million on derivatives trading in South Korea, Thailand, Indonesia and Malaysia. Société Générale is reported to have set aside $164 million, against a total exposure of $6.8 billion (the $4 billion lent in Korea is primarily lending to Korean companies; cf., Lavin, 1998). Commerz has $3 billion in loans (37% of equity), Dresdner 26% of equity and Deutsche 27% of equity in Asian loans.
8. Cf., *Korea Times* (1998a), which refers to an offshore investment fund created by LG Metal and SK Hannam Investment Securities Fund: 'The $18 million fund was called "Diamond Fund", and was guaranteed by Boram Bank ... JP Morgan had entered into a swap transaction with Boram in February 1997, involving an exchange of dollars for the Korean currency. [The fund lost an estimated $120 million.] Such derivatives as total return swaps were popular a year ago as they allowed investors to borrow yen at

low interest rates and invest in higher-yielding currencies such as the Thai bat [*sic*] or Indonesian rupiah.'

9. The Korean 'Securities Supervisory Board said that brokerage houses have more than a 10 percent stake in 66 funds. Another 23 funds were invested in by parent offshore funds of securities firms ... The offshore funds were reported to have invested 68.3 percent of their money in Korean securities' (*Korea Times*, 1998b). The Board also reports that the losses that SK Securities companies and investment trust companies suffered in offshore funds are estimated at 1.5 trillion won (krw) ($1 = krw 1,672) as of the end of last year. 'Four investment trust companies are running 19 offshore funds, which were reported to have suffered about 400 billion won' (see AP-DJ News Service, 1998a).
10. 'Boram had agreed to a trade of two revenue streams, giving Morgan the stream linked to the prevailing US interest rate in return for the revenue from a basket of derivatives linked to the value of South-east Asian securities and the Thai baht ... A year ago, investment bankers eagerly pitched derivatives to SK companies. With benchmark Japanese rates at 0.5 percent, it made sense to sign contracts that would allow investors to borrow in yen and invest in higher-yielding Asian currencies, many of which were linked to the dollar until last year. "It's not an accident that a lot of derivatives got sold in Korea", said John Ellis, head of the Asia derivatives debt at Bank of America in Honk Kong. "It was as good as lending money"' (see *Wall Street Journal*, 1998).
11. Although Boram was prepared to pay Morgan, SK filed a suit in a Korean court to block the payment, thus hoping to exonerate it from having to pay Boram the funds which would have ended up being paid to Morgan.
12. One of the 30 recently created investment banks, it was suspended by the Korean Government at the beginning of December and closed at the end of the year. In September it was listed as having 66 billion won in equity, 3,125 billion won in total outstanding loans, 3.66% of which were classified.
13. Again, the legal cases are peripheral to these considerations. Housing and Commercial Bank (a government-owned bank ranked 24th in North Asia with over $1 billion in equity in 1996 at 1996 exchange rates) apparently offered credit enhancement by offering to guarantee the foreign exchange payments of the offshore trusts. Morgan has filed a suit against the bank (and SK Securities) for failing to make payments missed by the offshore trusts). Housing and Commercial, however, contends that their exposure was limited to a maximum of $50 million for each swap, and is therefore not responsible for the total losses of the trusts. O'Brien (1998, p. D2) suggests that the original maximum was $100 million but that the contract was changed without the knowledge of the bank to unlimited exposure. Morgan contends that an officer of the bank authorized removal of the limiting clause before closure of the contract. According to O'Brien's account, 'SK and M had a close working arrangement. SK had established offshore funds to manage the derivatives, and those funds also purchased other securities directly from Morgan.' SK was also sued as parent of the trusts. The total value of the suit is $300 million.

14. '[T]here are about 40 other local funds that operated in similar agreements with J. P. Morgan, ... J. P. Morgan has a total exposure of $3.4 billion to Korea, of which $2 billion is to derivatives products' (see Kang, 1998).
15. The Bank of Korea reported (AP-DJ, 1998b) that trading in financial derivatives by South Korean banks increased by 60.1% in 1997 to $556.5 billion. Foreign exchange forwards comprise about two-thirds of the total. It also reported that Korea's 26 banks booked losses for 1997 of 3.92 trillion won, while the 39 branches of foreign banks reported net profits of 930.48 billion won (Industrial & Commercial Bank of China and Credit Suisse First Boston were the only foreign banks reporting losses) (Park, 1998).
16. This glossary provides definitions of some of the terms employed above. The interested reader is invited to consult Federal Reserve System, 1998, for a more complete listing of terms and instruments.

References

Andrews, E. L. (1998) 'Huge German bank covering risks in Asia', *New York Times*, 29 January.

AP-DJ News Service (1998a) 'S. Korea banks sec cos from making offshore fund guarantees', 20 February.

AP-DJ News Service (1998b) 'S. Korean banks' derivatives transactions rose 60.1% '97', 5 March.

Brown, S., Goetzmann, J. and Park, J. (1998) 'Hedge Funds and the Asian Currency Crisis of 1997', NBER Working Paper 6427, Boston, MA, February.

Chew, L. (1996) *Managing Derivative Risks: The Use and Abuse of Leverage*, New York, John Wiley.

Federal Financial Institutions Examination Council (FFIEC) (1998) *Country Exposure Lending Survey/1*, Washington DC, 8 April.

Federal Reserve System (1998) *Trading and Capital-Markets Activities Manual*, Washington DC, February.

Ghose, R. (1997) 'What are credit derivatives?', in *Credit Derivatives: Key Issues*, British Bankers' Association.

International Monetary Fund (IMF) (1998) *World Economic Outlook*, Washington DC, April.

Kang, C. (1998) 'Korea Housing/J. P. Morgan–3: calls inaction inappropriate', AP-DJ News Service, 18 February.

Korea Times (1998a) 'ASK Securities, JP Morgan heading for int'l court battle over derivatives', 16 February.

Korea Times (1998b) 'Brokerage firms incur 1.5 tril won losses from offshore funds', 19 February.

Lavin, D. (1998) 'Profit at Société Générale up 34%; bank sees 'robust growth trend', *Wall Street Journal Interactive Edition*, 12 March.

O'Brien, T. L. (1998) 'J. P. Morgan in Korea battle on derivatives: more US implications seen from Asian crisis', *New York Times*, 27 February, D1.

Park, K. (1998) 'Foreign banks in S. Korea combined '97 net profit KRW930.48B', AP-DJ News Service, 13 March.

Partnoy, F. (1997) *F.I.A.S.C.O. Blood in the Water on Wall Street*, New York, Norton.

Wall Street Journal (1998) 'Review & Outlook: busting contracts', 23 February.

Watzinger, H. (1997) 'Credit derivatives in emerging markets', in *Credit Derivatives: Key Issues*, British Bankers' Association.

5

From 'Miracle' to 'Cronyism': Explaining the Great Asian Slump

*Robert Wade**

Explanations are about the only thing not in short supply in the Asian crisis. For all their diversity they can be collapsed into two 'meta' interpretations reflecting deeper differences in beliefs about rationality and markets. Those whose world view emphasizes rationality, self-adjusting markets, and market failure as exceptional except when governments introduce distortions, tend to see the crisis as the result of rational calculations in a situation of market-distorting government interventions and institutional weaknesses in Asian economies. Those whose world view stresses non-rationality (or a different kind of rationality than that assumed by neoclassical theory), routine failure of well-working markets, and the need for government interventions to modify market outcomes, tend to see it as the result of non-rational calculations in under-regulated financial markets, both national and international.

The debate about the causes has been less a debate than paradigms ('parrot-times') talking past each other. Some hard testing is needed. The problem is that even in one country several different explanations may each contain truth. But '[t]here are not eighteen good reasons for anything', as George Stigler once said (quoted in Lipton, 1998). This paper aims, modestly, not at the necessary hypothesis formulation and testing but at an interpretative account. It gives prominence to the non-rational elements as an offset to the tendency of economists to be much more accepting of stories based on the assumption of rational calculation simply because more congruent with neoclassical theory. And, unlike other accounts, it encompasses both the crisis *and* the prolonged prior success.

Scale of the crisis

Table 5.1 shows the change in exchange rates and stock prices in East and South-east Asia between June 1997 and late March 1998. The three countries identified as the worst affected – South Korea, Thailand, Indonesia – have had the biggest falls in exchange rates, ranging from 36% to 72%. However, Malaysia and the Philippines, generally regarded as having escaped lightly, have had exchange rate declines of not much less than Thailand and Korea. Adding the fall in the stock market to the fall in the exchange rate to get a broader measure of impact, we have to put Malaysia with the group of worst affected countries, with the Philippines just behind. In short, the conventional understanding that only Korea, Thailand and Indonesia have been badly affected is not true by these measures. Malaysia and the Philippines have been hurt almost as much. Even Japan, Hong Kong and Singapore have taken substantial hits. Taiwan and China look to be least affected.

As of July 1998, the crisis is not yet in the clearing-up-after-the-storm stage; not a 'V' nor a 'U' but an 'L' or an 'S'. After a respite in early 1998 a second great wave of capital outflow occurred in May and June, and forecasters resumed chasing the economies downhill. It is not an exaggeration to liken the Asian crisis to the Great Depression of the 1930s in terms of the scale of the falls in output and consumption and the increase in poverty and insecurity. Countries have been pushed

Table 5.1 Change in exchange rates and stock prices in Asia (% between 2 June 1997 and 24 March 1998)

	Exchange rate against US$	*Stock index*	*Total*
East Asia			
Japan	–11	–17	–28
China	0.2	–11	–11
South Korea	–36	–34	–70
Hong Kong	–0.1	–22	–22
Taiwan	–15	10	–5
South-east Asia			
Thailand	–36	–17	–53
Malaysia	–31	–34	–65
Indonesia	–72	–24	–96
Singapore	–11	–20	–31
Phillippines	–29	–18	–47
United States	–	+24	+24

back down the hierarchy of world income to where they were 10 years ago and more.[1] Meanwhile, the international lenders have escaped with, at most, small losses, disproving once again the adage that 'if you owe the bank $1 million you have a problem, if you owe the bank $1 billion the bank has a problem'.

The high debt→debt deflation story

Most commentators agree that the sharp pullout of funds by investors across the region was the trigger, and that the pullout was panicky. The whipsaw movement from capital inflows to capital outflows was on a scale that could not but tear apart the social fabric of countries subjected to it, especially where political structures are only weakly institutionalized. *Net* private flows to or from the five Asian economies (the ASEAN four plus South Korea) were plus $93 billion in 1996, turning to minus $12 billion in 1997. The swing in one year of $105 billion (with most of the outflow concentrated in the *last quarter* of 1997) equals 11% of the combined GDP of the five countries. Asia's experience was worse even than Latin America's in the 1980s. The swing between 1981 inflows and 1982 outflows in the three biggest debtors (Brazil, Mexico, Argentina) amounted to 8% of their combined GDP.

An interpretative account has to explain why the inflows were so big, why the outflows were so big, and why the contraction of economic activity has continued to be so sharp. It has to link the banking crisis, the currency crisis and the corporate crisis, and the politics with the economics, without becoming so luxuriant as to be obscure.

The bank-based high debt model

Thanks to relatively equal income distribution, the large majority of Asian households are net savers (in contrast to Latin America). They deposit much of their savings in banks. Banks have to lend. But not to households and not to governments, which are not sizeable net borrowers. Banks have lent largely to firms seeking to borrow in order to invest.

Large Asian firms have tended to finance a high proportion of their investment from bank borrowings, and to carry a large amount of debt relative to equity compared to western or Latin American firms.[2] High debt/equity ratios allowed them to invest much more than through retained earnings or equity finance alone, and high corporate investment helped to propel the region's fast economic development over several decades.

Corporate sectors with high levels of debt are vulnerable to shocks that cause a fall in cash flow or an increase in fixed payment obligations – systemic shocks such as a fall in aggregate demand, a rise in interest rates, or devaluation of the currency (when part of the debt is foreign).[3]

This bank-based system of financial intermediation encourages close relations between bankers and corporate managers, and is sometimes called 'relationship' banking. The system often includes government incentives to direct lending to particular sectors or functions. And it includes a closed or partially closed capital account, such that financial capital cannot move freely in and out of the country. The whole apparatus buffers highly leveraged corporate sectors from systemic shocks and from the prudential limits of western banks, allowing them to sustain levels of investment well above what the risk preferences of equity holders would allow. Very high domestic savings permit the investment to be financed domestically (Wade, 1990, chs 10 and 11).

Financial liberalization

Asian governments, encouraged by the IMF and the World Bank as well as by national business elites, liberalized their financial systems through the 1990s, including the external capital account.[4] Liberalization permitted domestic agents to raise finance on foreign markets and gave foreign agents access to the domestic financial market. Hence locals could open foreign bank accounts; banks could extend credit in foreign currencies in the domestic markets; non-bank financial institutions and private corporations could borrow abroad; foreigners could own shares listed by national companies on domestic stock markets; foreign banks could enjoy wider freedom of entry into the domestic banking sector; and off-shore banks could borrow abroad and lend domestically (Islam, 1998). All this took place in the context of a more or less fixed nominal exchange rate regime tied to the US dollar.

With liberalization, governments gave up their capacity to coordinate foreign private borrowing. The IMF, the World Bank and the OECD acknowledged the need for *pari passu* strengthening of bank regulation and supervision, but did not constrain their push for liberalization by the pace of regulatory strengthening *on the ground*.

Liberalizing the financial sector and opening the capital account is dangerous when the banks have little experience in international financial markets and when non-banks also borrow abroad (Wolf, 1998a). It is doubly dangerous in the context of a bank-based financial system and a high debt-to-equity corporate sector. It is triply dangerous when the exchange rate is pegged. When, in addition, the banks and non-banks are essentially unsupervised a banking-cum-currency crisis is just waiting to happen. In Asia, swift external financial liberalization with unsupervised banks and fixed exchange rates undermined the previous system of industrial and banking cooperation and exposed fragile debt structures to unbuffered shocks.

Inflows

The capital inflow side of the story starts with the extraordinary growth of international capital flows in recent years, that now amount to well over 70 times the volume of world trade. The flows are mostly short term; 80% of net global foreign exchange transactions have a maturity date of seven days or less (Eatwell, 1997, p. 4). The growth of these flows reflects, in part, the efforts of central banks in Europe and Japan to stimulate their economies by means of loose monetary policy.

The growth also reflects the imbalance between savings and investment in Japan. For many years the Japanese, the fastest ageing population in the world, have been saving hard for the approaching years of long retirement. The economy is mature, among the richest in the world, and not able productively to utilize enough investment to absorb the savings. The result is an excess of domestic savings over domestic investment that manifests itself in chronic current account surpluses matched by capital exports (Wolf, 1998b).

In the decade 1985 to 1995, the yen appreciated hugely against the US dollar, from about 238 to 80. East and South-east Asian currencies, linked to the dollar, depreciated against the yen. Real exchange rates moved similarly. At the depreciated exchange rates, East and South-east Asia provided much more competitive production sites. Japanese capital flooded out to Asia, much of it in export-oriented production aimed at the US. Capital from other core economies joined in. With such high rates of investment, much of it in tradables, the economies grew at speeds rarely equalled in human history. Thailand had about the highest growth rate in the world from 1985 to 1994.

Japan's imbalance between saving and investment grew after the early 1990s because of the bursting of the property, stock market and currency bubbles. Japanese banks found themselves with many bad loans. Banks near to insolvency tend to take big risks unless they are recapitalized, merged, or forced into bankruptcy. Rather than follow one or other of these solutions the Japanese government decided to allow them to write off the bad loans gradually (to 'trade through'), giving them extra profits via a low bank rate and tax-avoiding declarations of losses. Meanwhile, the voracious Japanese appetite for savings continued, the savings going mostly into the banks. The banks had to lend. The 'near to insolvency → high risks' pressure therefore continued.

Japanese banks aggressively sought high returns from foreign lending, much of it in risky loans to South-east Asia. They found themselves able to borrow both domestically and abroad at low rates. They lent short term to South-east Asian banks and firms at appreciably higher rates, confident that South-east Asian currencies would remain pegged to the US dollar. European banks also lent heavily, especially after the flight from Mexico in the wake of the Mexican crisis of 1994–5.

On the demand side, banks and firms in Korea and South-east Asia rushed to borrow abroad. Borrowing aborad at roughly half the cost of borrowing domestically seemed to be a one-way bet. You could only win. The proviso was that the currency tie to the US dollar be maintained, precluding exchange rate risk. (The higher credit-rated banks and enterprises of Korea not only borrowed abroad and lent domestically, they also lent on to South-east Asia.)

At the same time, capital flowed in to accommodate the excess of investment over savings. High-speed growth generated gross domestic investment demand even higher than gross domestic saving, itself about the highest in the world.

In short, the inflows were driven both by the need to accommodate the excess of investment over savings (manifested in current account deficits, see below), and by the opportunity, thanks to capital account opening, for foreign creditors to get higher returns and domestic borrowers to borrow more cheaply. They were also driven by the image of 'miracle Asia'. Nobody was paying much attention to the growing imbalances in the banking systems or to other risk factors.

The inflows put *upward* pressure on the exchange rate. The attention of the monetary authorities and of speculators and investors was on the chances of preventing appreciation of the nominal exchange rate. Nobody was thinking depreciation. Nobody was hedging against a currency sell off.

Real vulnerabilities

The proximate source of real economy vulnerability was the deterioration in the current account in all the affected countries, especially in 1995 and 1996. Falling export growth was the main cause of the rising deficits. This reflected, first, a fall in demand for some of the main exports, notably semiconductors in the case of Korea (semiconductors being Korea's biggest single export item). Falling export growth reflected, second, declining competitiveness as a result of domestic costs rising faster than productivity. Capital inflows combined with the currency peg caused appreciation of the domestic currency. The real exchange rate appreciated in all five of the most affected countries in 1995–6, choking exports (Kaplinsky, 1998).

Third, the nominal exchange rate rose sharply against the yen from the spring of 1995 onwards, as the yen fell against the dollar (from a peak of 80 in 1995 to 147 in June 1998). Investments that had been competitive at the earlier exchange rate were now less competitive, especially against Japan and China. Much investment now looked to be 'excessive'. Fourth, the terms of trade (export prices over import prices) were trending downwards, owing especially to competition from China. Fifth, China gobbled up export markets in the US and Japan over the 1990s.

As investment surged throughout the region, much of it into a narrow range of sectors, productivity and profits began to suffer. At the margin, companies put more and more investment into non-tradable speculative ventures, including property and land. Thailand, Malaysia, and Indonesia all experienced speculative property balloons inflated by foreign finance. The borrowers received returns in local currency and had to repay in foreign currency. They began to accumulate a massive currency mismatch.

Over and above the condition of each country was the fact that they were fairly highly integrated (roughly half of total trade was intra-regional) *and* moving cyclically rather than countercyclically. Had they been less integrated or less cyclical, the regional multiplier effects would have been much smaller. (Taiwan has survived relatively unscathed partly because it had had its boom and bust in the early 1990s. By the time this crisis hit the region, Taiwan's banks were in relatively good shape [Wade and Veneroso, 1998, p. 11].) The third vital element in the regional picture, after integration and cyclicality, was the stagnation of Japan which accounts for two-thirds of the East and South-east Asian economy.

In short, the vulnerability of the real economy in Asia did increase in the few years before the crisis. Price and investment trends led to growing current account deficits. Also, at least in Thailand and Korea, new civilian democratic regimes corrupted the central policy-making technocracy and lost focus on *national* economic policies.

Government–bank–firm collaboration came to be steered more by the narrow and short-term interests of shifting coalitions. Their experience is bad news for the proposition that more competitive politics yield better policies.

Outflows

Granted that the whipsaw movement of capital inflows and outflows is the main proximate cause of the crisis, could it have happened without serious vulnerabilities in the real economy? Almost certainly, yes. We know from history that financial crises can occur in the absence of *ex ante* signs of rising vulnerability (though any self-respecting analyst can find vulnerabilities *ex post*). Indeed, when times are good and demand is fast growing, firms tend to assign increased weight to past positive experience and reduce the probability of loss associated with some of their investment projects. They may cut back their cushion of safety (probable cash flow minus probable fixed payments) and thereby become *more* vulnerable to a downturn (Kregel, 1998). This is how, paradoxically, the passage from a sound to a fragile to an unstable financial system can occur even faster after a period of good times than after a period of uncertain times.

Also, we know that bankers and money managers tend to exhibit herd-like behaviour, based on the premise that any individual banker or individual bank will be faulted by management or shareholders for missing out on business that others are getting, but will not be faulted for making losses when everyone else is making losses. The effect is compounded by information cascade, such that the entry (exit) of one prominent actor is interpreted by other actors to signal that the situation is better (worse) than they thought. They then enter or exit for reasons related not to their own independent assessment of risk and reward but to their presumption that the first actor knows something which they do not.

The fall in export growth and rising current account deficits by 1995 and 1996 made for mild concern among international banks and money managers, especially about Thailand. However, doubts were held at bay by the continuing fast growth and the image of miracle Asia. Then the outlook for speculators and investors in the European and US markets improved in 1997. Interest rates looked set to rise, presenting lenders with opportunities for higher risk-adjusted returns than they had had before. Equity markets soared (Rude, 1998). In Japan, on the other hand, the outlook turned for the worse in the second quarter of 1997. In early May 1997, Japanese officials, concerned about the decline of the yen, hinted that they might raise interest rates. The threat never materialized. But the combination of the threat of a rise in Japanese interest rates in order to defend the yen, plus the worries that were circulating about Thailand's currency, plus the brighter opportunities in the US and Europe, raised fears among commercial bankers, investment bankers, and others about the safety of big investment positions throughout the region that were predicated on currency stability.

The Asian crisis proper began as a huge liquidity crisis in Thailand. First, the Thai property and stock market bubbles burst. Later, the foreign banks realized they had large short-term foreign exchange loans to Thai borrowers that were unhedged and uncovered by Thai reserves. Knowing that the profitability of their loans depended on the currency peg, they raced for the exits at the first signs that the peg might not hold. As they sold holdings in Thai baht the reserves ran out. The baht was floated in early July 1997, and sank. The IMF entered Thailand in August 1997 with a support package and conditionality measures that included the freezing of many finance companies. This was the start of what Jeffrey Sachs has called the IMF's screaming fire in the theatre (Sachs, 1998). The freezing of finance companies sent uninsured depositors into a panic. Later, the IMF imposed the closure of some domestic banks in Indonesia with the same result (inevitable where deposits are uninsured).

Taiwan's small (12%) devaluation in October, despite its towering foreign exchange reserves, acted as a firebridge from South-east to East Asia. After Taiwan's unexpected devaluation, the Hong Kong dollar and the Korean won suddenly looked set for a catch-up devaluation. As holders of these currencies, too, tried to pull out the crisis grew from a 'South-east Asian' crisis to an 'Asian crisis'. In October to December, Japanese, US and European bankers demanded full repayment of interest and principal from their Korean borrowers as short-term loans came due, and the Korean government had no option but to turn to the IMF. The IMF and the Korean government signed a $57 billion rescue package in early December. In mid-December the Koreans revealed that their short-term debt was nearly double what they had said just the previous week, or $95 billion. The gap between $95 billion and $57 billion left scarcely a dry pair of pants in the official community on either side of the Pacific.

A very big rescue package at this point could have stopped the crisis from spreading. Better information about bank and corporate balance sheets might also have checked the panic by enabling investors to discriminate between good and bad assets.

Instead, the perception shifted from 'miracle Asia' to 'Asian crony state capitalism' almost over night. 'Crony capitalism', originally coined by activists in the anti-Marcos struggle in the Philippines, was now appropriated to convey a told-you-so moral about the dangers of government intervention.[5,6]

Debt deflation and import inflation

Once floated, the currencies fell in vicious iteration with domestic bankruptcies. As foreign banks that had been routinely rolling over their short-term loans began to demand repayment of not only the interest but also the whole of the principal, highly leveraged firms found their cash flow insufficient to cover their now much higher payment obligations. A fast rising number of often well-managed and profitable firms were cut off at the knees. They started to reduce their cash outflows by delaying payments to suppliers, cutting back on expenditures, raising cash by selling inventories at cut-rate prices, selling assets at whatever they could fetch, and firing employees.

The process fed through from firms to banks as banks wrote off loans and wrote down assets. Their calling in of loans put pressure on their borrowers, and those that went bankrupt put pressure on their depositors. The financial economy and the real economy dragged each other down.

This is 'debt deflation', akin to the Great Depression of the 1930s (Kregel, 1998; Wade and Veneroso, 1998; Wade 1998a). Debt deflation is a downward pressure on prices of both products and assets at a time when investment demand is falling, resulting in a *rising* real value of debt. It is given a vicious twist in Asia by the steep rise in the price of imports, including intermediate goods and medicines. Asia is now caught in the slow, painful unfolding of debt deflation with import inflation. It is all the worse because of Asia's high debt/equity ratios, which for any increase in interest rates, fall in cash flow, or devaluation impart a bigger contractionary effect than where debt/equity ratios are lower. This is how, in the chaos theory metaphor, the butterfly that flapped its wings in Thailand caused a hurricane across Asia.

The IMF's role

The IMF's interventions in Thailand, Indonesia and Korea (and informally in Malaysia, without funding) have made things worse than need be, according to this story. Misdiagnosing the problem as a macroeconomic balance-of-payments problem (the type of problem it is used to dealing with) rather than as a microeconomic debt deflation problem, and as a crisis of excess consumption rather than excess investment, it insisted on a domestic austerity package and on fundamental structural reforms in return for bailout funds. It justified big increase in real interest rates on the grounds that high rates would encourage domestic capital to stay at home and foreign lenders to resume lending, which would boost the currency. The currency boost would both make it easier for domestic firms to repay their foreign debts and check the dangers of competitive, 1930s-style devaluations.

This was the theory. In practice, the increase in real interest rates combined with other elements of the austerity package (tax increases, cuts in government expenditure), only depressed firms' cash flow and raised their fixed-payment obligations, tipping more and more into insolvency, accelerating the outflows and reducing the inflows. In prioritizing the return of capital flows, the IMF forgot that private capital flows are cyclical rather than countercyclical. When a whole economy is sinking and instability abounds, foreign capital will not return whatever the interest rate. Certainly the high real interest rates did not have the effect of reversing the currency falls in Asia. And the cross-country evidence shows no clear relationship between the level of real interest rates and changes in the exchange rate (Stiglitz, 1998).

A sharp dose of austerity may make sense for a Latin American-style excessive consumption crisis. But the Asian crisis was related to excessive investment (much of it in non-tradables), not excessive consumption. IMF demand compression worsens already existing problems of excessive production capacity.

Similarly, being required to undertake fundamental structural reforms at the height of the crisis worsened confidence, reinforcing the 'cronyism' image. Requiring a sharp rise in bank capital adequacy standards in the midst of the crisis caused a cut in credit, a rise in non-performing loans, and further bankruptcies. The Asian experience confirms that the middle of a liquidity crisis is a bad time to make radical financial reforms.

The IMF also required governments to guarantee the foreign debts of local firms and banks. Protected from default, foreign creditors hung back on rescheduling or rolling over the debt. This worsened the hard currency squeeze on local debtors, pushing them to buy foreign exchange to cover their increased dollar needs and adding to the exchange rate collapse.

These various policy mistakes help to explain why the crisis has been so protracted. Their effects are compounded by the high debt/equity ratios of the corporate and financial systems, by the relatively high level of regional integration, the synchronous movement of all the regional economies except Taiwan, and by Japan's stagnation. Mexico in 1994 recovered relatively quickly by exporting to the giant to the north, whose political structure was sufficiently institutionalized to accommodate a $20 billion swing in trade balances in one year. Had Japan been expanding it might have played a similar role as the US to Mexico. Fears of further falls in the Japanese yen (even after the steep fall of June 1998 to 147 yen to the US dollar) add to the continuing reluctance to invest and raise fears of competitive devaluations, notably in China and Hong Kong.

The future

As of July 1998, governments of the region are beginning to follow an expansionary policy, lowering real interest rates, expanding the monetary base, and running bigger fiscal deficits. This represents a considerable change of direction.[7] It sets aside the central bank orthodoxy that has dominated the discussion, according to which very low inflation, restrained demand, and high real interest rates are the top priorities. Governments now have to channel credit into export industries, generate an export boom taking advantage of exchange rates, and let the profits therefrom reinforce inflationary expectations in reflating domestic demand. Hopefully, inventory depletion will be followed by a bounce-back in demand.

Governments may have to reintroduce some form of cross-border capital controls for this strategy to be viable. Indeed, it is not obvious why Asia needs to draw capital from the rest of the world (except in the form of foreign direct investment, a small proportion of the total). Its savings are more than enough to support the volume of investment that is productive and profitable without being speculative. Of course, the reintroduction of some form of capital controls in Asia would be a major setback in the current Big Push for liberalization of capital movements worldwide, and would be fiercely resisted by western financial interests (see Wade and Veneroso, 1998; Wade, 1998a; Rude, 1998). If capital controls are not re-established the exchange rate must float. The Asian crisis shows only too clearly the dangers of free capital movements with fixed rates.

The escape from crisis could be much accelerated through regional cooperation between the governments and their central banks. The lack of regional cooperation whether over debt negotiation or expansion is one of the most striking features of the whole story. The region has the means to solve the crisis if only it could put them to work: some $700 billion of foreign exchange reserves between China, Hong Kong, Taiwan and Japan, growing current account surpluses in the crisis-affected countries (even if due more to import compression than export expansion), net creditor positions in terms of foreign asset ownership, and huge savings. The magnitude of the neighbourhood contagious effect gives an incentive for such cooperation.

These endowments could easily provide the basis for an Asian Financial Facility. The fund would help member countries replenish reserves as soon as signs of distress become obvious, thereby reducing the chance of investor pullout. It would be designed to be quick disbursing and lightly conditional. Even the first moves towards an Asian Facility might trigger a shift of image from 'failure' to 'recovery' and send western capital cartwheeling to take positions before prices rise – especially when western stock markets fall from current valuations that are, in the US case, twice the previous historic highs.[8]

The main obstacle is political. Japan's proposal for an Asia Fund, made in mid-1997, was shot down by the US Treasury, which wanted any such thing to be within the IMF. Japan has since exercised negligible leadership, and remains paralysed by the power struggle between big manufacturing, wanting a weak yen, and banks, wanting a strong yen. China has shown a moderate amount of leadership, and emerges from the crisis with its reputation enhanced relative to Japan's. But it is the US Treasury under Secretary Rubin and Under-Secretary Summers that has been shaping the overall strategy, both directly and indirectly via the IMF.[9] The US emerges from the crisis with much greater power in the region than it had before. And the US does not want an Asian initiative that would exclude it from a central role. Nor does China want a Japanese-led fund.

Until Asian governments adopt expansionary policies, take control of short-term capital movements, and cooperate within the region, the crisis is likely to drag on and on, like water torture, bringing poverty and insecurity to hundreds of millions of people and turning part of Asia into a dependency of the IMF and its number one shareholder. Recent policy changes suggest that this lesson is slowly being learned.

Conclusion

'Real' or 'financial' causes? Rational behaviour, boundedly rational, or non-rational? Individually rational, collectively non-rational, socially suboptimal? Specific and exceptional market failure or normally working financial markets producing massive economic, political and social failures (as in 'the operation was a success but the patient died')?

The capital inflows were a function of capital account opening, fixed exchange rates, lack of bank supervision adequate for an internationalized system, depreciation of domestic currencies against the yen (because linked to the falling dollar), and higher returns to financial assets in Asia than in the US and Europe. The outflows were a function of capital account opening, appreciation of domestic currencies against the yen after spring 1995 (because linked to rising dollar), falling export growth and rising current account deficits, the combination of the last two giving rise to fears of devaluation.

The causation also has another strand, relating to herd behaviour, information cascades and the like, that links individual rationality with collective non-rationality or sub-optimality. What is striking about the Asian crisis is the abrupt shift of confidence from 'miracle Asia' to 'crony Asia' – a 'gestalt shift' in the language of cognitive psychology. In the famous drawing of a vase or a pair of inturned faces we see either one or the other, not some of one and some of the other, and the shift takes place instantaneously, not by degrees. This is a long way from the idea of rational, weighing-up-risks-and-rewards calculation.

The notion of a gestalt shift lends support to the 'panic' story – that the crisis was caused in large part by speculator and investor pullout from economies that but for the pullout would have remained viable enough to generate returns within the normal range. The panic, in other words, was not simply the 'trigger' or messenger of a crisis. The panic was a primary cause. The change in behaviour was much bigger than the changes in 'real' factors could warrant.

This line of argument suggests that had the massive outflow not occurred in Thailand, or had it been reversed in a matter of a couple of months, the Asian crisis would not have happened. One can see several turning points where things might have gone differently. Had the Japanese government not made the colossal macro error in the spring of 1997 of raising taxes as the economy was slowing, the Japanese economy might have still been expanding. Had the Japanese government in August 1997 matched its pledge to play a big role in promoting financial stability in the region with a contribution to the Thai bail-out of $10 billion rather than $4 billion, confidence might have been restored. Ditto had the US Treasury not shot down Japan's Asia Fund proposal. Ditto had the US Congress not declined to provide more funds to the IMF in November 1997 because of a dispute about an *abortion*-related amendment to the country's foreign aid programme. It took an unlikely conjuncture of these and several other events that might easily have been different to produce a crisis on anything like this scale. In this sense the crisis was under-determined.[10]

This same line of argument throws doubt on the popular moral hazard argument for why the inflows were so big. The moral hazard argument says that lenders lent appreciably more than otherwise because they believed they would be covered by implicit government or IMF guarantees. But the hypothesis is advanced without evidence that, for example, lenders lent more to companies, banks, sectors and countries where there was a stronger *ex ante* presumption of bail-out. It is equally plausible that lenders were paying no attention to downside risks, being carried along by the gestalt of miracle Asia and the incentives for herd behaviour. (Life insurance policies are not normally blamed for suicides.)

Much the same point applies to the popular 'lack of transparency' hypothesis about the size of the *inflows*: that lenders lent more than they would have had they been better informed about balance sheets, foreign exchange reserves and foreign debts. In fact, plenty of relevant information was publicly available; for example, the Bank for International Settlement's commentaries from early 1995 onwards stressed the build up of short-term foreign debt (BIS, 1996a, p. 5; 1996b, p. 141). But investors were not reading – until after the crisis hit. At which point they refocused from macro indicators towards the micro indicators of debt maturity structures and the like, which they could have been tracking all the while had they a mind to. On the other hand, lack of transparency may have a significant role in explaining the magnitude of the panic, and hence the size of the *outflows*, for the reason given earlier.

The IMF argues that its far-reaching conditions for austerity and institutional reform boosted confidence as investors saw the governments taking firm action to repair the underlying vulnerabilities. The gestalt shift argument says, in contrast, that the news that a country was negotiating conditionalities with the IMF aggravated the loss of confidence, prompting a bigger rush for the exits; as did the signal that far-reaching institutional reforms were essential for growth to be restored.

The latter argument raises an interesting question of causality. IMF critics have pointed out that no sizeable *changes* occurred in indicators of national institutional strength in the year or two before the crisis, and go on to ask how, given this, institutional factors could be assigned a large role. (For example, the ratio of short-term to total debt had been constant since 1993, and not so much above the rising Latin American average.) But weaknesses such as lack of bankruptcy codes and creditor rights may exist for years without causing difficulties provided growth remains high. Once growth falters, these same *constant* weaknesses may help to bring on a crisis and hinder the resumption of growth. The question remains, however, whether the IMF should have insisted on such reforms in the middle of a liquidity crisis.

However the explanation is parsed, capital account opening is central. It exposed domestic financial structures – that had been strong enough to allocate huge domestic savings to generally productive and profitable investments over many years – to unbearable strain.[11] Yet the IMF and the US and UK Treasuries now insist that the crisis demonstrates the importance of liberalizing the capital account even more – though in an 'orderly' way. Orderly means with a proper regulatory and supervisory regime in place. The way to create that regime, they say, is to bring in foreign banks and financial services firms to operate in the domestic market. They will demand an effective regime and help to supply the skills to operate it with. In return, they will require freedom to enter and exit as they wish, and national treatment (parity with domestic firms, or better).

Even with a sizeable sector of foreign financial firms, developing an effective regime will take many years. And duration aside, regulation according to whose norms? The norms of a capital-market-based Anglo-American system are very different to those of a bank-based Asian system. The latter reflect the functioning of a system that allows firms to carry much higher levels of debt than are consistent with Anglo-American prudential limits. The system has powerful developmental advantages as well as higher risks of financial instability. And it also seems to be a response to very high levels of household savings that are deposited in banks. A regulatory regime based on Anglo-American norms of prudent debt/equity ratios will probably not work in these conditions.

The idea that the way to avoid more Asian-style crises is to integrate national economies even more fully into world capital markets is implausible. As Dani Rodrik remarks, 'Thailand and Indonesia would have been far better off restricting borrowing from abroad instead of encouraging it. Korea might just have avoided a run on its reserves if controls on short-term borrowing had kept its short-term exposure to foreign banks, say, at 30% rather than 70% of its liabilities. On the other hand, which of the recent blowups in international financial markets could the absence of capital controls conceivably have prevented?' (Rodrik, 1998; see also Bhagwati, 1998). There is little empirical evidence that capital account opening improves economic performance.[12]

The greatest concern about capital account convertibility, however, is that it brings economic policy in developing countries even more under the influence of international capital markets – the influence of a small number of country analysts and fund managers in New York, London, Frankfurt, and Tokyo. Even if it were the case that free capital movements do lead to efficiency *in the allocation of capital* and as such do maximize the returns to capital worldwide, governments have much more than the interests of the owners of capital in view – or ought to have. They want to maximize the returns to labour, to entrepreneurship, to technical progress, and to maximize them within their own territory rather than somewhere else; they want to provide public goods that contribute to the good life. Only blind faith in the virtues of capital markets could lead one to think that maximizing the returns to capital and promoting development goals generally coincide.

Postscript

By 1999 commentators declared the Asian Crisis to be over, as export-driven growth resumed. By early 2001, however, pessimism again prevailed. A report in the *International Herald Tribune* captured the mood: 'East Asian governments apparently are retreating from free-market principles and abandoning key reform efforts just as their export-oriented economies are slowing because of shrinking sales to the United States. The backsliding is expected to intensify ... But the cost, economists and bankers warn, will be bigger debts and slower growth that will further undermine business and investment confidence, already sagging as a result of political instability in the region' ('As Asian reforms go into eclipse, growth outlook darkens', 24 January 2001). Among the several indicators of 'backsliding', the report identified curbs on the free movement of capital. Notice how changes of policy not in a free market direction are by definition not 'reforms'.

Notes

* This paper builds on Wade, 1990; Wade and Veneroso, 1998; and Wade, 1998a. It benefits from conversations with Nesli Basgoz, Keith Bezanson, Jagdish Bhagwati, Manfred Bienefeld, Donald Brash, Robert Brenner, Leonardo Burlamaqui, Alessandra Casella, Richard Doner, Ronald Dore, Barry Eichengreen, Peter Garber, Stephanie Griffith-Jones, Jan Kregel, Stephan Haggard, Barry Herman, Michael Lipton, Arvid Lukauskes, my *ad hoc* research assistant Robert K. Merton, Percy Mistry, Kevin Muehring, Loren Ross, Eric Wanner, David Weiman, and especially Frank Veneroso.

1. Per capita income measured at current exchange rates.
2. See Wade and Veneroso, 1998, for discussion of the problems of the empirical evidence on debt/equity ratios.
3. See 'Shocks and debt', appendix in Wade and Veneroso, 1998.
4. Japan resisted the push for financial liberalization in developing countries. See Wade, 1996, pp. 3–36.
5. Donald Emmerson, personal communication, 2 May 1998.
6. The IMF has endorsed some relaxation, whether because it has changed its mind or because it is making the best of *fait accomplis*. See Wade, 1998b.
7. Hard-nosed economists embraced a completely unanalysed political concept to escape the conclusion that well-working markets had produced a terrible result.
8. The record-breaking rise in American stocks has been propelled partly by capital coming out of Asia. See Fuerbringer, 1998.
9. The State Department, Commerce Department, National Economic Council, National Security Council and CIA have had virtually no role.
10. The analytical challenge is to marry the contingent aspects of the crisis with the propensity of the world economy to generate rotating credit balloons and investment excesses.
11. See Wade, 1990, p. 367 for the stability conditions of the bank-based high debt model.
12. See Stiglitz, 1998; Rodrik, 1998; Bhagwati, 1998. For evidence favourable to capital account opening see Quinn, 1997.

References

Bank for International Settlements (BIS) (1996a) *The Maturity, Sectoral and Nationality Distribution of International Bank Lending, First Half 1995*, January, BIS, Basle.

Bank for International Settlements (BIS) (1996b) *66th Annual Report*, 10 June, BIS, Basle.

Bhagwati, J. (1998) 'The capital myth: the difference between trade in widgets and dollars', *Foreign Affairs*, May.

Eatwell, J. L. (1997) 'International Financial Liberalization: The Impact on World Development', Discussion Paper, Office of Development Studies, UNDP.

Feuerbringer, J. (1998) 'Markets are bolstered as investors flee rout in Asia', *New York Times*, 14 May.

IMF (1998) *IMF Survey*, vol. 27, no. 6, March.

Islam, A. (1998) 'The Dynamics of Asian Economic Crisis and Selected Policy Implications', Development Reseach and Policy Analysis Division, UN ESCAP, July.

Kaplinsky, R. (1998) '"If You Want to Get Somewhere Else, You Must Run at least Twice as Fast as That!": The Roots of the East Asian Crisis', paper for Asian Crisis Conference, Institute of Development Studies, Sussex University, 13–14 July.

Kregel, J. (1998) 'Yes, "It" Did Happen Again – A Minsky Crisis Happened in Asia', Jerome Levy Institute, NY, mimeo.

Lipton, M. (1998) 'The East Asian Crises, Banking, and the Poor', paper for Asian Crisis Conference, Institute of Development Studies, Sussex University, 13–14 July.

Quinn, D. (1997) 'The correlates of international financial deregulation', *American Political Science Review*, September, 531–51.

Rodrik, D. (1998) 'Who Needs Capital Account Convertibility?', unpublished paper, Harvard University.

Rude, C. (1998) 'The 1997–8 East Asian Financial Crisis: A New York Market-informed View', Department of Economic and Social Afairs, United Nations, July.

Sachs, J. (1998) The IMF and the Asian flu, *The American Prospect*, March–April, 16–21.

Stiglitz, J. (1998) 'Knowledge for Development: Economic Science, Economic Policy, and Economic Advice', Annual Bank Conference on Development Economics, World Bank, Washington DC, April.

Wade, R. (1990) *Governing the Market: Economic Theory and the Role of Government in East Asian Industrialization*, Princeton University Press.

Wade, R. (1996) Japan, the World Bank, and the art of paradigm maintenance: the East Asian miracle in political perspective, *New Left Review*, no. 217, May–June, 3–36.

Wade, R. (1998a) The Asian debt-and-development crisis of 1997? Causes and consequences, *World Development*, August.

Wade, R. (1998b) Asian water torture, *Financial Times*, 23 June.

Wade, R. (1998c) 'IMF and US Treasury playing catch up on Asia strategy', *Financial Times*, 14 July.

Wade, R. and Veneroso, F. (1998) 'The Asian crisis: the high debt model vs. The Wall Street–Treasury–IMF complex', *New Left Review*, no. 228, March–April.

Weisberg, J. (1998) 'Keeping the boom from busting', *New York Times Magazine*, 19 July.

Wolf, M. (1998a) 'Caging the bankers', *Financial Times*, 20 January.

Wolf, M. (1998b) 'Saving Japan: a permanent cure', *Financial Times*, 7 April.

6
Thailand's Crisis: Neo-Liberal Agenda and Local Reaction

Pasuk Phongpaichit and Chris Baker

In the eighteen months following the flotation of the Thai baht on 2 July 1997, analysis of the Asian Crisis went through dramatic changes. The neo-liberal faith in free markets and free capital flows, which framed both analysis and policy-making in the early stages, gave way to calls for 'coordinated Keynesianism' and restrictions on capital movements. The IMF's hubris collapsed into a limited admission of error. The debate on the Crisis was conducted on a global scale, moved along by the statements of participants (Camdessus, Rubin, Stiglitz), landmark actions (Suharto's fall, Mahathir's revolt), and academic interventions (Krugman, Sachs, Bhagwati). However, the debate was also moved ahead more subtly by events within the key countries (Thailand, Indonesia, South Korea), specifically by the interaction between IMF policies and the realities of local political economy. Because Thailand was the first to collapse and because Thailand became the most apparently compliant subject of IMF tutelage, this interaction in Thailand was especially important.

This chapter traces the crisis in Thailand from July 1997 to the major policy modifications in the third quarter of 1998. It offers two principal suggestions about this local–international interaction. First, Thailand's readiness to surrender sovereignty over economic policy effectively invited the IMF (and its US patron) to adopt an imperial mode in managing the crisis. Second, the failures of the IMF's inappropriate fiscal and monetary measures provoked opposition which ultimately drove Thai policy-makers to revolt against IMF tutelage and make major changes in policy, dramatically at odds with the neo-liberal agenda.

Background: into crisis[1]

Most accounts of events leading up to the unpegging of the baht in July 1997 cover the following four main points (Ammar and Orapin, 1998; Lauridsen, 1998; Warr, 1998; Hewison, 1998):

1. Rapid growth of export-oriented industrialization from the mid-1980s, aided by a large inflow of foreign direct investment, created large structural problems which undermined export competitiveness. First, the supply of some factors of production was rapidly exhausted – particularly skilled labour and infrastructure – leading to supply constraints and rising costs. Second, capital inflows inflated the price of non-traded goods (especially property) relative to traded goods, causing a misallocation of resources and real appreciation of the currency to the detriment of exports.
2. These difficulties created a slowdown by the early 1990s, but were then masked by financial liberalization. Deregulation and capital account convertibility in 1991–3 – carried out in the context of over-enthusiasm about Asia in the international financial markets – led to massive money inflows. Total foreign debt doubled within two years. Gross domestic investment rose to above 40% of GDP, more than the economy could absorb. A large proportion of the debt was short-term and vulnerable to market sentiment.
3. The financial inflows generated a rise in domestic consumption, a decline in the current account balance, an asset price bubble, and over-investment in many domestically-oriented sectors (steel, cars, petrochemicals, services).
4. Economic policy-makers failed to control these forces either by unpegging the baht from the dollar, properly sterilizing the inflows, or by using fiscal measures to manipulate resource allocation. In fact, they seriously compounded the crisis by attempting to maintain the existing policy regime. They sacrificed financial reserves in a futile defence of the currency value,[2] and created a financial stopgap fund (FIDF)[3] which allowed the financial industry to accumulate massive bad debts.

However, there remains a difficulty of explaining *why* all this happened – why Thai policy-makers opted for such rapid liberalization of the financial sector in 1991–3, and why the government defended the policy regime in 1996–7 so ardently and with such disastrous results.

We have argued elsewhere (Phongpaichit and Baker, 1995, 1998a) that for three decades from the mid-1950s to the mid-1980s, Thailand's policy regime can be interpreted as a variant of the East Asian developmentalist model.[4] First, a handful of banks dominated the capital market and played a key planning role – identifying high-potential sectors, and channelling capital towards them. Second, the government helped to cultivate protected oligopolies in banking and in other key sectors. These policies, along with restricted access to capital, allowed a small number of conglomerates to dominate the urban economy. Third, these conglomerates invested heavily in the political power needed to maintain this system, first through military dictators, and later through political parties. Fourth, with the relative stability of the Bretton Woods system, no free capital convertibility, and occasional back-stopping by international patrons (the US, later Japan), Thailand was able to conduct a stable macroeconomic policy, founded on a dollar-pegged currency, which ensured only minor cyclical disruption to steady GDP growth.

From the mid-1980s, this policy regime was systematically taken apart (Phongpaichit and Baker, 1998b). The main agents were a group of technocrats, whose influence on policy-making expanded from the 1984 currency devaluation (a typical 1980s crisis caused by oil price hikes and excess public-sector borrowing) and grew further when business needed the technocrats' skills to manage transition to export-oriented industrialization. Many of this technocrat cadre had been educated in the US and were drawn to free-market policies. They argued that the potential of the Thai economy was restricted by oligopolies and particularly by the power of the banking cartel. In 1991–3, they enthusiastically fell in with the World Bank/IMF project to liberalize financial markets. In a short space of three to four years, full capital convertibility was introduced, the role of the stockmarket greatly expanded, and the financial sector broadened.

But having liberalized the financial market, this alliance was unable to control the economic and political consequences. Portfolio and loan funds poured in, doubling the level of private sector foreign debt within two years, then doubling it again in the next two. At the same time, the technocrats lost control over economic management. From 1995, the cabinet was dominated by provincial business-politicians and new entrepreneurs, many of whom were made richer by the inflows (Handley, 1997), and none of whom understood much economics. Technocrats who tried to impose restraint were removed, while others simply withdrew. While academics pointed out the incompatibility between capital account liberalization and the pegged exchange rate, Japanese firms fretted over the neglect of the export economy, and leading bankers pointed to the excess of property development, the politicians refused to contain a bubble economy from which they (temporarily) benefited.

Alienating sovereignty over economic policy

From late 1995, the economy was clearly slipping towards crisis. Academics and business groups criticized the government heavily (Phongpaichit and Baker, 1998a, pp. 121–3). Ineffectual attempts to bail out the stock and property markets further reduced urban trust in the government. By early 1997, the severity of the economic decline was evident. Export growth disappeared. The largest finance company collapsed. The rating agencies down-graded Thailand. By September, the formal business associations, the army, and street demonstrations of white-collar workers and businessmen demanded that the government resign. This collapse of urban faith in the government's ability to manage the economy provided the setting for the arrival of the IMF. There was no significant voice raised in opposition. The IMF was tacitly welcomed as a saviour.

The initial negotiations with the IMF in August 1997 were cloaked in secrecy, and the first letter of intent (LOI) was never published in full.[5] The Bank of Thailand issued a summary a week after the signing, and the IMF posted a similarly short statement a week later. These summaries revealed no data or assumptions. The Thai ministers and officials involved gave the impression that they simply acceded to all IMF demands.

In the absence of opposition, the IMF grew more aggressive. Over the next four months, IMF officials castigated the Thai government for failing to comply with conditions, and blamed the crisis on the Thai failure to follow past IMF advice to unpeg the currency and regulate the financial sector. The second LOI in November went far beyond the usual fiscal and monetary conditionality to include a major project to transform the economy by rapid infusion of foreign capital. Basle provisioning rules would force banks to recapitalize, while restrictions on foreign equity in the financial sector were effectively removed. Privatization would begin quickly with sale of government shares in the national airline and Bangchak petroleum company 'by mid-1998'. A week after this LOI, the American Chamber of Commerce in

Bangkok called for removal of all barriers to foreign ownership (*Bangkok Post*, 3 December 1997).

In November 1997, the prime minister abruptly stepped down. Insider accounts (widely believed) claimed that he was acceding to an IMF/US demand, endorsed by the Thai army. The change signalled the return to influence of the technocrats who had presided over the earlier phase of financial liberalization. The two key economic ministers in the new Democrat Party-led government were Tarrin Nimmanhaeminda (finance) and Supachai Panitchapakdi (commerce), committed liberalizers who had managed economic reforms in the 1992–5 cabinet. Anand Panyarachun, who had been premier during the 1991–2 stage of liberalization, was commissioned to form a think-tank to plan reforms across the spectrum of government, business and society. Anand branded this task with the phrase 'good governance' popularized by the World Bank. Technocrat veterans of the mid-1980s and 1991–3 policy reforms were recruited to serve in Anand's think-tank, lead the commission investigating the central bank, head the agency to auction assets of collapsed finance companies, and chair an expanded state-owned bank.

As the Thai economy fell, the neo-liberal agenda rose. On the day after the IMF entry into Thailand, the US deputy treasury secretary, Lawrence Summers, said 'countries will only enjoy the benefits of a truly global marketplace if our [financial] firms are given greater access to their markets' (speech at Congressional Leadership Institute, *Nation*, 16 August 1997). American journalists claimed 'the latest crisis marks the triumph of the American economic system of open markets over [Asian] state-run economies' (James Flanagan of *LA Times* in *Nation*, 5 November 1997). On 2 December at the New York Club, Alan Greenspan claimed that market liberalization had 'fostered the growth of trade and standards of living worldwide' and hectored: 'markets should be allowed to work'.

In sum, the urban constituency's loss of faith in the government's ability to manage the economy invited the IMF to adopt an aggressive imperial role, dictating change in the structure of the economy. By the end of 1997, the IMF had presided over the installation of a government heavily weighted with the technocrats who had managed the earlier, aborted phase of financial liberalization. The IMF contributed significantly to a dominant discourse which blamed the crisis on the failings of Asian-style capitalism. The IMF and western companies expected the crisis would be overcome by an infusion of foreign capital induced by privatization, liberalization, legal reforms and very low entry prices.

The decline of the numbers

In August 1997, the IMF envisioned a relatively mild recession, with GDP growth of 3.5% in 1998. The first LOI did not specify how this would be achieved, but it can be derived from the LOI's macroeconomic framework (see Table 6.1). With currency depreciation, exports would grow 8.6% while import growth would shrink to 1.6 %. As a result of the IMF presence and the correction in the current account balance, international confidence would rapidly return and the 1998 capital account would show a net inflow of 1.8% of GDP. Overall economic activity would suffer only slightly, with consumption flat and gross domestic investment running at 35.9% of GDP.

The IMF imposed the package which had been designed to manage the public sector debt crises in Latin America in the 1980s. The package made available US$17.2 billion to supplement the depleted reserves, of which US$4 million came from the IMF and the rest mainly from Asian sources. The two main conditions were those applied to profligate governments, namely a 1% budget surplus and caps on public sector borrowing. A third condition demanded a tight monetary policy to deter capital outflow and stabilize the exchange, but it was expected this would be temporary.

The package was devised for an economy where the government had borrowed too much and spent too much, provoking capital to flee in fear that the currency would collapse and the government default. In the environment for which it was devised, the package worked (at least for a short while) by providing both short-term and long-term solutions to the government's debt problem, thereby leading to a rapid return of confidence and an upsurge in private-sector activity.

The IMF clearly imagined the Thai package would result in a similarly rapid confidence bounce, and projected that six months would see a return of stability. But the nature of the Thai crisis had very little in common with the Latin American model. The Thai government's debt was small, and the budget had been in surplus for a decade. The large current account deficit was mostly the flip-side of massive capital inflows. Thailand's problem was the very high level of private-sector foreign debt which had resulted from these inflows. The weight of this debt increased as the currency floated downwards. The risk was not

Table 6.1 Macroeconomic framework for 1998 in the IMF letters of intent (LOI)

	LOI-1 *8/97*	*LOI-2* *11/97*	*LOI-3* *2/98*	*LOI-4* *5/98*	*LOI-5* *8/98*	*Estimates* *10/98*
Real GDP growth (%)	3.5	0/1.0	–3.0/3.5	–4.0/5.5	–7.0	–8.0/–10.0
Consumption	0.8	–1.1	–5.0	–8.0	–	–8.0/–14.0
Gross fixed investment	–0.8	–6.5	–21.0	–24.0	–	–22.0/–28.0
Gross domestic investment (% of GDP)	35.9	34.3	29.1	28.2	–	26.0
Exports in US$, growth (%)	8.6	7.9	6.2	1.4	–	–6.0
Imports in US$, growth (%)	1.6	0.2	–7.7	–17.7	–	–35.0
Current account balance (% of GDP)	–3.0	–1.8	3.9	6.9	10.0	11.0/12.0
Capital account balance (% of GDP)	1.8	0.3	–12.0/14.0	–14.0/16.0	–	–15.0
CPI inflation (period average, %)	8.0	10.0	11.6	10.5	9.2	8.8

Note: The fifth LOI contained only a very abbreviated set of macro assumptions. The last column is based on estimates by the Bank of Thailand and various analysts in October 1998.

that government would suffer financial collapse, but that the private sector would, especially the banking sector. The deflationary implications of the IMF package worsened the problem.

After the LOI was signed, the IMF pressed the Thai government to implement the fiscal tightening and make 'significant increases' in taxes. The 1997/98 government expenditure budget was revised downwards successively in August, October and November, resulting in a total reduction of almost 20%. The revenue side was bolstered by raising VAT from 7 to 10%, increasing the tax on petrol, and raising prices of some public utilities. These measures contributed to a rapid lowering of the level of demand. Retail figures for the first half of 1998 showed a drop of 10–15% for everyday consumer purchases, and 50–75% for durables.

The IMF moved rapidly to the second stage of the programme, financial restructuring and privatization. The second LOI in November included disposal of bankrupt finance companies, introduction of Basle provisioning rules for banks, a new bankruptcy law, and rapid progress on privatization. In August, the government had suspended 42 more finance companies, bringing the total to 58, of which 56 were subsequently closed leaving 33 in operation. The August suspension sparked a minor panic with runs on many financial institutions. The abrupt suspensions and subsequent closures made no distinction between good and bad debtors, and deprived many borrowers of access to credit. Remaining financial institutions restricted new lending and by the end of the year the formal credit system had collapsed.

While the IMF anticipated a rapid return of international confidence, it did not pay attention to the reaction of international finance. Several firms voiced doubts as to whether the IMF credit was adequate. Partly this response was real, and some firms published projections showing that the IMF credit line would not cover the Bank of Thailand's forward commitments (resulting from the currency defence) and the expected outflows. Partly, this response was psychological. The package was one-third the size of the 1994 Mexico bailout, signalling a lack of commitment. The US Deputy Treasury Secretary, Lawrence Summers, explained, 'Thailand is not on our border'. Furthermore, some international financial firms stated they could find nothing in the package which addressed the problem of high private sector debt, and the likelihood of bad loans and low or negative returns on portfolios. As a result, the package did not deter capital outflow but stimulated it. In the year from July 1997, the capital account (net of IMF and other government loans) showed a deficit of 550 billion baht, reversing over half

Table 6.2 Thailand's balance of payments, 1990–9 ('000 million US dollars)

	1992	*1993*	*1994*	*1995*	*1996*	*Q12/97*	*Q34/97*	*Q12/98*	*Q34/98*	*Q12/99*
Current account	–6.3	–6.4	–8.1	–13.6	–14.7	–5.3	2.2	7.0	7.3	6.0
Exports	41.5	47.6	56.3	70.6	71.7	36.4	36.4	32.8	33.7	34.4
Imports	–46.8	–53.4	–63.8	–82.6	–83.8	–39.8	–33.1	–24.1	–24.8	–26.5
Income & transfers	–1.1	–0.7	–0.6	–1.6	–2.6	–1.9	–1.2	–1.6	–1.6	–1.8
Capital account	9.5	10.5	12.2	22.0	19.6	–1.5	–7.1	–5.4	–4.5	–2.9
Government	–0.3	–0.2	0.0	0.3	0.4	–2.6	1.9	0.2	4.7	5.4
Private	9.8	10.7	12.2	21.7	19.1	1.1	–8.9	–5.6	–9.2	–8.3
Direct investment	2.0	1.6	0.9	1.2	1.4	0.8	2.6	4.5	2.4	2.9
Portfolio	0.6	5.2	1.8	4.0	3.1	1.8	2.7	0.1	0.0	0.8
Loans	4.9	4.4	8.9	15.8	9.2	2.0	–9.2	–6.5	–8.3	–7.9
Currency & deposits	1.8	2.7	2.0	3.4	2.9	–3.5	–2.4	–1.1	–1.7	–1.4
Other	0.6	–3.1	–1.4	–2.7	2.5	0.0	–2.6	–2.6	–1.5	–2.7
Errors & omissions	–0.1	–0.2	0.1	–1.1	–2.6	0.7	0.9	–2.0	–1.0	–0.6
Balance of payments	3.0	3.9	4.2	7.2	2.2	–6.0	–3.9	–0.4	1.8	2.5
GDP (current prices)	111.8	125.7	144.9	168.8	182.2	89.4	66.3	53.5	60.6	62.5
Baht/US$	25.3	25.2	25.0	24.8	25.2	25.8	36.5	43.3	38.7	36.8

Source: Bank of Thailand.

of the inflow of 1,039 billion in 1995–6 (Table 6.2). The stock market index fell from 550 at the float to 207 a year later, largely as a result of foreign withdrawals. Driven largely by the outflows, the baht dropped from its 26/US$ level before the float to bottom at 56. In response, the government tightened money even further, confirming the credit crunch.

From late 1997, the problems of the Thai economy were compounded by the contagion of crisis through the region. The impact of the baht depreciation on exports was largely annulled by a generalized currency depreciation in the region, and capital flight became more driven by herd instinct. Yet the slide in the Thai economy had begun before contagion came into play, and the response elsewhere in the region, particularly in terms of capital flight, was partly a replication of the Thai pattern.

The IMF maintained its strategy. The second LOI in November 1997 noted the 'slower return of confidence' and 'much sharper decline in private investment and consumption than originally anticipated', but proposed 'determined implementation' of the programme and predicted 'overall growth is still expected to be positive' through 1997–8. The third LOI in February 1998 made only a small concession on the 1997/98 budget (no further cuts).

Over the year spanned by the first five LOIs, the projection for the economy in 1998 slid from mild recession to disaster – from a GDP change of +3.5% to –7% (Table 6.1). This 10.5-point swing was driven by two main changes. First, expectations for the capital account changed from a small inflow to an outflow of around 15% of GDP. Second, calculations of domestic demand slid downwards, with consumption growth dropping from +0.8% to –8%, and import growth from +1.6% to –35%.

Reaction 1: business nationalism

While in July–November 1997 there was little opposition to the IMF's control of economic policy, resistance built up rapidly through the first half of 1998. This resistance came from two main sources and agendas. First, businessmen demanded that the government adjust the IMF policy to minimize the impact on the real economy and on domestic capital. Second, farmers and activists demanded measures to soften the impact on the poor.

At the time of the float, Chatri Sophonpanich, head of Bangkok Bank, predicted that two-thirds of Thailand's tycoon families would be wiped out. Through the first half of 1998, Bangkok businessmen mounted increasing opposition to a recovery programme which implied that most of them would be ruined. The beginnings of resistance had a touch of irony. Some leading business figures slated the IMF and its US patron as 'imperialist' and 'neo-colonial'. When an old radical called the crisis a 'political and economic war' between the US and Asia, and insisted 'we must not offer to sell everything to foreigners ... we have to preserve our important resources, state enterprises, occupations and businesses for future national development', business leaders voiced support (*Bangkok Post,* 10 January 1998). Some businessmen joined with a rump of dependency-school Marxists to hold a conference on the neo-colonialism theme.

Between March and May 1998, this growing business nationalism focused on the programme of privatization. The union in the electricity generating authority (EGAT) objected successfully to a board revision designed to facilitate progress towards privatization. A coalition of businessmen, activists and NGOs opposed plans to sell the government stake in the Bangchak oil refinery to foreign interests. Business leaders argued that privatization, conducted at a time when the country was desperate for capital inflows, would allow foreign capital to buy cheaply without adequate safeguards for Thai customers of public utilities.

The companion strategy was direct action. A steel magnate advised businessmen whose debt had ballooned with the baht depreciation to stop paying interest. By mid-year, the finance industry reckoned that there were large volumes of 'strategic non-performing loans'. The steel magnate and others used their position as appointed senators to modify (in favour of debtors) a bankruptcy bill mandated under the IMF programme to expedite the disposal of indebted companies.

In early 1998, the business lobby argued that the recovery programme, as mandated by the IMF and conducted by the finance minister, Tarrin, concentrated too much on fiscal discipline, external stability and financial restructuring and paid no attention to the real economy. In particular the tight money policy and high interest rates continued to depress business activity.

This agitation peaked in May, while the fourth LOI was under negotiation. Some businessmen and academics proposed that Thailand should declare a debt moratorium as prerequisite for pumping liquidity into the economy. The deputy finance minister countered that a moratorium 'would be like triggering an atomic bomb', and government lobbied businessmen to drop the proposal. Soon after, the Commerce

Minister, Supachai Panitchapakdi, broke ranks and sided with the business lobby on the issue of liquidity. Chatri of Bangkok Bank announced that although he had survived to this point because of prudent preparation, if the tight money policy continued, he (and by implication just about everybody else) would be finished.

Reaction 2: the poor and populism

Responsibility for managing the social impact of the crisis was initially divided between the Labour Ministry, focusing on unemployment, and a scheme of 'social safety nets' organised by a consortium headed by the Asian Development Bank (ADB). The second LOI expected the ADB scheme to begin 'by early 1998', but planning moved slowly and the scheme was announced only in the third quarter.

The Labour Ministry's scheme had two main parts. First, the Ministry would repatriate many of the 1.3 million foreign workers (mainly Burmese) who had in-migrated during the boom. Second, the Ministry would facilitate Thai rural–urban migrants to return to their villages.

In March 1998, the ministry began rounding up Burmese and pushed over 200,000 across the border. However, few were convinced that the authorities had the will or ability to prevent them returning. Besides, forcibly returning people to Burma attracted international criticism. When Thai employers (especially in rice mills and the fishing industry) objected, the Ministry quietly abandoned the policy. To assist urban–rural back-migration, the government established a fund to provide loans. But the machinery for processing applications was inadequate. By October 1998, only 12,000 loans had been approved, less than a sixth of applications. Moreover, reports showed that many workers made unemployed in this way were over 30 (especially women), had little prospect of finding other employment in the formal sector, had been working in the city for one to two decades, and had no route home to a village base (Vatikiotis, 1998).

Statistics for February 1998 showed that the number in employment had fallen over the previous year by 853,000 – 2.7% of the labour force of 32 million. The number of unemployed increased by a little less (781,000) bringing the total to 4.6% of the labour force. However, the net loss of employment was significantly larger. The construction industry alone had shed 941,000 jobs, while employment in services and commerce had increased by 328,000 and 139,000 respectively, indicating a transfer of now-unemployed workers to the informal sector (Voravidh and Thiranat, 1998). Average real income had fallen by around 16% (Kakwani, 1998).

These figures preceded the major reductions in industrial employment. In March, the Asian Development Bank (ADB) predicted unemployment would rise to 1.8 million in 1998 and 'could be a very big problem' (*Bangkok Post/Nation*, 13 March 1998). In July, a large textile plant (Thai Mellon) closed down and laid off the last 5,000 of what had once been a 40,000 strong workforce. The International Labour Office (ILO) predicted unemployment would reach 1.93 million in 1998, and worsen in 1999. By late 1998, predictions of unemployment had risen to 3 million.

Estimates also began to be made of the impact on poverty. The economic boom had brought down the numbers below the poverty line from 23% in 1981 to under 8% (under 5 million) at the last count in 1996. But now these gains were being reversed. Rough estimates suggested the figure could rise to 12–13 million by the end of 1998 (Warr, 1998; World Bank estimate reported in *Nation*, 30 October 1998).

Until early 1998, the government faced mounting criticism for bailing out the rich and ignoring the poor. This campaign peaked in May–June. On the eve of the parliamentary debate on measures which would salvage the finance industry by socializing its debts, a leading social critic (Thirayudh Boonmee) urged MPs to make passing the measures conditional on a tax restructuring to shift the burden onto the rich (land, luxury goods, inheritance), and on prosecution of white-collar criminals. Tarrin protested that passing of the decrees was a matter of 'life or death' for the economy, but subsequently conceded the need for tax reform.

In February and April, farmers' groups staged demonstrations for relief of agrarian debts, and then proposed to mount a massive demonstration in the capital on 24 June. Fearing demonstrations would further disrupt international confidence, ministers hastily negotiated a compromise. Farmers' leaders threatened that if the government made no concessions to the poor, they would 'bring their followers to see the Asian Games' scheduled for Bangkok in December. This agitational pressure fed through to a growing populist strain in politics. The main opposition party adopted the proposals on tax reform and rural debt relief to embarrass the government and to build its populist credentials.

With growing evidence of IMF failure, and with growing pressure from business nationalism and populism, criticism of the IMF strategy spread even to some staunch supporters of liberalization. Anand

Panyarachun called attention to the dangerous 'polarization' between rich and poor, and the potential for violent consequences. Leading conservative economists in Thailand argued that the IMF's programme of restructuring the economy went far beyond its mandate. When the US Treasury Secretary, Robert Rubin, visited Bangkok in July to restate the need to adhere to the IMF programme, two leading establishment economists used the occasion to voice their dissent. Virabhongsa Ramangkura, an ex-Finance Minister who had been appointed as link-man with the IMF in late 1997, stated 'I doubt the US has a true understanding of the local economy' (*Nation*, 1 July 1998). Supachai, the Commerce Minister, said: 'The IMF was wrong ... we had to warn them that we would face a severe recession' (*Nation*, 3 July 1998). Supachai also openly dissented from the neo-liberal position on financial deregulation: 'movements of money and capital ... cannot be left entirely to market forces without incurring tremendous risks' (*Nation*, 16 June 1998).

Revising the strategy

In the third quarter of 1998, the strategy for managing the crisis underwent a fundamental revision. Some of the changes evolved over a longer time. Some were enacted independently of the main negotiation with the IMF. But together they amounted to a substantial redirection.

The revision in part reflected a change in the macroeconomic circumstances. The problems which IMF packages were classically supposed to solve (current account deficit, weak reserves) had been overcome, although not at all through the mechanisms (export recovery, return of confidence) which the IMF had assumed. Rather, the collapse of demand and of imports had resulted in a large current account surplus (Table 6.2). Net capital outflow slowed because of reduced capacity to repay and some inflow from distress sales. The government was able to buy dollars to restock the reserves. Pressure on the baht eased, bringing it back to a fragile equilibrium around 37–40/US$. With stability restored, the problem was the continuing contraction of the economy.

But the change in strategy went beyond an adjustment in macroeconomic strategy, and to this extent it was a response to the growing protests by domestic capital and by the poor. As these protests crested in May, Tarrin began a campaign of public lobbying among academics, businessmen, and the press. He appeared to be rallying support for the coming fourth LOI, and at the same time manoeuvring to present a weakening IMF with a *fait accompli* over its contents.

Fiscal

The fourth LOI (May 1998) showed the first signs of harder bargaining by the Thai side. The letter began by noting the improvements in the exchange rate and reserves, but went on to stress that 'conditions in the real economy are still deteriorating' with 'more pronounced weakness in private consumption and investment demand, and continued liquidity shortages'. The priority was 'to minimise further decline and bring about early recovery'. The major change was to allow a public sector deficit of 3% of GDP in 1997/98. The fifth LOI planned a 3% deficit for 1998/99, with an additional 1.5% to finance interest costs from the financial bailout, and targeted use of the deficit 'to maximise the impact on the real economy and on the social safety net'. Deflationary stringency was reversed into a policy of mild Keynesian stimulus.

Banking

The original IMF programme envisioned a complete overhaul of Thailand's protected financial sector, including large-scale transfer to foreign ownership. In the imagination of some neo-liberal commentators, the crisis would also reduce the banks' dominant role in the capital market in favour of an American stock-based model.

Foreign ownership of banking did increase significantly. Two banks were bought outright and another expected to find a buyer. But the changes finalized in the third quarter embraced a very different model. The state role in banking also increased significantly. In August 1998, the government took over six of the fifteen commercial banks, merging four with state-owned institutions and reserving two for sale at a later date. The state-owned Krung Thai Bank became the largest bank, and government installed new management in the expectation it would play an expanded role in the recovery. The government also geared up some specialized state-owned financial institutions, which originated from the 1960s development era but had been virtually dormant for some years, to channel funds from the Japanese Ex-Im Bank and similar sources into the economy. Supachai noted that the government would direct the banks to apply the new sources of credit to priority sectors. The government also made funds available to recapitalize other domestic banks, on condition of capital write-downs and management changes. These measures were linked to a scheme for restructuring corporations' bank debts in order to unwind the credit crunch.

These measures helped the major commercial banks to survive. After the 'establishment' Siam Commercial Bank entered the government's recapitalization scheme, some smaller banks followed. The two large commercial banks (Bangkok and Thai Farmers) recapitalized with foreign funds by up to 49%, while the Bank of Ayudhya group sold off non-banking businesses. Tarrin commented: 'we never wanted to sell the banks cheap' (*Nation*, 18 August 1998). These changes left Thailand with a banking sector trisected into foreign-owned, state-owned and private-domestic segments.

In May 1998, Chatumongkol Sonakul was appointed governor of the Bank of Thailand and announced his priority to loosen monetary policy and bring down interest rates. In early June, Bank of Thailand officials publicly criticized the IMF for blocking their attempts to reduce interest rates. By the end of the month, the Bank began to reduce the overnight repurchase rate, which fell from 22% to 9.5% by the end of August. By the end of the year, commercial bank lending and deposit rates had slid down by 7–10%.

Asset sales

Decrees enacted in June conclusively socialized the debts of the 56 closed finance companies. However, the method for disposing of these companies changed from the good bank/bad bank model based on the US experience with the savings and loan crisis. Instead, a Financial Restructuring Authority was empowered to auction all the assets (good or bad) in packages. This avoided the problem that identifying particular debtors as 'bad assets' would effectively condemn them as bankrupt and reduce their chances of survival (Chatumongkol in *Nation*, 17 August 1998). This technique also made it difficult to assess the pricing of the asset packages, and placed a premium on local knowledge. While some foreign buyers (notably GE Capital) bought heavily, local buyers were prominent, and some were able (through proxies) to buy back their old assets at a discount.

The central bank's involvement in debt restructuring, and the changed technique for asset disposal, increased the survival chances of private businesses stricken by debt. Similarly, the government stepped quietly back from the fire sale of public corporations. The fifth LOI argued that 'market opening policies ... which aim at increasing the role of the private sector in Thailand's economy, need to be implemented with great care, and based on an overall social consensus'. It pushed back the time scale for privatization, and retreated to a policy statement which differed little from those proposed (but never implemented) by Thai governments over the previous decade.

Industrial planning

Separate from the IMF negotiations, the government broached sectoral-level industrial planning on a scale not seen since the 1960s. The project was justified by the need to upgrade competitiveness in export industries. Japan's MITI supplied the technical expertise. Key sectors were food processing, textiles and car parts. The model employed was the Japanese technique of sectoral institutes providing skills training, technical upgrading and management consultancy, with linkages to specialized financial institutions. The agriculture ministry also announced a return to planning, with the emphasis on increasing the value-added from agricultural exports.

Social spending

From the beginning, the LOIs contained sections on the 'social safety net'. But the first three LOIs did little more than protect education and health from the full severity of budget cutting. The fourth LOI in May gave the social issue higher prominence, and allocated 0.5% of GDP to employment-generating public works programmes. The fifth LOI for the first time mentioned 'rising unemployment' and allocated more funds for education loans and rural health care. The government also extended public welfare provision significantly by passing a labour protection law, and committing itself to introducing an old-age pension scheme.

While the ADB-led social fund was delayed by bureaucratic process, political parties sensitive to the growing popular resentment, and aware of forthcoming elections, moved much faster. The opposition party NAP mobilized its own funds to support a programme of minor irrigation works. Parties in the governing coalition used their access to budget funds to launch various schemes of self-reliant agriculture, cattle banks, community development, seed and fertilizer distribution.

Turning east

In September 1998, Japan announced a US$30 billion fund to support Asian recovery (the Miyazawa Initiative). A year earlier, the US had crushed the Japanese attempt to launch a similar plan independent of the IMF (the Asian Monetary Fund). With its moral authority to dominate crisis management severely weakened, the US accorded the new

Japanese plan a terse acceptance. Tarrin was the first Asian petitioner to travel to Tokyo to discuss the scheme.

Conclusion

By 1994–5, Thailand's economy was already falling out of its unprecedented boom cycle. But massive financial inflows from 1994 to 1996 determined how the cycle would end. First, they created a speculative bubble that meant that the crash would ultimately be more dramatic. Second, the inflows cemented a political coalition which resisted reforms. The steepness of the crash, and the urban public's loss of confidence in political management of the economy, removed any opposition to IMF conditions and encouraged the IMF to adopt an imperial role. The IMF expanded its programme beyond the usual macroeconomic conditionality to include plans for restructuring the financial sector and significantly increasing the role of foreign capital. Western businessmen, political leaders and commentators imagined the Crisis would result in the 'creative destruction' of much domestic capital, admission of foreign capital at bargain prices, and transformation of the state, moving away from the Asian 'developmental model' in which the state takes responsibility for promoting the domestic economy, to a 'regulatory model' (Jayasuriya, 1998) in which the state provides a safe environment for capital.

Some of this agenda was implemented in the early months of the Crisis. Several restrictions on foreign ownership and business activity were removed. Japanese firms bought out their joint-venture partners in manufacturing. Some western firms bought into finance, insurance, retailing, and petrochemicals. The legal framework of the finance industry was overhauled, and plans laid to transform the role of the central bank – a key issue for the regulatory model.

But the IMF macroeconomic package, designed to chastise a profligate government, was totally inappropriate for a crisis brought on by excessive speculative money flows. While the IMF strategy assumed a rapid return of investor confidence, the deflationary implications of the package only spurred capital flight. By May 1998, the macroeconomy had begun to stabilize – not in the way the IMF had intended, but because the collapse of imports delivered a current account surplus which replenished the reserves and hardened the currency. From this point onwards, the macroeconomic tutelage of the IMF became irrelevant. The problems now for Thailand's economic managers were how to channel the growing pool of public resources into reviving the debt-saddled and demand-starved private sector, and how to prevent the vicious downturn (GDP shrank at an annualized rate of 12% over the first half of 1998) provoking social disorder.

Between May and August 1998, a series of changes altered the overall direction of policy. Fiscal and monetary stringency gave way to mild Keynesian stimulus. Plans to liberalize and internationalize the financial sector were rolled back in favour of a balance between foreign, state and private-domestic ownership. The possibility that the Asian bank-based model of the capital market would be replaced by a western stock-based model was removed when the government resolved to preserve a significant proportion of the domestic banking sector. Both private and public assets were afforded some protection against a fire sale. The government revived sector-based industrial planning, and significantly increased public interventions to assist the poor.

While the details of negotiations between the Thai economic managers, the IMF and Washington are not known, there is evidence that these changes were negotiated in the face of some reluctance from Washington and the IMF.[6] The prime minister claimed they were the result of 'hard bargaining' (*Nation*, 21 January 1999). A deputy finance minister said that 'it took a lot of effort to persuade the international institutions' to accept the Thai version of the fourth LOI (Pisit Leeahtam at Foreign Correspondents Club of Thailand, 11 November 1998). The policy changes were responses to popular pressure, and represented a return to some key long-term objectives of Thai economic policy, namely, the promotion of domestic capital, and the protection of social cohesion. Seeing the dangers of reliance on foreign capital, even ardent pro-liberalizers became more convinced of the importance of promoting domestic capital.

The Thai case shows the difficulty of enforcing international policy agendas in a country where a relatively democratic political system ensures economic policy is sensitive to the local political economy. The long-term impact of these policy changes is unclear. But they offer the possibility that, in the exit from the Asian Crisis, the neo-liberal model will be challenged by an updated Asian model which aims to preserve the state's power and freedom to protect domestic capital and pursue social goals.

Notes

1. The section is adapted from Phongpaichit and Baker (1998b), which traces the background to the Thai crisis in greater detail.

2. At the start of 1997, Thailand's foreign reserves stood at US$38 billion. The announcement of the IMF package on 21 August implied that the remaining reserves, net of foreign commitments, were US$6.6 billion. Later, the true figure was revealed as US$ 0.8 billion.
3. The Financial Institutions Development Fund (FIDF) paid out 700,000 billion baht to assist ailing financial institutions, mostly from mid-1996 to mid-1997.
4. Here we mean the UNCTAD version of the East Asia model, not the World Bank version.
5. The LOIs can be found on the Bank of Thailand site, www.bot.or.th. The first LOI is posted in a form which is slow and discouraging to read or download. The macroeconomic assumptions in the first LOI were revealed when the second LOI published revisions.
6. Of course, both the IMF/US and the Thai side had an interest in maintaining the myth of Thailand's good pupillage.

References

Ammar, Siamwall and Orapin, Sopchokchai (1998) *Responding to the Thai Economic Crisis*, Bangkok, TDRI (August).

Handley, P. (1997) 'More of the same? Politics and business, 1987–96', in Hewison, K. (ed.), *Political Change in Thailand: Democracy and Participation*, London and New York, Routledge.

Hewison, K. (1998). 'Thailand's capitalism and economic recession', in Robison *et al.* (eds) (1998).

Jayasuriya, K. (1998) 'Authoritarian liberalism, governance and the emergence of the regulatory state in post-crisis East Asia', in Robison *et al.* (eds) (1998).

Kakwani, N. (1998) *Impact of Economic Crisis on Employment, Unemployment and Real Income*, Bangkok, NESDB and ADB.

Lauridsen, L. S. (1998). 'Thailand: causes, conduct, consequences', in Jomo, K. S. (ed.), *Tigers in Trouble: Financial Governance, Liberalisation and Crises in East Asia*, London, Zed Books.

Phongpaichit, P. and Baker, C. (1995) *Thailand: Economy and Politics*, Kuala Lumpur, Oxford University Press.

Phongpaichit, P. and Baker, C. (1998a). *Thailand's Boom and Bust*, Chiang Mai, Silkworm Books.

Phongpaichit, P. and Baker, C. (1998b) 'The political economy of the Thai crisis', *Journal of the Asia Pacific Economy*, vol. 4, no. 1, February.

Robison, R., Jayasuriya, K., Beeson, M. and Hyuk Rae Kim (eds) (1998) *From Miracle to Meltdown: The End of Asian Capitalism?*, London, Routledge.

Vatikiotis, M. (1998) 'No safety net', *Far Eastern Economic Review*, 8 October 1998.

Voravidh, Charoenloet and Thiranat, Kanchana-akson (1998) 'Wikrit thang sethakit panha kan wang ngan lae khwam yak jon' [Economic crisis, unemployment and poverty], in Narong Petprasoet (ed.), *Ton jon thai nai pawa wikrit* [The Thai poor in the crisis], Bangkok, Political Economy Centre.

Warr, P. (1998) 'Thailand', in McLeod, R. and Garnaut, R. (eds), *East Asia in Crisis: From Being a Miracle to Needing One?*, London, Routledge.

7
Malaysian Débâcle: Whose Fault?

Jomo K. S.

In the immediate aftermath of the outbreak of the East Asian financial crisis in July 1997, the first generation of currency crisis theories – which had focused on public sector debt related to fiscal deficits – were very soon seen as irrelevant to South-east Asia, since most of the affected governments had consistently maintained budgetary surpluses in recent years. Many observers immediately assumed that the crises were due to poor macroeconomic management, as suggested by the second generation of theories seeking to explain currency crises.

However, it also soon became clear that all the governments affected had been maintaining decent macroeconomic balances except for balance-of-payments current-account deficits, especially in the case of Malaysia and Thailand. These had been bridged by massive capital inflows, mostly of a short-term nature, in the form of portfolio investments and also foreign borrowings. With the debt – including foreign borrowings – mainly involving the private sector, and with continued high savings and growth rates as well as low consumer price inflation despite huge financial inflows, the monetary and financial policies in the region had been largely encouraged by the international financial community.

Once it was clear that the region's macroeconomic balances were not seriously awry, various commentators, including US Federal Reserve Board chairman Alan Greenspan, began to focus on alleged cronyism and its supposed consequences as the new explanation for the crises. Nebulous catch-all terms, such as cronyism and Asian values, as well as business practices seemed to provide ready-made explanations for the crises. Differences in organizations, relations, practices and norms – which had previously been credited with the East Asian miracle by some commentators – were now condemned as the sources of the financial débâcle. Popular versions of the political economy of rent seeking are now readily invoked and deployed in the post-crisis discourse as if to explain all, while, in fact, often explaining nothing.

Despite ongoing debates about the significance of macroeconomic fundamentals and crony capitalism in contributing to the East Asian economic crises since mid-1997, there is now little disagreement that they began as currency and financial crises. It will be argued here that the currency and financial crises in Malaysia became a crisis of the 'real economy' mainly as a result of the government's policy responses, and partly as a result of financial market demands and the IMF. Related work (Montes, 1998; Jomo, 1998) shows that the crises have been caused by the undermining of previous systems of international and national economic governance due to deregulation and other developments associated with financial liberalization and globalization. Thus, the erosion of effective financial governance at both international and national levels created conditions that led to the crises.

This analysis of the crisis in Malaysia since mid-1997 is also based on recognition of major structural and systemic differences among the eight high-performing Asian economies (HPAEs) studied by the World Bank (1993), namely Japan, South Korea, Taiwan, Hong Kong, Singapore, Malaysia, Thailand and Indonesia. The last three may be distinguished as second-tier or second-generation South-east Asian newly industrializing countries (NICs), with characteristics quite different from the others, and, of course, even among themselves. Industrial policy or selective state intervention has been of much poorer quality and less effective in these economies for various reasons; instead, there has been much other state intervention motivated by other (non-developmental) considerations, especially in Malaysia and Indonesia (Jomo *et al.*, 1997).

Such interventions – now often cited as evidence of 'crony capitalism' – bear some of the responsibility for the vulnerability of the second-tier South-east Asian NICs to the factors that precipitated the financial crisis in the region in mid-1997. More importantly, such interests have influenced government policy responses in ways that have exacerbated the crisis. In other words, while crony capitalism does not really explain the origins of the crisis, except in so far as crony financial interests were responsible for the financial policies from the mid-1990s which led to the crisis, it has certainly exacerbated the crisis in Malaysia.

This contribution to the debate will begin by outlining recent financial developments in Malaysia before considering the broader macroeconomic situation. It will show how financial interests and financial liberalisation led to the overvalued currency and its adverse macroeconomic and developmental consequences. It will then review the official policy responses to the currency and financial crises, and show how they have contributed to the crisis of the real economy. Although Malaysia has not been subject to IMF conditionalities in return for receiving credit facilities, since December 1997 it has adopted similar contractionary policies. Other policy biases in favour of politically influential 'cronies' have also exacerbated the situation, undermining the efforts to restore confidence which are considered so crucial to recovery.

Recent financial developments before the crisis

The turn of the decade saw two important developments with enormous implications for the future of Malaysia's financial system. In 1989, the Banking and Financial Institutions Act (BAFIA) was passed by Parliament, with vast implications for governance of the financial system. Soon after, the Kuala Lumpur Stock Exchange (KLSE) broke off from its Siamese twin, the Stock Exchange of Singapore (SES), paving the way for its subsequent rapid expansion. In 1992, the Securities Act was passed to enable the establishment of a new Securities Commission (SC), which took over the role of the Capital Issues Committee (CIC), previously controlled by the central bank, Bank Negara Malaysia (BNM).

Despite the relatively recent rapid growth of securities markets in Malaysia (first established in the early 1960s by MIDF, or Malaysian Industrial Development Finance), the banking system remains the main source of funds raised by the private sector, in both absolute and relative terms. Being a former British colony and greatly influenced by financial trends in the US and UK since independence, the Malaysian financial system has exhibited many features of the 'Anglo-Saxon model', restricting banking activities to accepting deposits, granting loans and other specified activities. Banks in Malaysia are kept at arm's length from involvement in corporate governance and management. Shares held by a commercial bank in manufacturing companies should not exceed 10% of the paid-up capital and reserves or 5% of a foreign bank's net working funds, whichever is lower. Malaysian banks also tend to be conservative, mainly extending loans on the basis of collateral, rather than project viability. 'These policies ... impose on industry a similarly cautious and short-term view of investment, profitability and profit allocation and inhibit long-term or high-risk industrial investment' (Hing, 1987, p. 422).

The first half of the 1980s saw many abuses by directors and staff of banks and finance companies in lending operations. Some major Bumiputera-controlled conglomerates[1] emerged at this time, usually with the patronage of powerful politicians, e.g., in the form of soft loans from state-owned banks and the award of major projects and licences as well as other lucrative business opportunities. The ownership of financial institutions as well as top corporations by the government and by state-owned enterprises and, later, the privatization of some of them served to encourage such developments. Huge loans could be obtained without going through proper procedures, and were often given for speculative get-rich-quick schemes, rather than for productive investments. As such, other national developmentalist priorities, e.g., entailing industrial policy, were neglected.

Meanwhile, many major corporate groups controlled by non-Bumiputeras[2] have also grown as a result of political patronage, arising from close ties with powerful, often Malay politicians (Gomez and Jomo, 1997). During the height of implementation of the ethnic redistributive New Economic Policy (NEP), many Chinese capitalists minimised their vulnerability to long-term risks by moving capital abroad, mainly from the mid-1970s until the late 1980s (Jomo, 1990). Within the country, many preferred short-term investments in construction, commercial property and residential housing at the expense of more productive investments, e.g., in manufacturing. In addition, Malaysian banks have little incentive to operate as long-term agents (because of the lower franchise value for banks) as the government has done little to ensure that the banking system effectively finances productive investments, especially in potentially export-oriented manufacturing (Chin and Jomo, 1996).

Emphasis on loan security has encouraged loans to the property sector for share purchases and for consumption rather than for production. The share of bank credit to the property sector rose from 21.6% in 1977 to 35.9% in 1988 following the liberalization of interest rates, which coincided with a property boom. This huge increase contrasted with the modest increase in the relative importance of building and construction in GDP, and reflected the greater profitability of property investments owing to rapid price appreciation. Loans by the banking system for consumption credit also rose together with loans for the purchase of stocks and shares. As a result, the share of credit to the manufacturing sector declined during this period despite a sharp increase in manufacturing's share of GDP.

A BNM Survey of Private Investment in Malaysia found that this reduction in the share of bank credit to the manufacturing sector caused firms to rely increasingly on internally generated funds. On average, the surveyed firms financed 52% to 66% of their capital expenditure from internally generated funds in the period 1986–90. Bank financing only accounted for between 10% to 14% of total financing. Although banks still provided a larger share of external finance than the capital market (ranging from 1% to 8%), this probably reflected the less developed state of the capital market *vis-à-vis* the banking system then. Company size was also found to be an important determinant of access to credit, with larger companies enjoying lower credit costs on average. This could be due to the less stringent requirements imposed by financial institutions on bigger companies with better track records and reputations (see Zainal *et al.*, 1994, p. 313). Such 'discrimination' was more pronounced during the recessionary years of 1985–86, when the average cost of credit for large companies was almost 11% lower than for small and medium-sized enterprises.

The absence of any incentive for Malaysian bankers to favour long-term lending for productive investments is one reason for the limited development of Malaysian manufacturing capabilities, especially in non-resource-based export-oriented industries (which are instead dominated by foreign investors). Export-oriented manufacturing only accounts for a very small percentage of total outstanding loans extended by commercial banks. With the exception of export credit and some relatively minor financial institutions, there is little other evidence of financial policy serving as an important tool of industrial policy in Malaysia (Chin and Jomo, 1996). Only slightly over a quarter of Malaysian commercial bank lending goes to manufacturing, agriculture, mining and other productive activities; the percentage is likely to be even smaller with foreign borrowings, most of which have been collateralized with assets such as real property and stocks. Hence, despite considerable government intervention in the financial sector, more than 70% of bank lending in Malaysia has not been for productive investments in manufacturing, agriculture and mining, but for other purposes, especially property and share purchases and consumption credit (Chin and Jomo, 1996).

In the mid-1990s, well before the crisis, the BNM began trying to consolidate Malaysian banks, in anticipation of further financial liberalization. A new two-tier regulatory system was introduced in

December 1994. The new system sought to provide incentives for smaller banks to recapitalize and merge. To qualify for tier-one status, banks must have an equity base of at least RM500 million. Tier-one banks have the exclusive privilege of handling certain lucrative kinds of transaction denied to other banks, such as opening foreign currency accounts.

Hence, while financial restraint exists in Malaysia, it has primarily sought to ensure bank profitability, especially with increasing Bumiputera dominance of the Malaysian banking system from the 1970s. Banks in Malaysia have been heavily used by the state for the wealth redistribution policies of the New Economic Policy (NEP). As Bumiputeras advanced their interests in the financial sector, rents were created by limiting competition in some areas, especially from foreign banks. However, this was not complemented by other policies to restrict wasteful competition in the banking sector that would erode these rents. Instead, the lucrative banking margins have fostered wasteful competition, e.g., with too many bank branches competing for limited business in particular areas resulting in a socially wasteful duplication of services, which undermines the likelihood of scale economies in the provision of banking services (Chin and Jomo, 1996).

The almost singular preoccupation with inter-ethnic economic redistribution has compromised the purpose, nature and quality of state intervention generally and of financial restraint in particular. Though utilised to support inter-ethnic economic redistribution and other related public policies, financial restraint in Malaysia has not been much used to favour long-term productive investments, especially in non-resource-based export-oriented manufacturing, which continues to be dominated by foreign direct investment (FDI). As a result, an alternative agenda for financial restraint more conducive to late industrialization efforts has been thwarted.

However, it is not this system of financial restraint in itself, despite all its problems, that has caused the recent financial problems culminating in the crisis. Rather, the roots of the crisis can be traced to partial and improperly sequenced liberalization of the Malaysian financial system; after all, 'in a deregulated, liberal environment, banks are prone to speculate or lend excessively in areas such as in real estate, stocks or commodities' (Park, 1994, p. 20). Malaysia should have been more prudent in liberalizing and deregulating the domestic financial sector. Prudent regulation by the government is necessary to help maintain a balance between the competitive efficiency of markets and the security of the banking system (Park, 1994, p. 21; Chowdhury and

Islam, 1993, p. 144). Appropriately sequenced deregulation as well as continued regulation of the capital account to constrain exit might have been able to mitigate some of the worst excesses which have contributed to the recent financial crises in Malaysia and South-east Asia.

In recent years, promotion of stock markets all over the world by the International Finance Corporation (IFC), a World Bank subsidiary, has resulted in the growing significance of equity finance and stock markets in the South-east Asian region, especially in Malaysia, with its British colonial heritage. As noted earlier, the split between the Kuala Lumpur Stock Exchange and the Stock Exchange of Singapore at the end of the 1980s gave momentum to the growth of the stock market in Malaysia. The 1992 passage of the Securities Act and the subsequent establishment of the Securities Commission (SC) gave further impetus to stock-market growth in Malaysia, with the SC taking over the role of the Capital Issues Committee (CIC) previously under the central bank's jurisdiction, and thus reducing the latter's role in overall financial management.

The successful promotion of the stock market in recent years has been accompanied by significant financial disintermediation from the banking system to the securities markets, particularly in the bull-run years of the early 1990s, though corporate savings continue to account for much corporate financing. Imminent financial liberalisation is expected to exacerbate most of these trends, and to reduce further the financial sector's support of productive long-term investments. Hence, the stock-market boom in recent years does not seem to have raised funds for productive investment more effectively. In June 1995, the finance minister announced a package of incentives to attract foreign fund managers to Malaysia, thus further liberalizing the capital market for foreign financial institutions. Inevitably, this made the national economy much more vulnerable to both international macroeconomic fluctuations as well as capital flight, and rendered the tasks of exchange rate management and controlling inflation much more difficult.

It has been estimated by stock-market analysts that, by mid-1997, about a quarter of the stock in the Kuala Lumpur Stock Exchange was in foreign hands, another quarter was held by Malaysian institutions, with the rest constituting the 'retail trade' of price-takers. While most Malaysian shareholders only operate within the Malaysian stock market, foreign institutional investors see the Malaysian market as only one of many different types of financial market in a global financial system including many national markets, i.e., the global financial system is hardly a market of equals. Although always in the minority, foreign investment institutions 'made' the stock markets in the region, shifting their assets among securities markets as well as among different types of financial investment options all over the world. In the face of limited transparency, the regional nature of their presence, the nature of fund managers' incentives and remuneration and the short-termism of their investment horizons, foreign financial institutions were much more prone to herd behaviour and contributed most to the regional spread of contagion. To quote Mansor (1995, p. 10): 'Although only about 20% of daily market activity has been attributed to foreign funds, the influence of foreign funds is more than their share of the volume of activity, as they are generally considered market leaders. Their presence is crucial to lending credibility and international standing, which are important elements in raising future capital, locally and overseas.'

Stock-exchange listing has often been a means to access more bank borrowings on better terms. The establishment of the Labuan International Offshore Financial Centre (IOFC) in Malaysia in 1993 facilitated greater access on better terms to international funds. Increased competition among 'debt-pushing' Japanese and continental European banks (who appreciated the higher interest rates available for dollarized short-term loans to the region) eased access to foreign funds. These and other reforms, as well as the growth of 'private banking' and 'relationship banking' in the region, also weakened the scope and efficacy of national-level prudential regulation.[3]

From currency to economic crisis

The Malaysian economic boom from the late 1980s had been helped by the significant depreciation of the ringgit against the US dollar from late 1985. Meanwhile, the Japanese yen and then the Korean won, the new Taiwanese dollar and the Singapore dollar, all appreciated against the US dollar and, hence, even more against the ringgit. Labour shortages and the 1988 withdrawal of privileges under the General System of Preferences (GSP) from the first-tier East Asian newly industrializing economies of South Korea, Taiwan, Hong Kong and Singapore encouraged the relocation abroad of production facilities from these NIEs. Meanwhile, reforms, selective deregulation and other new incentives made relocation in South-east Asia as well as China more attractive. Malaysia's resource wealth and relatively cheap labour sustained production for export of agricultural, forest, mineral and, more recently, manufactured products. Much of the wealth generated was captured by business cronies of those in power, who in turn contributed to growth by re-investing in the 'protected' domestic economy, mainly in import-substituting industries, commerce, services, property, privatized utilities and infrastructure.

However, the recent crisis suggests that Malaysia's economic boom of the last decade was built on some shaky and unsustainable foundations. Recent growth was increasingly heavily reliant on foreign resources, both capital and labour. It was becoming quite clear that Malaysia's future economic progress could no longer be secured by continued reliance on its previous economic strategy emphasizing cheap labour and other production costs. Yet, limited and inappropriate investments in human resources continued to hold back the development of greater industrial and technological capabilities in the country, as elsewhere in the region (Jomo and Felker, 1999; Jomo, Felker and Rasiah, 1999). Export-led growth since the late 1980s was thus followed by a construction and property boom, fuelled by financial interests favouring such 'short-termist' investments – involving loans with tangible asset collateral which bankers like – over more productive, but also apparently more risky investments in manufacturing and agriculture. The exaggerated expansion of investment in such 'non-tradables' also exacerbated current-account trade deficits.

Although high growth was sustained for almost a decade, during most of which fiscal balances were in order, monetary expansion was not excessive and inflation was generally under control, some other indices have been awry. Foreign savings supplemented the already high domestic savings rates in the region to accelerate further the rate of capital accumulation, albeit in increasingly unproductive activities owing to the foreign domination of most internationally competitive industries in the region. Malaysia's savings – investment gap, which was 5% of GNP in 1997, lay behind the current-account deficit, which has exceeded RM12 billion since 1994. Before the 1990s, the gap had been bridged by foreign direct investment. But high FDI and foreign debt have, in turn, caused growing investment income outflows abroad. In recent years especially, the current-account deficit was increasingly covered by short-term capital inflows. Much portfolio investment went into the stock market in 1993 and again from 1995 until mid-1997, with disastrous consequences following their hasty exit. Many recent confidence-restoring measures seek to induce such short-term inflows once again, but they obviously cannot be relied upon to address the underlying problem of the persistent current-account deficit in the medium to long term.

Companies and banks in Malaysia were also borrowing heavily from abroad, thus increasing capital inflows. According to the central bank,[4] commercial banks' net foreign liabilities increased from RM10.3bn at the end of 1995 to RM25.2bn in June 1997, while their net external reserves position deteriorated from –RM5.3bn to –RM17.7bn over the same 18-month period! Fortunately, a lower proportion of foreign borrowings was of a short-term nature[5] compared to Thailand and Indonesia, and a greater proportion was hedged, owing to the lower costs of hedging for Malaysian borrowers. One reliable estimate of the foreign borrowings of almost 90 of Malaysia's largest listed companies estimates their total borrowings at around RM35bn, with the three largest borrowers alone accounting for three-quarters of this corporate foreign debt. Malaysia's medium and long-term debt as a percentage of net external reserves rose dramatically over two and a half years from 102% at the end of 1994 to 176% in June 1997, after declining since the aftermath of the mid-1980s crisis (Jomo, 1990).

Capital inflows – to the stock market as well as through bank borrowings – helped bridge current-account deficits due to the growing proportion of non-tradables being produced in Malaysia, much of which involved (infrastructure as well as property) construction activity. These flows were 'sterilized' to minimize consumer price inflation, and instead fuelled asset price inflation, mainly involving property and share prices.[6] Consequently, by mid-1997, several related economic problems had emerged from the rapid growth of the last decade.

Despite the central bank's claim that the ringgit has been pegged to a basket of the currencies of Malaysia's major trading partners, for all intents and purposes it has been virtually pegged to the US dollar for many years. Such quasi-pegging offered certain advantages including the semblance of stability – and low inflation – so much desired by the financial interests. The 1990 and then the 1994 devaluations of China's renminbi put greater competitive pressure on the emerging second-tier or second-generation South-east Asian NICs, including Malaysia.

The problem was exacerbated by the failure to 'progress' more rapidly to higher value-added production, mainly owing to inadequate or misallocated public investments in education and training as well as limited indigenous internationally competitive industrial capabilities. As the US dollar strengthened with the US economy, especially against the Japanese yen from mid-1995, the ringgit and other regional currencies followed suit, adversely affecting South-east Asian export competitiveness. This reflected the political weakness – especially in terms of influencing economic policy-making – of export manufacturer interests in Malaysia – where almost all internationally competitive non-resource-based industrial capability is foreign-owned – compared to financial interests.

With exports and growth more generally affected most adversely in Thailand, and the property market, construction activity, stock market and financial institutions also under strain, Thailand was the choice target in the region for a currency attack. Several currency attacks from late 1996 severely depleted the Bank of Thailand's reserves, forcing it to let the baht float from 2 July 1997. With the baht down, currency speculators turned their sights on the other economies in the region that had maintained similarly unsustainable US dollar quasi-pegs for their currencies. Both the Indonesian and Filipino monetary authorities gave up defending their currencies after very brief but nonetheless costly defence attempts. Only the Malaysian central bank put up a more spirited – and expensive – defence of its currency. In mid-July, the ringgit rose to RM2.47 against the US dollar from RM2.53, before the authorities finally gave up ringgit support operations after hefty losses of several billion US dollars.

There was widespread consensus that the ringgit had become overvalued by the 'quasi-peg' against the US dollar as the American economy and dollar had strengthened significantly in recent years.[7] Hence, the ringgit was expected to depreciate to around RM2.7–3.0 against the dollar, the supposed 'equilibrium' exchange rate based on calculations taking account of purchasing power parity, etc. However, since mid-July 1997, the Malaysian ringgit has fallen precipitously, reaching RM4.88 to the US dollar in early January 1998, its lowest level ever; this represented a collapse by almost half within less than half a year from a high of RM2.47 in July 1997. The stock market has fallen more severely, with the main Kuala Lumpur Stock Exchange (KLSE) Composite Index (KLCI) dropping to less than 500 in January 1998 from over 1,300 in the first quarter of 1997.

This sudden and massive collapse of the ringgit – politely referred to in the financial community as 'overshooting' – by about two ringgit against the dollar, much more than the anticipated 'correction' of RM2.7–3.0, raises serious questions about the very nature of the international monetary system. Other international, regional and domestic speculators also contributed to the collapse by reacting in their own self-interest to perceived and anticipated market trends. As investors scrambled to get out of positions in ringgit and the other regional currencies, the currencies fell further, and, with them, the stock and other markets. With financial liberalization, fund managers have an almost infinite variety of investment options to choose from and can move their funds much more easily than before, especially with the minimal exit restrictions Malaysia and the other countries in the region prided themselves on. The operations and magnitude of hedge funds have also exacerbated these phenomena, with disastrous cumulative consequences.

Policy responses: deepening the crisis

The ringgit's collapse has been portrayed by Malaysian Prime Minister Mahathir as exclusively due to speculative attacks on South-east Asian currencies. In a study published in mid-April 1998, the IMF acknowledges that currency speculation precipitated the collapse of the baht, but denies the role of currency speculation in the collapse of the other East Asian currencies. While currency speculation *per se* may not have brought down the other currencies, the contagion effect undoubtedly contributed to the collapse of the other currencies in the region not protected by the large reserves held by Japan, China, Taiwan, Hong Kong and Singapore. Thus, contagion – exacerbated by the herd-like panicky investment decisions of foreign portfolio investors who perceived the region as much more similar and integrated than it actually is (e.g., in terms of trade links) – quickly snowballed into massive capital flight.

The ringgit probably fell much further than might otherwise have been the case owing to international market reactions to Mahathir's various dissenting statements, including his tough speech in Hong Kong on 20 September 1997, at a seminar before the joint World Bank–IMF annual meeting. Arguing that 'currency trading is unnecessary, unproductive and immoral', Mahathir suggested that it should be 'stopped' and 'made illegal' and, most damagingly, seemed to threaten a possible unilateral ban on foreign exchange purchases unrelated to imports by the Malaysian authorities (which never happened). Before his Hong Kong speech, Mahathir had railed against George Soros (calling him a 'moron') and international speculators for weeks, even suggesting dark Western conspiracies to undermine the East Asian achievement. Mahathir's remarks continued to undermine confidence and to exacerbate the situation until he was finally reined in by regional government leaders and, perhaps, his cabinet colleagues.

The Prime Minister's partly – but not entirely – ill-founded attacks reinforced the impression of official denial, with blame for the crisis attributed abroad. The fact that there was some basis for his rantings was hardly enough to salvage his reputation in the face of an increasingly hostile Western media. Thus, until Suharto's illness (in December 1997) and subsequent recalcitrant behaviour (in the eyes of the international financial community) in 1998, Mahathir was demonized as the regional 'bad boy'. Meanwhile, other governments in the region went 'cap in hand' to the IMF and Western governments in desperate efforts to restore confidence and to secure funds to service the fast-growing foreign debt liabilities, despite the fact that they were privately held.

Other official Malaysian policy responses did not help. The authorities' designation of the supposedly indicative top 100 KLCI share counters – by requiring actual presentation of scrip at the moment of transaction (rather than later, as was the normal practice), ostensibly to check 'short selling', which was exacerbating the stock-market collapse – also adversely affected liquidity, causing the stock market to fall further. The government's threat to use repressive measures against commentators making unfavourable reports about the Malaysian economy strengthened the impression that the government had much to hide from public scrutiny. The announcement of the 1998 Malaysian Budget was seen by 'the market', i.e., mainly foreign financial interests, as only the latest in a series of Malaysian government policy measures tantamount to 'denial' of the gravity of the crisis and its ostensible causes.

A post-Cabinet meeting announcement on 3 September 1997 of the creation of a special RM60 billion fund for selected Malaysians was understandably seen as a bail-out facility designed to save 'cronies' from disaster. Although the fund had not been institutionalized, and many government officials denied its existence, public funds, mainly in the Employees Provident Fund (EPF) and the Petronas, were increasingly deployed to bail out some of the most politically well-connected and influential, including Mahathir's eldest son, his party cooperative (KUB) and the country's largest conglomerate (Renong), previously controlled by Mahathir's party and now believed to be ultimately controlled by Mahathir and his confidante, former Finance Minister Daim. The protracted UEM–Renong saga was probably most damaging. This 'bail-out' – to the tune of RM2.34 billion – gravely undermined public confidence in the Malaysian investment environment as stock-market rules were bent at the expense of minority shareholders.

The situation was worsened by the perception that Mahathir and Daim had taken over economic policy-making from Deputy Prime

Minister Anwar, who had endeared himself to the international financial community. The emergence of this troika caused ambiguity about who really was in charge and what to expect. Some of the measures introduced by the Finance Ministry and the central bank since early December 1997 and in late March 1998 have also been perceived as pre-empting the likely role and impact of the National Economic Action Council (NEAC), chaired by the prime minister with Daim as executive director.

The possibility of IMF intervention in Malaysia enjoys a certain mystique as various groups have rather different perceptions of the IMF's actual record and motives. For many of those critical of Malaysian government policy (not just in response to the crisis), IMF intervention is expected to put an end to all or at least much they consider wrong or wish to be rid off. In the wake of the protracted wrangling between the IMF and Suharto's government in Indonesia, this pro-IMF lobby sees the IMF as the only force capable of bringing about desirable reforms which domestic forces alone cannot bring about. Ironically, most of them fail to recognize that the contractionary measures[8] introduced since December 1997 and elaborated in March 1998 have been precisely what the IMF would like to see. Such measures have transformed the financial crisis into a more general economic crisis for the country.[9]

The currency and financial crises have also contributed to new macroeconomic problems besides undermining economic development efforts more generally:

- with the massive ringgit devaluation, imported inflation is inevitable, especially for Malaysia's very open economy, whose gross exports are equivalent to over 80% of what it produces; it only imports slightly less, but the high import content of many manufactured exports exaggerates these measures of openness;
- over-zealous efforts to check inflation in these circumstances could exacerbate deflationary tendencies;
- business failures, growing unemployment and reduced incomes will exacerbate deflationary tendencies;
- the stock market collapse (by more than half since its peak in the first quarter of 1997) is bound to affect adversely both consumption and investment ('wealth effect');
- credit restraint policies adopted by the government since December 1997 will further dampen economic activity;
- the flight of foreign funds cannot be easily replaced by domestic funds which would have to be diverted from alternative uses;

- difficulties in recovering loans will further constrain the financial system and economic activity;
- the depreciated ringgit has increased the relative magnitude of the foreign debt as well as the external debt-servicing burden;
- despite the massive ringgit devaluation, there has not been a commensurate export boom for many reasons including: greater uncertainty and reduced confidence in the Malaysian investment environment; a limited price competitive effect owing to other devaluations in the region; greater uncertainty about foreign demand owing to international economic uncertainties; reduced commodity (especially petroleum) prices; reduced agricultural output due to climatic (E1 Niño drought) and environmental (haze) factors; lag time needed for new investments to begin production;
- technological progress is likely to slow down because of the greater costs of foreign technology acquisitions, as well as the greater attraction of falling back on cheap labour and production costs instead of making the human resource investments to achieve higher productivity.

Conclusion

The Malaysian currency and financial crises since mid-1997 can be traced to financial liberalization and its consequent undermining of national monetary and financial governance (Jomo, 2001). The ringgit's virtual peg to the US dollar facilitated huge foreign capital inflows, which were necessary to cover the current-account deficit, exacerbated by the peg. Thus, foreign savings supplemented the already high domestic savings rate (40% in 1996) to raise the investment rate to 45%. This contributed to an asset price inflationary bubble involving shares and property.

As elsewhere in the region, besides encouraging portfolio investments as well as bank borrowings from abroad, the quasi-peg also became a target for currency speculators, as regional currencies appreciated with the US dollar despite its adverse consequences for export competitiveness and growth. Meanwhile, financial liberalization had also created lucrative opportunities for taking advantage of falling, once over-valued currencies, thus accelerating and exacerbating the collapse of the region's currencies and share markets. All this, together with injudicious official responses in Malaysia, transformed the inevitable 'correction' of the overvalued ringgit into a collapse of both the ringgit and the Kuala Lumpur stock market as panic set in, made worse by 'herd' behaviour and 'contagion'. Government efforts to 'bail out' politically influential business interests and otherwise to protect or advance such interests – usually at the expense of the public (the public purse, workers' forced savings, taxpayers or minority shareholders) – have exacerbated the crisis in Malaysia by undermining public and foreign confidence.

To make matters worse, the 1998 Commonwealth Games and Asia Pacific Economic Cooperation (APEC) summit in Kuala Lumpur and various government efforts to prop up the property market, especially its residential component, may only serve to delay its apparently inevitable collapse. Given the heavy exposure of so many companies to the sector, especially among the KLCI's top 100 counters, this could drag out the crisis in the country much longer than in neighbouring countries, where property markets have already collapsed.

Yet, in other respects, Malaysia is relatively better off than its neighbours also affected by the crisis. Although prudential regulation had been weakened in recent years by various changes, especially those relating to financial liberalization, it has remained better than in most other countries in the region besides Singapore and, possibly, the Philippines, thus saving Malaysia from some of the worst excesses witnessed elsewhere in the region. Lower domestic interest rates also limited the extent of foreign borrowings, most of which was hedged, owing to the relatively lower costs of hedging in Malaysia.

Despite various weaknesses, this Malaysian brand of ersatz capitalism – involving changing relations and institutions of 'crony rentierism' – sustained rapid growth for four decades since independence in 1957 (Gomez and Jomo, 1997). It has come unstuck owing to the economic consequences of and policy reactions to massive currency devaluation and asset price deflation due to 'irrational' herd behaviour greatly exaggerating the impact of 'rational' (i.e., rent-seeking) speculative market behaviour to gain advantage from the region's unsustainable currency appreciations. The overvalued ringgit and other regional currencies emerged in the mid-1990s owing to some unintended consequences of partial financial liberalization,[10] which also created the conditions for the asset price inflationary bubble that has now burst with devastating consequences for the region.

In Malaysia, the gravity of the crisis and the difficulties of recovery have been exacerbated by injudicious policy responses, compromised by nepotism and other types of cronyism, though there is little persuasive evidence that cronyism in itself led to or precipitated the crisis. Failure to recognize the nature of the processes of accumulation and growth prevented the design and implementation of an adequate proactive strategy of well-sequenced liberalization in the face of pressure from international financial interests. Fortunately, Malaysian central bank regulation and managed consolidation of the banking sector helped ensure its greater robustness compared to its neighbours, though the new restructuring attempted in the wake of the crisis is less well conceived and less likely to serve its intended ends. The authorities' push for the very rapid merger of banks and financial companies has been made particularly difficult by the uncertainties of such turbulent times and has a limited chance of success, especially in light of the recent failure of a similar Thai attempt. While the consolidation of the financial sector may be desirable to achieve economies and other advantages of scale in anticipation of further financial liberalization, the acceleration of its pace in response to the crisis seems to be less well conceived.

Appendix tables

Table 7.A1 Malaysia: key macroeconomic variables, 1989–96 (percentages)

	1989	*1990*	*1991*	*1992*	*1993*	*1994*	*1995*	*1996*
GDP growth rate	9.2	9.7	8.7	8.0	9.0	9.1	10.1	8.8
Share of GDP								
Gross national savings	29.0	29.1	28.4	31.3	33.0	34.0	34.7	36.0
Consumption expenditure	65.2	66.6	66.5	63.5	62.3	61.2	60.5	58.1
Private	50.8	52.6	52.6	50.5	49.2	48.6	47.9	46.9
Public	14.4	14.0	13.9	13.0	13.1	12.6	12.6	11.2
Gross capital formation	29.3	32.4	36.4	36.0	38.3	40.1	43.0	41.8
Private	18.5	20.9	25.9	24.8	26.7	27.2	30.5	29.2
Public	10.8	11.5	10.5	11.2	11.7	13.0	12.6	12.6
Balance of payments								
Current account	–0.7	–2.1	–8.8	–3.8	–4.8	–6.3	–8.5	–5.2
Official long-term capital	–2.4	–2.5	–0.5	–1.9	0.6	0.3	2.7	0.3
Private long-term capital	4.4	5.5	8.3	8.9	7.8	6.0	4.7	4.5
Long-term capital, net	2.0	3.0	7.8	7.0	8.4	6.2	7.4	4.8
Basic balance	2.7	0.9	–1.0	3.2	3.6	–0.1	–1.1	–0.4
Private capital: net	1.5	1.2	3.9	8.0	8.4	–4.5	1.1	4.5
Private capital: commercial Banks	1.1	2.0	2.7	6.2	6.6	–7.0	0.1	3.4
Private capital: others private	0.4	–0.8	1.2	1.8	1.8	2.5	1.0	1.1
Errors and omissions	–1.0	2.6	–0.3	0.1	5.7	0.2	–2.0	–1.6
Overall balance	3.2	4.6	2.6	11.3	17.7	–4.3	–2.0	2.5
Implicit capital inflows	3.9	6.8	11.4	15.1	22.5	2.0	6.5	7.7
Short-term capital inflows	1.9	3.8	3.6	8.1	14.1	–4.2	–0.9	2.9

Source: Montes (1998).

Table 7.A2 Malaysian ringgit exchange rates with US dollar and Japanese yen, 1984–98 (annual/monthly averages)

Year/month	*RM equivalent for one unit of* US$	¥
1984	2.34	0.0099
1985	2.48	0.0105
1986	2.58	0.0154
1987	2.52	0.0175
1988	2.62	0.0204
1989	2.71	0.0197
1990	2.70	0.0188
1991	2.75	0.0205
1992	2.55	0.0201
1993	2.57	0.0232
1994	2.62	0.0257
1995	2.51	0.0268
1996	2.52	0.0231
1997	2.81	0.0232
June 1997	2.52	0.0202
July 1997	2.57	0.0223
Aug. 1997	2.75	0.0233
Sept. 1997	3.01	0.0249
Oct. 1997	3.29	0.0271
Nov. 1997	3.39	0.0271
Dec. 1997	3.77	0.0291
Jan. 1998	4.40	0.0338
Feb. 1998	3.82	0.0304

Source: Bank Negara Malaysia.

Table 7.A3 Malaysia: economic growth, inflation, unemployment and interest rates, 1984–97 (percentages)

Year/month	*Growth*	*Inflation (CPI)*	*Unemployment*	*Fixed deposit interest rate*
1984	7.8	3.6	6.3	10.5
1985	-1.1	0.4	7.6	7.3
1986	1.2	0.6	8.7	6.3
1987	5.4	0.8	8.2	2.5
1988	8.9	2.5	8.1	3.3
1989	9.2	3.9	7.5	5.0
1990	9.7	2.0	5.1	7.0
1991	8.7	4.4	4.3	8.0
1992	7.8	4.7	3.7	7.9
1993	8.3	3.5	3.0	6.5
1994	8.5	5.0	2.9	5.3
1995	8.8	3.5	2.8	6.6
1996	8.7	3.4	2.8	7.18
Jan. 97		3.2		7.26
Feb. 97		3.1		7.25
Mar. 97		3.2		7.25
Apr. 97		2.6		7.26
May 97		2.5		7.30
June 97		2.2		7.38
Jul. 97		2.1		7.52
Aug. 97		2.4		7.56
Sept. 97		2.3		7.63
Oct. 97		2.7		8.54
Nov. 97		2.6		9.11
Dec. 97		2.9		9.31
Jan. 98		3.4		9.34
Feb. 98		4.4		9.55
Mar. 98		5.1		9.81

Source: Bank Negara Malaysia; thanks to Mohd Aslam.

Notes

1. Bumiputera refers to the indigenes of Malaysia, mainly the Muslim Malays of Peninsular Malaysia.
2. Non-Bumiputeras refer to those not considered indigenous to Malaysia, mainly ethnic Chinese and Indians.
3. After the 1992 débâcle, when Bank Negara Malaysia lost tens of billions of ringgit after sterling devalued under pressure from hedge fund managers associated with George Soros, the central bank's prestige was greatly diminished and its powers reduced.
4. With financial liberalization, it is likely that official measures of such flows underestimate the actual extent of these borrowings.

5. According to the Bank of International Settlements (BIS) (*Asian Wall Street Journal*, 6 January 1998), 56% of Malaysian foreign borrowings from commerical banks were short term in nature. According to the Malaysian central bank, however, only 30% of all foreign borrowings were short term in nature, with another 9% due in the next year, i.e., 39% in all.
6. Some commentators claim that the resultant property price bubble has its roots in Japanese-type or more generically East Asian culture, norms and relationships which compromise relations between the state and the private sector as well as among businesses, invariably involving welfare-reducing, if not downright debilitating rent-seeking behaviour. In so far as such relations are believed to exclude outsiders, their elimination is believed to contribute to levelling the playing field and bringing about an inevitable convergence towards supposedly Anglo-American-style arm's-length market relations. See Chang (1994) for a critique of this view.
7. For example, the yen fell from less than 80 yen to the US$ in mid-1995 to over 120 yen by mid-1997, while the Deutschmark had floated against the US dollar before mid-1997.
8. After tightening bank credit from December 1997, the financing of special funds for investment in food production and for small and medium industries (SMIs) as well as for car purchases (especially for the 'national cars') was increased. Nevertheless, the severe contractionary consequences of tighter liquidity have continued to slow down the economy fairly indiscriminately.
9. Subsequent developments have been covered in Jomo (2001).
10. Full liberalization would not have approved of the currency peg desired by the dominant financial interests.

References

Bank Negara Malaysia. *Annual Report*, various years, Kuala Lumpur.

Bank Negara Malaysia (1994a) *Money and Banking in Malaysia*, 35th Anniversary Edition 1959–94, Kuala Lumpur.

Bank Negara Malaysia (1994b) *Quarterly Bulletin*, vol. 9, no. 2, March–June.

Chang, Ha-Joon (1994) *The Political Economy of Industrial Policy*, London, Macmillan.

Chin K. F. and Jomo, K. S. (1996) 'Financial Liberalisation and Intermediation in Malaysia', paper for the conference on 'Globalisation and Development', Faculty of Economics and Administration, University of Malaya, Kuala Lumpur, August. To appear in Jomo, K. S. and Nagaraj, S. (eds), *Globalisation and Development: Heterodox Perspectives*, forthcoming.

Chowdhury, A. and Islam, I. (1993) *The Newly Industrialising Economies of East Asia*, London, Routledge.

Eatwell, J. (1997) *International Financial Liberalisation: The Impact on World Development*, Discussion Paper Series, Office of Development Studies, United Nations Development Programme, New York, May.

Gomez, E. T. and Jomo, K. S. (1997) *Malaysia's Political Economy: Politics, Patronage and Profits*, Cambridge, Cambridge University Press.

Hing, A. Y. (1987) 'The financial system and industrial investment in West Malaysia', *Journal of Contemporary Asia*, vol. 17, no. 4, 409–35.

Jesudason, J. (1989) *Ethnicity and the Economy: The State, Chinese Business and Multinationals in Malaysia*, Singapore, Oxford University Press.

Jomo K. S. (1990) *Growth and Structural Change in the Malaysian Economy*, London, Macmillan.

Jomo K. S. (1998) *Tigers in Trouble: Financial Governance, Liberalisation and Crises in East Asia*, London, Zed Books.

Jomo K. S. (2001) *Malaysian Eclipse: Economic Crisis and Recovery*, London, Zed Books.

Jomo K. S. with Chung, C. Y., Folk, B. C., ul-Haque, I., Phongpaichit, P., Simatupang, B. and Tateishi, M. (1997) *Southeast Asia's Misunderstood Miracle: Industrial Policy and Economic Development in Thailand, Malaysia and Indonesia*, Boulder, Westview.

Jomo K. S. and Felker, G. (1999) *Malaysian Industrial Technology Policies*, London, Routledge.

Jomo K. S., Felker, G. and Rasiah, R. (1999) *Technology, Competitiveness and the State: Technology Development in Malaysia*, London, Routledge.

Keynes, J. M. (1936) *The General Theory of Employment, Interest And Money*, New York, Harcourt Brace and Company.

Malaysian Ministry of Finance, *Economic Report*, various years, Kuala Lumpur.

Mansor, M. I. (1995) 'Malaysian Capital Market: Recent Development and Future Challenges', paper prepared for the Fifth Tun Abdul Razak Conference, Ohio University, 21–23 April.

Montes, M. F. (1998) *The Currency Crisis in Southeast Asia*, Singapore, Institute of Southeast Asian Studies (ISEAS).

Park, Y. C. (1994) Concepts and issues', in Patrick, H. T. and Park, Y. C. (eds), *The Financial Development of Japan, Korea and Taiwan: Growth, Repression and Liberalisation*, New York, Oxford University Press.

Singh, A. (1992) *The Stock Market and Economic Development: Should Developing Countries Encourage Stock Markets?* UNCTAD Discussion Paper No. 49, October.

World Bank (1993) *The East Asian Miracle*, New York, Oxford University Press.

Zainal, A. Y. *et al.* (1994) 'Financial reform in Malaysia', in Caprio Jr., G. (ed.), *Financial Reform: Theory and Experience*, New York, Cambridge University Press.

8

Indonesia: From Showcase to Basket Case

*Jonathan Pincus and Rizal Ramli**

Introduction

In the year after the onset of the East Asian financial crisis a diverse set of national crises began to take shape. Among these, Indonesia's is by far the most severe. National income was expected to contract in 1998 by between 10 and 15%, and the decline to extend into 1999.[1] According to government estimates, the proportion of the population below the poverty line has risen to 40%, and 15 million workers have lost their jobs (Thoenes, 1998b).[2] A severe drought has complicated matters, driving up food prices and causing shortages in some locations.[3] The banking system is essentially defunct, suppressing exports and reducing whole industries to resort to barter as the last remaining source of working capital.[4] The nation's currency, the rupiah, was still trading in July 1998 at around 15,000 to the US dollar, levels at which it ceases to function as a meaningful store of economic value.

Like Thailand and South Korea, the severity of Indonesia's economic crisis is all the more remarkable because of the country's successful record of development. Grouped as one of its 'East Asian Miracle' economies, Indonesia has for years been a favoured client of the World Bank, frequently held up as an example of the benefits of market-oriented reforms (World Bank, 1993).[5] Real GDP growth averaged 6.6% per annum over three decades, and average real incomes in the bottom quintile of the population nearly trebled over the same period. Growth in recent years has been spurred by an emergent industrial sector that expanded at an annual rate in excess of 10% from 1990 to 1995.

In an attempt to explain this sudden turnaround, economists have identified a number of factors that contributed to the onset of the crisis and the subsequent deepening of economic distress. These include over-reliance on short-term overseas borrowing, inherent instability in global financial markets (Radelet and Sachs, 1998a), under-regulated and poorly monitored domestic financial systems (Stiglitz, 1998), and moral hazard resulting from 'patrimonial' ('crony capitalist') relations between Asian governments and big businesses (Krugman, 1998). Added to these are policy errors made by governments and the International Monetary Fund during the early stages of the panic (Feldstein, 1998; Wade and Veneroso, 1998), and political uncertainty resulting from mounting pressure on weak or non-existent democratic institutions.

All of these factors were at play in the Indonesian case to varying degrees. We should not lose sight of the fact, however, that, much like the 'Asian miracle' that preceded it, the recent crisis was in fact not one but several distinct national crises sharing a common external environment. This essay represents an early attempt to situate these various factors within the context of Indonesia's political economy. It is now generally agreed that the onset of the crisis was due to over-reliance on short-term borrowing followed by an unexpected and massive outflow of capital in the second half of 1997. However, we shall argue that the *intensity* of the crisis in Indonesia owes more to a series of policy errors and to the nature of the state and economic policy-making under the Suharto regime. More specifically, we trace the roots of the collapse to the attempt, beginning in the 1980s, of a weak, patrimonial[6] Indonesian state to carry out a wide-ranging programme of economic liberalization.

Two important consequences arise from the inherent contradiction between patromonialism, limited state capacities, and the liberalization effort. First, although economic ministers (or 'technocrats' as they are generally known) did at times possess sufficient influence to enact wide-ranging reforms, they lacked the power to enforce new rules, or to build the required supervisory and regulatory powers within the bureaucratic apparatus. Second, the orthodox strategy pursued by the technocrats succeeded mainly in weakening their own control over fiscal and monetary policy. Paradoxically, although successive rounds of liberalization failed to achieve their stated objective of reducing the level of rents in the system, they had the unintended effect of limiting the technocrats' capacity to intervene in a meaningful way to adjust to external shocks.

The rest of the essay is organized as follows. The next section recounts the events of the deepening crisis, and in doing so points out how weaknesses in the banking sector and a series of policy errors plunged the economy into depression. This is followed by a discussion of the nature and sequencing of the financial reforms, and the role of the liberalization process in creating the conditions that led to the current crisis. The paper concludes with some comments on prospects for recovery and restructuring of the state in post-Suharto Indonesia.

The onset of the crisis

When the Thai government allowed the baht to float in July 1997, Indonesia's position appeared to be relatively strong. Trouble had been expected in Thailand for some time, and the government had taken steps to withstand the probable contagion effects. As recently as June 1997 the country was still winning praise from the IMF for 'prudent macroeconomic policies, high investment and savings rates, and reforms to liberalise markets' (Wessel *et al.*, 1997). Despite some concerns over weaknesses in the banking system and a slight slowdown in non-oil export growth, the general prognosis remained positive (World Bank, 1997). There had been no major corporate bankruptcies analogous to the Hanbo collapse in Korea. The 1996 current-account deficit of 3.5% was comparable to previous years, and less than half the level in Thailand. The government had maintained a nominal budget surplus equivalent to 1% of GDP for the previous four years, and Bank Indonesia (BI) had substantially increased its stocks of international reserves. BI had also entered into a number of stand-by agreements with neighbouring countries, including Japan (World Bank, 1997, p. 16). The rupiah trading band was widened twice in 1996, moves intended to improve Indonesia's capacity to adjust quickly to an external shock.

The first real signs of danger appeared in early August 1997 with renewed pressure on the rupiah. The government took immediate action to dampen what was generally considered to be a serious, but temporary, speculative burst against the currency. BI abandoned the rupiah trading band, raised its three-month interest rate from 11 to 28% and intervened massively in the foreign exchange markets. The ministry of finance announced the postponement of investment projects worth about US$16 billion.

With the benefit of hindsight we know that the problem was neither confined to speculation nor temporary. According to the Bank for International Settlements, US$34.2 billion of Indonesia's total private foreign debt of US$55 billion – equivalent to 16% of GDP – was due to mature in less than one year. From the end of 1995 to mid-1997, Indonesian firms had doubled their exposure to take advantage of the spread between international and domestic interest rates. Not only had the government failed to curb excessive borrowing, but Bank Indonesia was unaware of the scale of overborrowing or the fact that most of the short-term credits were unhedged against exchange-rate risk (Wessel *et al.*, 1997).

The extent of overborrowing was symptomatic of deeper pathologies in the financial system. A decade of banking reforms beginning in 1983 had removed most controls on interest rates, entry, credit allocation and had lowered reserve requirements. By the early 1990s, Indonesia possessed one of the most liberal banking systems in the world. Bank credit expanded rapidly as the number of institutions mushroomed to over 240. The private banks were particularly aggressive, expanding credit at an annual rate of over 40% from 1988 to 1996. Both the legal framework and supervisory capacity lagged behind this rapid growth, with some predictable results. Non-performing loans exceeded 12 billion dollars according to 1996 official statistics, although this is almost certainly an underestimate (World Bank, 1997, p. 128). A series of spectacular bank failures in the 1990s underscored the fragility of the banks' balance sheets (Cole and Slade, 1996, p. 135).

Demand for dollars continued to build as domestic bank and non-financial firms scrambled to cover their foreign exchange positions, and it become clear that new credits were not forthcoming.[7] For the five countries most affected by the crisis, Radelet and Sachs estimate the net outflow of commercial bank lending in the second half of 1997 at US$34 billion.[8] They compare this to a net inflow of $55.5 billion in 1996 and $13 billion for the first six months of 1997 (1998a, p. 6). This sudden shift in the availability of foreign credits placed Indonesian banks, already weakened by non-performing loans, in immediate distress. Since the banks were themselves large-scale dollar borrowers, currency depreciation resulted in a contraction of bank capital. Domestic borrowers found that they were unable to roll over their short-term loans, and were forced into default.

Rising interest rates only made it more difficult for banks and non-bank firms to meet their short-term obligations. Ironically, while the government's official policy emphasized squeezing domestic liquidity to shore up the exchange rate, in its capacity as guardian of the state banking system BI was quietly injecting liquidity into the system to forestall a wholesale collapse. An estimated Rp 80 trillion (the equivalent of $30 billion at the pre-crisis exchange rate) were released between July and February.[9] In the context of an open capital account, this effective monetary expansion nullified the effects of the interest rate rises but could not save the state banks from default.

In September the government went further, installing what BI Governor Sudradjad Djiwandono called 'a self-imposed IMF programme', including the cancellation of $62 billion worth of investment projects, another liquidity shock and a promise to shut down insolvent banks (Thoenes, 1998a). But by then the first defaults on private foreign debt had been announced, and foreign and domestic investors, realising the scale of the crisis, were crowding the exits. After a temporary respite, the rupiah again came under pressure, and the government called in the IMF on 8 October (see Figure 8.1).

The three-year, $23 billion IMF programme signed on 31 October fared no better than BI's self-imposed austerity measures. Like the Thai and Korean plans, Indonesia's recovery plan called for maintenance of a fiscal surplus equivalent to 1% of GDP, bank closures and high interest rates. Capitalizing on its new-found bargaining power, the IMF also insisted on a comprehensive backlog of reforms including the winding-up of domestic monopolies closely associated with the Suharto family. As critics of the IMF have noted, many of the structural reforms – although desirable over the medium term – were unrelated to the immediate problem of overcoming the country's short-term liquidity

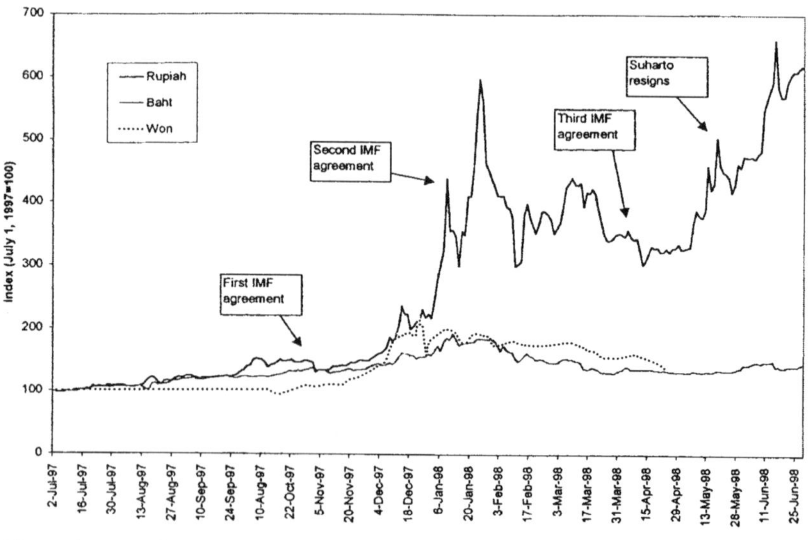

Figure 8.1 Exchange rate indices, July 1997 to June 1998 (1 July 1997 = 100)

crisis (Feldstein, 1998, p. 24). Their inclusion constituted a direct confrontation with Suharto that the President came to view – correctly, as it turns out – as a challenge to his leadership.[10] IMF demands for an end to fuel subsidies that mainly benefit the urban lower and middle classes were also politically naive, as was demonstrated in May 1998 when the attempt to finally implement this provision sparked the chaos that eventually led to Suharto's resignation.

The immediate cause of the programme's collapse, however, was bank liquidation. On 1 November the government closed 16 private banks in line with the agreement. With public confidence in the banking system already low, failure to publish the criteria used in deciding which banks would close sparked a generalized bank run as depositors scrambled to retrieve their savings.[11] An announcement that deposits would be guaranteed only up to a level of \$5,000 contributed to the panic. Confidence in Suharto's resolve to implement the IMF programme was further undermined when his second son, Bambang Trihatmodjo, was allowed to acquire the licence of a second bank which he used to continue operations from the same premises of his closed Bank Andromeda. The government also reversed its previous decision to postpone 15 infrastructure projects with close connections to the Suharto family.

The wheels finally came off in mid-December when rumours that Suharto was seriously ill raised fears of imminent political instability. The rupiah broke the 10,000 to the dollar barrier on 6 January in the wake of IMF and US Treasury criticism of a draft budget ostensibly violating spending limits set in the agreement.[12] A new pact with the IMF later in the month collapsed in due course. But by then Suharto's continued presence was itself a destabilizing factor, and the nation girded itself for what has turned out to be a prolonged, and painful, period of political transition.

What is most notable about the second agreement (as well as the third in April and fourth under President Habibie) is the doggedness with which the IMF has held to its original programme. Although fiscal targets have been relaxed because of the continued weakness of the rupiah and a decline in oil prices, the IMF still insists that 'tight monetary policy continues to be essential if the exchange rate is to stabilize and inflation decline' (IMF, 1998, p. 2). Yet 11 months after the first interest rate hike the rupiah is still trading at around 15% of its pre-crisis value and prices are rising at an annual rate of 80% (Figure 8.2). As Radelet and Sachs conclude, the proposition that high interest rates could stabilize the rupiah has been tested and proved incorrect (1998b,

p. 36). Continuing along this course only serves to undermine the credibility of the IMF, which in Indonesia – and to a lesser extent in Thailand and Korea – has left itself open to the charge that its strategy amounts to little more than halting the progress of the disease by killing the patient.

'Putting the cart before the horse'

Financial liberalization was a central plank of the neo-liberal resurgence in development policy. Yet by the early 1980s the experiences of Argentina, Chile and Uruguay – where deregulation had been followed by rapid credit expansion, a build-up of short-term foreign debt and bank failures – had dampened earlier enthusiasm for the benefits of 'unrepressed' financial systems. In response, the main proponents of liberalization emphasized the importance of ordering the various phases of deregulation correctly. Deregulation of domestic and international trade should precede financial deregulation, with full convertibiltiy on the capital account coming in the final stages of the process (McKinnon, 1993).

Indonesia has often been cited as an example of a country that has pursued an idiosyncratic ordering of deregulation with no apparent ill effects (Cole and Slade, 1996, p. 356). In *The East Asian Miracle*, The

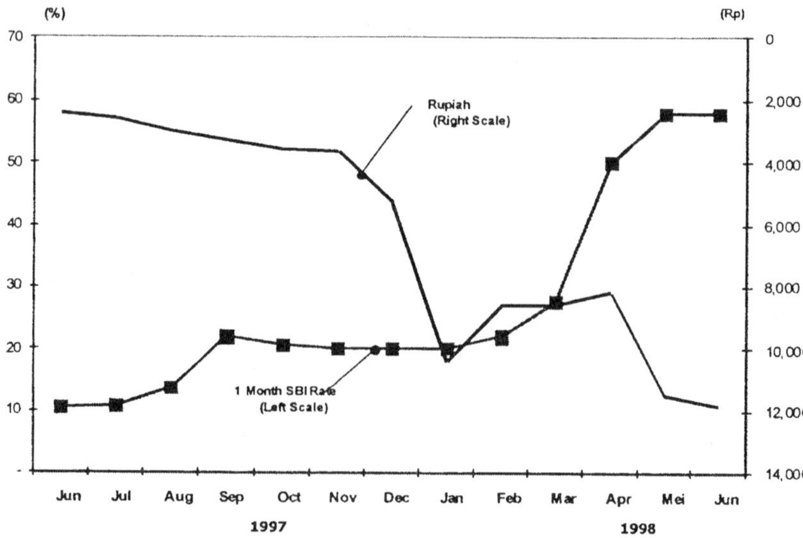

Figure 8.2 One month SBI rate and dollar exchange rate

World Bank praised Indonesia's financial reforms in a section entitled, without apparent irony, 'Indonesia Moves Ahead by Putting the Cart Before the Horse' (1993, p. 238). Flouting the conventional wisdom, Indonesia had opened its capital account in the early 1970s, followed by radical bank deregulation in the 1980s. Meanwhile monopolies and cartels still dominated key non-financial domestic markets. Anxious to support any form of deregulation in Indonesia, the World Bank applauded Indonesia's unorthodox approach and concluded that the opening of the financial system would stimulate deregulation of the real side of the economy and thus propel the process of economic growth.[13]

The pace and sequencing of liberalization in Indonesia had in fact less to do with theoretical debates in economics than with the political isolation and powerlessness of the technocrats. Like the crony capitalists and self-styled 'nationalists' (including the newly appointed president, B. J. Habibie) who opposed them, the technocrats depended entirely on their relationship with Suharto to implement their policy initiatives. This has often meant waiting for periodic economic crises when their influence was at its highest.[14] Moreover, their lack of an independent political base and patrician management style led them to rely heavily on measures that could be implemented through central directives. The result has been that liberalization has proceeded in a piecemeal fashion, driven in fits and starts by immediate political opportunities and lacking a coherent medium-term strategy or assessment of risks (Winters, 1998).

An example is the balanced budget law, adopted in the early years of the regime to prevent a return to the huge fiscal deficits characteristic of the Sukarno government of the 1960s. The law itself does not in fact call for a balanced budget in the sense that revenues must equal expenditures, but only requires that deficits be covered by corresponding inflows of aid and overseas borrowing. Although largely devoid of economic meaning, the rule has performed a valuable *political* service for the technocrats, who – lacking direct influence on line ministries – needed an external constraint on total government spending. This victory, however, came at a cost: namely, the loss of meaningful adjustments to fiscal policy in the management of the economy. As Hill notes, 'Consequently, monetary policy and quantitative restrictions on bank credit (up to 1983) have been the primary instruments of short-run macroeconomic stabilisation' (Hill, 1996, p. 62).

Yet even as an approximate spending target, the impact of the balanced budget principle was more apparent than real. Suharto himself did not feel bound by the rule, and permitted substantial off-budget spending for political purposes. Examples include spending on electoral campaigns, and the use the so-called 'reforestation fund' to help finance a then Minister of Research and Technology Habibie's national jet project in 1994. The need continually to tighten liquidity to adjust for unplanned oscillations in fiscal policy was an important underlying cause of the persistent wedge between domestic and overseas interest rates, and hence the problem of overborrowing.

Much the same could be said for Indonesia's open capital account, introduced in 1970. The initial impetus for a unified, fully convertible exchange regime was the desire to avoid the problems of corruption and disincentives to trade that had plagued the Sukarno regime (*ibid.*, p. 41). Convertibility can also be seen as part of the regime's implicit social compact with the politically weak Chinese–Indonesian community, which in time came to encompass the growing indigenous capitalist class. With little prospect of 'voice' in the political system beyond a limited number of well-connected individuals, the right to 'exit', financially at least, provided some insurance against arbitrary rule. Moreover, the technocrats viewed an open capital account, combined with a fixed exchange rate or crawling peg, as an additional means of imposing macroeconomic discipline on an unwieldy government structure. Again, this constraint placed a heavy burden on monetary policy and restrictions on the expansion of bank credits to adjust for exchange-rate shocks and unfavourable capital movements (Cole and Slade, 1996, p. 40).

Aside from a small number of isolated incidents, however, this would not emerge as a major problem in the 1970s and early 1980s owing to the sheer weight of the government in total foreign exchange transactions. This is illustrated in Figure 8.3, which shows net oil and gas revenues plus aid disbursements as a percentage of GDP. Combined with the state banks' dominance in the financial system, the government's leverage in the currency market imparted some protection against unfavourable exchange rate movements. This was lost with the advent of bank liberalization and the fall of oil and aid receipts relative to private capital flows.

The banking reform of 1988 removed restrictions on opening new banks and branch offices, and sharply reduced reserve requirements. These measures followed the removal of bank credit and interest rate ceilings on state banks in 1983. The immediate intent of these reforms was to mobilize domestic sources of financing to replace oil revenues, which had fallen with the oil price in the 1980s. Unable to push

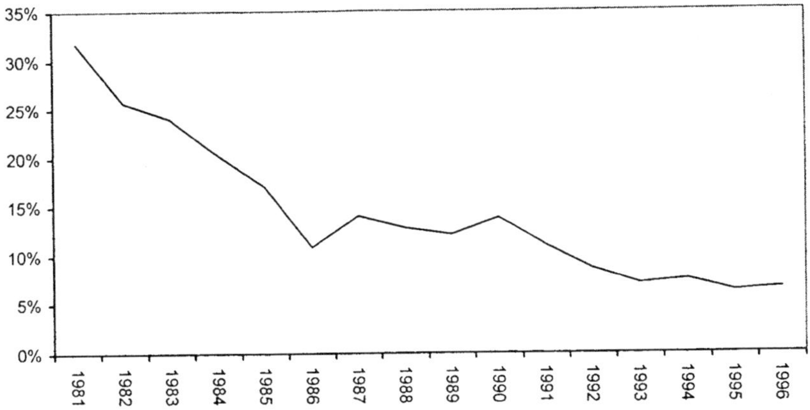

Figure 8.3 Net oil and gas exports and aid disbursements as share of GDP (1981–96)

through reform of the state banks, which remain an important source of funds for the patronage system, the technocrats instead opted for liberalization to introduce more competition into the financial sector.[15]

The cumulative effect of deregulation was to leave Indonesia with one of the world's most unregulated financial industries. Having eased entry and lowered capital requirements, banks were required to hold no more than about $16 million in capital. This created an environment in which banks were encouraged to take excessive risks, a problem compounded by lax supervision, inadequate accounting procedures, an absence of restraints on borrowing and lending practices and ambiguous procedures relating to bank liquidation. Although the technocrats understood the risks involved, by the early 1990s they no longer possessed sufficient influence with Suharto to regain control over the freewheeling banking system. An attempt in 1991 to limit foreign borrowing, for example, came to grief when second son Bambang and timber-baron Prajogo Pangestu managed to circumvent the new rules in launching the $1.8 billion Chandra Asri petrochemical project (MacIntyre, 1994, p. 260).

Successive rounds of deregulation have thus left the government with few remaining instruments to manage the economy and adjust to external shocks. Having surrendered control over capital movements, interest rates, credit creation and (to a large extent) fiscal policy, the monetary authorities were left with interest rates on Bank Indonesia securities (SBIs) and the exchange rate as the main levers of macroeconomic adjustment. The Finance Ministry's lack of control over fiscal expenditures under Indonesia's version of the balanced budget rule, virtually guaranteed that domestic interest rates would remain high as a counter to persistent inflationary pressures.

Combined with an open capital account, implicit government guarantees on deposits and persistently high domestic interest rates, the financial liberalization amounted to a high-risk strategy that relied heavily on the confidence of domestic and foreign investors to paper over the system's underlying fragility. Devaluation of the currency was held out as a measure of last resort, a logical result of the country's huge foreign debt burden. Yet Bank Indonesia's reluctance to repeat the experience of the maxi-devaluations of the 1970s and early 1980s left the country vulnerable to periodic speculation against the rupiah. Beyond the crawling peg and exchange rate band, the government found that on occasion it had to rely on draconian liquidity shocks to shore up the value of the rupiah and contain runaway credit creation. In what became known as the 'Sumarlin Shock',[16] state enterprises were forced in June 1987 to withdraw time deposits from state banks and purchase SBIs from the central bank. Bank Indonesia also pressed private banks to buy their money market securities (SBPU),[17] which in effect forced them to sell foreign exchange to the central bank to meet their reserve requirements (Cole and Slade, 1996, p. 53). A similar intervention (Sumarlin Shock II) was carried out in February 1991 when the rupiah once again came under pressure.

We now know that the monetary shocks of 1987 and 1991 were merely dress rehearsals for the 1997 crisis. Responding to domestically generated pressure on the rupiah, the two Sumarlin shocks succeeded in averting a destabilizing loss of confidence in the currency. But the use of such crude measures signalled that the authorities had lost control over monetary policy, and that corrective measures were needed. The technocrats' inability, or failure, to heed these warnings in the end proved fatal.

Conclusion and prospects

Indonesia was destined to suffer a recession in 1997. Like Thailand, Korea and Malaysia, Indonesia maintained an open capital account and had accumulated short-term dollar-denominated debt in excess of international reserves. All four countries were therefore vulnerable to a sudden change in market sentiment. When the change came it came quickly, and on a scale previously unimagined, let alone experienced in the region.

Yet, as we have argued in this essay, the intensity of the Indonesian crisis cannot be explained by external factors alone. The attempt to implement a radical programme of financial liberalization in the context of deeply entrenched patrimonial state structures increased the likelihood of collapse, while at the same time undermining the mechanisms needed to restore stability. Far from dismantling the patronage networks that tied capitalists to the regime, liberalization expanded the range of opportunities available to these groups to profit from their political connections. Meanwhile, the weakness of state oversight, regulation and enforcement enabled them to socialize the risks of these new ventures, particularly in the banking sector.

Indonesia now faces the immediate problem of reversing the descent into economic disintegration propelled by the implosion of the financial system. Indonesia also shares with Thailand and Korea a poorly designed IMF programme, most notably the bungled bank liquidation and a failure to shift from an orthodox tight money policy despite the absence of a credible strengthening of the currency over a period of eight months. It has yet to be demonstrated, for example, that the interest rate still has the power to exert upward pressure on the rupiah, given the extent of corporate bankruptcies and the collapse of the banking system. Moreover, there seems little point to maintaining an open capital account in a country that is unlikely to attract new, voluntary commercial lending. Based on humanitarian considerations alone, the IMF should now consider sacrificing ideological purity in favour of experimenting with more innovative approaches to the crisis (see, for example, Wade and Veneroso, 1998). This is likely to involve a full or partial closing of the capital account, a relaxation of monetary policy and lower interest rates. The IMF should also take direct responsibility for organising an orderly rescheduling of Indonesia's overseas private debt. Government targeting of strategic export industries – for example, industries in imminent danger of losing hard-won markets in the US and Europe – is also urgently needed. Acceleration of bank restructuring, including mergers, closings and selected nationalizations, should be given the highest priority.

Realistically, this is not likely to occur. Just as improbable are new initiatives from the Habibie Government to redirect the recovery effort. Widely viewed as a transitional figure, President Habibie lacks the legitimacy and independent power base required to effect a major change in policy. Having come to power on his predecessor's coat-tails, he represents a continuation of the political uncertainty that has marked Indonesian politics since the onset of the crisis.

Over the longer term, the country's future hinges largely on the formation of new political structures and traditions that can accommodate the country's tremendous diversity while avoiding a descent into sectarianism or mindless nationalism. This will not be an easy task. Thirty years of depoliticization under Suharto leave behind a legacy of bureaucratic coercion and a woefully impoverished political culture. Ethnic and religious intolerance, skilfully manipulated by Suharto to weaken his opponents, remains a serious obstacle to reform. The severity of these problems was evident in the brutality directed at the Chinese–Indonesian community during the May riots (Schwarz, 1998), and the inability of opposition leaders to present a unified front against Suharto despite their shared moral revulsion at the scale of the regime's venality.

Driven by these moral concerns, Indonesia's first attempts to reinterpret the Suharto years have focused largely on the 'corruption, collusion and nepotism' of the President's family. This is understandable, given the years of enforced deference to Suharto (opposition figures were routinely imprisoned for 'insulting' the President) and the severity of the economic depression. But condemnation of the Suharto family will not substitute for more careful analyses of the country's political economy. Suharto may have engineered his New Order regime – and profited handsomely from it – but he was not alone. A cheap, politically disenfranchized labour force, low and easily evaded taxes and flexible rules underpinned the fortunes of a wide swathe of the capitalist class extending well beyond the President's inner circle. The regime's functionaries extracted their share of the spoils through a tight web of patron–client relations that reached from the presidential palace to the lowliest village chief. 'Cronyism', far from existing as an aberration, was (and is) the predominant mode of accumulation.

One of the many dangers facing post-Suharto Indonesia is that no real alternative to this system will emerge, and that the faces will change but the methods remain the same. For some, including the Bretton Woods agencies, an accelerated programme of economic liberalization is the most attractive option. The 1980s shibboleth that 'government failure is always worse than market failure' appears at first glance to offer a simple solution to the twin problems of state incapacity and patrimonialism. But, alas, some things are in fact too good to be true. If we have learned anything from the Indonesian crisis it is that where governments fail, markets are bound to fail as well sooner or later. The idea that economic liberalization is a substitute for a fair and effective state is a dangerous fallacy, and one that Indonesia's new leaders should resist at all costs.

Notes

* The authors wish to thank Adam Schwarz, Jeffrey Winters and an anonymous reader for insightful comments on an earlier draft. The usual caveats apply.

1. In June the IMF forecast a decline in GDP of 10% for the year (IMF, 1998, p. 1). Goldman Sachs predicts a 15% contraction, as compared to 6% and 1.9% in Thailand and South Korea, respectively (Sender, 1998, p. 63).
2. These figures were reported by the Central Bureau of Statistics (CBS), which estimated the incidence of poverty before the crisis at 11.3% of the population (Solomon, 1998). This is most likely an underestimate given that CBS has set the poverty line at the low levels of Rp 227,720 per family per month in urban areas and Rp 177,997 in the countryside. At the current rate of exchange these poverty lines are equivalent to US$15.25 and $11.90, respectively.
3. The problem of food shortages has been compounded by anti-Chinese violence that has disrupted normal distribution networks.
4. Footwear exports, for example, have declined sharply despite a backlog of one billion dollars worth of orders. Companies are unable to organise trade credits or obtain foreign exchange for the purchase of inputs (Radelet and Sachs, 1998b, p. 35). Total exports fell from US$4.2 billion in July 1997 to $1.4 billion in March of 1998.
5. A 1992 World Bank report cited Indonesia as 'one of the Bank's greatest success stories overall in the 1980s', and that '[t]he impressive growth of Indonesian industry was a testimony, among other things, to the Bank's sound analysis, advice and influence' (World Bank, 1992, cited in MacIntyre, 1994, p. 264).
6. 'Patrimonialism' refers to a style in which vertical patron–client relations, primarily between the bureacratic apparatus and business, take precedence over other forms of political mobilization and control (see MacIntyre, 1994, for a discussion of patrimonialism in the Indonesian context).
7. In contrast to Korea, about three-quarters of private overseas debt in Indonesia was held by non-bank firms. However, since every major conglomerate operates a private bank, the distinction in most cases is not particularly meaningful. Pressure on the banks was also amplified by the extent to which they had violated prudential bank rules. The first audits undertaken by the Indonesian Bank Restructuring Agency (IBRA) have revealed that Indonesian banks were trading heavily in repurchase agreements and complex foreign currency derivatives, and that some banks were exposed to single borrowers beyond the 20% lending limit set by BI (Witcher, 1998).
8. The five countries are Korea, Thailand, the Philippines, Malaysia and Indonesia.
9. One result was that the IMF, which had been tracking base money, changed its monitoring criteria to Net Domestic Assets as part of the third agreement with the government in January 1998.

10. Suharto reportedly told former Vice-President Walter Mondale, in Jakarta as a special US emissary to urge implementation of the package: 'If I do these things, they will throw me out of office' (Sanger, 1998).
11. The legal basis for the bank closures was also unclear. The December 1996 regulations on bank liquidation had failed to set out clear criteria for closure, leaving the decision up to the discretion of the Ministry of Finance and Bank Indonesia (World Bank, 1997, p. 127).
12. Radelet and Sachs point out that the proposed 32% budget increase was mainly due to exchange rate movements, and thus did not justify the harsh reactions that it attracted from the IMF and US Treasury. 'Within three weeks', they wrote, 'the Fund had quietly approved a new budget with a 46% increase in spending, but the damage to market perceptions had been done' (1998a, p. 23, fn. 11).
13. The Bank did not specify the mechanism through which this link between financial and real side deregulation would operate. In fact, cartelization of domestic and international trade proved to be perfectly consistent with financial deregulation. Groups with access to trade and licensing privileges were more than happy to leverage their capital through entry into the banking sector.
14. See Winters (1996) for a detailed description of the technocrats' political fortunes and misfortunes.
15. Symptomatic of the technocrats' frustration with their lack of control over state bank lending was the circulation of a list in 1994 of non-performing loans, in which members of the Suharto family figured prominently. It was widely acknowledged in Jakarta that the technocrats had leaked this document to draw attention to the perennial problem of uncontrolled patronage at the state banks.
16. Named for then Acting Finance Minister J. B. Sumarlin.
17. *Surat berharga pasar uang*, or SBPU.

References

Cole, D. C. and Slade, B. F. (1996) *Building a Modern Financial System: The Indonesian Experience*, Cambridge, Cambridge University Press.

Feldstein, M. (1998) 'Refocusing the IMF', *Foreign Affairs*, vol. 77, no. 2, March–April.

Hill, H. (1996) *The Indonesian Economy Since 1966*, Cambridge, Cambridge University Press.

International Monetary Fund (1998) 'Memorandum of Economic and Financial Policies of the Government of Indonesia', Jakarta, 24 June, mimeo.

Krugman, P. (1998) 'What Happened to Asia?', Cambridge, MA, MIT, mimeo.

MacIntyre, A. (1994) 'Power, prosperity and patrimonialism: business and government in Indonesia', pp. 244–67 in MacIntyre, A. (ed.), *Business and Government in Industrializing Asia*, St. Leonards, NSW, Allen and Unwin.

McKinnon, R. I. (1993) *The Order of Economic Liberalisation: Financial Control in the Transition to a Market Economy*, 2nd edn, London, Johns Hopkins University Press.

Radelet, S. and Sachs, J. (1998a) 'The Onset of the East Asian Financial Crisis', Cambridge, MA, Harvard Institute for International Development, 30 March, mimeo.

Radelet, S. and Sachs, J. (1998b) 'The East Asian Financial Crisis: Diagnosis, Remedies, Prospects', Cambridge, MA, Harvard Institute for International Development, 20 April, mimeo.

Sanger, D. E. (1998) 'One year later, Asian economic crisis is worsening', *New York Times*, 6 July.

Schwarz, A. (1998) 'In Indonesia, protect and integrate the ethnic Chinese', *International Herald Tribune*, 19 June.

Sender, H. (1998) 'A new wave of pain', *Far Eastern Economic Review*, 25 June, 62–4.

Solomon, J. (1998) 'Poor Indonesians are facing hunger as crisis mounts', *Asian Wall Street Journal*, 10 July.

Stiglitz, J. (1998) 'Sound Finance and Sustainable Development in Asia', Washington DC, World Bank, 12 March, mimeo.

Thoenes, S. (1998a) 'Indonesia: the offshore borrowing trap', *Financial Times*, 12 January.

Thoenes, S. (1998b) 'Indonesia's next crisis: workers on barricades', *Christian Science Monitor*, 3 July.

Wade, R. and Veneroso, F. (1998) 'The Asian Crisis: The High Debt Model vs. The Wall Street-Treasury–IMF Complex', Russell Sage Foundation, 2 March, mimeo.

Wessel, D., McDermott, D. and Ip, G. (1997) 'Money trail: who ruptured the rupiah?', *Asian Wall Street Journal*, 31 December, 1.

Winters, J. A. (1996) *Power in Motion: Capital Mobility and the Indonesian State*, London, Cornell University Press.

Winters, J. A. (1998) 'The Politics of Created Crisis: Indonesian Banking Reform in the 1980s', Northwestern University, mimeo.

Witcher, S. K. (1998) 'Hidden loans, derivatives raise cost of Indonesian bank bailout', *Asian Wall Street Journal*, 25 June.

World Bank (1992) *World Bank Support for Industrialization in Korea, India and Indonesia*, Washington DC, World Bank Operations Evaluations Department.

World Bank (1993) *The East Asian Miracle: Economic Growth and Public Policy*, New York, Oxford University Press.

World Bank (1997) *Indonesia: Sustaining High Growth With Equity*, Washington DC, 30 May.

9

Interpreting the Korean Crisis: Financial Liberalization, Industrial Policy and Corporate Governance

*Ha-Joon Chang, Hong-Jae Park and Chul Gyue Yoo**

Introduction

As the interpretation of its economic 'miracle' has been, so the interpretation of the recent crisis in Korea remains highly controversial.[1] Although there are many important issues which have been raised by the Korean crisis, such as exchange rate policy, labour market policy, and the architecture of the international financial system (Chang, 1998a), three issues have been especially controversial in the debate: financial liberalization, industrial policy and corporate governance.

In this paper, we examine these three issues and argue that the recent crisis in Korea was *not* the result of excessive government intervention that encouraged 'moral hazard', as is often believed. We show that the crisis resulted from uncoordinated and excessive investments by the private sector, financed by imprudent amounts of short-term foreign debt, which in turn had been made possible by rapid and ill-designed financial liberalization (especially capital account liberalization) and a serious weakening of industrial policy. We also point out that, while it has some important shortcomings, Korea's supposedly pathological corporate governance system was neither the main source of the recent crisis, nor something that has to be radically restructured if Korea is to regain its growth momentum, as many observers outside and inside Korea currently believe.

Financial liberalization: capital account liberalization and the debt crisis

While there are those who believe that the recent crises in Korea and other Asian countries were mainly the results of some systemic malaise, comparable even to that found in the former communist countries before the fall of the Berlin Wall (Brittan, 1997; Krugman, 1998), many commentators agree that they are largely the products of mismanaged financial liberalization and financial market panic (Stiglitz, 1998; Radelet and Sachs, 1998; Wade, 1998; Chang, 1998a).

In the 'traditional' system, the Korean government controlled all the internal and especially cross-border financial flows very tightly (Chang, 1993).[2] Although there was a series of financial liberalizations during the 1980s, these were 'cautious and slow in terms of ... order and speed' (Park, 1996, p. 252), and the system remained a rightly controlled one until the early 1990s (Amsden and Euh, 1990). However, from the early 1990s, the Korean government started significantly relaxing its control over the financial sector and, under the Kim Young Sam government, which came to power in 1993, the liberalization process was greatly accelerated (see Table 9.1).

The five-year financial liberalization plan announced by the Kim government in 1993 was regarded as the first such plan to have a relatively well-defined (although not precise) timetable and unambiguous policy content. It aimed at, among other things, interest rate deregulation, abolition of 'policy loans', granting of more managerial autonomy to the banks, reduction of entry barriers to financial activities and, most importantly, capital account liberalization, something that Korea's previous plans for financial liberalization had characteristically failed to include (Choi, 1993).

Table 9.1 Major financial liberalization measures in Korea during the 1990s

(1) Interest rates deregulation (in four stages: 1991 to July 1997)
- By 1997, all lending and borrowing rates, except demand deposit rates, were liberalized

(2) More managerial autonomy for the banks and lower entry barriers to financial activities
- Freedom for banks to increase capital, to establish branches, and to determine dividend payments (1994)
- Enlargement of business scope for financial institutions (1993):
    - continuous expansion of the securities business of deposit money banks (1990, 1993, 1994, 1995)
    - freedom for banks and life insurance companies to sell government and public bonds over-the-counter (1995)
    - permission for securities companies to handle foreign exchange business (1995)
- Abolition of the limits on maximum maturities for loans and deposits of banks (1996)

Table 9.1 (continued)

(3) Foreign exchange liberalization
- Adoption of the Market-Average Foreign Exchange Rate System (1990)
- Easing of the requirement for documentation proving 'real' (i.e., non-financial) demand in foreign exchange transactions (1991)
- Setting up of foreign currency call markets
- Revision of the Foreign Exchange Management Act (1991):
  changing the basis for regulation from a positive system to a negative system
- Introduction of 'free Won' accounts for non-residents (1993)
- Allowance of partial Won settlements for the export or import of visible items (1993)
- Foreign Exchange Reform Plan (1994):
  a detailed schedule for the reform of the foreign exchange market structure
- A very significant relaxation of the Foreign Exchange Concentration System (1995)

(4) Capital market opening
- Foreign investors are allowed to invest directly in Korean stock markets with ownership ceilings (1992)
- Foreigners are allowed to purchase government and public bonds issued at international interest rates (1994), equity-linked bonds issued by small and medium-sized firms (1994), non-guaranteed long-term bonds issued by small and medium-sized firms (Jan. 1997), and non-guaranteed convertible bonds issued by large companies (Jan. 1997)
- Residents are allowed to invest in overseas securities via beneficiary certificates (1993)
- Abolition of the ceiling on the domestic institutional investors' overseas portfolio investment (1995)
- Foreign commercial loans are allowed without government approval in so far as they meet the guideline established in May 1995
- Private companies engaged in major infrastructure projects are allowed to borrow overseas to pay for domestic construction cost (Jan. 1997)
- Liberalization of borrowings related to foreign direct investments (Jan. 1997)

(5) Policy loans and credit control
- A planned termination of all policy loans by 1997 is announced (1993):
  a step-wise reduction in policy loans to specific sectors (e.g., export industries and small and medium-sized firms)
- Simplifying and slimming down the controls on the share of a bank's loans to major conglomerates in its total loans

The decision to liberalize the capital account substantially was in a sense a consequence of Korea's economic success. Until 1986, Korea had suffered from chronic current account deficits, which motivated and enabled its government to have strict foreign exchange controls, the two pillars of which were the so-called Foreign Exchange Concentration System, under which all foreign exchange had to be surrendered to the central bank, and the Foreign Exchange Management Act, which put severe restrictions on the use of foreign exchange (e.g., limits on overseas remittances, on overseas real estate acquisition, or even on expenditure on foreign tourism, which was severely restricted until the late 1980s).

However, given the Foreign Exchange Concentration System, the large trade surpluses between 1986 and 1989 generated excess liquidity in the system, prompting the government to scale it down. Although the trade surpluses disappeared subsequently, the surge of capital inflow in the 1990s that made up for it provided the justification for the continued raising of the ceiling on foreign exchange holdings, until the system was finally reduced to near insignificance in 1995. At the same time, the increased credit ratings of Korean corporations and banks in the international financial markets meant that the private sector began to regard government involvement in their foreign exchange transactions as a burden rather than a necessity (previously they simply had not had the creditworthiness to borrow in the international capital market without government guarantees).

Adding to these 'structural' pressures was the continued pressure from the US government to open up the financial market. The March 1992 bilateral talks were its culmination, and it was the agreement arising from these talks that formed the basis for the 1993 financial liberalization programme. The decision of the Kim government in 1993 to apply for membership of the OECD also subjected Korea to further external demands for financial market liberalization.

By 1995, government regulations on foreign borrowing had been significantly reduced, and the result was a mushrooming of foreign debt, which nearly trebled from $44 billion in 1993 to $120 billion in September 1997 (it fell slightly to $116 billion by November 1997).[3] This debt build-up was almost twice as fast as that of 1979–85, the period of the country's earlier (near) debt crisis – Korea's foreign debt grew at 17.8% per annum during 1979–85, while it grew at 33.6% per annum in 1994–6.[4]

What has to be noted here, however, is that, although Korea's foreign debt was large and fast-growing, it was *not* at an obviously unsustainable level. The World Bank considers countries with debt/GNP ratios under 48% as low-risk cases, but Korea's debt/GNP ratio was only 22% in 1996, and was still around 25% on the eve of the crisis.[5] The corresponding figures at the end of 1995 were 70% for

Mexico, 57% for Indonesia, 35% for Thailand, 33% for Argentina, and 24% for Brazil (World Bank, 1997). Also, in terms of another common indicator of debt burden, i.e., debt service ratio (total debt service to exports of goods and services), Korea was well below the World Bank 'warning' threshold (18%) at 5.4% in 1995 and 5.8% in 1996. These compare very favourably with those of countries like Mexico (24.2%), Brazil (37.9%), Indonesia (30.9%) and Thailand (10.2%) in 1995 (World Bank, 1997).

However, the overall debt figures mask one critical problem with Korea's foreign debt, namely, its maturity structure. The share of short-term debt (which is defined as debt with less than a year's maturity) in total debt rose from an already high 43.7% in 1993 to an astonishing 58.3% at the end of 1996 (BAI, 1998). The magnitude of these figures can be put into perspective if we recall that, on the eve of the 1980s debt crisis (between 1980 and 1982), the average ratio of short-term over overall debt for the non-OPEC developing countries was only 20% (Koener *et al.*, 1986, p. 8, table 1.1).

Leading this rapid build-up of short-term foreign debt were the inexperienced merchant banks (officially called 'merchant banking corporations'), newly licensed by the Kim government in the name of financial liberalization – nine of them in 1994, and fifteen in July 1996, in addition to the six that existed before the 1993 financial liberalization programme. The total foreign debt stock of the merchant banks rose by around 60.1% per annum during 1994–6, from $7.27 billion to $18.62 billion (BAI, 1998), vastly outpacing the growth of total foreign debt at 33.6% per annum that we have already referred to as unprecedented. Moreover, supervision of the merchant banks, unlike that of the deposit banks, was virtually non-existent, to the extent that the Kim government was apparently unaware of the huge mismatch in the maturity structures between their borrowings (64% of their $20 billion total foreign borrowings were short term) and lendings (85% of them were long term) that existed on the eve of the crisis.

The rapid debt build-up itself can be explained by the investment boom among Korean corporations, which benefited from the demise of the country's famous industrial policy that had put a break on excessive competition (see below for further details), and from the relaxation of financial policies that traditionally controlled the amount and term structure of foreign borrowing. However, the large share of short-term debt needs more explanation.

First, liberalization was much more extensive in relation to short-term foreign borrowing than to long-term foreign borrowing. For example, while those who were contracting long-term loans were required to provide detailed information and obtain permission from the Ministry of Finance and the Economy (MOFE), as the combined finance and planning ministry was called in President Kim Young Sam's day, short-term borrowers were not required to do this. Combined with the stricter information requirements for long-term loan applications that foreign lenders typically require, this gave the borrowers the incentive to go for short-term loans in order to cut the 'overhead' costs of borrowing.

Second, given the Kim government's commitment to financial liberalization, there was an expectation that Korea's credit rating in the international financial market would keep on improving and that international lending rates for Korean banks and companies would therefore fall. And, given the uncertainty over the exact dates of various liberalization measures announced in 1993 (only the year and not the month in which these steps were to be taken had been announced), many Korean borrowers seem to have taken a 'wait and see' approach by continuously rolling over short-term loans rather than taking our long-term ones, an approach supported by the international lenders who were perfectly willing to roll over Korean loans until the eve of the crisis.

To summarise, the post-1993 financial liberalization in Korea was critical in generating the current crisis as, for the first time in the country's history, it instituted a very substantial, if not full-scale, capital account liberalization. It was not simply the extent of the liberalization but also its design that contributed to the crisis, as it gave the incentive to borrowers to contract short-term loans and allowed poor asset-liability management to go unchecked. However, this cannot be the whole story; we need to explain why the investment boom that demanded all this borrowing was so strong. This is where we turn to the issue of industrial policy.

Industrial policy: over-investment and 'crony capitalism'

It has now become an almost conventional wisdom that the Korean government encouraged, and sometimes even forced, corporations into unprofitable business through its industrial policy. However, we shall argue here that it was the demise of industrial policy, rather than its perpetuation, which drove the Korean economy into crisis.

On its assumption of power in 1993, the Kim Young Sam government abolished the practice of five-year planning, which had provided an overarching policy coordination framework since its introduction in 1962, in favour of the poorly constructed '100-day Plan for the New Economy', which is now regarded by many people as little more than a publicity stunt. At the same time, in the name of government administrative 'rationalization', the planning ministry, the Economic Planning Board (EPB), was merged with the Ministry of Finance (MOF), forming a super-ministry, the Ministry of Finance and Economy (MOFE), which symbolized the demise of (indicative) 'planning' in Korea.

Most critically, the Kim Young Sam government accelerated the dismantling of selective industrial policy that had started in the late 1980s. The rising domestic and international criticism of selective industrial policy since the late 1970s had culminated in the introduction of the Industrial Development Law (IDL) in 1986 by the then government of Chun Doo Hwan. Although the IDL emphasized a 'functional' rather than sectoral approach to industrial policy, it had provisions for sectoral rationalization programmes (with a limited time duration), and thus allowed for a selective industrial policy, had the government the will. And, indeed, in the early days of the IDL, this was the case – several major rationalization programmes were implemented throughout the late 1980s and the early 1990s, covering, among others, industries such as cars, heavy construction machinery, heavy electrical machinery, ferro-alloys, naval diesel engines, dyeing, textiles, and coal mining (for more details, see Chang, 1993, pp. 142–4).

However, the will to conduct selective industrial policy started to wane from the late 1980s with the rise of neo-Liberal ideology and the growing power of the *chaebols* (conglomerates), which now hankered for greater freedom in their investment decision-making (Chang, 1998b). We see the first sign of such a change in 1989, when the then government of Roh Tae Woo for the first time openly refused to coordinate investments in the petrochemical industry, despite the looming threat of massive overcapacity; however, it later had to make a U-turn and intervene when the industry ran into serious trouble owing to overcapacity (for example, by imposing a compulsory export quota).

The ambiguity that the Roh government showed over industrial policy was replaced by the unambiguous aversion to it held by the Kim Young Sam government, which seriously weakened, if not completely negated, most industrial policy measures (the notable exception being the promotion of R&D in some high-technology industries). Given that 'traditional' Korean, and other East Asian, industrial policy provided an investment coordination mechanism that checked 'excessive competition' (for further theoretical discussion, see Chang, 1994, ch. 3), this led to overinvestment. This is turn resulted in falling profitability owing to low capacity utilization and/or falling export prices (many Korean exporters account for large shares in the world markets and therefore are not price-takers), and eventually in major corporate failures in a number of leading industries, including electronics (more specifically, semiconductors), cars, steel, petrochemicals, and shipbuilding. Let us consider a couple of prominent examples in order to illustrate how the demise of industrial policy affected Korean industry.

In the steel industry, the Kim government supported what many, if not all, people regarded as an over-ambitious steel venture by Hanbo, a medium-sized *chaebol* with a dubious track-record in manufacturing. The decision was emphatically *not* taken as a part of any coherent industrial policy, and looked particularly strange when the government had already refused to endorse the largest conglomerate Hyundai's entry into the steel industry. As it turned out, Hanbo collapsed in early 1997, and it was subsequently revealed that behind the government support for Hanbo lay corruption involving the then president's closest aides and probably his son, thus delivering the first blow to foreign confidence in the Korean economy.

The Kim government also licensed Samsung to enter the already overcrowded car industry in 1993. What is fascinating about this entry is that it destabilized the industry before it produced a single car – Samsung's cars did not come on the market until 1998. Relatively lacking in strength in machine-related industries and having deliberately located the factory in the president's hometown, Pusan, despite the fact that the (reclaimed) site needed massive fortification, Samsung's venture looked questionable from the beginning. In the event, it saw a solution in the acquisition of the then third (but previously second) largest car manufacturer, Kia, whose manufacturing capability was highly regarded but whose financial strength was in doubt. Kia, a unique *chaebol* in that it was not family-owned and did not have a particularly diversified industrial portfolio despite its size (it was the eighth largest *chaebol*), tried to defend itself from the threat of takeover by Samsung in two ways, both of which proved unsuccessful. First, it tried to stabilize its cash flows by further diversifying its portfolio. In this context, the expansion of its specialized steel business proved particularly disastrous. Second, it made further pre-emptive investments in the car industry, which did not prove very successful. What followed is well known. The Kim government dithered over the fate of Kia for an extended period of time, until it finally decided to nationalize it, thus seriously weakening foreign confidence in Korea (for further details, see Chang, 1998a).

The stories of Hanbo's steel venture and Samsung's car venture not only illustrate the perils of dismantling the investment coordination mechanism in a high-investment–high-growth regime, but also suggest that the relationship between the state and business in Korea had undergone an important change under the Kim government (see Chang, 1998b for further details).

The corruption surrounding the Hanbo case was, despite current perceptions, *not* typical of what was going on in the country under its state-led model of development. In the traditional model, large sums of money did flow from big business to politicians and top bureaucrats. These flows were often tied to particular projects in areas like urban planning and government procurements, but they were rarely directly related to particular projects *in the main manufacturing sectors*, such as we see in the Hanbo case.

Moreover, under the Kim government, for the first time in post-1960s Korean history, we heard the names of particular *chaebols*, such as Samsung, talked about as being 'close to the regime'. Under the old regime, the *chaebols* as a group were preferentially treated, but rarely was any of them regarded as being closer to the government than others. Under the Kim government, there was a fundamental transformation in the state–business relationship in Korea, which meant that the major manufacturing sectors became less insulated from corrupt political exchanges than they had been previously.

The abolition of five-year planning and the serious weakening of sectoral industrial policy played a very important part in this process. With the well-publicized 'rational' criteria for intervention previously provided by the five-year plans and sectoral policies gone, it became much easier to 'bend the rules' for political reasons. This meant the end of the 'generalistic' state–business relationship that characterized the Korean model and the rapid rise of 'particularistic' (or 'cronyistic', to use the currently popular expression) relationships, and, more importantly, as we have seen, their spread into the major manufacturing industries which were previously largely insulated from corruption. In this sense, it may be said that, contrary to common perception, it was only under the Kim Young Sam government that genuine 'crony capitalism' was born in Korea.

The above discussion suggests that industrial policy in Korea was *not* responsible for the over-investments that are behind the current crisis. It was rather its abolition by the Kim Young Sam government that made such investments easier. In addition, our discussion suggests that the abolition of industrial policy also made it easier to 'bend the rules', facilitating the rise of 'particularistic' (or 'cronyistic') state–business links in relation to the critical manufacturing sectors.

Corporate governance: moral hazard and high debt

One currently popular account, advocated, among others, by Krugman (1998), acknowledges that the recent crisis in Korea and other Asian countries is the direct result of private corporate sector profligacy, but argues that this would not have been possible without the implicit guarantee provided by the government for the banks and industrial corporations. It is argued that this system led to 'moral hazards' among the Korean corporations that resulted in reckless investments and low efficiency, as reflected in low corporate profitability.

This view is also reflected in the IMF programme for Korea, with its demands that the country take measures that will weaken, and eventually dismantle, the large, diversified, family-owned *chaebols*. The proposed measures for this purpose include the banning of mutual payment guarantees among the member firms of the same *chaebol*, the demand for the publication of consolidated balance sheets for the whole *chaebol* (rather than for individual firms), the strenghtening of minority shareholder rights through stricter disclosure requirements, and in general measures that are supposed to make high corporate gearing difficult, if not impossible.

The first obvious problem with Krugman's account is that the ostensibly low corporate profitability in Korea is mainly due to high interest payments, rather than to inefficiency. Table 9.2 shows that Korea's post-interest-payments profitability (the ratio of 'ordinary income' to

Table 9.2 An international comparison of corporate profitability (%)

	Korea (1973–96)	*Korea (1996)*	*Japan (1955–73)*	*Japan (1995)*	*Taiwan (1995)*	*USA (1995)*
Operating income/sales	7.4	6.5	7.2*	3.3	7.3	7.7
Financial expenses/sales	5.5	5.8	3.4	1.3	2.2	n.a.
Ordinary income/sales	2.8	1.0	4.3	2.9	5.1	7.9
Total borrowing/ total assets	n.a.	47.7	n.a.	34.8	26.2	26.4
Debt/equity	338.4	n.a.	320.7	n.a.	n.a.	n.a.

Definitions: Operating income = gross profit – selling and general administrative expenses. Ordinary income = operating income + net non-operating income.
Note: * 1961–73.
Sources: Bank of Korea (various years) and *Japan Statistical Yearbook* (various years).

sales) was low owing to high corporate gearing – 2.8% as opposed to 7.9% in the USA (1995), 5.1% in Taiwan (1995), 4.3% in Japan (1955–73) and 2.9% in Japan (1995). However, this should not be interpreted as showing Korean corporate inefficiency, as Korea's corporate profitability before interest payments (measured by the ratio of 'operating income' to sales) has *not* been low by international standards. Over the 1973–96 period, this figure for Korea averaged at 7.4%, which was similar to that for the USA (7.7%) and Taiwan (7.3%) recorded in 1995. Moreover, low post-interest profitability did not harm investment momentum in Korea, since the government used a range of methods to ensure that the income appropriated by the financial sector was recycled to the manufacturing corporate sector (see Akyuz *et al.*, 1998).

At this point, it may be argued that, whatever the 'real' efficiency of the Korean corporations, they were prone to failure because of their high debt burden, and that therefore the government had to bail them out routinely, thus creating the incentive for moral hazard (for more detailed criticisms, see Chang, 2000).

However, first, there has been no instance, at least in the last two decades, where the Korean government has bailed out a failing *chaebol*. Between 1990 and 1996 alone, as many as three of the 30 biggest *chaebols* went bankrupt (Hanyang, Yoowon, and Woosung), not to speak of the six that went bankrupt in 1997 (Kia, Hanbo, Sammi, Haitai, Jinro, and Halla). Certainly, there were occasions where individual firms belonging to a *chaebol* were assisted, but this invariably involved a government-mediated takeover of the firm (by another *chaebol* or by the government-owned banks), or the imposition of terms of enterprise restructuring that severely restricted managerial autonomy (e.g., Daewoo shipbuilding in the late 1980s). In this situation, there is little room for moral hazard, as the managers know that they will lose control over the enterprise if they fail to perform. The important point in relation to the moral hazard story is *not* that some struggling enterprises have been helped by the government, but whether or not bad management is punished.[6] During the 1990s, notwithstanding the rise of 'cronyistic' relationships with a few particular *chaebols*, the overall government–*chaebol* relationship has been strained as never before, and therefore whatever little prospect of government bail-out previously existed is likely to have diminished even further.[7]

Second, if the *chaebols* were counting on government bail-out, they would not have increased as they did their exposure to the non-bank financial institutions (NBFIs), such as the merchant banks, since it was generally accepted that, given their greater freedom from government regulation and their small size, NBFIs were themselves highly unlikely to be bailed out in cases of failure. The share of the top 30 *chaebols* in total bank loans fell from 19.5% in 1991 to 13.9% in 1995, despite the fact that from 1994 there was some relaxation of restriction on bank lending to *chaebols*. In the case of the six chaebols that went bankrupt in 1997, in particular, reliance on NBFIs, especially on merchant banks, was very heavy. For example, the Halla group borrowed 50% of its 6.5 trillion Won debts from the merchant banks (*Maeil Business News*, 8 December 1997).

And, third, the investments that the *chaebols* had made in the build-up to the crisis were mainly in industries with stable returns, rather than 'high risk, high return' industries, which those investors operating under moral hazard will be inclined to choose. Table 9.3 shows how, during the few years leading up to the crisis, investment in the six 'stable' leading export industries where the *chaebols* were particularly heavily represented – namely, petrochemicals, petroleum refining, iron and steel, cars, electrical and electronics, and shipbuilding – grew much faster than investment in manufacturing in general as well as overall investment.[8] Of course, these industries did not remain 'stable', since, in the absence of investment coordination, overcapacity and falling profitability resulted. It is instructive to note that, of the six *chaebols* which failed in 1997, five failed in one or other of these six industries. For example, Hanbo, Kia, and Sammi failed mainly owing to their failures in steel; Halla failed in shipbuilding; while Haitai, a food-processing conglomerate, stalled owing to its ill-fated foray into the electronics industry.

In addition to the 'moral hazard' argument, the currently popular view of Korea's 'pathological corporate governance' sees high corporate gearing as another major problem. The most obvious problem with

Table 9.3 Trends in facility investment in Korea (growth rates, %)

	1972–9	*1980–2*	*1983–91*	*1992–3*	*1994*	*1995*	*1996*
All industries	43.3	1.3	20.0	–1.0	36.7	37.9	17.3
Manufacturing	43.6	–11.3	29.6	–8.9	56.2	43.5	17.1
The 'six' industries	n.a.	n.a.	20.3*	–6.8	68.2	48.7	25.1
Non-manufacturing	49.9	21.8	10.1	15.5	9.5	26.9	17.7

Notes: The 'six' are petroleum refining, petrochemicals, iron and steel, electrical and electronics, cars and shipbuilding.
* 1987–91.
Source: KDB (Korea Development Bank) (various years).

this view is that Korea's corporate financing system had served the country well until the crisis. While the argument by Wade and Veneroso (1998) that high corporate gearing is an inevitable consequence of high household savings may be debatable (after all, as seen in Table 9.2, Taiwan, despite its high household savings ratio, has a corporate gearing ratio as low as that of the USA), their argument that the high-corporate-debt system has been an effective way of generating 'patient' long-term investments deserves to be emphatically repeated (also see Dertouzos *et al.*, 1989; Albert, 1991; Hutton, 1995).

It may be reasonably argued, of course, that despite its desirable features the high-corporate-debt system is still a very risky one, as is proved by recent events in Korea. At one level, this is obviously true, but the fact that Japan had nothing remotely approaching the current Korean crisis (or for that matter Korea's early 1970s or early 1980s crises), despite a corporate gearing ratio that was as high as Korea's until the 1980s, shows that high corporate debt *per se* cannot be the cause of the current crisis. During its 'high-growth' period, that is, between 1955 and 1973, the debt–equity ratio of Japanese manufacturing corporations was 320%, which was at an equivalent level to the Korean figure of 338% between 1973 and 1996 (JBS, various years; BOK, various years). The Japanese debt–equity ratio peaked at around 500% in the mid-1970s, and was still as high as 385% in 1980 (JBS, various years). This comparison suggests that, had it not been for the ill-designed financial liberalization policy and the demise of industrial policy that led to over-investment, high corporate debt in Korea would not have produced a crisis.

Our questioning of the currently popular view of the Korean corporate governance system does not mean that there was nothing wrong with that system. Features like continued family control (which runs counter to meritocracy) and the poor quality of financial reporting should certainly be rectified. However, our view is that most of these problems could be eliminated without changing the fundamental nature of the system – such as portfolio diversification (as long as it is not excessive) and the flowing-back of the profits transferred to the financial sector. Trying to Americanise the corporate governance system may only adversely affect the Korean corporations' ability to invest and upgrade, the features that made them so formidable in international markets.

Conclusion

In this paper, we have examined some common views on the recent Korean crisis, focusing on issues relating to financial liberalization, industrial policy, and corporate governance. We have presented evidence that shows how these views lack a solid empirical basis, and have argued that it was the dismantling of the traditional mechanisms of generating and coordinating long-term investment, rather than the perpetuation of the traditional regime, that made Korea's corporate debt and foreign borrowing situations difficult. We have also argued that although things were difficult they were not obviously near to crisis point, and therefore what actually happened cannot be explained without reference to the panic that gripped the financial markets following the South-east Asian crises and the high-profile corporate bankruptcies (Hanbo and Kia). We have examined the forces behind the policy changes that led to the crisis and concluded that, while there were certain structural and external forces that were difficult to resist (e.g., the growing power of the conglomerates, growing US pressures for market opening, etc.), policy failures certainly have to take a large portion of the blame.

When what remains of the 'traditional' Korean economic system after the Kim Young Sam government's liberalization drive has been dismantled by the IMF programme, it may seem pointless to talk about the merits of the old system, whatever they were. However, changes in formal institutions, which can never specify the full universe of individual and institutional interactions, cannot fully determine the future, and, in that sense, it may be too early to predict what will happen to the Korean economic system in the long run. After all, was it not out of the very American system imposed on Germany and Japan by the American Occupation Authority that the famous German and Japanese economic systems emerged?

Notes

* We thank Lance Taylor and two anonymous referees for their useful comments on an earlier version of the paper.

1. See Chang (1993) for a review of the earlier phases of the debate on the Korean experience. The most recent phase of the debate has been prompted by the World Bank (1993). See Fishlow *et al.* (1994) and Akyuz *et al.* (1998) for criticisms of the World Bank view.
2. In fact, Korea experimented briefly with domestic (but not international) financial liberalization in the late 1960s. This exercise was once hailed as a model for financial liberalization in developing countries, but later researches revealed that it was not as extensive as had been supposed, and it was subsequently abandoned following the little-known (outside Korea) financial crisis of the early 1970s, which was resolved by a state-imposed moratorium on all 'curb market' loan servicing in 1972 through the infamous '3 August Decree' (see Harris, 1987 and Chang, 1993, for further details).

3. The definition of foreign debt here follows the World Bank definition, and therefore is different from the concept of 'external liabilities', which include the offshore borrowings of Korean banks and overseas borrowings of the overseas branches and subsidiaries of Korean banks. The IMF and the Korean government started using this definition from 28 December 1997. At the end of November 1997, Korea's external liabilities amounted to $157 billion, of which $92 billion was of less than a year's maturity.
4. By 1997, the Bank of International Settlement (BIS) data, which is also frequently used, showed that the growth of Korea's foreign debt was already slowing down. Its foreign debt increased from $105 billion at the end of 1996 to $120 billion in September 1997 – an annual growth rate of 19% – and actually decreased to $116 billion by the end of November 1997.
5. In the World Bank classification, a country is 'less indebted' when the debt/GNP ratio is less than 48%, 'moderately indebted' when this ratio is between 48% and 80%, and 'severely indebted' when it is over 80%. For the exact definitions, see World Bank, 1997, Vol. 1, pp. 49–50.
6. There was little room for moral hazard on the part of domestic lenders either. Defaulted loans have remained as 'non-performing loans' on their balance sheets, damaging their profitability. As for international lenders, it is implausible that they should have increased their exposure in Korea in the belief that the IMF would bail them out. Until the very eve of the crisis, no one expected Korea to find itself in a situation requiring IMF intervention.
7. Since the 1980s, successive Korean governments have introduced a series of 'anti-*chaebol*' policies, including ceilings on the share of the top 30 *chaebols* in total bank loans, restrictions on mutual payment guarantees among member firms of the same *chaebols*, and pressures on the *chaebols* to sell 'non-business' property. The *chaebols* for their part have stepped up their publicity campaign against government regulation since the early 1990s.
8. In these six industries, investment by the top 30 *chaebols* accounted for 82.3% of total investment on average between 1994 and 1996. See Choi (1995, 1996, and 1997).

References

Akyuz, Y., Chang, H.-J. and Kozul-Wright, R. (1998) 'New perspectives on East Asian development', *Journal of Development Studies*, vol. 34, no. 6.

Albert, M. (1991) *Capitalism vs. Capitalism*, New York, Four Walls and Eight Windows.

Amsden, A. and Euh, Y. (1990) 'Republic of Korea's Financial Reform: What are the Lessons?' Discussion Paper, no. 30, Geneva, United Nations Conference on Trade and Development (UNCTAD).

BAI (Board of Audit and Inspection)(1998) *The Analysis and Evaluation of the 1997 Foreign Exchange Crisis*, Seoul, Board of Audit and Inspection, Government of Korea.

BOK (Bank of Korea) (various years) *Financial Statement Analysis*, Seoul, Bank of Korea.

Brittan, L. (1997) 'Asian Model R.I.P.', *Financial Times*, 4 December 1997.

Chang, H.-J. (1993) 'The political economy of industrial policy in Korea', *Cambridge Journal of Economics*, vol. 17, no. 2.

Chang, H.-J. (1994) *The Political Economy of Industrial Policy,* London and Basingstoke, Macmillan.

Chang, H.-J. (1998a) 'Korea: the misunderstood crisis', *World Development,* vol. 26, no. 8.

Chang, H.-J. (1998b) 'An Alternative View on Regulatory Reform in Korea', paper presented at the conference on 'Korea's transition to a high-productivity economy', University of Hawaii, Honolulu, February.

Chang, H.-J. (2000) 'The hazard of moral hazard – untangling the Asian Crisis', *World Development,* vol. 28, no. 4.

Choi, B. (1993) 'Financial policy and big business in Korea: the perils of financial regulation', in Haggard, S., Lee, C. and Maxfield, S. (eds), *The Politics of Finance in Developing Countries,* Ithaca, New York, Cornell University Press.

Choi, S.-N. (1995 and 1996) *Analysis of the 30 Korean Big Business Groups,* Seoul, Korea Economic Research Institute.

Choi, S.-N. (1997) *The Korean Big Business Group for 1997,* Seoul, Centre for Free Enterprise.

Dertouzos, M., Lester, R. and Solow, R. (1989) *Made in America,* Cambridge, MA, MIT Press.

Fishlow, A., Gwin, C., Haggard, S., Rodrik, D., and Wade, R. (1994) *Miracle or Design? – Lessons from the East Asian Experience,* Washington, DC, Overseas Development Council.

Harris, L. (1987) 'Financial reform and economic growth: a new interpretation of South Korea's experience', in Harris, L. *et al.* (eds), *New Perspectives on the Financial System,* London, Croom Helm.

Hutton, W. (1995) *The State We're In,* London, Jonathan Cape.

JBS (Japanese Bureau of Statistics)(various years) *Japan Statistical Yearbook,* Tokyo, Japan Bureau of Statistics.

KDB (Korea Development Bank) (various years) *Survey of Facility Investment,* Seoul, Korea Development Bank.

Koener, P., Maass, G., Siebold, T. and Tetzlaff, R. (1986) *The IMF and the Debt Crisis,* London, Zed Books.

Krugman, P. (1998) 'What Happened to Asia?', mimeo, Department of Economics, Massachusetts Institute of Technology.

Park, W.-A. (1996) 'Financial liberalisation: the Korean experience', in Ito, T. and Krueger, A. (eds), *Financial Deregulation and Integration in East Asia,* Chicago, University of Chicago Press.

Radelet, S. and Sachs, J. (1998) 'The onset of the East Asian financial crisis', *Brookings Papers on Economic Activity,* no. 1.

Stiglitz, J. (1998) 'Sound Finance and Sustainable Development in Asia', paper delivered at the Asia Development Forum, 10–13 March, Manila.

Wade, R. (1998) 'The Asian debt-and-development crisis of 1997: causes and consequences', *World Development,* vol. 26, no. 8.

Wade, R. and Veneroso, F. (1998) 'The Asian crisis: The high debt model vs. The Wall Street–Treasury–IMF complex', *New Left Review,* March–April.

World Bank (1993) *The East Asian Miracle,* New York, Oxford University Press.

World Bank (1997) *Global Development Finance,* World Bank, Washington, DC.

10
Fashioning a New Korean Model out of the Crisis: The Rebuilding of Institutional Capabilities

*John A. Mathews**

Introduction

The financial meltdown in East Asia in 1997–8 had dramatic effects not only on the countries of the region itself, but on the scholarly debates over the sources and limits of the 'East Asian Miracle' model of development as well.[1] The achievements of the fast-growing East Asian economies are not in question: as Joseph Stiglitz put it, the East Asian Miracle was real.[2] But the methods used by the East Asians in constructing this miracle were cast in a pitiless spotlight through the financial chain-reactions of 1997, and, in many cases, were found wanting. Positions adopted before the crisis have thus had to be revised.

The case of Korea is of particular interest, in that it grew so fast and so effectively up to 1997, and then fell so heavily. In the trauma of November and December 1997, the Korean economy, which had grown to become the eleventh largest in the world, was reduced to a wreck, tossed on the seas of international finance. Practices which had seemed smart before the crisis, like extended debt leveraging in order to expand businesses, came to be seen as folly when external conditions turned adverse, and repayment obligations could not be met.

Every crisis is pregnant with opportunity, as the Chinese characters *wei ji* tell us. The Korean case is of particular interest in the way that the country has recovered from the worst effects, relatively quickly, and by the middle of 1998 was rebuilding a new version of a 'Korean model' – turning the crisis to its own advantage by reforming the political–economic structures, which were in fact long overdue for reform but which could not be tampered with in the absence of a major crisis. The key to the transformation lies in the role played by the twin IMF agreements of December 1997. While many saw these agreements as yet another case of heavy-handed IMF intervention looking to dampen economic activity at the very time that it needed to be revived, and many also saw them as instruments of US foreign and economic policy, few have interpreted the agreements as embodying the interests of institutional reform in Korea. Yet the case is strong that this is indeed the role they have played, providing the *external sanction* needed to drive reform. This paper seeks to substantiate this proposition, by reference to the IMF agreements themselves, their concordance with earlier Korean reform initiatives, and to the subsequent reform and restructuring efforts mounted under their mantle in 1998 in Korea.

The year 1997 is certainly not the first time that Korea has fallen into the arms of the IMF. In 1971, just ten years after the unleashing of the export-oriented growth model, and again in 1980–3, at the stormy conclusion to the crash-through programme of heavy and chemical industrialization, the pattern was strikingly similar. A period of breakneck expansion of industrial capacity and output, fuelling exports and capitalized by borrowed funds, ended in an overheated blow-up as external conditions turned adverse and made interest and capital repayments problematic. In each case IMF intervention calmed things down and stabilized the economy, and domestic 'rationalization' cleaned out the weaker corporate players, preparing the system for its next period of breakneck expansion.[3] It is a remarkably simple, remarkably effective model of accelerated economic development. The catch is that there has to be some institution to salvage the wreckage when the process gets overheated – otherwise the foreign borrowings that drive it will dry up and capital investment will henceforth be dependent on national savings.[4]

The 'old' Korean model, that died on 30 November 1997 and was finally buried on 24 December 1997, was built on three foundations:

- strong industrial conglomerates (*chaebol*) able to penetrate new markets and industrial sectors;
- a financial system that channelled capital, chiefly through foreign borrowings, to the *chaebol* ('policy loans'); and
- strong 'pilot agencies' to set the lead for investment in new sectors and the standards for judging corporate performance (e.g., export levels).

This model must be counted as one of the most successful 'engines' of accelerated industrial development ever devised and put into practice.

Its strengths were the capacity to move rapidly into new sectors – first into labour-intensive industries in the 1960s; then into capital-intensive heavy and chemical industries in the 1970s; and then into knowledge-intensive industries in the 1980s – and to mobilize the resources necessary to do so. Its weaknesses were, first, its extreme dependence on foreign borrowing, and hence vulnerability to externally generated downturns. Second, the dependence on strong and large industrial firms turned into a fetter as these firms grew ever larger and more powerful. In the 1980s, and increasingly in the 1990s, they became a political force that was in many ways out of control. The concentration engendered by the model threatened to choke off all other forms of development and initiative in the Korean economy. Only something drastic – like a major crisis – could loosen the grip that the *chaebol* came to exercise over the economy. Third, the role of state agencies in directing development, combined with financial non-transparency, could and did lead to excessive cronyism and outright bribery and corruption, as revealed in the case of Hanbo Steel (discussed below). The strong 'envelope' of regulatory controls and restrictions also became increasingly incompatible with the decision-making imperatives of nimble, high-technology firms competing in international marketplaces, and its dismantling proceeded in a jerky, on-off process of deregulation followed by re-regulation without a clear goal or sense of purpose.

The 'old' Korean model, like its counterpart in Japan in the 1930s (which it resembles in many striking ways), threatened to become a political force beyond the control of existing state agencies and newly created democratic institutions. It was unstoppable, or, rather, could be stopped only by a major crisis. Hence the tendency among the political and business elite in Korea, particularly within the circles grouped around the new president, Kim Dae-Jung, to regard the 1997–8 meltdown as a 'blessing in disguise'.

The unravelling of the Korean model in 1997

By the crisis year 1997, Korea's rapid industrial development through borrowed capital was nearing the end of its fourth decade. The government-induced 'policy loans', which had made so much sense in the years of heavily regulated finance, made less and less sense as the financial system was slowly liberalized and deregulated.[5] Indeed, the continuation of strong policy direction over investment and open market sourcing of capital borrowings made for an explosive mix in which cronyism and corruption could – and did – flourish. Nonetheless, an external crisis that no one foresaw brought the system down. How it happened is a matter of great interest, since it also affects how the new model is being fashioned, in 1998, out of the ruins of the old.

The Korean crisis of 1997 had many elements, but there were at core three processes whose interactions catapulted the country to the brink of insolvency. There was a debt default crisis, triggered by adverse external circumstances that made it difficult for companies and banks to service their loans. Korea has always lived with high debt levels, making it vulnerable to external downturns. But this crisis saw company collapses imposing huge losses on domestic banks, which in turn created a liquidity crisis as letters of credit could not or would not be honoured. The liquidity crisis forced further companies and banks into difficulties, so that foreign banks and investors started to withdraw, and external credit-rating agencies downgraded Korean stocks and bonds. This created a run on the currency, which had been gently devaluing after two years of appreciating along with the US dollar.

All these factors came together in a downward vicious spiral in November and December of 1997. The more the exchange rate fell, the more companies had to hedge their foreign operations, and withhold their foreign earnings, putting further pressure on the exchange rate, and exacerbating the debt repayment problems (since the external debts were largely denominated in US dollars). In this way, a crisis feeds on itself and amplifies processes that would normally be self-correcting.[6]

How did Korean corporations get themselves into a level of indebtedness that made them critically vulnerable to any economic downturn or demands for capital redemption from creditor banks? This is easily answered. They simply continued to do what they had always done. High levels of debt-to-equity ratios, and high levels of cross-divisional debt guarantees by one affiliate supporting fellow affiliates, have always been a part of the 'Korean model'. In the 1990s, it was merely being practised on a larger and riskier scale, and by smaller and less experienced *chaebol*, anxious to become players in the international Big League.

Across the board, Korea's top 30 *chaebol* were leveraged to the extent of debt exceeding shareholders' equity by nearly 4 times (actually, a ratio of 3.87) – compared with the situation in other countries, such as Taiwan (0.85), Japan (2.0) and the US (1.6). With hindsight, such a degree of leveraging might be dismissed as foolish. Yet it sustained

Korea's rapid growth in the 1980s and 1990s very nicely, particularly in the case of the top five *chaebol*, which fluctuated around this average (Hyundai being the most daring, at a ratio of 4.4, and Samsung the most conservative, with a ratio of 'only' 2.7 – as shown in Table 10.1).

Table 10.1 Debt–equity and debt–asset ratios and cross-group debt guarantees for 30 largest *chaebol*, 1997

Company	*Debt–asset ratio (top 20)*	*Debt–equity ratio (%)*	*Debt guarantee (trillion won)*	*Guarantee–equity ratio (%)*	*No. of subsidiaries*
Hyundai	376	436.7	4.04	41.1	57
Samsung	206	267.1	1.92	13.6	80
LG	313	346.5	1.29	15.5	49
Daewoo	337	339.5	3.74	47.8	32
Sunkyong	320	383.8	0.71	15.1	46
Sangyong	297	409.4	2.20	68.4	25
Hanjin (Korean Air)	619	555.8	0.84	39.4	24
Kia*	418	519.0	2.09	91.3	28
Hanwha	619	751.4	1.77	142.6	31
Lotte	179	192.2	0.56	20.8	30
Kumbo	465	481.8	1.01	78.9	26
Halla*	2,930	2065.4	0.42	138.4	18
Dong-Ah	320	354.7	1.04	75.3	19
Doosan	625	688.2	0.43	52.9	25
Daelim	344	423.3	1.19	106.7	21
Hansol	290	291.9	0.62	50.5	23
Hyusung	315	370.1	0.15	16.9	18
Dongkuk	190	218.4	0.48	42.6	17
Jinro*	2,532	3075.0	0.51	462.0	24
Kolon	350	318.0	0.59	64.1	24
Kohap	–	590.5	0.42	78.8	–
Dongbu	–	251.5	0.58	61.2	–
Tongyang	–	307.8	0.56	85.0	–
Haitai*	–	658.5	0.21	45.6	–
New Core*	–	1225.6	0.36	172.5	–
Anam	–	478.5	1.62	349.4	–
Hanil	–	576.8	0.17	44.6	–
Keopyung	–	347.6	1.86	353.2	–
Miwon	–	416.9	0.64	144.2	–
Shinho	–	489.3	1.12	290.2	–
Totals	–	386.7 (av.)	33.15	47.04	–

* Company under court protection.
Sources: Bank of Korea for debt–asset ratios for top 20; Korean Fair Trade Commission for debt–equity ratios, debt guarantees, and subsidiaries.

The high ratio reflects not imprudence on the part of the top *chaebol*, but the structure of capital institutions in the country, with banks supplying much more developmental capital than equity markets.[7] So the problem was not the high debt–equity ratios themselves, but the abuse of this system by some of the smaller and medium-sized *chaebol*, who were anxious to grow and move up the ladder by whatever means available.[8]

There was a further twist to these practices, in the form of 'cross-group debt-guarantees'. Mutual guarantees were a secret weapon of Korea's *chaebol*, enabling them to expand rapidly and diversify with minimal collateral. But in the hands of weaker and inexperienced players they became a trap that could ensnare the entire group when one marginal affiliate stumbled – with Kia and Halla being two of the most spectacular cases of this effect at work. Table 10.1 reveals that Halla's debt guarantees amounted to 1.38 times its equity base; the situation was even worse for Jinro, whose debt guarantees amounted to 4.6 times its equity base.

A catastrophic series of corporate bankruptcies in 1997 revealed how vulnerable firms with these kinds of debt–equity ratios and cross-divisional debt guarantees could be. Hanbo Steel folded in January 1997, with debts totalling more than 5 trillion won ($5.85 billion) – the largest collapse in Korea's history. But this was only the beginning. Other affiliates of the Hanbo group, which had been forced to act as guarantors of Hanbo Steel's debts, also collapsed, effectively bringing down the entire group, Korea's 14th largest *chaebol*.[9] Why the banks had continued to lend to such a poor risk subsequently became clear: they were being bribed by Hanbo's founder, Chung Tae Soo, to do so. Chung, it turned out, had been indicted twice before for bribery, but somehow had managed to stay in business. Eventually he was forced to default because even the banks, despite the bribes, refused to go on lending to him, and demanded his removal from the company's management. Eventually the bribery scandals spread, reaching even into the President's office, thus effectively tying the hands of the government at the very moment when strong leadership was called for to stem the mounting crisis.

Korea's crisis, therefore, had elements that were imported from the wider crises of the region, and in particular from the difficulties facing banks in Japan and Hong Kong who had lent short to Korean firms and merchant banks, but it also had elements that were entirely self-generated, such as the *chaebol* collapses of 1997 and government inactivity due to mounting bribery scandals. The system was in considerable disarray at the time of the November and December financial crisis which saw the intervention of the IMF.

The IMF agreements of December 1997

There were three agendas at work in the twin IMF agreements signed with Korea on 5 and 24 December 1997. First, a conventional IMF agenda called for monetary rectitude, some financial austerity, and fiscal responsibility. Macroeconomic targets were set, and austerity measures demanded. While the targets themselves were relatively pointless, the austerity measures raised interest rates and tightened liquidity at a time when it was already severely contracting. The IMF argued that this was necessary to restore 'health' to the banking sector. While this is no doubt true, it tightened an economic noose that was already squeezing healthy businesses.

The second component was a conspicuous American agenda to open up the Korean economy to foreign investment. This was contained in the 'restructuring and reform measures' clauses of the IMF agreement. It called for accounting standards and disclosure rules to be strengthened to meet international practice and audit standards; for acceleration of the schedule allowing foreign entry into the Korean financial sector, including allowing foreign firms to establish bank subsidiaries and brokerage houses by mid-1998; for liberalizing foreign investment in the Korean stock market, increasing the ceiling on aggregate foreign ownership in firms from 26% to 50% by the end of 1997 and to 55% by the end of 1998; for allowing foreign banks to purchase equity in Korean domestic banks in excess of the 4% limit requiring supervisory authority approval; for allowing foreign investors to purchase, without restriction, domestic Korean money market instruments and corporate bonds; and for reducing restrictions on foreign direct investment in Korean industrial and other firms through simplification of procedures.[10] These matters are not normally the subject of IMF agreements, and they reflect a clear concern by the American sponsors of the IMF, who wanted a substantial opening of the Korean market to US investors as *quid pro quo* for the bail-out.[11]

The Koreans fought these provisions, but not very strenuously, partly because there is a strong lobby within Korea that supports such liberalization and opening up of the Korean economy (in the name of imposing discipline on domestic firms), and partly because there existed a Korean agenda which had to find a way into the negotiations. Reaching a *quid pro quo* with the American agenda was the point of leverage. The Korean side in the negotiations knew exactly what it was doing and made use of the extraordinary opportunity created by the IMF intervention to transform the Korean 'model' from a developmental system to a more mature system. The Korean-instigated reforms (which had not been part of any comparable IMF agreement with a country in trouble) cover matters such as: corporate governance and structure (e.g., transparency of corporate balance sheets and full implementation of international accounting standards for Korean *chaebol*, and consolidated financial statements for business conglomerates); reducing the levels of mutual debt repayment guarantees between affiliates within a single business group; easing restrictions in the labour market over redundancies (to enable businesses to move from one industry to another); opening the way to corporate bankruptcy procedures; and, above all, reform of the financial sector, including separation of the Bank of Korea from the Ministry of Finance and the creation of a new office for the supervision of all financial institutions. Taken as a group, these constitute a quite remarkable set of structural reforms, all incorporated into the agreement at the instigation of the Korean side.[12]

Reforming the Korean financial sector

While international attention has been focused on Korea's renegotiation of external debts and the floating of a successful government-backed bond issue, the real reform process has continued quietly at home. Central to the reform of the Korean model has been a restructuring and 're-engineering' of the financial sector, and in particular an overhaul of its regulatory and supervisory processes. This is in clear recognition of the damage inflicted by the dismantling of previous regulatory controls (e.g., over capital inflows) and by the inadequacy of supervisory structures. The reforms have been very much in line with those mandated by the IMF agreements, which can be interpreted to mean that there has been an opening up to foreign intervention (the US agenda) complemented by complete overhaul of the regulatory structures (the Korean agenda).

First, the worst affected and worst performing financial institutions were quickly closed. The greedy merchant banks that borrowed short and lent long were singled out for disciplinary action. As part of the December IMF Accords, a total of 14 merchant banks were placed in provisional liquidation by the Kim Young Sam administration. At the beginning of February, the new Kim Dae-Jung government announced that ten of these would actually be shut down and arrangements made to provide some protection for their creditors. To minimize the impact on creditors – i.e., the companies that borrowed from these banks – the government set up at the beginning of February a 'bridging bank' that would temporarily assume some of the debt held by the suspended banks until they could be liquidated, merged, or sold. The remaining 20 of the 30 merchant banks were given until the end of February to devise plans to stay afloat. Subsequently, in July, five commercial banks were ordered to close their doors definitively, under orders from the newly established Financial Supervisory Commission (to be discussed below).

The second element in the restructuring involved clearly separating the Bank of Korea (the central bank) from the Ministry of Finance and Economics, and stripping both of supervisory functions. The Bank of Korea is being consolidated as the principal instrument of the country's monetary policy, in charge of setting prime interest rates.[13] Such a restructuring is critical to breaking the nexus between monetary policy and supervision of financial institutions, which was one of the factors allowing situations like the Hanbo scandal to flourish. The independence of the Bank of Korea is thus protected and reinforced, while its supervisory powers are diminished and transferred. The Ministry of Finance and Economy is to retain the authority over macroeconomic and broad financial policy and license the establishment of financial institutions.

The third element involves restructuring completely the mechanisms for supervision of financial institutions, and the creation of a powerful new office for such a purpose, to be located within a strengthened prime minister's office. The new consolidated institution is to consist of a Financial Supervisory Board (FSB) and Financial Supervisory Agency (FSA) together with a Securities and Futures Trade Commission.[14] The Financial Supervisory Agency is to be the special juridical body responsible for inspecting, auditing and sanctioning financial institutions. Until the new structures are established, an interim Financial Services Commission has been established and began operating in early April 1998 to act as financial watchdog and to direct reforms of the industrial conglomerates.[15] The Commission revealed that it had teeth when in July 1998, only three months after its establishment, it ordered the closure of five non-viable commercial banks, and gave seven further banks 'conditional approvals' requiring them to undergo substantial restructuring, including replacement of senior management.[16]

Finally, the non-performing loans that lie at the heart of the Korean debt crisis, and continued through 1998 to cripple the operations of the banking sector, have been addressed through the creation of the Korea Asset Management Corporation (KAMCO), which is empowered to purchase the assets of shaky institutions (such as collateralized non-performing loans) and sell them off to domestic and foreign bidders. This institution, like similar bodies created for similar purposes in Thailand, Indonesia and Malaysia, is modelled not on a Japanese institution but on the US Resolution Trust Corporation, which played an important role in resolving the savings and loan crisis of the 1980s.[17]

The implications of these changes are likely to be profound. The FSB and FSA are likely to become central players in monitoring the future health of the financial sector in Korea and preventing any repetition of the suicidal short-term borrowings that characterized the activities of the newly established and deregulated merchant banks in the mid-1990s and that helped trigger the 1997 crisis. The clarification of the role of the Bank of Korea, and its separation from any supervisory function, is likely to diminish the scope for bribery and corruption. The KAMC has moved rapidly to cleanse the bad debt problems, in striking contrast with the painfully slow progress made in solving a comparable problem in Japan. The restructuring carries the full mandate of the IMF, and indeed would not have been politically feasible in Korea without its intervention, but it has been driven by the Korean government itself, under the fresh administration of Kim Dae-Jung.

Reforming the industrial sector: reining in the *chaebol*

Underpinning the Korean crisis lay the expansionary practices of the mid-sized *chaebol*, extending their activities through debts that far exceeded their equity base or their capacity to repay. While these practices had been exposed and denounced by many before, both within and outside Korea, they went on unchecked – with the disastrous results of 1997, and the bankruptcies of Hanbo, Sammi, Jinro, Halla and many others. So reform of *chaebol* practices has been near the top of the political agenda for a long time in Korea, but until 1997 the necessary will or sense of crisis was lacking.[18] The IMF intervention and agreements, and then the election of Kim Dae-Jung as president on 18 December, changed all that. The IMF Accords contained several clauses explicitly targeted at reforming the structures and operations of the *chaebol*, as mentioned. However, it was up to the Korean Government (and Kim Dae-Jung's transition team in the first instance) to act on them and drive through the changes – something that had eluded previous administrations. The President-elect showed that he meant business by calling a meeting of the country's top five business leaders – the heads of the leading *chaebol* – in January 1998, only three weeks after his election and six weeks before his inauguration, to secure their agreement to a binding five-point undertaking. This historic compact between the *chaebol* leaders and the President-elect committed them to:

- producing consolidated balance sheets, prepared according to international accounting standards;
- terminating the cross-divisional payment guarantee system for raising loans;
- requiring affiliates to perform profitably, and merging or divesting those that are not profitable;
- promoting partnerships between the *chaebol* and small and medium-sized enterprises;
- placing their personal wealth into their companies to improve their equity base.

This compact captured the essential reforms needed to rein in the *chaebol* and give more life to other elements in the Korean economy, particularly small and medium-sized enterprises. While the abuses have generally occurred within the ranks of the mid-sized *chaebol*, and the top five have generally been responsible in their behaviour, the top five chairmen nonetheless took responsibility for the practices of their colleagues in mid-sized *chaebol* and for having failed to take the lead in reform.

The key strategic weapon of the *chaebol*, and the factor that has enabled them to expand so rapidly, has been the lack of transparency in their accounting and shareholding details. Behind the veil of secrecy, owners and their senior managers have been able to manipulate profit and loss flows, channelling profits from one business into another to get it started or prop it up during downturns. This has been a powerful technique for entering new businesses, such as semiconductors – and when it worked it served the firms, and Korea, very well indeed.[19] But such a system can, and does, lead to abuses.[20] Even in the case of the top five *chaebol*, the lack of consolidated balance sheets has presented company presidents with too many temptations for unaccountable diversification and expansion.[21]

The complement to insisting on transparent accounting is the elimination of the practice whereby a *chaebol* affiliate can raise loans backed by the security, indeed the total repayment guarantee, of its associated affiliates. The practice of using affiliates to guarantee loans is to be outlawed eventually, with *chaebol* individually seeking to reduce the level of their guarantees as fast as possible.[22]

Requiring affiliate management to ensure the profitability of their businesses is code for extensive restructuring of *chaebol* operations. One after another, the top 30 *chaebol* have been making announcements to this effect.[23] These involve plans to sell off assets, to merge unprofitable businesses into others, and to abandon ambitious plans for diversification (as in Hyundai's announcement that it would give up plans to enter the steel industry). All the major *chaebol* put a freeze on their overseas expansion plans. The net effect of these initiatives, if indeed they are implemented as announced, will be to reduce debt-to-equity ratios and slim down the *chaebol*, making them leaner and more focused competitors.

Calls for a better relationship between the *chaebol* and small and medium-sized enterprises are intended to end *chaebol* predatory practices that have gone on far too long in Korea. *Chaebol* are being urged to find ways of encouraging small and medium-sized enterprise growth and participation in the economy, either by striking up alliances with selected firms or leaving other sectors of the economy free of *chaebol* influence. This is why Kim Dae-Jung also announced steps to boost funding, export support, and services for small and medium-sized enterprises that will bring them into a position of being able to compete with *chaebol* on their own terms.

These promise to be the most thoroughgoing reforms to *chaebol* structures and practices in a generation. And Kim Dae-Jung appears to have every intention of driving the changes through.[24] The days of huge investment rates are behind them. They are likely to continue to be formidable competitors in international markets, particularly in areas where they have built up considerable internal know-how, such as semiconductors, steel, and shipbuilding. But now they move into a long-anticipated 'consolidation' phase, after the frantic growth and diversification of the past three and a half decades.

Prospects for a new Korean model

It is only very rarely that one glimpses the complete overhaul of an entire national political economy. Yet this is what is being undertaken in Korea under the mantle of the IMF agreements and driven by the political reform credentials of the Kim Dae-Jung administration.[25] How can the new model, which is being established through the reforms to the financial, industrial and political structures in Korea, be expected to work? The first point to note is that, in spite of all the 'liberalization' and 'deregulation' of the financial sector, the Koreans have no intention of replacing their former highly interventionist model of development with an Anglo-American style non-interventionist economy based on unfettered market forces. While the new Korean model will have at its centre an economy which is much more open and transparent, it will be closely supervised and regulated, and the sources of corruption and excessive risk-taking, such as too close ties between the Bank of Korea, commercial banks and lesser *chaebol*, will be much reduced. If these reforms succeed, the 'renovated' Korean economy is likely to benefit in terms of competitiveness; moreover, it could have new sources of competitive advantage.

The first of these new sources of advantage would be the emergence of the *chaebol* as genuine 'industrial groups' or clusters, on the Japanese model of *keiretsu*. Thus the restructured top five *chaebol* could emerge each as a tightly knit group of firms involved in a range of industrial sectors, knitted together by common ownership of financial institutions such as insurance companies, securities firms and (part ownership in) retail and merchant banks. Each could specialize in certain industrial sectors, but each would span manufacturing and service firms, and would have at its core financial institutions that would eventually provide a first preference channel for future capital needs. Such a structure if it emerges would give the Korean economy great responsive and adaptive capacities.

The second feature of the new industrial structure is likely to be flourishing small and medium-sized firms, many of which would be based on new and advanced technologies – unfettered or unobstructed by the *chaebol*. The emergence of such firms has been choked off in the past by the concentrated power of the *chaebol*. In the future, *chaebol* will stand to benefit by entering into alliances with such small and medium-sized enterprises as they seek to span as many of the emerging technologies as possible.

The strength of the former Korean model lay in its power to coordinate investment, partly through the operation of a 'pilot agency' such as the Economic Planning Board, and partly through the state controls over the financial system. Both have now disappeared. The Economic Planning Board was abolished (or rather 'absorbed' within the Ministry of Finance and Economics) in the mid-1990s, in an excess of deregulatory zeal. But a pilot agency of this kind is widely missed in Korea, and discussions are proceeding as to what kind of institution might take its place.[26] Other East Asian successes, like Taiwan and Singapore, maintain their pilot agencies – the Council for Economic Planning and Development in Taiwan, and the Economic Development Board in Singapore – adapting them as needed to new circumstances but never abandoning their coordinating and lead-taking role.[27] State controls over financial flows are unlikely to be reintroduced, but the vacuum created at the centre by the excess deregulation of the mid-1990s has been filled by the new financial supervisory structures.

Although these are early days, such signs of change lend plausibility to Korea's reemergence as a strengthened and highly competitive economy. The new Korean model is likely to rely on accounting and financial transparency as devices to drive competitiveness and to extirpate any remnants of cronyism and corruption. This aspect of the new Korean model will be complemented by a greater reliance on the institutions of democracy in its supervision and its guidance. While Korea has made enormous advances in democratization since the ending of the military regime in 1988, there is still much to be done to embed the processes of democracy in the institutional fabric of the country. This is precisely what the new Kim Dae-Jung regime is dedicated to accomplishing.[28] Extensive reforms are envisaged: a strengthening of the authority of the prime minister's office; a shift towards parliamentary authority and a reduction in direct presidential authority; a streamlining of the bureaucracy, and creation of new agencies such as the Office for Planning and Budget; a revitalization of local government; a renewed mandate for trade unions to engage in political activities, thus inducting them as legitimate members of the Korean body politic. Kim Dae-Jung apparently has no intention of rescuing the economy and making it strong only to see it repossessed by an anti-democratic military and industrial elite.

Other analysts are less sanguine about Korea's prospects. Wade and Veneroso (1998) argue that Korea's highly leveraged development model needs strong government coordination if it is to work and that this is what is being dismantled at the insistence of the IMF (Wade and Veneroso, 1998). This analysis stems from a very pessimistic view of the role of the IMF. It does not seem to take into account the positive moves being made towards re-regulation currently under way within Korea. It is based on consideration of four ways of reducing a mountain of debt – through inflation, through declaring bankruptcy, through repayment of debt out of cash flow, and through debt-to-equity swaps. Wade and Veneroso see Korea as being precluded by the

IMF from acting decisively on any one of these fronts. My disagreement with this analysis rests on two considerations. First, Korea has been able to use the IMF intervention to attack its debt problem directly, such as in the negotiated rollover of short-term loans and conversion of some of the short-term debt to longer-term securities. Second, the Wade and Veneroso 'solutions' such as inflation are oriented towards public sector debt of the Latin American kind in the 1980s, not to private sector debt of the East Asian 1990s kind. In Korea, the *chaebol* are restructuring in order to reduce their own debt-to-equity levels, thereby changing the debt structure of the country as a whole. Thus transformed, the firms will seek to trade their way out of their difficulties, and eventually retire the present debts.

The argument presented, then, is that while the 'East Asian Miracle' process in Korea expired in 1997, another process that might be called the 'rebuilding of institutional capabilities' is now under way. In some countries, such as Taiwan and Singapore, the institutions of the East Asian Miracle were sufficiently strong and resilient to enable the country to weather the storms of 1997 relatively unscathed. These countries did not succumb to rapid financial deregulation in the mid-1990s and did not abandon their governmental 'pilot' agencies that provided coordination and leadership in times of crisis. However, Korea has long been a country of greater extremes. It sought more rapidly accelerated growth rates; it indulged in higher investment rates and it relied more heavily on foreign debt to finance these investment rates than any other country. It thus ran bigger risks than others, and it therefore fell more heavily when the crunch came, as it did in November 1997. But Korea is also picking itself up more rapidly and re-establishing the institutional foundations for more balanced and more responsible growth in future. Where some profess to see in the events of 1997 and 1998 a definitive 'end' to East Asia's rise, and its Americanization, this paper has argued instead that the crisis has seen a reinvention and reconsolidation of the institutional capacities needed to sustain a sophisticated and competitive economy.

To be sure, the 'new' Korean economy will have to ride out one or two very difficult years, in 1998 and 1999, while the full effects of the 1997 financial crisis work their way through. There will be many more bankruptcies of otherwise quite healthy companies; there will be layoffs and upheavals in the labour market; there will be further debt hiccups as the legacy of the past is only slowly dismantled. But these will represent the symptoms of the dying model, not those of the model in the making.

Notes

* This article is adapted from the author's longer working paper, 'Fashioning a New Korean Model out of the Crisis', Working Paper No. 46, Japan Policy Research Institute, May 1998. The paper was written when the author was ACT Government Visiting Professor in the Australia-Asia Management Centre at the Australian National University, Canberra. The paper was prepared partly under the auspices of the 'Building Institutional Capacity in Asia' project of the Research Institute for Asia and the Pacific of the University of Sydney. The assistance of Ms Hye-Jin Lee, in Seoul, and of Ms Elizabeth Thurbon, in Sydney, is gratefully acknowledged. The comments of many policy-makers in Seoul served as the foundation for the arguments developed in the paper, buttressed by helpful discussions with Professor Chalmers Johnson and Associate Professor Linda Weiss and the comments of an anonymous referee.

1. See World Bank (1993) for the 'East Asian Miracle' analysis, which has sparked a wide debate, and effectively put an end to the polarization between those analysing East Asian success in terms of neoclassical market analysis, and those analysing it in terms of institutional capabilities.
2. See Stiglitz (1998) for a review, and Radelet and Sachs (1997) for an extended defence of the East Asian Miracle process.
3. See Park and Song (1997) and Johnston, Darbar and Echeverria (1997) for analyses of Korea's capital liberalization and earlier experiences of crisis. Loriaux (1997) provides a more general discussion.
4. These are not inconsiderable in Korea (as in Japan and other East Asian countries such as Singapore) – but they would not on their own provide the leverage for the accelerated growth that Korea has enjoyed. See Cho (1994) for an overview of savings and investment in the Korean development model.
5. See Woo (1991) for the definitive account of the role of finance and its regulation in Korea's development, and Cumings (1997) for the most recent and comprehensive account of this experience in the wider political setting of Korea's development.
6. For further details, see Mathews (1998) for analysis of the debt repatriation demands that triggered the crisis in Korea, based on capital flow data provided by the Bank for International Settlements and the International Institute for Finance.
7. The Korean debt–equity ratios are far from unknown in advanced industrial countries. In the case of leveraged buyouts, where debt is involved far more than shareholder equity, such ratios would be considered conservative.
8. Worst offenders in this regard were Hanbo, whose collapse in January 1997 signalled the start of the souring of the Korean miracle, and other *chaebol* such as Halla, Kia, Jinro and New Core.
9. Hanbo Steel and Hanbo Construction were badly affected by a downturn in the building industry in Korea, but the default was actually on debt raised to build a huge steel mill. In 1988, Hanbo Steel had raised 2.7 trillion won to build the mill, when it had an equity base of 90 billion won, giving it a debt to equity ratio of 30 to 1. Costs ran well over the original estimate, and banks were continually pressed for more funds, rising by 1998 to more than

5 trillion won, against the company's equity base in January of 224 billion won, a debt to equity ratio of 22 to 1.

10. These requirements have subsequently been enacted by the Koreans, in successive reforms implemented by the new Kim Dae-Jung administration.
11. That these matters constitute a US agenda is not hard to prove, the US Congress, and US officials such as the Special Trade Representative, having repeatedly called for these very measures to be implemented, without success, until the financial crisis enabled them to incorporate these points into the IMF agreement.
12. According to my informants in the Ministry of Finance during extensive discussions in January 1998.
13. The restructured Bank is to consist of a Monetary Board as the supreme decision-making organ of the central banking system and an executive body headed by the Governor of the Bank of Korea, who will concurrently hold the position as Chair of the Monetary Board.
14. The Board is to be responsible for the promulgation and amendment of supervisory rules, licensing of business activities and operations of the financial institutions, other than their establishment.
15. The head of the interim Commission is Lee Hun-Jai, a former mandarin of the financial ministry who fell foul of his masters and then spent a decade working in the private sector. He has emerged as a powerful enforcer of reform in the financial sector, complementing the equally tough role played by Park Tae-Joon in reforming the industrial sector.
16. The five banks ordered to close or merge were the three national banks, Daedong, Dongnam and Donghwa, and the two regional banks Kyunggi and Chungchong. The seven institutions given 'conditional approvals' were the Korea Exchange Bank, Cho Hung, Commercial Bank of Korea, Hanil, the Peace Bank of Korea, Kangwon and Chungbuk.
17. The US Resolution Trust Corporation, established in the mid-1980s, was empowered to conduct audits of suspect savings and loan bodies, shut down insolvent bodies, and sell off their loans and underlying collateral as repackaged securities ('securitization of debt') or through public auctions, normally at considerable discounts to their face value.
18. For discussion of the general practices of the *chaebol*, and case histories, see, for example, Kang (1996).
19. See Mathews and Cho (1998) for a discussion of the case of semiconductors.
20. In the case of Hanbo, for example, funds raised to build the steel mill were being siphoned off to start new, unrelated businesses, as well as to bribe bank presidents, legislators, government officials and presidential aides into maintaining the flow of funds.
21. Samsung, generally reckoned to be the best-managed company in Korea, berates itself for having entered the car industry, at the cost of losses that will last until well into the next century and draining profits from the company's successful operations such as semiconductors.
22. On the other hand, a too sudden outlawing of the guarantees, as originally demanded, could tip some groups into unnecessary bankruptcy.
23. The Hyosung group (Korea's 14th largest *chaebol*) was first off the mark, announcing major restructuring initiatives in March 1998, designed to reduce its debt-to-equity ratio to 2.0 by the year 2002.

24. His enforcer is the formidable Park Tae-Joon, founder of the steel giant POSCO, and now a member of the National Assembly and chairman of the United Liberal Democrats, the coalition partner with Kim Dae-Jung's National Congress for New Politics.
25. While political reform has not been the focus of analysis in this article, it too has been an essential part of the restructuring. President Kim achieved enormous moral authority in driving through the reform process, not just through his own personal history (involving several jail terms as a dissident and attempted assassinations) but through gestures such as releasing former presidents Roh Tae-Woo and Chun Doo-Hwan.
26. One of Kim Dae-Jung's initiatives is the creation of a new Office of Planning and Budget to be located in the Presidential Blue House, separate from the Ministry of Finance and Economics. This institutional innovation will go some way to redress the loss of coordination experienced with the demise of the EPB.
27. The theoretical underpinnings of such structures are provided by Weiss (1995, 1998).
28. Many of the reforms have been canvassed by Kim in earlier speeches and writings; see Kim (1994) for a selection.

References

Chang, H. J. (1998) 'The Korean economic crisis: the result of under-regulation', *JPRI Critique*, vol. 5, no. 2, February.

Cho, S. (1994) *The Dynamics of Korean Economic Development*, Washington DC, Institute for International Economics.

Cumings, B. (1997) *Korea's Place in the Sun: A Modern History*, New York, W. W. Norton.

Fischer, S. (1998) 'The Asian Crisis: A View from the IMF', Address to the mid-winter conference of the Bankers' Association for Foreign Trade, Washington DC, 22 January.

Johnston, R. B., Darbar, S. M. and Echeverria, C. (1997) 'Sequencing Capital Account Liberalization: Lessons from the Experiences in Chile, Indonesia, Korea and Thailand', IMF Working Paper WP/97/157, Washington DC, International Monetary Fund.

Kang, M. H. (1996) *The Korean Business Conglomerate: Chaebol Then and Now*, Korea Research Monograph No. 21, University of California, Berkeley, Institute of East Asian Studies.

Kim D.-J. (1994) *Korea and Asia: A Collection of Essays, Speeches and Discussions*, Seoul, The Kim Dae-Jung Peace Foundation Press.

Loriaux, M. *et al.* (eds) (1997) *Capital Ungoverned: Liberalizing Finance in Interventionist States*, Ithaca, Cornell University Press.

Mathews, J. A. (1998) 'Fashioning a New Korean Model out of the Crisis', JPRI Working Paper No. 46, San Diego, Japan Policy Research Institute.

Mathews, J. A. and Cho, D. S. (1998) 'Combinative capabilities and organizational learning in latecomer firms: the case of the Korean semiconductor industry', *Journal of World Business*.

Park, Y. C. and Song, C. Y. (1997) 'Managing foreign capital flows: the experiences of the Republic of Korea, Thailand, Malaysia and Indonesia', in Helleiner, G. (ed.), *International Monetary and Financial Issues for the 1990s*, Geneva, UNCTAD.

Radeler, S. and Sachs, J. (1997) 'Asia's reemergence', *Foreign Affairs*, vol. 76, no. 6 (November/December), 44–59.

Stiglitz, J. (1998) 'Restoring the Asian miracle', *Asian Wall Street Journal*, 2 February.

Wade, R. and Veneroso, F. (1998) 'The Asian crisis: The high debt model vs the Wall Street–Treasury–IMF complex,' *New Left Review*, March–April.

Weiss, L. (1995) 'Governed interdependence: rethinking the government–business relationship in East Asia', *The Pacific Review*, vol. 8, no. 4, 589–616.

Weiss, L. (1998) *The Myth of the Powerless State*, Cambridge, Policy Press, and Ithaca, Cornell University Press.

Woo, J.-E. (1991) *Race to the Swift: State and Finance in Korean Industrialization*, New York, Columbia University Press.

World Bank (1993) *The East Asian Miracle: Economic Growth and Public Policy*, New York, Oxford University Press.

11
Japan's Crisis: Evolution and Implications

D. Hugh Whittaker and Yoshitaka Kurosawa

Introduction: Japan and the Asian Crisis

Japan is linked to the Asian Crisis in two principal ways. First, it is deeply involved in the economies of the crisis countries (see Table 11.1), and their crises in various ways. It has been claimed, with some justification, that Japan exported its bubble to other Asian countries following the collapse of its own bubble in 1990. From just $40 billion in early 1994, Japan's loans to Asia surged to some $265 billion in 1996, helping to finance current-account deficits in the run-up to the crisis. Following the baht fall on 2 July 1997, Japan played an important role in putting together the financial aid package for Thailand, but after its attempt to forge a regional Asian Monetary Fund (AMF) was squashed by the US, it was sidelined in the remaining packages.[1] Instead, Japan was portrayed, again with some justification, as part of the continuing problem, unable to help the crisis countries get back on their feet, and threatening to cause further turmoil by its inability to deal with its own problems.

Second, these problems amounted to what may be called a Japanese crisis, which was multifaceted, but at the core of which was a massive $500 billion worth of bad loans. Ironically, the causes of the crisis are now often attributed to the very institutions hailed as keys to the Japanese economic juggernaut in the late 1980s. For some commentators, Japan's woes are ultimate proof of the limitations of the 'Japanese model' – and by extension the 'Asian model' – and its current reforms represent the termination of that model. The implications, needless to say, are profound.

The two are interconnected, but our primary focus is on the second. While we focus on Japan's crisis, we are mindful of the 'model causes

Table 11.1 US, EU and Japanese involvement in East Asian international transactions (%)

	Exports (1996)					*Imports (1996)*				
	US	*EU*	*Japan*	*East Asia*	*Total*	*US*	*EU*	*Japan*	*East Asia*	*Total*
Singapore	18.4	13.0	8.2	46.8	100.0	16.4	14.5	18.2	37.9	100.0
Hong Kong	21.3	14.9	6.6	45.1	100.0	7.9	11.1	13.6	60.4	100.0
Taiwan	26.8	13.6	12.9	45.0	100.0	18.2	15.3	25.7	23.0	100.0
Korea	16.7	10.8	12.3	35.9	100.0	22.1	14.1	20.9	15.9	100.0
Malaysia	18.2	13.7	13.4	43.2	100.0	15.6	14.5	24.7	32.6	100.0
Thailand	18.0	16.0	16.8	32.7	100.0	12.6	14.5	27.8	24.3	100.0
Philippines	33.9	15.9	17.9	25.3	100.0	19.7	9.4	21.8	28.3	100.0
Indonesia	16.4	16.6	28.5	29.7	100.0	10.2	22.2	23.2	29.4	100.0
China	17.7	13.1	20.4	35.0	100.0	11.7	14.3	21.0	34.0	100.0
Vietnam	4.5	24.3	26.4	24.1	100.0	5.0	13.0	9.2	57.1	100.0
East Asia	19.8	13.7	13.5	40.0	100.0	14.3	14.0	20.3	35.1	100.0

	Foreign direct investment flows (1995)					*Outstanding loans (BIS-Reporting Banks, June 1997)*				
	US	*EU*	*Japan*	*Asian NIEs*	*Total*	*US*	*EU*	*Japan*	*Asian NIEs*	*Total*
Singapore	42.8	31.1	23.8	n.a.	100.0	2.5	53.7	30.8	n.a.	100.0
Hong Kong	13.7	18.0	53.2	0.3	100.0	4.0	44.7	39.3	n.a.	100.0
Taiwan	43.6	8.3	19.5	13.9	100.0	10.0	57.4	12.0	n.a.	100.0
Korea	33.2	24.5	21.5	6.8	100.0	9.6	35.1	22.9	n.a.	100.0
Malaysia	19.7	7.9	22.9	35.3	100.0	8.3	44.0	36.4	n.a.	100.0
Thailand	15.7	13.7	47.8	32.0	100.0	5.8	28.5	54.4	n.a.	100.0
Philippines	9.4	2.7	75.1	11.9	100.0	20.0	48.1	14.9	n.a.	100.0
Indonesia	6.9	22.4	9.5	11.2	100.0	7.8	38.3	39.4	n.a.	100.0
China	8.2	7.0	8.3	64.1	100.0	5.1	48.5	32.3	n.a.	100.0
Vietnam	8.1	16.8	17.3	35.3	100.0	6.9	67.3	16.6	n.a.	100.0
East Asia	20.1	15.2	29.9	21.1	100.0	5.5	44.7	34.3	n.a.	100.0

Sources: *IMF Direction of Trade Yearbook*, 1996; JETRO White Paper on FDI, 1997; *BIS The Maturity, Sectoral and Nationality Distribution of International Bank Lending – First Half 1997*, Basel, 1998; compiled by Kawai, 1998.

crisis, crisis ends model' arguments that are directed towards East Asia in general. These arguments may be intellectually comforting for some critics, but they severely distort our understanding of what is happening in the region in two ways. First, the Asian Crisis of 1997 was primarily a financial and currency crisis. It had much in common with other recent crises, the result of post-Bretton Woods financial liberalization, international currency flows, and poor policy choices.[2] Such crises will continue to occur in the future; indeed, Japan's current financial deregulation programme which will release some of the $8.5 trillion of individual deposits onto world markets will virtually ensure they will.[3] That is not to deny that there were institutional problems in East Asia, or that these problems to some extent facilitated and prolonged the crisis. But they were not the principal cause.

Second, if the 'model causes crisis' argument is problematic, so is the 'crisis ends model' argument.[4] The vulgarized conception is of a static 'Asian model', any change to which is proof of collapse.[5] Such change, however, could represent evolution rather than dissolution. The Asian Crisis is clearly an important milestone in the region, and, if nothing else, external pressures or rescue-package conditions will bring about basic institutional changes, but we cannot assume that they mean model dissolution/convergence. (Conversely, and given that these countries are characterized by change anyway, the model[s] may be undermined by developments unrelated to the Asian Crisis, even by their own success.) Japan's crisis and reforms provide insight into such distinctions.

Japan's crisis

Many of Japan's financial woes can be traced to its programme of liberalization and policy mistakes in the 1980s, but they have been exacerbated by uncertainty, prevarication and, to an extent, by the institutional features of the 'Japanese system'. Japan came under strong pressure to stimulate domestic demand as its trade surpluses mounted in the late 1970s/early 1980s. Monetary policy was relaxed in 1983, and further relaxed after the yen appreciation in 1985. A programme of incremental financial deregulation was also launched in the late 1970s, starting with large-scale deposits, while interest rates for small individual accounts were still regulated. Easy money for large companies and investors set in train a sharp appreciation in asset prices, focusing initially on land, which Japanese banks had traditionally demanded for collateral. In mid-1985 the value of residential land in Tokyo was about half of Japan's GDP; by the end of 1987 it was one and a half times. Starting from a similar base line, the value of stocks listed on the first section of Tokyo's stock exchange grew more slowly, but they, too, overtook the size of Japan's GDP by 1988. Japan had developed an asset 'bubble' (Noguchi, 1992).

A shift from indirect to direct corporate finance also preceded the 1985–86 yen appreciation, and accelerated after it. The shift was prompted by increased risk – floating exchange rates, strengthening of the Anti-monopoly Law, financial deregulation – and since the corporate bond market was still regulated in Japan much of the finance was raised abroad. But rising land and share prices made it very attractive to raise money through new share issues as well, the more so since dividends were not rising in tandem (Kurosawa, 1993). It is estimated that companies raised some $600 billion in equity finance between 1985 and 1990. Some of this money was funnelled into capital spending, which recorded double digit increases in the late 1980s, but 70% went into financial investments unrelated to core corporate activities (Noguchi, 1992).[6]

Losing business from their major corporate customers, meanwhile, banks turned to small firms, and especially property. Japan's financial institutions provided $220 billion in new loans to the property sector between 1985 and 1990 (compared with total outstanding loans of two-thirds of this figure at the end of 1984), and an estimated $75 billion through 'non-bank' financial institutions, notable among which were the now infamous housing loan companies (*ibid.*).

In retrospect, monetary policy should have been tightened much earlier than 1989. There were several reasons why it was not. The international agreement to maintain loose monetary conditions after Black Monday was one factor, but West Germany, also with a buoyant economy, raised its interest rates in 1988. Japanese authorities were under pressure not to follow suit, not just from the US, but from domestic manufacturers already struggling to adapt to the yen appreciation. A former senior Ministry of Finance (MOF) official has also suggested that there was a shared belief that it was now Japan's duty as the world's largest creditor nation to maintain low interest rates, and that Japan's economy was strong enough to do so (Teramura, 1998).[7]

The delay substantially increased the size of the bubble, and the subsequent fallout. From an index peak of almost 40,000 in late 1989, share prices dropped 40% in 1990, held in 1991, and plunged again in 1992 to just over a third of their peak value. Land prices began to drop in 1990 and plummet in 1991. The heady asset price spiral now became a vicious cycle of bad debts and declining asset values. By 1992 a few nervous voices were raised about the possibility of a 'China syndrome' meltdown. The Nikkei average had broken ¥15,000, dangerously close to the level at which hidden assets, which were supposed to cover bad debts, would disappear.[8]

In the absence of rigorous disclosure, government pronouncements on bad debt levels were slanted towards maintaining investor confidence. Various asset price support measures were implemented, and the official discount rate was lowered. When Toyo Credit failed in May 1992, the MOF decided on a policy of rescue rather than (US) Savings & Loan-style pay off. More failures followed, becoming progressively larger. It did not help, of course, beginning with small institutions in early 1994, that Japan's financial institutions began to face a 'Japan premium' in overseas markets. Around $8 billion in 'special' (no collateral) loans was poured into the Cosmo and Kizu credit unions and Hyogo Bank in mid-1995. By this time, too, the $8 billion reserves of the deposit insurance system were exhausted.

Stronger banks, already struggling to meet BIS capital requirements, became increasingly loath to bail out weaker institutions in the traditional 'convoy system' manner. The spate of failures in November 1997, including the first major 'city' bank, Hokkaido Takushoku, followed a week later by the fourth largest securities company, Yamaichi, were the culmination of this process. Whether or not it was calculated, as some suggest, the failure of these institutions paved the way for a (direct) infusion of public money into the financial sector, and in mid-1998, after considerable international pressure – and the prospect of a difficult election for the Liberal Democratic Party of the then Prime Minister Hashimoto – a 'bridge bank' scheme was announced.

As Japan's bubble collapse gradually developed into a full-blown crisis, criticism mounted over mismanagement by the authorities.[9] The threat to the world economy encouraged all manner of politicians and economists to lecture them on how to resolve it. Why then was there such prevarication, and is it related to the now castigated 'Japanese model'? Part of the indecisiveness was related to questions over how the blame – hence the pain – for imprudent loans should be apportioned.[10] Perhaps this is a flip side of a feature of Japanese capitalism discussed below, namely profit distribution, often under bureaucratic guidance, incorporating social distribution and stability objectives, as opposed to profit maximization through market competition based on clear and legally enforceable rules. Large institutions benefiting from the 'convoy system' (of moving stronger and weaker institutions along together) in good times were expected to make sacrifices in bad times. This is systemic, but it should not be equated with 'crony capitalism'. Whether the gangster-related scandals, which reached core financial institutions and even bureaucrats and complicated the clean-up, are also systemic, or are primarily the result of bubble excesses, depends in part on how the 'system' is defined, as we shall see below. Perhaps, too, fiscal conservativeness is systemic, but some measures were simply ill-judged, ill-timed or unlucky, and set in train further developments, an example being the Toyo Credit rescue in 1992.

The crisis was not being limited to the financial sector. In their enthusiasm to gain orders during the bubble boom, construction companies offered collateral or guarantees to allow developers to secure loans, which then turned sour. Government stimulus packages in the 1990s kept them afloat, but plans to rein in public works expenditure drove their share prices down in 1997, fuelling rumours of major bankruptcies. The massive new public works package announced in April 1998 may have given them breathing room, but ultimately there is likely to be extensive restructuring in this sector as well.

Elsewhere in the real economy, after overinvestment in the late 1980s, a substantial cyclical adjustment was to be expected. At the same time, a massive rise in foreign direct investment (FDI) in the 1980s and early 1990s – the result of intense trade friction and a rapidly appreciating yen – left many companies struggling to restructure or reorient their domestic operations towards higher value added, knowledge-intensive goods and services, and to overhaul their personnel management systems. Employment in manufacturing began to decline. In the SME (small and medium-sized enterprise) sector, this has brought about a decline in 'traditional' firms, combined with difficulties in nurturing new enterpreneurial business (Whittaker, 1997). Such simultaneous adjustments created what some dubbed a 'composite recession' (Miyazaki, 1992).

Furthermore, the sense of malaise has been deepened by demographic and social change, including a declining birth rate and a population ageing more rapidly than any other OECD country. This sense is potently expressed in former bureaucrat-turned-critic Sakaiya's serialisation of 'Japan 2018' in the daily *Asahi Shinbun*. By 2018 the consumption tax rate has increased to 20%, average incomes are taxed at 40%, and people must wait until they are 67 for a meagre pension. Real economic growth hovers around 0%, and the yen is now worth ¥230 to the dollar ...

More immediately, voters, savers and consumers, who are now urban, relatively affluent and educated, wanted a more direct say in matters that affect them. Their needs have become more diverse, and governance/regulatory structures evolved for an industrializing Japan have as yet been unable to adapt to meet these demands and complexities. The inability to bring about a successful transition in the 1980s, the scandals associated with the worst of bubble excesses, and the subsequent downturn have intensified these demands.[11] The Liberal Democratic Party's 38-year reign came to an end in 1993, with voter disgust at the ongoing series of scandals paraded before them, notably graft in construction deals.[12] Angered by the way they have been treated by, and scandals in, Japan's large financial institutions, small investors and depositors voted with their feet, to the immediate benefit of foreign institutions. And the boom in discount shopping – bringing 'price destruction' deflation – indeed the resistance to spending at all, had an undercurrent of protest at the regulatory framework which favours producer interests over those of the consumer.

Even if flaws in the 'Japanese model' are not the fundamental cause of Japan's financial crisis and wider economic malaise (in some respects its successes have prompted them), for an increasing number of Japanese critics, nothing short of a complete systemic overhaul will suffice to bring about a cure. Are they right? Is this the end for the 'Japanese model'?

'Japanese model' RIP?

Whether or not the 'Japanese model' is facing – or should face – extinction depends in part on how it is defined. We should perhaps first distinguish between a macro-level model and a micro- or corporate-level model, although, as Dore's article in this issue suggests, there is considerable institutional interlock as well as 'psychological consonance' between the macro, micro and intermediary institutions.

The macro-level model concerns governance of the economy. Johnson's (1982) 'developmental state' formulation assigned a key role to MITI bureaucrats as the general headquarters staff of Japanese capitalism. As interest in Japan's financial institutions grew, the role of the MOF and policy-based finance has received closer attention (e.g., JDB/JERI, 1994). Even more recently, however, interest has grown in the Ministry of Construction and its associated network of national and local politicians and the recipient companies of public works contracts. Should they also be included in the model? Perhaps not, since they are less directly linked to the corporations which powered Japan's economic growth, but public works receive policy-based finance to such an extent that increasing criticism has been directed at Japan's 'public works state complex' (*doken kokka*), likened to the US military-industrial complex.[13]

It is not simply a matter of *who* is included in the model, but *what*. Earlier models stressed catch-up (with the West) policies focused primarily on economic growth. More recently it has been recognized that distribution of the fruit of that growth, with few obvious losers, was also a key concern[14] Ruthless, 'strong devouring the weak' (*jakuniku kyoshoku*) capitalism was frowned on; social stability and distribution objectives were incorporated into economic policy. The Large-Scale Retail Store Law; recession cartels and numerous exemptions from the Anti-monopoly Law; the Delayed Payment Law (aimed at preventing exploitation of subcontractors); the 'convoy system' in finance; not to mention active labour market policy emphasizing work and living stability, all reflected these concerns.[15]

Then there is the question of whether the role of the bureaucrats has been over-emphasized, both in policy formation and economic development. In the micro-level model, the focus moves from bureaucrats to corporations as the value creators which have powered Japan's economic growth. There is less controversy over the characteristics of the micro-level model, although it might be argued that excessive attention has been directed to large corporations at the expense of small firms: Japan, after all, has the highest proportion of small firms – and employment in them – of any major OECD country. In the (large firm centred) micro-level model, the interests of shareholders are not given overriding priority by senior managers, most of whom are promoted employees and have spent their whole working life in the same corporation. Instead, shareholders are given a virtually fixed return, the bulk of profits is reinvested, and companies pursue market share competition.[16] Linked to corporate governance is 'Japanese-style management', which features long-term employment and human resource development for core regular employees in 'corporate communities'. In addition, in manufacturing there is a heavy emphasis on shop-floor-based improvement, production methods such as just-in-time, and interfirm coordination management.

The 'Japanese model', particularly the micro-level variant, has been condemned to oblivion for as long as it has been recognized. The crux of the current argument is that a combination of Japan's financial crisis, increasing foreign participation and the Big Bang will bring about fundamental changes in Japan's financial markets. Not only will this change the nature of macroeconomic management, but, through corporate finance, it will have a major impact on corporate governance, bringing a decisive end to the model (and a convergence towards 'normal' Anglo-Saxon capitalism).

Thus, according to the *Economist*, '[t]he changes in the financial system will have profound consequences for the way Japanese companies are run. Much of what is special about Japanese capitalism simply reflects the *inadequate* rewards that capital has attracted. Now companies will have to start counting the *true* cost of money' (28 June 1997, p. 8; emphasis added). Ide (1998) makes the same argument, predicting that changes in financial markets will lead to the demise of 'Japanese-style management' and 'lifetime employment'. (The *Economist*, of course, has a history of predicting the demise of lifetime employment: 20 years ago it declared, '[c]ompanies are no longer as smug as they once were about lifetime employment' and that it would probably not outlive the decade.)[17]

The case is plausible. We have seen that deregulation in the 1980s was already beginning to change one pillar of corporate finance, the 'main bank' system, through internationalization of fund raising and a shift to direct financing. This reduced the ability of the main banks to act as monitors for other lenders and shareholders (main banks are also major shareholders), which hitherto had lowered agency costs, and at the same time it made it harder for bureaucrats to control corporate behaviour through the banks. As the pace of deregulation accelerates, accounting and disclosure practices are being reformed. Credit-rating agencies are growing in importance, in effect replacing main banks as judges of creditworthiness. It does seem that Japan will move towards 'global standards' in terms of regulations and transparency. And also possibly in terms of capital costs. 'Stable' or 'mutual' shareholding, another pillar of corporate finance in which a high proportion of shares is held by *keiretsu* (corporate group) companies, or other companies related by business, is weakening. Mutual shareholding not only suppressed hostile takeovers, but reduced pressure on managements to prioritize shareholder returns. Now, however, the poor performance of such shares is being weighed against the need for funds for restructuring. Banks are selling shares of their erstwhile close customers, trading companies are selling shares of corporations which do less and less business through them, and life insurance companies are also selling corporate shares, in return for which the corporations are reducing the share of pensions they entrust to life insurance companies (*Nikkei*, 3

July 1997, 11 July 1997). All in all, it is unclear how far 'mutual shareholding' will unravel, or just what proportion needs to be maintained for the system to function, but the downward trend is significant. Changes to the Anti-monopoly Law and associated laws allowing holding companies are in part intended to offset this development, but they will also facilitate corporate restructuring, including mergers and acquisitions.

There is evidence of change in corporate governance. 'Shareholder measures' (*kabunushi taisaku*) no longer simply mean paying off gangsters, or giving major shareholders a factory tour before the AGM. By 1997 companies were giving their shareholders presents and discounts, even rushing overseas to do 'IR' (investor relations – a new buzzword) presentations to foreign fund managers, who now owned over 10% of Japan's shares, with the proportion rising rapidly. Major corporations like Toshiba, Hitachi and NEC have also begun publishing return on equity (ROE) targets, although they fall well short of them. By mid-1998, prominent companies were shaking up their boardrooms, typically reducing the number of board members and separating board functions from executive functions. In some cases, external directors were being appointed, while others (like NEC, Toyota) were creating international advisory boards. Some CEOs were being appointed from April, to correspond with financial years, in order to clarify responsibility.

Such developments are significant, but they do not signal a fundamental shift to maximizing shareholder returns as an overriding management priority. As NEC's president said: 'I don't think ROE is absolute, but as we are engaged in global competition, we have to adopt management indices of an international standard' (*Nikkei*, 21 July 1997). In fact, a stronger case could be made that a new variant of 'stakeholder capitalism' is emerging in Japan, in which shareholder interests are given explicit recognition, *as a key stakeholder*, and profitability is an explicit objective, *as a management tool*.[18]

Although it is not clearly articulated as a 'new model', many employers and policy-makers are struggling to find a 'third way' to reform. Thus, for instance, the Japan Federation of Employers' Associations (*Nikkeiren*) set out its vision for reform in a report titled. 'Structural reform aiming at qualitative improvements in peoples' living and employment stability: searching for a third way'. By 'third way' it meant avoiding the high unemployment levels of continental Europe, on the one hand, and large income disparities of the neo-liberal Anglo-Saxon countries, on the other. This report called on employers to reaffirm their commitment to social responsibility, which is 'all the more important since the goal is small government, and a private sector-led economy and society. Corporate roles become broader and employers' responsibilities increase' (*Nikkeiren*, 1997, p. 39). The reluctance of employers to downsize aggressively by laying off workers in the recessionary 1990s, and their cautious personnel management reforms (though often couched in revolutionary language), reflect this orientation, particularly among the large, long-established companies.[19]

In brief, the slow pace of reform in Japan, and, in particular, the reticence to embrace unfettered market capitalism, reflects: (a) a reluctance to adandon past successful formulae; (b) the complexity of the structural issues involved; and (c) a desire to preserve the 'social' dimension of the 'Japanese model' both at the corporate and macro levels. In other words, the quest for a 'third way' to reform. The general public is growing agitated at the slowness of political and administrative reform, and of deregulation, which would benefit them as consumers and savers, and is becoming more inclined to interpret this as the protection of vested interests (a mood intensified by continued recession). However, to some degree they also support the social dimension of the 'Japanese model', particularly those who experienced the Second World War or the hard times after it.

Concluding comments: Japan and East Asia

Japan's economic power, and its position as world's leading creditor nation, derive from the strength of its manufacturing, especially its machine industries, and the strength of these has increasingly little to do with government policy. Japan's production base has now expanded throughout Asia, and it is fitting to return to East Asia for our concluding comments.

As Table 11.1 shows, Japan is the biggest source of imports for all the East Asian economies, with the exception of Korea and Vietnam. A high proportion of the imports from Japan are for capital goods or sophisticated parts necessary for the export industries; many in fact are for Japanese transplant facilities. In addition, a substantial chunk of intra-regional trade involves Japanese companies. Japan was also the largest source of FDI in the ASEAN countries (except Indonesia), as well as China and Vietnam, in 1995. The picture is quite different when it comes to exports. For all East Asian countries, with the exception of Indonesia and former Cold War adversaries China and Vietnam, the US absorbs more exports than the EU or Japan. Crudely put, Japan has supplied the capital resources for these countries, while the US has supplied the export markets.

For better or worse, it is hard to see this structure changing in the near future. In the short term, the Asian Crisis and Japan's crisis will affect each other negatively. The weakness of the Japanese economy, particularly muted consumption, limits its ability to absorb Asian exports. Conversely, depressed conditions in the crisis countries are having a negative impact on Japan's attempts to deal with its problems. However, the basic characteristics of the 'East Asian integrated production network' appear to be unchanged. Interviews with executives of Japanese transplants in ASEAN countries in late 1997 suggest that the Asian Crisis prompted caution in terms of new investments and capacity increases, but in the medium term there would be no fundamental shift in the basic commitment to the region, or the strategic division of labour that has been adopted (Takii and Fukushima, 1998). In the longer term, East Asian countries will seek to reduce their dollar dependence, while Japan will seek a greater regional – international – role for the yen through financial deregulation. These developments will provide a new spur for the creation of currency and financial coordination mechanisms in East Asia.

Notes

1. The AMF proposal was squashed ostensibly because of fears that its terms would be lax, inviting moral hazard problems. However, an underlying reason was Japanese leadership, despite Japanese assurances that it would be tied in with the IMF. By the time the Indonesian package was debated, the US and the IMF were willing to mobilize significant sums of money, and Japan fell into line behind the IMF. The AMF proposal limped from the Manila Meeting of Asian Finance and Central Bank Deputies (18–19 November 1997) as 'a cooperative financing arrangement that would supplement IMF resources' (*Nikkei*, 20 September, 8 October, 2, 4, 5, 6, 25 November 1997).
2. Had the countries in question responded to the dollar rise in 1995 by floating or lowering their exchange rates, tightening economic policy at the expense of growth (suppressing expansion of the current-account deficit), and/or controlling the inflow of capital from abroad, replacing short-term portfolio finance with long-term finance (whose payment schedules they could meet), they may have had a rocky spell, but not a crisis. Of course, these comments have the benefit of hindsight.
3. The Ministry of Finance (MOF) gives the following rationale for its deregulation programme: '*Goal – to produce an international market comparable with New York and London by 2001*. A well-functioning financial system forms the base of an economy. In order to maintain Japan's economic vitality as its

society ages in the 21st century, our citizen's financial assets must be deployed more effectively, and funds must be provided to next generation growth industries. And, in order to fulfil our global responsibilities, we must ensure the smooth supply of capital to the world. For this, we must utilise fully the ¥1,200 trillion of individual savings, ensuring the optimal distribution of resources through financial markets' (translated from http://www.mof.go.jp/big.bang/bb7.htm).

4. Cf., Samuel Brittan, '"Asian Model", R.I.P.', *Financial Times*, 4 December 1997. In his defence, Brittan is speaking of the 'Asian model' as a notional concept, but this qualification is frequently lost.
5. Or, alternatively, convergence towards a 'normal' (Anglo-Saxon) model, since the framework is dichotomous – a homogeneous 'Asian model' versus a 'normal' Western'/Anglo-Saxon model.
6. Was moral hazard at work here? More accurately, there were intense pressures on individuals making investment decisions to jump on the bandwagon, and, at the systemic level, a lack of preparedness for risk, partly as a result of the 'land myth' (land prices never drop), and the legacy of pre-deregulation risk-dispersion mechanisms. Excessive capital investment was not the result of state direction, but was exacerbated by 'match thy competitor' competition.
7. Overconfidence in the strength of the Japanese economy was a factor in cautious responses to the collapse of the bubble as well.
8. The level was estimated at somewhere around ¥13,000. 'Hidden' assets are the result of valuing assets at purchase price.
9. 'The extent of Japanese mismanagement of its own economy in the last seven years, particularly under Herbert Hoover Hashimoto, is one of the overwhelming themes of the modern era' (W. Overholt, a managing director at Bankers Trust Company in Hong Kong, cited in the *New York Times*, 17 December 1997. Cf. also L. Thurow in *The New York Review*, 5 February 1998.)
10. For example, *Bungei shunju*, 1995.
11. UNCTAD's (1996) argument that real wages in Japan should be increased to effect a 'positive deindustrialization' would have been easier to achieve in the late 1980s. In 1986 and 1987 the Maekawa Commission called for a change in economic policy to domestic demand-led growth, one consequence of which was a 'leisure boom'. A national campaign was launched to reduce working hours, but it was introduced cautiously so as not to undermine export competitiveness, and frustration at 'rich companies, poor employees' increased.
12. Leaders of the subsequent reformist government were themselves caught up in scandals, and the LDP made a comeback to dominate the current coalition, but as a result of voter resignation at the lack of a viable alternative.
13. According to MOF's Vice-Minister for International Affairs: '[G]overnment fixed capital formation is on a far higher level in Japan than other major industrial nations. Recently it has amounted to 6.6% of gross domestic product and 41% of government expenditures ... When one reviews the process of this system's formation, one can feel justified in calling Japan a public works state' (Sakakibara, 1998, p. 32. See also McCormack, 1996).

14. Vestal, for instance, argues that '[t]his tradeoff between maximizing growth and minimizing social disruption is not only the key to this dynamic development framework, but is also the single most important characteristic of post-war industrial policy in Japan', and '[t]he single most important lesson of Japanese industrial policy lies in its management of employment' (1993, pp. 68, 146. Cf. also Sugeno, 1996).
15. This environment, in which corporate profits were to some extent fixed, encouraged growth orientation, which increased absolute profits, benefiting employees and enabling greater R&D and investment in plant and equipment. 'Good' companies were ones that grew and increased their market share.
16. Imai and Komiya (1994) introduce some of the variations and features of this model. Also Aoki and Dore (1994).
17. *The Economist*, 1 October 1977, p. 92. Long before the Western media were interested in 'Japanese-style management' and 'lifetime employment', leading Japanese academics were predicting the demise of 'managerial familism' as it was called then: 'Lifetime employment makes it difficult for modern companies to adjust workforces with technological innovation. Henceforth the demerits of maintaining managerial familism will come to outweight the merits. Because of this, it is necessary to grasp the new management in the context of the dissolution of managerial familism' (Hazama [1960], 1987, p. 23).
18. It remains to be seen to what extent other 'stakeholder' interests – such as the environment, local communities – will be integrated into this new evolved model.
19. This is not to deny that significant reforms increasing workforce diversity and flexibility are being introduced in these companies: cf., Kameyama, 1997, 1998.

References

Aoki, M. and Dore, R. (eds) (1994) *The Japanese Firm: Sources of Competitive Strength*, Oxford, Oxford University Press

Brittan, S. (1997) 'Asian Model', R.I.P., *Financial Times*, 4 December

Bungei shunju (1995) 'Nihon keizai chinbotsu no hi (The day Japan's economy smks), November.

Feldstein, M. (1998) 'Refocusing the IMF', *Foreign Affairs*, March/April.

Hazama, H. (1960) 'Keiei kazoku shugi no ronri to sono keisei katei' (The theory of management familism and its formation process). Reprinted in Inagami, T. and Kawakita, T. (eds) (1987) *Nihon no shakaigaku: sangyo, rodo* (Japanese Sociology: Industry, Labour), Tokyo, Tokyo University Press.

Ide, M. (1998) *Japanese Corporate Finance and International Competition*, Basingstoke, Macmillan.

Imai, K. and Komiya, R. (eds) (1994) *Business Enterprise in Japan: Views of Leading Japanese Economists*, Cambridge, MA, MIT Press.

Japan Development Bank/Japan Economic Research Institute (JDB/JERI) (1994) *Policy-Based Finance: The Experience of Postwar Japan*, World Bank Discussion Papers 221.

Johnson, C. (1982) *MITI and the Japanese Miracle*, Stanford, Stanford University Press.

Kameyama, N. (1997; 1998) 'Human resource management in Japan', *Labour Issues Quarterly*, Japan Institute of Labour, nos 36–40.

Kawai, M. (1998) 'Higashi ajia no tsuka doyu to kinyu kiki' (East Asia's currency upheavals and financial crisis), MOF Institute of Fiscal and Monetary Policy seminar paper.

Kume, I. (1995) 'Institutionalizing the active labour market policy in Japan: a comparative view', in Kim, H.-K. *et al.* (eds), *The Japanese Civil Service and Economic Development*, Oxford, Oxford University Press.

Kurosawa, Y. (1993) 'Corporate finance in Japan', *Financial Digest*, no. 26, Tokyo, Japan Credit Rating Agency.

McCormack, G. (1996) *The Emptiness of Japanese Affluence*, Armonk, M. E. Sharpe.

Miyazaki, Y. (1992) *Fukugo fukyo* (Composite Recession), Tokyo, Chuo koron.

Nikkei (Nihon keizai shinbun), various dates.

Nikkeiren (1997) *Koyo antei to kokumin seikatsu no shitsuteki kaizen o mezasu kozo kaikaku: 'daisan no michi' no mosaku* (Structural reform aiming at qualitative improvements in peoples' living and employment stability: searching for a 'third way'), Tokyo.

Noguchi, Y. (1992) *Baburu no keizaigaku* (Economics of the Bubble), Tokyo, Nihon keizai shinbunsha.

Sakakibara, E. (1998) 'Moving beyond the public works state', *Japan Echo*, February.

Sugeno, K. (1996) *Koyo shakai no ho* (Laws of an Employment Society), Tokyo, Yuhikaku.

Takii, M. and Fukushima, M. (1998) *Ajia tsuka kiki* (Asia's Currency Crisis), Tokyo, JETRO.

Teramura, Y. (1998) '1990 nendai no Nihon' (Japan in the 1990s), unpublished paper, Cambridge University, Oriental Studies.

Thurow, L. (1998) 'Asia: the collapse and the cure', *The New York Review*, 5 February.

UNCTAD (1996) *Trade and Development Report*, Geneva.

Vestal, J. (1993) *Planning for Change: Industrial Policy and Japanese Economic Development, 1945–1990*, Oxford, Oxford University Press.

Whittaker, D. H. (1990) 'The end of Japanese-style employment?', *Work, Employment and Society*, vol. 4, no. 3.

Whittaker, D. H. (1997) *Small Firms in the Japanese Economy*, Cambridge, Cambridge University Press.

12

Responses to the Crisis: Constraints to Rapid Trade Adjustment in East Asia's Electronics Industry

Dieter Ernst

Introduction

The initial triggers of the Asian Crisis that resulted from an exposure to global financial markets are now well understood: research highlights *endogenous* failures of international capital markets[1] and domestic policy failures, especially for financial regulation.[2] It is time to move on to an analysis of possible responses. Elsewhere, I have analysed how the Crisis has reshaped the region's longer-term industrial upgrading options (Ernst, 1998b, 2001d). In this paper, I focus on *short-term* responses and discuss a *puzzle* related to rapid trade adjustment.[3]

A puzzle

Both Japan and important East Asian countries are currently in the grip of debt deflation. In a debt deflation, companies devote income to trying to reduce excessive debt rather than spending it on consumption or investment. But what makes sense for individual companies does not make sense for economies. In an economy gripped by private sector debt deflation, activity can be sustained only by expanding fiscal deficits, improved external balances, or both. Most Asian countries do not have the first option, as it is excluded by IMF agreements. They are thus forced to rely on the second option, which indicates how drastic are the pressures to export one's way out of the crisis.

It has been argued that 'trade adjustment in East Asia ... will be rapid and sizable, lifting aggregate growth in these economies even as the domestic non-tradable sectors continue to suffer a decline (as in Mexico)' (World Bank, 1998a, p. 5).[4] Much hope has been pinned on the electronics industry to come through with rapid growth through expanding exports.

Two arguments appear to bolster such an expectation: the severity of the region's currency depreciations has lowered the cost of much of its electronics supply base relative to its competitors; and the electronics industry's proven track record as an engine of export-led growth shows that it can be quickly started and accelerated in response to changes in the market.[5] Since July 1997, the countries worst affected have seen the value of their currencies fall by between 35% and 70% against the US dollar[6] – which in principle should feed into a substantial reduction of export prices. And rapid export expansion in line with shifting comparative advantages has been one of the great achievements of the region's electronics industry.

Yet, it was not until mid 1999 that a brief and short-lived export boom in electronics materialized. What explains the puzzling delay in post-Crisis trade adjustment? We first introduce a taxonomy of East Asia's electronics firms and market segments to distinguish different capacities to ride out the crisis. We then discuss three constraints to an East Asian export boom in electronics: (i) *supply-side constraints* that result from limited access to trade finance, and from the cost-increasing impact of local currency depreciations in highly import-dependent countries; (ii) *demand-related constraints*, resulting from deteriorating growth perspectives in East Asia's electronics export markets; and (iii) *deflationary pricing pressures*, resulting from a narrow specialization in high-tech commodities that are characterised by periodic surplus capacity and price wars. Combined, these barriers have produced a vicious circle: once exports increase, net volume gains are likely to be offset by pricing losses.

A taxonomy of firms and market segments

A stylised taxonomy of East Asia's electronics firms and market segments highlights a strictly hierarchical industry structure: global brand-name multinationals dominate and shape the development of all the other layers of East Asia's electronics industry. Clearly, some firms are 'more equal than others', to paraphrase George Orwell, in terms of their capacity to ride out the crisis. We shall see that multinationals have little difficulty in adjusting, and that it is local firms, primarily low-end suppliers to global production networks,[7] that are most likely to be negatively affected. Five layers can be distinguished.

- At the top, the industry is dominated by foreign MNCs which control global brands and architectural design standards (Henderson and Clark, 1990) for computer, communications and consumer applications.[8]
- A second layer consists of large firms (mostly foreign MNCs) that dominate the production of key sub-assemblies and components like hard disk drives (HDD), picture tubes or displays, and semiconductors (especially DRAM – dynamic access random memory).[9]
- A third layer consists of small group of local original-brand-manufacturers (OBM), such as Samsung and LG in Korea, Acer in Taiwan and Creative Technology in Singapore.
- A fourth layer comprises contract manufacturers which can be foreign firms like Solectron and SCI, or Asian firms like for instance Venture Manufacturing, Flextronics, in Singapore, and many others.[10]
- Finally, a fifth group of actors consists of many small and medium-sized suppliers of a great variety of components and support activities, located all over the region. This includes for instance plastic moulding, metal stamping, tool and die making, precision parts and components, electroplating and finishing, mould making, jigs and fixtures, casting and industrial automation equipment. Apart from a number of Japanese suppliers, many of these suppliers are small, local companies with very limited capital resources.

This stylized taxonomy can help to improve and fine-tune the findings of macroeconomic analysis: it enables us to highlight some fundamental differences in terms of size-related economies of scale and scope, financial clout, technological capabilities and market access that only emerge once the analysis has been pushed down to a sufficiently disaggregated level. The firms in the top layer obviously have much greater opportunities to cope with the impact of the crisis than do firms on the lower layers.

Supply-side constraints to an export expansion

One fundamental constraint is that Asian exporters now have trouble finding containers to ship their goods, because so few are arriving carrying imports.[11] In addition, two of the most pressing obstacles are (i) a shortage of credit that results from the devastation of the financial sector – Asian exporters face very serious constraints in their access to trade finance, and (ii) the negative impact of devaluation on the cost of imported materials and machinery.

Access to trade finance

Access to trade finance is no problem for affiliates of multinational corporations (MNCs), especially if they are located in a country that has an open capital account. In Singapore, for instance, foreign affiliates can bring in US dollars and transfer them abroad at their discretion. There are no foreign exchange regulations. Furthermore, MNC affiliates have no problems in obtaining letters of credit. Under pressure from the IMF, most countries in the region have moved in a similar direction and have opened up their capital accounts.

Especially in the EA-5 countries, the IMF's prescriptions, such as tight monetary policies and the restructuring of financial systems, have hit exports severely. Local electronics firms are squeezed by high interest rates, and they have great difficulty in finding a bank willing to provide trade credit. Such pressures are severe for the highly leveraged Korean *chaebol*. They all actively court foreign multinationals for merger and acquisition (M&A) arrangements, in order to reduce their huge debts. An additional financial constraint to exports is the difficulty of securing letters of credit through local banks, none of which is now regarded internationally as creditworthy. This has caused a dramatic decline in Korea's input imports: 'Importing capital goods has become very difficult for most South Korean companies ... No signs of recovery in imports can be seen' (Yoshiaki Usami, director of the Seoul branch of JETRO, as quoted in *Nikkei Weekly*, 9 February 1998).

Access to trade finance is clearly a major problem for Asian contract manufacturers and subcontractors. By the spring of 1998, many of these companies were in default on both interest and principal repayments, working capital had dried up, and letters of credit were impossible to obtain.[12]

In general, the lower a firm is positioned along a particular product's supply chain, the more it has been affected negatively by restricted access to trade finance. This increasing inequality also applies in geographic terms: suppliers that are located in Malaysia and Thailand are much more affected by these credit constraints than Singapore-based suppliers. Indonesian suppliers are in the worst position: many of them have now lost for good their long-term supply contracts.

This has two important negative implications for the long-term upgrading potential of East Asia's electronics industries. First, for each individual country, it strengthens an industry structure that is characterized by an *inverted production pyramid*: the pyramid's top, i.e. final assembly, keeps expanding, *despite* the weakness of the pyramid's base, i.e. an immature set of support industries. In other words, capacity expansion proceeds without industrial deepening. Second, and more generally, this reduces the role that smaller firms can play as engines of export growth. Overall, the crisis is likely to have a negative cascading effect that increases inequality and that may block further industrial upgrading.

In order to counter such negative trends, corrective policy instruments have been discussed in various forums, but so far very little has been achieved. The Singaporean government for instance established a 2 billion US$ trade financing scheme to enable Indonesia to buy essential supplies (*Financial Times*, 31 March 1998, p. 1), but apparently it has failed to draw sufficient support. Likewise, the Japanese government has announced various measures to assist its Asian neighbours in their access to trade finance, as part of the US$ 30 billion Miyazawa initiative, but so far no details have been disclosed.

Devaluation and import prices

East Asia's electronics industries depend heavily on imports of key components, subassemblies and production equipment. While import content ratios are not available,[13] it is possible to construct proxy indicators. Table 12.1 documents the critical rôle played by electronic components, and especially semiconductors (SC) both for electronics imports and merchandise imports. In the extreme cases of Malaysia and Thailand, electronic components account for almost 30% and 25% respectively of merchandise imports. And among the four leading East Asian electronics producers (Korea, Taiwan, Singapore and Malaysia), components on an average account for three-quarters of their electronics imports.

The tenacity of the region's import dependence in electronics becomes clear when we look at the two most prominent success stories: Korea's semiconductor industry and Taiwan's PC industry. Despite all their impressive achievements, both industries remain heavily dependent on imported inputs. Korea's semiconductor industry is based on an extremely weak foundation, in terms of the materials and production equipment required. Korea's current annual consumption of semiconductors materials is approximately $600 million, with 70% of total consumption being imported (40% from Japan and 20% from the

Table 12.1 Share of components in electronics imports and merchandise imports, 1996 (%)

Country/share	*Electronics imports*	*Merchandise imports*
Korea	Components: 74.3 – SC: 49.2	Comp: 10.1 – SC: 6.7
Taiwan	Comp: 81.3 – SC: 53.1	Comp: 16.9 – SC: 11.0
Singapore (1997)	Comp: 61.0 – SC: 37.5	Comp: 24.2 – SC: 15.0
Malaysia	Comp: 82.7 – SC: 53.5	Comp: 29.6 – SC: 19.1
Thailand (1995)	Comp: 69.4 – SC: 33.3	Comp: 25.1 – SC: 6.5
Philippines	Comp: 74.2 – SC: 55.5	Comp: 20.3 – SC: 15.2
Indonesia	Comp: 65.2 – SC: 5.0	Comp: 3.2 – SC: 0,2
Hong Kong (1997)	Comp: 51.6 – SC: 24.3	Comp: 13.3 – SC: 6.3
China	Comp: 67 – SC: 23.3	Comp: 7.6 – SC: 2.6

Source: Ernst, 1998b.

United States). As for production equipment, 90% has to be imported, with 50% originating from Japan.

In Taiwan's PC industry, a rapid expansion of production capacity and international market share has not been matched by industrial deepening. For most of the key components that determine the price and the performance features of its major export products, Taiwan continues to rely heavily on imports, primarily from Japan. Picture tubes for computer monitors provide an example: nearly two-thirds have to be imported, either from Japan or from Japanese affiliates in South-east Asia. The situation is equally severe for display panels, a key component for Taiwan's thriving portable PC industry. Taiwan has to import virtually all of the high-end flat panel displays that are used in its portable PCs, and the supply of these devices is controlled by a tightly knit oligopoly consisting of Sharp, a Toshiba–IBM joint venture and NEC, with Hitachi and Matsushita being important second-tier producers.[14]

High import dependence constitutes an important barrier to export expansion. It implies that local currency depreciations will lead to substantial price increases in the key components and machinery required for Asia's electronics production. For both products, import prices are normally quoted in US dollars.[15] As a result, the massive devaluation imposed by the Asian crisis has led to an equally massive increase in import prices, at least for Asian companies that rely on open market purchases (author's interviews, September 1998). This is likely to be very different for Asia-based MNC affiliates. Many of their transactions take place as intra-firm trade, where sophisticated *transfer pricing* techniques can shield these affiliates from an increase in import prices.[16] To the degree that they buy from independent sources, they engage in global sourcing: large orders usually enable them to request substantial price discounts. This is an option which does not exist for most Asian electronics firms, with the exception of some *chaebol* and some large Taiwanese business groups.[17]

Demand-related constraints

The scope for trade adjustment depends to a very large degree on *demand-related* factors. This raises two questions: Where are the main export markets for East Asia's electronics industry? And can these markets absorb a substantial increase in the region's electronics exports?

A basic dilemma

The outbreak of the Asian crisis has brought back into the limelight a basic dilemma that has accompanied the development of the region's electronics industry almost from its beginning: How should it balance the different markets for its products? Should the focus primarily be on the US and Europe, or should there be a shift toward *intra-regional* trade?

Initially, a heavy reliance on exports to the US and Europe helped to compensate for insufficient domestic market size and lack of sophisticated demand; it also helped to insulate individual Asian economies from economic turmoil within the region. Until well into the second half of the 1980s, the lion's share of these exports went to the US and Europe. In 1987, for instance, both markets together accounted for 84.4% of the exports of the four leading Asian newly industrializing economies (NIEs); for ASEAN countries, this share was even higher, at 93.2%.[18] The US market alone accounted for more than 58% for NIE exports, and 67% for those originating from ASEAN countries – only

Mexico, unsurprisingly, displayed a higher degree of US market dependence. Both the Japanese market and the East Asian markets accounted for a very small share of East Asia's electronics exports.

The flipside of this strategy, however, has been a heavy exposure to the highly volatile business cycles of a handful of electronics exportables. The response to this dilemma has been a rapid growth of intra-regional trade which, especially since the early 1990s, became one of the hallmarks of the 'Asian Miracle'.[19] In 1996, the main concern was a demand glut for DRAM and consumer electronics which had caused a dramatic crash in the region's exports. Trade regionalization was considered to be a powerful countervailing force that could help to mitigate this fundamental weakness. The result has been a significant increase in intra-regional exports, including exports to Japan.

Intra-regional trade

Over the last few years before the Crisis, East Asia had become a strategic growth market for its own electronics industry. Table 12.2 shows that an increasing share of the region's electronics exports is now staying within the region (exclusive of Japan).

Similarly, East Asia has become an important source of Japanese electronics imports.[20] Until the outbreak of the crisis in 1997, Japan's imports of electronics products had been growing very rapidly, and Asia had become the most important source of these imports. Asia's share in Japan's total electronics imports surged from less than 31% in 1988 to almost 58% in 1996 (Ernst, 1998b).[21]

Table 12.3 documents these dramatic changes for Korea's electronics exports: between 1991 and 1996, the combined share of North America's and Europe's markets decreased from almost 51% to slightly more than 41%, leading to a massive increase in the share of East Asia

Table 12.2 An increasing share of intra-regional electronics exports, 1991–6 (%)[a]

Country/year	*1991*	*1996*
Korea	21.5	31
Taiwan	20.5	27.9
Singapore	26.2	37.6
Malaysia	39.5	41.6

[a] That is to say, share of each country's electronics exports to East Asia (exclusive of Japan) out of its total electronics exports (%).
Source: Ernst, 1998b.

Table 12.3 Korea: direction of electronics exports, 1991–6 (%)

Share/year	*1991*	*1996*
North America (NA)	32.5	27.5
NA & EU-15	50.5	41.2
Japan	10.1	10.8
NA, EU & Japan	60.6	52.0
East Asia	21.5	31.0
East Asia & RoW	39.4	48.1

Source: Ernst, 1998b.

and other emerging markets. The result is that almost 60% of Korea's electronics exports are destined for markets where demand is now either stagnating or declining. This includes Japan, with 10.8%, and a 48.1% share for emerging markets in East Asia,[22] Latin America, Eastern Europe, Russia and the rest of Asia, up from 39.4% in 1991. These figures indicate a disturbing dependence on markets that are highly vulnerable to contagion from the Asian Crisis: demand is falling in most of these markets. In addition, a high dependence on emerging markets has three substantial disadvantages: (i) there is less pressures to upgrade product performance and quality; (ii) there is less exposure to sophisticated customers; and (iii) it gives rise to an extreme vulnerability to exchange rate fluctuations. Given Korea's sticky pattern of specialization, it is no longer possible to claim that Korean firms 'make products that sell in the most demanding markets – if the exchange rate is right' (Wade and Veneroso, 1998, p. 1).

The impact of the Crisis: East Asia's shrinking markets

The outbreak of the Crisis again reversed the agenda. Paradoxically, *intra-regional trade* has now become a liability because it provides a perfect channel for the contagion to spread swiftly through East Asia. The primary concern now is to reduce the industry's vulnerability to economic turmoil within the region: debates centre on the role that the electronics industry could play in sheltering the region from crisis contagion.

Has there been a shift in East Asia's electronics exports away from Japan and East Asia, throwing the region back into a heavy reliance on exports to the US and Europe? We still lack systematic trade data for the electronics industry, covering the period since July 1997. Proxy indicators, however, clearly indicate a dramatic downward trend in East Asia's electronics markets. During 1998, the computer market in Asia (including Japan) has declined by 7% on a yearly basis. It is thus safe to assume that electronics exports to the rest of the region will fall drastically, as all these countries are now struggling with a severe decline in domestic demand, and as most of them lack the financial resources for new investment and imports.

Exports of consumer electronics and of related components are most vulnerable to the impact of the financial crisis, for two reasons: (i) East Asia has already substantial surplus production capacities; and (ii) demand for these products in EA-5 countries has dropped sharply by about 70–80% on a year-to-year basis during 1998. But demand in most of these economies is also likely to decline for computers and telecommunications equipment, given the massive decline projected for capital expenditures in the region.

As Japan is in the throes of a severe recession, its imports from Asia have fallen drastically: while overall, Japan's imports fell by 15% (during the first half of 1998), imports from every Asian country were down, with Malaysia, Vietnam and Indonesia suffering the biggest falls, down respectively 22%, 23% and 30%. Taiwan's exports to Japan, its third largest export market, fell by almost 24% during the first quarter of 1998.

In short, the coexistence of the Asian financial crisis and Japan's deflationary downward spiral has created an explosive mixture of forces that could play havoc with the region's established trade patterns. In response to a drastic fall of their intra-regional exports, most Asian countries, including China, are now under tremendous pressure to shift their exports away from Asia as well as from Japan, to the US and Europe. The question of course is whether they will succeed in implementing such a shift in their export markets.

It is a disturbing thought that the US trade deficit is at its highest level in nine years, even though the full impact of the Asian Crisis has yet to be felt. In 1997, the US trade deficit in manufactured goods rose by 4.1% to a record $172.6bn. Most of the increase was accounted for by rising deficits with China and Japan: in December 1997, the US trade deficit with China had increased by 45% on a year-to-year basis (*Nikkei Weekly*, 16 March 1998); and Japan's trade surplus with the US rose 66% from a year earlier (*Financial Times*, 20 February 1998, p. 22, citing Japan's Ministry of Trade and Industry trade figures). This, no doubt, is an unfortunate starting-point for the US to absorb an expected export boom from Asia. Since then, the combined effect of the declining demand in Asia and a surging US dollar has produced a further sharp deterioration in the US trade position. Sooner or later, this may well invite a protectionist response.

In short, Asian economies should not expect too much from devaluation-induced export expansion: there is very little chance that exporting one's way out of the crisis will produce the expected results. One reason is the familiar *trade restriction trap*: once a substantial increase in Asian exports had caused the US current account to deteriorate, this might lead to vigorous trade restrictions. A second reason could be a *worsening of East Asia's terms of trade*: whatever expansion occurs in its export volume, these gains are likely be more than compensated for by substantial price declines. We shall now turn to an analysis of such effects.

Constraints resulting from deflationary pricing pressures

Deflationary pricing pressures dominate many if not most sectors of the electronics industry that are of relevance to East Asia. This has given rise to a further set of constraints to a devaluation-induced export expansion: even if the East Asian electronics industries succeed in expanding their export volumes, negative pricing effects may erase such gains.

It is important to emphasize that local Asian firms are likely to be more vulnerable to such negative pricing effects than MNC affiliates. Established market leaders with a strong global brand image can cope with these pressures: they can charge premium prices, and they can shift the burden of cost reduction onto other shoulders, primarily their Asian suppliers. For the latter companies, this magnifies the pressure to reduce prices. At the same time, they are under tremendous pressure to broaden their capability base and to increase their investment outlays, simply to sustain their link with their main global customers. There is a substantial risk that, once devaluation is reversed, Asian suppliers will find themselves caught in a higher-cost production structure than before the Crisis. But now they will be unable to back away from the price reductions which they have granted in response to the currency depreciation.

Asian producers of final electronics products are caught in the middle: they must increase hard currency export revenues at almost any cost, in order to service their mounting debt; at the same time, they have to bear the full brunt of this ruthless cost-reduction pressure, as they do not have anyone else to whom they could pass it on. The root cause of this vulnerability is a narrow specialization in high-tech commodities that are characterized by periodic surplus capacity and price wars.[23] This leaves Asian electronics firms very little room for price increases; there is a constant squeeze on their profit margins, with the result that the funds required for continuous upgrading may dry up even further.

Deflationary pricing pressures on Asian suppliers

How does devaluation affect the prices paid by MNC affiliates to their Asian suppliers? In order to understand this important issue, let us look at the impact of devaluation on the production cost of a Malaysian supplier to a global original equipment manufacturer (OEM) customer based in Singapore (author's interviews in Singapore, March 1998). Most of the materials need to be purchased in US dollars, owing to the very high import content ratios of production; non-material costs (e.g., labour and overheads) on the other hand are overwhelmingly in local currency. This implies that depreciation should lead to a reduction in the share of non-material costs (both labour costs and overheads).

The Singapore-based OEM customer requests that this reduction in non-material costs be translated in proportional price reductions. The supplier does not have much choice but to give in to such pressure. Its main concern is to sustain the link with its OEM customer, at almost any cost. Lower-end suppliers, in particular those located outside of Singapore, have been pushed to the limit in granting such price reductions. This reflects the intense price wars in most sectors of the electronics industry (see next section).

This is a very problematic development: it deprives lower-end suppliers of the means that they need urgently for upgrading their product and technology portfolios. Such upgrading requirements are now much more demanding. The dominant global PC manufacturers have drastically reduced the duration of contracts for printed circuit board assembly (PCBA): typically, PCBA suppliers can now be dropped within a week. PC manufacturers have also off-loaded so-called *back-end* activities (related to logistics and global supply chain management) to contract manufacturers, in order to concentrate on their core competencies. This has forced Asian contract manufacturers to move beyond PCBA to the final assembly of PCs (so-called 'box-build' contracts). The main concern is to stabilize the link with their main customers: the duration of box-build contracts typically is around six months. This, however, requires substantial investments which may no longer be possible.

Even more problematic is a somewhat longer-term effect: once local currencies start to appreciate again, this will leave lower-end suppliers in a very vulnerable position where they will be stuck with a higher-cost production structure that cannot sustain the currently-granted price reductions. It is unlikely that they will be able to back away from these price reductions which they have granted in response to the currency crisis. In other words, there is a real danger that current price reductions may force many of these suppliers out of the market.

In short, price pressures which were already intense before the financial crisis, have now become even more severe. At the same time, however, Asian suppliers are under tremendous pressure to recapitalize. In order to survive, they need to upgrade their product mix and their efficiency; they also need to proceed with a regionalization of their production base. This dual pressure has resulted in severe cash-flow problems, especially for smaller local suppliers. Asian contract manufacturers are now saddled with a higher-cost production structure than before the crisis, and thus are potentially more vulnerable to its impact.

A narrow and sticky specialization in high-tech commodities

Specialization is an important indicator of the degree of industrial upgrading that a country has achieved. Industrial economists distinguish specialization patterns that reflect differences in the product mix (homogeneous versus differentiated products[24]), and in the types of production process (mass production versus flexible production). A fundamental problem of East Asia's electronics industries is a narrow and sticky specialization on a few high-tech commodities that are prone to periodic surplus capacity and price wars. With few exceptions, the region has failed to upgrade into higher-end and rapidly growing market segments for differentiated products that provide sufficient scope for premium pricing (Ernst, 2001d).

Take Korea (Ernst, 1994, chs 1 and 2; Ernst, 1998a). Almost without exception, the *chaebol* have targeted those segments of the electronics industry that require huge investment outlays and sophisticated mass production techniques for fairly homogeneous products like microwave ovens, TV sets, VCRs, computer monitors, picture tubes, displays, and computer memories, especially DRAM. Overwhelmingly, the focus has been on consumer electronics and components, with only limited inroads into industrial electronics. Burdened with unimpressive 'me too' products, the *chaebol* have all failed to establish themselves as credible competitors in the more design-intensive sectors of the computer industry.

A particularly disturbing feature of Korea's specialization pattern is that it typically combines high investment thresholds and highly volatile income streams. This poses a considerable risk. For instance, the minimum efficient scale for producing DRAM devices is now more than $1 billion of annual sales. This implies that only firms that have reached the critical threshold of 5% of world production can compete successfully.[25] Competition in DRAM centres on the capacity to invest in huge mega-plants churning out a limited variety of standard products and on the capacity to improve yields and productivity as quickly as possible.

The very high entry barriers typical for DRAM and other high-tech commodities are due less to their R&D intensity than to an explosive combination of high capital-intensity, very high economies of scale and an extremely volatile nature of demand for these devices. High-tech commodities are prone to periodic boom-and-bust cycles and hence do not generate a steady flow of profits. For companies with a high debt–equity ratio, this is obviously not an optimal choice.[26]

Probably the most important weakness of Korea's semiconductor industry is a very narrow product range. The three leading Korean semiconductor producers are all heavily dependent on computer memories: 80% of Samsung's semiconductor revenues come from memories, and in the case of LG and Hyundai, this share is even higher, i.e., 87% and 90% respectively.[27] Korea's competitive position in semiconductors thus remains highly fragile.

The narrow focus on memory products has very negative implications for the overall structure of the electronics industry. Korea keeps exporting more than 90% of its total semiconductor output, while at the same time importing more than 87% of its domestic demand. Such an extreme imbalance between supply and demand makes it very difficult to broaden and deepen forward and backward linkages within the electronics industry and to place it onto a more viable basis.[28]

Surplus capacity and price wars

A narrow specialization on a few high-tech commodities has produced a paradoxical result: these products are more sensitive to price declines and negative terms of trade effects than labour-intensive ones. Between 1990 and 1997, world prices of high-tech products (based on US import prices) declined sharply, while those of labour-intensive products were unstable, but did not experience such a sharp decline (World Bank, 1998b, ch. 2). And while the average unit price index of Korean exports during the first quarter of 1998 declined by 19.4% from the corresponding period of 1997, much higher unit price reductions are reported for electronics (–38.6%) and semiconductors (–48.6%).[29]

It can be argued that deflationary price pressures result from persistent surplus capacity:[30] a persistent tendency for production capacity to overshoot demand characterizes especially the high-tech commodities that are the strength of East Asia. I shall illustrate this argument for two product groups that are of critical importance for East Asia's electronics industry: PCs and DRAM. Both product groups are less vulnerable to shrinking demand in Asia than, for instance, consumer electronics; they depend critically on market developments in the US, and to a lesser degree in Europe.

Pricing trends in PC markets

Since the beginning of 1997, the pace of price reduction has accelerated substantially. During 1997, the average selling price of a home PC dropped by 30% to $1,169; by Christmas 1998, these prices were expected to have fallen even further, by almost 49%, to below $600. Price wars have now also spilled over into the corporate computer market. During 1998, prices for computer hardware (from PC servers to notebooks) sold to private business have fallen by around 20%.

Such drastic price reductions have led to a scissors effect between growth of sales volume and sales revenue. During 1998, it is estimated that worldwide unit sales of PC producers have increased by around 16%, yet US dollar denominated sales revenues have increased by only 6.4% (Dataquest figures).

This has far-reaching implications for East Asia's export prospects for computer-related products. Export markets are likely to continue their rapid growth, especially in the US and Europe. As the Crisis-induced currency depreciation has dramatically improved the price competitiveness of Asian suppliers, much of these new export sales will originate from Asia, provided that supply-related barriers to an export expansion can be removed, and provided of course that there is no protectionist backlash. Yet, net volume gains will be offset by substantial pricing losses.

At the same time, we witness a drastic change in the rules of competition: cost reduction now needs to be combined with speed-to-market. The result is that Asian suppliers will have to assume most of the inventory risk and the time-to-market pressure by adopting just-in-time delivery schedules and by providing one-stop solution packages for global supply chain management. This requires a significant increase of upgrading investments at a time when pervasive price wars result in razor-thin profit margins, and when debt deflation has dried up investible resources.

DRAM price wars and their limits

Korean firms are among the leaders in this important market segment of the semiconductor industry.[31] In response to the demand glut for DRAM since late 1995, Korean producers have shared a common interest with Japanese producers in supply regulation and in the re-establishment of a stable oligopoly. The main objective was to fend off attacks from new entrants in Taiwan and Singapore, and to frustrate attempts by Micron Technology, one of the few remaining US manufacturers, and Siemens, to recapture market share.

These attempts are now in shambles. Since 1996, prices for DRAM have plunged owing to accumulated worldwide over-capacity:[32] while the price for a staple 16-megabit DRAM chip in late 1995 was $60, it had fallen to $3 in late 1997, and has increased slightly since then to $3.50. This price is at or below the manufacturing costs of all but the most efficient manufacturers in the industry.

All major DRAM producers are now desperate to generate foreign exchange through increasing exports at almost any cost. There is, however, reason to doubt whether drastic price slashing will be sustainable: the threat of dumping procedures is very real, and worsening terms of trade will make it more difficult to purchase essential input imports. A major drawback is that intensifying price wars will decrease export revenues, despite a possible substantial increase in export volumes, which is bound in turn to intensify further the already severe profit squeeze.[33]

An additional reason why price-slashing strategies are unlikely to last results from drastic changes in the competitive dynamics of this industry. Until recently, the established business model was to increase market share through aggressive forward price reductions based on incessant capacity expansion. This model was pioneered in the 1980s by Toshiba and NEC, and later successfully emulated by Samsung, LG and Hyundai. It apparently has reached its limits: aggressive price slashing has turned the DRAM business into the 'bleeding-edge' of the semiconductor industry, with all leading players now experiencing huge losses.

This has provoked two types of response. Within DRAM, an alternative business model is now emerging that focuses on *productivity improvements* and that tries to slow down the pace of capacity expansion.[34] The main emphasis is on squeezing the remaining profits out of a product at the end of its life cycle, and by doing so, to avoid getting trapped into endless capacity expansion wars. A related response, chosen in particular by second-tier DRAM producers, is to retreat from the general-purpose DRAM market and to diversify into higher value-added, less volatile market segments for specialized memories, ASIC and logic devices.[35]

East Asian countries are weak on both accounts. This is true even for Korea where much talk of radical change, and in particular diversification, has been followed by little action (Ernst, 1994a, 1998a): Korea's semiconductor industry is still stuck with a very narrow product range centred on DRAM. There are a few exceptions of successful diversification into higher value-added products. One example is synchronous DRAM,[36] for which prices are about 30% higher than for standard DRAM, where Samsung competes on equal terms with NEC and Fujitsu. But this does not change the overall picture. Despite their earlier impressive achievements in rapid capacity and international market share expansion, the Korean *chaebol* 'are too far behind and too focused on memory products to challenge the overall lead of companies in the US and Japan' (DRI, 1996, p. 12).

Conclusions

This paper has discussed why the electronics industry, East Asia's traditional engine of export-led growth, has failed to act as a carrier of rapid trade adjustment to the crisis. Three interrelated constraints are responsible for its declining capacity to generate the hard currency revenues with which to pay the accumulated debt: (i) *supply-side constraints* that result from limited access to trade finance, and from the cost-increasing impact of local currency depreciations in highly import-dependent countries; (ii) *demand-related constraints*, resulting from deteriorating growth perspectives in East Asia's electronics export markets; and (iii) *deflationary pricing pressures*, resulting from a narrow specialization in high-tech commodities that are characterized by periodic surplus capacity and price wars. Together, these barriers have produced a vicious circle: once exports increase, net volume gains are likely to be offset by pricing losses.

The expectations of a rapid trade adjustment in East Asia were based on the unrealistic assumption that the experience of Mexico's 1995 peso crisis could be repeated. But history never repeats itself. Then, after a deep devaluation of the peso, unit prices did not decline significantly during Mexico's phase of rapid export volume growth.

This was possible for three reasons: (i) the dollar value of world trade was rapidly expanding in 1995, unlike now; (ii) much of the Mexican rapid export growth was intra-firm exports to the US from export platform factories which contrasts with a much more complex pattern in East Asia (Ernst and Guerrieri, 1998); and (iii) there was no severe generalized regional crisis, as in East Asia today.

East Asia's experience has been very different. There has been some export volume growth, but less than one could have expected.[37] What really matters is that net volume gains have been offset by substantial pricing losses. This paper has identified some fundamental structural weaknesses of East Asia's electronics industries that are responsible for this puzzling outcome.

There are, however, also important *external* constraints to rapid trade adjustment that reflect a substantially more hostile international environment for what only a short time ago used to be called 'emerging markets'. The first such external constraint is the global trade crash: the fall in world export growth from its cyclical peak in 1995 was the largest in the past 15 years – from about 20% to about 4% (in US dollars) in just one year. The sharp depreciation of the yen in 1995 compounded the negative impact of the slowdown in world exports on many East Asian countries.[38]

Add to this the crisis of international capital markets, where panic and the Russian default have produced a flight into safe havens (US bonds), resulting in a drastic fall in international investment, especially to emerging markets. Furthermore, extremely volatile international currency markets obstruct potential advantages of local currency depreciations and have created a much more hostile international environment to exports and inward FDI.

This has dramatically intensified the competition among exporters, not only from East Asia, but from all emerging markets. 'This implies that if all East Asian countries lowered their export prices simultaneously, no one country would increase market share or export growth and the main effect would be lower export prices' (World Bank, 1998b, p. 29) This is precisely what happened in the electronics industry.

East Asia's response to the crisis should not count too much on rapid trade adjustment. Reinstating the electronics industry as an engine of growth necessitates industrial upgrading. The focus should be on improving profit margins on existing sales through productivity improvements and differentiation rather than on sharply increasing export volumes. The crisis poses a fundamental dilemma: it has dramatically increased the need for industrial upgrading, while at the same time reducing its chances of success. This precludes a return to the status quo ante – fundamental changes are required in the different Asian development models, and these changes are very different from the ones proposed by the 'Washington Consensus', with its focus on orthodox fiscal and monetary policies. While drastic changes in the financial system are important, they need to be supplemented by changes in the real economy. A new round of policy and institutional innovations is required that can help to remove the barriers to industrial upgrading (Ernst, 1999c).

Notes

1. Stiglitz, 1997; Sachs, 1997; Jomo, 1998; Wade and Veneroso, 1998; and Palma, 1998.
2. Chang *et al.*, 1998; Garnaut and McLead, 1998; and World Bank, 1998b and 1999.
3. If not mentioned otherwise, data on East Asia's electronics industry are based on interviews (March and September 1998, and from: Ernst, 1998b. See also Ernst, 1998a (for Korea); and Ernst, 2000 (for Taiwan).
4. 'Given their deep exchange rate depreciations, EA5 (Korea, Malaysia, Indonesia, Thailand and the Philippines) exports are expected to rebound by 18% in 1998 and 12 percent in 1999. Sharply lower GDP growth and real exchange rate depreciations are simultaneously expected to cut EA5 import growth to a negative 2 percent in 1998 and to 6 percent in 1999' (World Bank, 1998a, p. 6).
5. For case studies, see various contributions in Ernst, Ganiatsos and Mytelka, 1998.
6. Real effective exchange rates, courtesy of Morgan Guarantee Trust Company, Economic Research. Historical effective exchange rate indices are available through the Internet at: www.jpmorgan.com
7. The concept of an global production network (GPN) is an attempt to capture the spread of broader and more systemic forms of international production that cut across different stages of the value chain and that may or may not involve equity ownership. Such networks constitute an important organizational innovation that enable multinational corporations to cope with the conflicting requirements of specialization and coordination. The concept allows us to analyse the globalization strategies of a global network flagship with regard to the following four questions: (1) Where does a firm locate which stages of the value chain? (2) To what degree does a firm rely on outsourcing? What is the importance of inter-firm production networks relative to the firm's internal production network? (3) To what degree is the control over these transactions exercised in a centralized or in a decentralized manner? And (4) how do these different elements of the GPN hang together? For details, see Ernst, 1997a and b, 2001a, b and c. See also Borrus, Ernst and Haggard (eds), 2000.

8. Main actors include a handful of global players like Microsoft, Intel, Cisco, Compaq, HP, Dell, IBM, Sony, Fujitsu, Toshiba, Ericcson, Motorola, Siemens, Philips, Matsushita, Sharp and Canon.
9. For DRAM, for instance, this includes foreign multinationals (like Texas Instruments, NEC, Toshiba and Hitachi); Asian companies such as Samsung Electronics (the world industry leader); LG (from Korea), Acer Semiconductor Manufacturing (ASMI), Nanya Plastic and others (from Taiwan); and alliances between multinationals and state-owned enterprises, such Singapore's Chartered Semiconductor Manufacturing, Tech-Semiconductor and Tri-Tech.
10. While traditionally these firms have focused primarily on printed circuit board assembly, they have recently expanded into the final assembly and shipment of PCs and digital consumer and communication devices ('complete-box-build-and-ship').
11. During 1998, Maersk, the Danish shipping company, for instance, shipped its containers empty to Singapore and then filled them up with exports from the region (interview at Danish Industry Association).
12. *Far Eastern Economic Review*, 23 April 1998, quoting a report by Crosby Corporate Advisory, Singapore, on the trade finance bottleneck.
13. Import content ratios differ from product to product, and even for a given product, they differ from company to company. This obviously poses severe methodological problems for the collection of such data. An important objective for future research is to conduct a questionnaire survey to collect a representative set of product-specific import content ratios and to document how these ratios have developed over time.
14. This heavy dependence on component imports from Japan has been the root cause for Taiwan's exploding electronics trade deficit with Japan: Taiwan's trade deficit in components is currently responsible for around 70% of its total electronics trade deficit with Japan (Ernst and Guerrieri, 1998).
15. There is a debate in Japan as to whether a shift to Yen-denominated prices would enable Japanese suppliers of materials and machinery to preserve their important markets in Asia. Thus far, however, little has changed.
16. The role of transfer-pricing for inter-firm trade poses serious methodological problems for attempts to conduct a reliable quantitative analysis of price effects resulting from currency devaluations.
17. Kim (2000) provides a fascinating case of the difficulties faced by Samsung Electronics in its attempt to develop a global sourcing network.
18. Ernst and O'Connor, 1992, ch. 3, Table 13. NIEs here include Korea, Taiwan, Singapore and Hong Kong, while ASEAN countries exclude Singapore.
19. Over the last decade, intra-regional trade has made an increasing contribution to growth: in 1996, its share in East Asia's total exports accounted for about 40%, up from 32% in 1990. If Japan is included, the share of intra-regional trade rises to 50% (World Bank, 1998b). Trade theorists argue that this reflects the region's increasing specialization, based on shifting comparative advantages (Balassa, 1977). The most prominent version of this

argument has been the *flying geese* theory (based on Akamatsu, 1962). Recent research however has shown that the expansion of intra-Asian trade is due primarily to the spread of increasingly complex global production networks (GPN) (Ernst and Guerrieri, 1998).

20. Despite its close proximity, East Asia has surprisingly played a much less prominent role as a source of Japanese electronics imports than it did for the US (Ernst and Guerrieri, 1998). Until 1990, Japanese electronics imports overwhelmingly originated from the US, and even in 1993, East Asia's share was significantly lower than that of the US.
21. In absolute terms, Japanese electronics imports continue to be substantially smaller than those of the US: in 1996, Japan's total electronics imports were $47.439 billion, less than one-third of the US total of $151.5 billion. This however is a substantial improvement relative to 1991, when Japan's total electronics imports were worth only 20% of the US worldwide electronics imports. The most rapid increase has occurred for electronic components, where the import ratio shot up from 16% in 1985 to more than 35% in 1993. While in 1988, the US was the only source of imported ICs and computers, Japan now imports roughly the same amount of ICs and computers from Asia and from the US.
22. East Asia itself accounts for almost one-third of Korea's electronics exports, up from 21.5% in 1991.
23. This argument was first developed in Ernst, 1994. For a similar, independently developed argument, see the excellent paper by Kaplinsky (1998).
24. *Homogeneous* (standard) products are distinguished from differentiated (unique) products, in terms of the complexity of their technology and the demand patterns they are facing. Homogeneous products are based on widely accessible and mature technology and are thus easy to replicate. Changes in demand patterns are fairly predictable and interactions with customers plays a role only at the margin. *Differentiated* products, on the other hand, are based on new technology whose design features are still fluid and are thus difficult to replicate. This is due to the high entry barriers that result from the high R&D outlays required. Close interaction with customers is a critical prerequisite for success. It is argued that different market structures will result from these different product features: for *differentiated* products, firms can charge *premium* prices, while for *homogeneous* products, *price competition* is the overriding concern. See, for instance, Baumol, Panzer and Willig (1982) and Nilsson (1996).
25. For a detailed analysis of entry barriers in different sectors of the electronics industry, see Ernst and O'Connor (1992).
26. Until the outbreak of the financial crisis, this was not much of a problem. The *chaebol* had guaranteed access to 'patient capital' and ample opportunities for internal 'cross-subsidization' and thus were among the few firms worldwide that could cope with the demanding financial requirements of high-tech commodities. The *chaebol* could also built on sophisticated production and investment capabilities, both in typical mass production industries like cars and consumer durables and in resource-intensive process industries like the steel industry. After the financial crisis hit, this pattern is no longer sustainable.

27. In the case of the largest Japanese semiconductor producer, NEC, for example, only 35% of its semiconductor revenues were generated by MOS (metal oxide on silicon) memories.
28. It is probably fair to say that Korea's semiconductor industry represents a modern version of the classical mono-product export enclave, characterized by a minimum of linkages with the domestic economy. There is, however, one important difference: the cost for entering the semiconductor industry is exceedingly high, and certainly exceeds that of entering the plantation industry (Ernst, 1994, chapter 2).
29. Bank of Korea figures, quoted in Hak (1998).
30. There is no guarantee that demand growth will keep pace with supply – Say's law only applies under very restrictive conditions that are unlikely to occur in the real world. Krugman's claim to the contrary is not convincing. Neo-classical economists claim that *general* overproduction is impossible: 'all of the increased production in the world has as a necessary counterpart increased income – every dollar of sales must also represent a dollar of wages or profits to somebody. And there are only two things you can do with income: save it or spend it' (Krugman, 1998, p. 1). The conclusion drawn is that, short of a global excess of savings compared to investment opportunities, global oversupply is logically impossible. Such a conclusion is consistent with the basic assumptions of the maximization-and-equilibrium paradigm. Yet it fails to address the existence of persistent overproduction in specific industries and markets, which, as Richardson (1998) has convincingly demonstrated, explains why *concurrent coordination* is the basic rationale for the existence of the firm.
31. DRAM (Dynamic Random Access Memories) constitute the largest market segment for computer memories and make up roughly 24% of the world's total semiconductor demand (Dataquest, 1996). Intel and other American firms like Texas Instruments and Motorola had originally created the DRAM market. However by around 1986, five major Japanese firms (NEC, Toshiba, Hitachi, Fujitsu, and Mitsubishi) had taken over and had established a tight oligopoly that controlled roughly two-thirds of the world market for DRAM. Their share has now fallen to below 48%, and this is primarily due to the successful market penetration by Korean firms. By 1997, Korea firms controlled roughly one-third of the global market for DRAM, well ahead of the 20% market share of American companies.
32. The following DRAM price figures are courtesy of Dataquest, San José, CA.
33. For instance, Korean chip makers are estimated to have lost a combined $2.7bn in 1997. In response to such dramatic losses, they announced cuts in capital spending by around 40% in 1998. (These figures are courtesy of VLSI Research Inc, a market researcher in San José, California that specializes in the market for semiconductor production equipment, and hence is a reliable source for investment and capacity planning.)
34. The new model for DRAM manufacturing has been pioneered by Micron Technology from the US that had earlier greatly suffered from the success of the Toshiba–NEC–Samsung model. Rather than spending billions of dollars to be the first supplier to the market of an accelerating succession of DRAM generations (64 Mb, 256 MB, and 1-gigabit), Micron has optimized its manufacturing process to wring more money from 16 Mb devices.

35. Diversification beyond the DRAM market has been on the agenda already since the last demand glut of 1992/93. Since then, Japanese firms have drastically reduced their reliance on DRAM, and have developed strong positions in, for instance, specialized memories and ASIC.
36. Recent microprocessor generations for PCs, specifically Intel's new Pentium II chip, require a faster and more customized 64Mb chip, called Synchronous DRAM.
37. Based on earlier studies (Das Gupta, Hulu and Das Gupta, 1995), a 40% depreciation should have increased export volume in the crisis countries by 20 to 30% based on typical elasticities. Only Korean exports matched this expectation.
38. This is especially so for Korea whose export structure is similar to Japan's: in 1996, Japan's imports from Korea fell by 8.5%. Throughout the period 1990 to 1997, Korea's real export growth mirrors changes in the yen–dollar exchange rate, rising with an appreciation of the yen, and falling with its depreciation (World Bank, 1998b, figure 2.2, p. 21).

References

Akamatsu, K. (1962) 'A historical pattern of economic growth in developing countries', *Journal of Developing Economies*, vol. 1, no. 1, March–August.

Balassa, B. (1977) 'A "Stages" Approach to Comparative Advantage', World Bank Staff Working Paper, No. 256, Washington, DC, The World Bank.

Baumol, W. J., Panzer, J. C. and Willig, R. D. (1982) *Contestable Markets and the Theory of Industrial Structure*, New York, Harcourt Brace Jovanovich.

Borrus, M., Ernst, D. and Haggard, S. (eds) (2000) *International Production Networks in Asia: Rivalry or Riches?* London, Routledge.

Chang, H.-J., Park, H.-J. and Chul Gyue Yoo, C. G. (1998) 'Interpreting the Korean Crisis – financial liberalisation, industrial policy, and corporate governance', *Cambridge Journal of Economics*, vol. 26, no. 6.

Das Gupta, D., Hulu, E. and Das Gupta, B. (1995) 'The Determinants of Indonesia's Non-Oil Exports', Conference Paper on Deregulation, EDI/World Bank.

DRI (1996) *The Globalization of the Semiconductor Industry*, a DRI/McGraw-Hill study, Washington, DC, McGraw Hill.

Ernst, D. (1994) 'Network transactions, market structure and technological diffusion – implications for south–south cooperation', in L. Mytelka (ed.), *South–South Cooperation in a Global Perspective*, Development Centre Documents, Paris, OECD.

Ernst, D. (1997a) 'Partners in the China circle? The Asian production networks of Japanese electronics firms', in B. Naughton (ed.), *The China Circle*, Washington, DC, Brookings Institution Press.

Ernst, D. (1997b) 'From Partial to Systemic Globalization. International Production Networks in the Electronics Industry', report prepared for the Sloan Foundation, The Data Storage Industry Globalization Project Report 97-02, Graduate School of International Relations and Pacific Studies, University of California at San Diego.

Ernst, D. (1998a) 'Catching-up, crisis and industrial upgrading. Evolutionary aspects of technological learning in Korea's electronics industry', *Asia Pacific Journal of Management*, vol. 15, no. 2.

Ernst, D. (1998b) 'Destroying or Upgrading the Engine of Growth? The Reshaping of the Electronics Industry in East Asia after the Crisis', background study prepared for the World Bank report *East Asia – The Road to Recovery*, Washington, DC, The World Bank.

Ernst, D. (2000) 'Inter-Organizational Knowledge Outsourcing. What Permits Small Taiwanese Firms to Compete in the Computer Industry?', *Asia Pacific Journal of Management*, August, special issue on 'Knowledge Management in Asia'.

Ernst, D. (2001a) 'The economics of electronics industry: competitive dynamics and industrial organization', in Malcolm Warner and William Lazonick (eds) *The International Encyclopedia of Business and Management* (IEBM), International Thomson Business Press.

Ernst, D. (2001b) 'Global Production Networks and the Changing Geography of Innovation Systems. Implications for Developing Countries', special issue of the *Journal of the Economics of Innovation and New Technologies'*, on 'Integrating Policy Perspectives in Research on Technology and Economic Growth', edited by Bartzokas, Anthony and Teubal, Morris.

Ernst, D. (2001c) 'Placing the Networks on the Internet – A New Divide in Industrial Organization', paper presented at the Nelson and Winter Conference, Aalborg, Denmark, 12–15 June 2001, organized by DRUID.

Ernst, D. (2001d) 'Moving Beyond the Commodity Trap? Trade Adjustment and Industrial Upgrading in East Asia's Electronics Industry', in Newfarmer, R. S. and C. A. Wood, (eds), *East Asia: From recovery to Sustainable Development*, Discussion Paper Series, Washington, D.C., World Bank.

Ernst, D. and O'Connor, D. (1992) *Competing in the Electronics Industry. The Experience of Newly Industrialising Economies*, Development Centre Studies, Paris, OECD.

Ernst, D. and Guerrieri, P. (1998) 'International production networks and changing trade patterns in East Asia. The case of the electronics industry', *Oxford Development Studies*, vol. 26, no. 2, June.

Ernst, D., Ganiatsos, T. and Mytelka, L. (eds) (1998) *Technological Capabilities and Export Success – Lessons from East Asia*, London, Routledge.

Garnaut, R. and McLeod, R. (eds) (1998) *East Asia in Crisis. From Being a Miracle to Needing One?*, London, Routledge.

Hak, K. P. (1998) 'Excess Competition, Moral Hazard and Industrial Trauma in Korea', paper presented at World Bank conference on the Asian financial crisis, 13 May 1998.

Henderson, R. M. and Clark, K. B (1990) 'Architectural innovation: the reconfiguration of existing product technologies and the failure of established firms', *Administrative Science Quarterly*, vol. 35 (March), 9–30.

Jomo, K. S. (1998) 'Financial Liberalization, Crises, and Malaysian Policy Responses', paper presented at the Nordic Research Seminar on the Economic Crisis in East and South-east Asia, Centre for Development and the Environment (SUM), University of Oslo, Oslo, 23–24 January 1998.

Kaplinsky, R. (1998) '"If You Want to Get Somewhere Else, You Must Run At Least Twice As Fast As That!": The Roots of the East Asian Crisis', Institute of Development Studies, University of Sussex, unpublished paper.

Kim, Y. (2000) 'Technological capabilities and Samsung Electronics' international production networks in Asia', in Borrus, Ernst and Haggard (eds) (2000).

Krugman, P. (1998) Review of 'One World, Ready or Not: The Manic Logic Of Global Capitalism' by W. Greider, 3 August 1998, web.mit.edu/krugman/www/greider.html

Nilsson, J. E. (1996) 'Introduction: the internationalization process', in J. E. Nilsson, P. Dicken and J. Peck (eds), *The Internationalization Process. European Firms in Global Competition*, London, Paul Chapman.

Palma, G. (1998) 'Three-and-a-half cycles of "mania, panic and (one-sided) crash": East Asia and Latin America compared', *Cambridge Journal of Economics*, vol. 22 no. 6.

Richardson, G. B. (1998) 'Production, Planning and Prices', DRUID Working Paper no. 98–27, Department of Industrial Economics and Strategy, Copenhagen Business School, November.

Sachs, J. (1997) 'The wrong medicine for Asia', *New York Times*, 3 November.

Sachs, J. (1998) 'Global capitalism. Making it work', *The Economist*, 12 September.

Stiglitz, J. (1997) 'How to fix the Asian economies', *New York Times*, 31 October.

Wade, R. and Veneroso, F. (1998) 'The Asian Financial Crisis: The Unrecognized Risk of the IMF's Asia Package', paper presented at the Nordic Research Seminar on the Economic Crisis in East and South-east Asia, Centre for Development and the Environment (SUM), University of Oslo, Oslo, 23–24 January 1998.

World Bank (1998a) *Global Economic Prospects and the Developing Countries. Short-Term Update 1998. Special Topic on 'The Financial Crisis in East Asia: Implications for Developing Countries'*, SecM98-74, Washington, DC, The World Bank.

World Bank (1998b) *East Asia – The Road to Recovery*, Washington, DC, The World Bank.

World Bank (1999) *Global Economic Prospects for Developing Countries 1998/99: Beyond Financial Crisis*, Washington, DC, The World Bank.

13
Asian Crisis and the Future of the Japanese Model

*Ronald Dore**

Introduction

Asia's 'version of capitalism ... emphasising not markets but government planning and long-term relationships ... is now widely regarded as a problem rather than a solution.'[1] 'Gone are all the self-confident claims about the superiority of Asian values.'[2] And Asian gloom is matched by American triumphalism. Markets win. Goethe was right. America has it better.

We shall see when the recovery process has finished. Clearly, Korea is the test case. Whatever may be the nature of their small business sectors, any characterization of Malaysia and Thailand's form of capitalism surely turns on the multinational corporation (MNC) domination of their corporate sectors – which is not likely to change. It is Korea, of all the crisis countries, which has an indigenously evolved corporate sector. Shall we see fundamental change in Korea's corporations – their financing structure, their managerial objectives, their labour relations, their degree of cartelization, their relation to government? And will the Asian Crisis prove to have an impact on China's 'socialism with Chinese characteristics'? Or on Taiwan's prosperous agglomeration of medium enterprises? Or on Japan's 'Rhine model' capitalism? The last is the question which this paper addresses.

It is said[3] that some of the elements in the package the IMF sought to impose on Korea – those which were least obviously relevant to curing the financial crisis such as the 'flexibilization' of labour markets and corporate governance reforms – were in fact included at the behest of Korean officials in the Economic Planning Ministry (doubtless English-fluent, economics PhDs from leading American universities). If so, they were acting within a well-established Asian tradition – at least, one well established in Japan. *Gaiatsu* – foreign pressure, usually stemming from US–Japan trade talks – has long been a potent influence on Japanese policy, and hence a favourite weapon of those Japanese seeking reinforcement for a variety of material or ideological objectives – to break the power of the agricultural protection lobby, to shift tax burdens in the alcoholic drinks market, to clean up the stock exchange or to give more power to shareholders.

The deflationary crisis

At present, all the overt *gaiatsu* on Japan stemming from the Asian Crisis has concentrated on berating the government for letting its economy get into such a parlous state of gloom that it is importing ever less from Asia when it should be importing ever more to help in Asia's recovery. Since nobody in Japan in May 1998 needs telling that they need to do something and do it quickly, it has little effect,[4] except, when a Rubin or a Summers or a Camdessus says that Japan needs a fiscal stimulus package of at least 4% of GNP, or tells them that it should be in the form of tax cuts rather than public investment, to make that particular option more difficult for nationalist politicians to adopt even though they may have been on the verge of choosing it.

The contraction of Asian markets was certainly one factor in producing the current dire situation. It contributed to the declining spiral of consumer anxiety, reduced spending, increased savings and reduced producer investment, a declining spiral which has reversed what looked in 1996, with its 3.6% growth rate, to be the final stages of recovery from the debt deflation of the early 1990s. The timing could not have been worse – the Thai bust came just as Japanese consumers were recovering from the slow-down brought on by the sales tax increase, the end of a temporary income tax cut and increases in health charges. These were all measures which prudent bureaucrats and economists had demanded in order to deal with the alarming rise in the public debt – rapidly approaching 100% of GDP as a result of the, often quite bold, efforts to spend the economy out of its five-year recession. The deflationary impact of these 'for the sake of our grandchildren' measures was expected to be temporary, and was declared by commentators to have just about worked through, when the Asian Crisis hit.

There can be no doubt that as the Asian dominoes fell, the gloom-inducing effects were considerable. Of Japan's exports, 46% went to Asia in 1996 (compared with 30% in 1990);[5] the prospect loomed of increased Asian, especially Korean competition at their new, lower exchange rates; Japan's 11 billion Asian investments included many firms producing primarily for local domestic markets; Japanese banks with an estimated $264 billion at risk at the end 1996 (then about 35% of Asia's foreign loans) faced the prospect of more bad loans to add to the catalogue of misery hanging over them since the bursting of the bubble. Asia, however, was probably not as decisive a factor in lowering business confidence as the impact of the endogenously produced turmoil in the financial industry. (One Japanese steel executive showed an unusual confidence about the impact of Asia when he said [is this what they mean by 'crony capitalism'?] that the Korean steel-maker Posco would act responsibly and not take advantage of the cheap won to disrupt international markets, having recently had the presidency of the international steel federation.[6] And, indeed, in April 1998, the five big steel companies all announced an increase – on average of 5% – in their investment plans for the following year.)

It was not Asia but the difficulties of the banks and securities companies which dominated the headlines. For inducing anxiety in consumers there is nothing like big bankrupticies and the sight of the president of a major security company weeping on television. (Significantly, the tears came after an otherwise impassive performance, when he was asked what would happen to Yamaichi's 7,500 employees.) The strategy for dealing with the burden of bad debts left by the collapse of what must surely count as one of the biggest speculative bubbles in history had been, in one of Alan Greenspan's better phrases, to plod on against 'the head-winds of balance-sheet restructuring' – i.e., gradually to absorb them out of healthy profits – which, thanks to the mechanics of monetary policy, the banks had recently been getting. The downturn of the economy in 1997 made this strategy more difficult for the weaker banks. Nissai, one of the long-term credit banks, was rescued by the traditional 'convoy system' in the spring: all the other major banks – the faster ships – were induced to share in a new injection of capital. The decision not to provide the same helping hand to the Hokkaido bank and to Yamaichi seems to have been induced only partly by the marginally greater size of their problems. Two other factors were involved. First, there was exasperation on the part of the regulators, and of the other banks which might have been called on to help out, with the particularly gross – and in the long run fatally costly – forms of balance-sheet dressing of which the management of those firms (but particularly Yamaichi) had been guilty. Second, having taken the decision to open up the finance industry to foreign competition – the so-called Big Bang was due to happen on 1 April 1998 – the Ministry of Finance was particularly sensitive to criticism from the foreign financial community to the effect that the hugger-mugger methods of keeping lame ducks alive, and the unwillingness to cut out dead wood with a few salutary bankruptcies, involved a lack of accounting transparency which amounted to deception of 'the markets'.

Cyclical or structural?

The 'forms of capitalism' questions in all this are: how much is this a cyclical downturn, and how much evidence of deep structural problems? Even if it is deemed to be a cyclical phenomenon, how far will the downturn itself accelerate structural changes which were in any case under way?

Let us begin by listing the major features of the Japanese form of capitalism, in order to be clear about *what* it is whose transformation is in question.

Structure of corporations

(a) Governance by senior lifetime employees appointed through a seniority-constrained promotion system of bureaucratic type.
(b) Executive decisions guided by a much stronger sense on the part of senior executives of their responsibility to fellow employees than of their (legal) responsibilities to shareholders.
(c) That stance made possible by the 'stable shareholder system', a large part of it mutual cross-holdings between companies, which prevents hostile takeovers and reduces shareholder pressure.
(d) Dividends tend, as a result, to be treated as a fixed (small) charge – nowadays, even with depressed stock-market values, not much more than a 1% yield.
(e) High, though secularly diminishing, reliance on debt finance.
(f) Employment system based on job security – at the very least an obligation on the firm to find alternative jobs for surplus employees.
(g) Neither wages nor salaries based primarily on 'rate-for-the-job' criteria. Seniority-plus-merit criteria for rank promotion, and for movement up incremental pay scales, produce age–wage curves for manual workers approaching the steepness of those for managers.
(h) Negotiations with cooperative in-house unions lead to public disclosure of those incremental scales for blue-collar workers and managerial workers up to their mid-thirties. The undisclosed scales for more senior managers are extensions of the latter, which

sets a limit to top salaries. Presidents (apart from chauffeured cars for the rest of their lives and other perks) rarely get much more than ten times average pay.

Competition

Market competition is tempered by various forms of cooperation. First, there is a strong preference for long-standing 'relational contracting' between business firms: between banks, particularly a company and its 'main bank', between suppliers and their clients, particularly sub-contractors and assemblers in manufacturing and distribution. The maintenance of such relationships, and the long-term advantages accruing from them, are accepted as precluding immediate short-term maximizing responses to market signals. One form of such 'preferred partner' trading relations are those within the *keiretsu* groups, some formed on the basis of pre-war *zaibatsu* groups, centring on major banks.

Competition between market rivals is also moderated by sectoral industry organizations which (helped also by industry federations of companies' unions) help to keep alive a sense of 'the XY industry' as a kind of quasi-community with a settled hierarchical structure (former presidents of the 'big five' or the 'big three' rotate the industry association presidency) and a wide range of common interests – promoting research, standards and quality certification, etc., but primarily dealing with government. They serve to temper market competition with obligations of good neighbourliness (as when the other steel firms took over Kobe Steel's orders after the earthquake and gave the customers back when the blast furnaces were repaired).

Role of government

Although no longer playing as important a role in indicative planning, or in the allocation of investment resources, the high-prestige bureaucracy is still generally accepted as having an important role to play as umpire between competing private interests – between consumers and producers, between refiners and distributors, between small retailers and the big chains and department stores. And also, of course, in macroeconomic management.

Macroeconomic management

This has greater room for manoeuvre than in most countries by virtue of the brake on wage inflation provided by the 'spring struggle' system of the annual wage round. Negotiations, company by company, take place after a process of 'expectations convergence' over a period of several months from the staking of initial negotiating positions by the national employers' association and the national union federation. The percentage increase established by the wage leaders becomes a 'norm of fairness' which affects wages in un-unionized firms and acts to constrain the salary increases also of chief executives and others whose salaries are individually bargained.

Income distribution

The last factor may be one reason why the dispersion of wages/salaries is more compressed than in most other advanced industrial societies. There are other 'solidaristic' egalitarian features – a high degree of progressivity in income tax, high inheritance taxes, an expensive national health service and a fairly generous level of pensions.

How much 'a system'?

There are two ways in which these features 'hold together'. The first is institutional interlock. Cross-shareholding, lack of hostile takeovers, diminished shareholder pressure for high profits and high dividends, are obviously preconditions for the costly implicit commitment not to sack redundant workers in a recession, as is the ability to bear extra short-term costs to maintain relations with supplier 'cronies' in order to maintain a reputation for fair dealing and the advantages of the supplier's future cooperation. The bureaucratic form of the remuneration system, serving to compress wage differentials, is a major factor in the relatively egalitarian income distribution and that in turn functions to maintain the sense of the 'firm as community', which helps to provide non-financial work incentives and which makes the incentives of big wage differentials less necessary. Some features are clearly peripheral – they could change without forcing too many other changes. Some are 'core' and any change would have widespread ripple effects: the cross-shareholding system, for example, if it disappeared, could have far-reaching effects on the 'employee sovereignty' which now replaces the shareholder sovereignty prescribed by law.

The other form of 'systemic cohesion' comes from what one might call 'psychological consonance'. Various parts of the system all require people to behave in similar ways – call on similar behavioural dispositions, consistently emphasizing certain values. The most important are: (i) willingness to enter binding long-term commitments, i.e., a very moderate degree of liquidity preference; (ii) greater concern for long-term stable rewards than for short-term gain; (iii) a concern for the emotional and moral quality of the social relationships involved in economic transactions, the friendships and the mutual obligations they generate, as well as their material profitability (and note that 'friendships' include firm-to-firm relations as well as person-to-person – *vide* Honda's reaction when Rover ditched their long-standing collaborative relationship in favour of BMW); (iv) a tendency to view group solidarity as an important ingredient of that emotional and moral quality – the relevant 'group' being, depending on context, one's department, one's firm, one's industry, one's nation, Japan; (v) the egalitarian perception that group solidarity becomes impossible if inequalities, either of material reward or of respect, become too wide. (The journalists' 'crony capitalism', of course, seizes on (iii) and undiscriminately equates it with the corrupt distribution of favours by dictators.)

From cyclical to structural change?

So much for Japan's version of 'Asian capitalism' (a wartime and post-war growth out of a much more 'Anglo-Saxon' pre-war system). If the story of the cyclical crisis described above is correct, what effects is it likely to have on the long-term survival of that system?

The first question is whether it is feasible to expect the economy to get back into the sort of balance which produced the high growth rates, high national confidence and general air of prosperity of the late 1980s – without the asset price bubble of those years. One – pessimistic – interpretation goes as follows. The economy was well balanced in those years, the balance being characterized by high savings, high animal spirits and high levels of investment, but low returns to capital. As the low returns indicate, a lot of the investment was wasteful; the wastefulness *ex post* was a function of low hurdle rates *ex ante*. That situation was possible in the decades before 1990 because of a secular rise in the price of assets, which only accelerated to bubble-producing proportions at the end of the 1980s. The wealth which inflated company balance-sheets and private pockets and produced that sense of prosperity was partly an accumulation of value added by productive activity, partly conjured out of thin air – and destined to vanish into the same thin air with the pricking of the bubble.

But the asset price rise was an essential lubricant of the system, and there is no prospect of it being resumed. Equities are still priced at a level much higher than earnings could justify and have further to fall. The end of population growth and of the rural exodus means also the end of real-economy pressure for a rising price of land. Capital gains will no longer substitute for dividends. The providers of capital will require higher returns; the more so because of globalization and the far greater returns available in the Anglo-Saxon economies. (One direct effect of the crisis: Merrill Lynch has acquired the better part of the defunct Yamaichi's network and is now selling American mutual funds with great vigour.) Hence an end to the central feature of the system – the tendency to give higher priority to wages and employee welfare than to rates of return on capital – is inevitable.

The counter-argument is that exchange-rate fluctuations will keep the bulk of Japanese savings at home. Many Japanese investors in dollar securities will have their fingers burned if the 60% depreciation of the yen in 1995 is reversed. This could indeed happen if, as Japan's export surplus increases and its accumulated reserves mount, with the emergence of a strong euro as an alternative safe haven, the world's seemingly unshakeable confidence in the dollar takes a knock. The essential thing is that a system characterized by high savings and high investment does produce a high rate of growth in value added. And there is no reason why that system should not give a much smaller share of that value added to capital than is usual in Britain and America, if the sources of capital do not dry up.

And why should they? They have not dried up hitherto; savings ratios have in fact increased since the ending of the bubble. The true measure of efficiency in the use of capital is not the rate of profit or the return on equity but value-added output/capital ratios and although they have been declining in Japan in recent decades, as they decline in all economies as they mature, the decline has not been catastrophic.[7]

There will, undoubtedly, be difficulties restoring a viable balance among three manifestations of long-termism, namely:

- the concern to reduce the national debt and to bequeath a solvent treasury to future generations, the concern which prompted, as it turns out prematurely, the attempt in 1997 to get public finances back into balance;
- the prudence of households which maintains, and has recently increased their propensity to save; and
- the low-hurdle-rate willingness of corporate managers to invest.

A simple set of figures suggests the magnitude of the turn-around in confidence required. At the height of the last boom, in 1990, households' net savings amounted to nearly 8% of GDP, the government saved another 3.5% and the corporate sector's net absorption of new funds took 10%. By 1995, household net savings were still some 7%, the government was a 4% dissaver and corporations absorbed only 2%. (Net transfers abroad were closer to 2% at the end of the period compared with 1% at the beginning.)[8]

A gargantuan task indeed to get back to the 1990 balance (or one based on a slightly higher level of consumer spending and a lower level of saving), but not an impossible one, and not as serious in real economy terms as the two major readjustments the economy has already made – to higher oil prices in the 1970s and to the Plaza Agreement in the 1980s. Current reporting from Japan is dominated by the news that one company after another is downgrading its forecasts because the recession has convinced them that they have got to adjust to a *permanently* lower value of their (cross-held) securities and show them on their balance sheet at their reduced market value.[9] Ten years later the unwinding of the bubble is far from over, but managers retain the flexibility to reach eventually a new equilibrium – thanks to the fact that they do not have to make the (short-term) creation of shareholder value their dominant concern.

Longer-term sources of structural change

It is astonishing, however, how few of them seem actually to realize the importance of this structural condition for their ability to run their companies in what – by their values and objectives – is an optimal way. Every Tokyo lunchtime one can find gathering of senior businessmen which features some management guru declaring that 'we must in future pay more attention to our returns on equity' (for some reason the favourite measure), while everyone else nods sagely in agreement. The following conversation took place in April 1998; the respondent was the retiring president of a major trading company:

> – the cross-shareholding system has been one of the preconditions for maintaining lifetime employment. Will it survive?
> – I don't know about a connection with lifetime employment, but cross-shareholding will wind down and I've been encouraging that.
> – Why?
> – When I meet with our foreign shareholders in London or New York or wherever, they are constantly challenging me: why do you keep all those resources locked up in investments with such derisory returns? And I find it difficult to answer them.
> – But why do you need foreign shareholders anyway?

– I think a global company should have global ownership.

Greenspan's judgement about the end of Asian capitalism is not just a prediction. Given the current mood of Japan, it is also a factor making for its own fulfilment. Nationalist resentment at hectoring instructions from Washington is one thing. Accepting that the US offers a model of economic, and even of political, efficiency is quite another. And it is *nationalism* ('In the new era of global competition the only way we can compete is by adopting global standards') which drives the urge to adopt that model – in present-day Japan as among the modernizing samurai responding to Perry's Black Ships in 1853.

In part, the dominant attraction for things American is simply a reversion to 'normality'. The bubble boom when the world seemed at Japan's feet and American scholars were writing articles on a possible future Pax Japonica was, after all, only the second brief interlude of gung-ho national self-confidence in a century and a quarter of determined 'catch-up'. (The first such interlude was in 1942 from the capture of Singapore to the battle of Midway.) One obvious indicator of this return to normality is the frequency with which the phrase 'in the advanced countries of America and Europe, reform has already advanced to the point at which ...' comes up in arguments about change in anything from pensions and corporate governance to patterns of child care. The examplars of self-reliant entrepreneurship are found in Silicon Valley; the exemplars of bold and effective risk-taking in American venture capitalists; the exemplars of effective and honest corporate governance in American corporations; of 'transparency' in financial transactions in the American stock exchange; of consumer protection in American courts. The economists with PhDs from American universities by now have a large enough share of the posts in economics departments at top-flight universities to have a major effect in disseminating their true-believer perspectives in the financial and business press. And whereas Japanese businessmen used to be sent for 'know thine enemy' purposes to get their MBAs at American business schools and came back to their firms as loyal participants in a consciously different Japanese system, nowadays more of them either go under their own steam, or desert their sponsoring firm, to come back as 'consultants' teaching how to maximize shareholder value. (Ten people in Hays Consultants' Japan office are said to rack up a billion yen a year in fees advising companies on the fashionable 'annual salary system' for managerial salaries.)

To be sure, there is a minority in whom nationalism takes a different form – resentment of American superior power and of the arrogance which is often manifest in trade negotiations and advice on economic management. Such sentiments make them unwilling to see America as a model for anything. They can and do point to the continuing strength of Japanese R&D, the shipyards with three years' order books, the competitiveness of Japan's machine-tool industry. But they are today very much in a minority.

Genuine lock-stock-and-barrel imitators are also in a minority. The majority of Japanese managers have ambivalent feelings about the United States and the American way of life. The dominant line can be summed up as follows:

> Yes, we must do something about our insider-dominated companies; we must seek greater openness and transparency; we must give shareholders a better deal, we must pay more attention to return on equity; we must adopt American management methods; we must get away from seniority and move towards greater recognition for merit; we must break cartels and create real competition; but we should keep lifetime employment for those who want it, and the seniority element in wages may never disappear as it ideally should, and we may never achieve the flexibility and mobility in the labour market which makes for the greatest efficiency and is such a source of American strength. *And* – apart from these pragmatic concessions to the weakness of the flesh enforced by institutional inertia – we would not *want*, anyway, to see in Japan the level of executive salaries produced in America by sheer greed; that is individualism carried to extremes. We must aim for much greater individualism, but of the right kind, 'self-reliant', creative, entrepreneurial, and not voracious.

There are not many people who would argue that this is trying to have one's cake and eat it. It is not part of the *joshiki*, the 'common sense' which dominates these discussions, that it is precisely the 'bureaucratic' career-employment which constitutes the core of the system. It is not, in other words, part of 'everyday popular sociology' to perceive that system, with its relatively compressed wage differentials, and its use of a seniority element in promotion and pay, and the delicate balance of incentives which that implies, as an essential precondition for the combination of cooperation and interpersonal competition which is at the heart of 'Japanese-style management'. Nor is it generally perceived that maintenance of that pattern of career management and managers' relative autonomy from shareholder control are closely interrelated. Few people who discuss the issue draw a distinction between a certain amount of tinkering (like the appointment of some outside directors, for example, not as shareholder watchdogs but as contributors of useful business experience) which may not affect the fundamentals of the system, and more core elements like a shift to market-based labour mobility and rate-for-the-job wages: 'core elements' because if the majority of employees were no longer members of an enterprise community but 'labour' hired by the managers, it would probably entail in the long run a pattern of corporate governance which makes managers really the agents of shareholders, always ready to sell out to a takeover bidder if their interests are not given priority. And vice versa: a form of corporate governance which makes for the dominance of shareholder power would end the bureaucratic career system for the bulk of employees. And by either route there is no reason to suppose that, once those other elements have gone, mere cultural antipathy towards 'individualism carried to extremes' would stop the development of the American reward differentials which the proponents of change so often decry.

The view that the Japanese corporation is an integral system, with which, apart from a few peripheral changes, one tampers at one's peril – and a system which still has considerable merits – does have a few articulate academic exponents,[10] but they get little attention in the managerial press. They are often regarded as hopelessly 'nationalistic', the bulk of the media being strong adherents of that more competitive form of nationalism: We are losing. We must pull our socks up, we must imitate the successful 'more advanced' countries.

The whole tenor of such discussions in contemporary Japan demonstrates, if demonstration were needed, the importance of what Nye (1991) calls America's 'soft' power – the power its national prestige confers on the ideas and values it supposedly exemplifies. Another demonstration in contemporary Japan is the acceptance of the claims to authority by the American rating agencies. They are seen as issuing judgements somehow carrying great moral authority as well as financial consequences, even when they are rumoured to be considering downgrading Japan as a sovereign debtor – the country with the world's largest volume of foreign exchange reserves! A detailed investigation of the 'Japan premium' imposed by the international banking community on borrowings by Japanese banks would yield interesting results. A reasonable hypothesis is that – in part stimulated by the capacity for national collective action on the part of Japanese banks – American banks also acted collectively against the Japanese banks who stole so much business from them (exploiting Japanese banks' ability to operate at low profit margins) in the late 1980s. Though many Japanese bankers take this interpretation for granted, they say so only in private. The press rarely questions the alternative hypothesis that the premium results from the rigorous assessment of risk on the part of objective rating agencies. 'A just punishment for our deficiencies.'

Another sign of the dominant consensus: proposals for the transformation of corporate governance seem simply not to be controversial. In June 1997, an amendment of the Commercial Code made the payment of executives with stock options – earlier made available only to venture start-ups – legal for all firms; a clear bid to help persuade executives that they should identify their interests with those of shareholders. A trawl through the reporting of and commentary on the move through the major business newspaper, *Nihon keizai shimbun* found only one critical comment – from a steel executive who wondered mildly whether achievements through collective cooperation of the whole firm would not be damaged if the executives alone benefited hugely therefrom.[11] In April 1998 the Liberal Democratic Party, the overwhelmingly dominant party in a governing coalition with the Socialists plus other tiny groups, published its draft for a further amendment to the Commercial Code. It is concerned primarily with strengthening companies' Audit Committees; a 'greater transparency' move which also serves – and this is said to be a major intention – to dilute the threat to executives of being sued by shareholders for mismanagement. Content apart, the draft begins with a resounding declaration: 'The fundamental principle is shareholder sovereignty. The purpose of the company is to maximise the profits of the shareholders.' The draft got a short paragraph on an inside page of the same newspaper,[12] with no mention of that 'fanfare clause' and no suggestion that the proposed law could ever be a source of controversy.

Even longer-term sources of structural change

The power of the American model to invoke powerful demands for change in Japanese media discussion is today unquestionable, even if a collapse on Wall Street, a fall in the dollar, and a Japanese recovery could greatly reduce that power. The power of the admired model actually to *procure* change which goes against powerfully entrenched interest is, however, a different matter. If, for example, one examines the actual effect of some of the new managerial salary schemes of the kind introduced so expensively with the aid of Hays Consultants, it appears that the 'salary spread' – i.e., the difference between the top salary of a high-flying manager and the bottom salary of the most plodding of his age-and-seniority contemporaries – has hardly changed (a little above 20% over, and a little less than 20% below, the median).[13] The spread is in effect determined by current perceptions of fairness, and those perceptions do not radically change overnight.

So one has to look also for those factors which might change those current perceptions of fairness and the constellation of interests which sustain them. Four possibly long-term and accelerating trends of change come to mind. They can be only briefly sketched here. They are: (i) populist rejection of bureaucratic leadership; (ii) a consequent increase in competition in the non-tradeables sector; (iii) changes in the social selection/social mobility patterns determined by the school system and its ability-sorting mechanisms; and (iv) changes in the balance of party power and, relatedly, in the pattern of enterprise union leadership.

The bureaucracy

Japan has been living with bureaucratic arrogance for quite a while, and has even learned to accept it as the price of having a public-spirited, intellectually able and relatively honest administration. But the tolerance threshold has risen in recent years, particularly after one or two spectacular revelations of personal corruption on the part of senior officials. The central focus of this resentment since 1992 has been the hitherto unassailable Ministry of Finance (MOF), supposedly the *crème de la crème*. The revelation of the extent to which some senior officials were accepting treats from the people they were supposed to be regulating – shopping trips to Hong Kong, for instance – was the first shock which coincided with the unexpectedly contested nature of a plan to use public money to clean up (partly rescue, partly dissolve) the post-bubble mess in the mortgage loan credit agencies. (Contested because of the public nature of the battle between banks and agricultural credit cooperatives over who should bear the blame; the Ministry of Finance had failed in what had hitherto been one of its essential skills – getting the consent of all parties before going public.) The public prosecutors, having got the bit between their teeth, produced a succession of cases in 1998, all relating to accepting scandalous amounts of hospitality, a few combined with clear evidence of resultant lax regulation or blatant favours.

So far there seems not to have been much of an effect on the ability of the top ministries to recruit the best and brightest; and there are enough clear-conscience officials to keep morale reasonably high. The MOF was still able, in the spring of 1998 at the height of the scandals, to operate a capital-infusion scheme for the banks in which not only the endangered banks, but all the others, including the healthiest, agreed to take part in order that the banks which really needed the money should not be singled out. However, a prolongation of the kind of front-page media attention the MOF was getting in March and April 1998 could well have long-term effects – on, for instance, its ability to detect and deter bank scandals, and to organize collective action of the kind just illustrated.

Competition

What is already clear is that attacks on the bureaucracy have been a powerful element in furthering the deregulation drive, promoted by the press and politicians as a means of (i) shifting policy from a heavy bias in favour of the producer towards more solicitous concern for the consumer; and (ii) reducing the costs of the protected, cartelized non-tradeables sector whose excessive prices damage the competitiveness of the 'national champion' exporting firms facing tough competition in world markets. Bureaucratic interference bad; the market principle and free competition good: it is a bold person who challenges that equation in today's Japan, and public interest/public goods arguments in favour of retaining regulations are all too easily dismissed as simply an attempt by bureaucrats to retain the sources of their power.

The effects of greater competition in petrol retailing (for the first time self-service stations have been allowed), in transport, in energy supply, in construction, will be various. Even the most optimistic forecasts suggest a large increase in unemployment before the benefits to consumers of cheaper prices create more new jobs. If, as elsewhere, consumers choose to use the surplus thus generated on imports or the products of automated factories and the unemployment becomes endemic, that could well have knock-on effects on the normative force of the still-valid lifetime employment guarantee.

There will be other, less easily calculable, effects via the 'psychological consonance' mechanism described earlier. If 'convoy systems' disappear over whole sections of economic activity, if more and more people are forced to forget about any obligations to 'the industry' or to their competitors in order to survive the competition; if, in other words, acts of self-regarding individualism or my-firm-first-ism quantitatively increase, so such behaviour will tend to become the norm.

Social selection and egalitarianism

Only now is a generation of businessmen with only schoolboy memories of the immediate post-Second World War decade taking over control. Their predecessors, the men who are now retiring from the presidency to the chairmanship, or more likely from the chairmanship to the 'advisorship' role in their companies, are men who have vivid memories of the days of reconstruction just after the war, when they were working to rebuild their factories and their business networks, shoulder to shoulder with skilled craftsmen and labourers, with equally big holes in their socks, and an equal concern with how to get hold of some black-market rice. Indeed some of them, their pre-war academic Marxism turning to practical crusading, briefly interrupted their successful managerial career to became leaders of the white-collar unions who led the moves to amalgamate with the blue-collar unions.

The vast majority of them did not come from especially well-heeled families. They spent their first six years of schooling in the local primary school, and may still attend their class reunions in company with those who became carpenters, greengrocers and welders. If it is common background, instinctive fellow-feeling and shared hardship that makes for social solidarity and a sense of benevolent responsibility among those who rise to the top, then they have it. The compressed wage differentials and the other egalitarian elements of the Japanese system owe a great deal to those underlying sentiments, and not just to the Confucian, or rather Mencian, prescriptions about the duties of benevolence in which those sentiments are sometimes expressed.

But younger generations (who do not read Mencius, and may have no idea of the Confucian origin of some of the proverbs they use) are of a different sensibility. They have been brought up in affluence. Their smooth career paths have given them no such background of shared experience with those on the receiving end of their orders. For the last 20 years an increasing proportion of them have been siphoned off at the age of 11 into the élite private secondary schools and have no more contact with their less well-off countrymen than an Etonian has with his. Social mobility appears to be declining; an increasing proportion of the graduates of the top universities (who owe their places there not at all to personal influence but to their performance in a genuinely competitive national test) are the children of graduates of similar universities. And it is they who become the people in the top ministries who draft reports on the 21st-century future of Japan's corporations, or the university economists who sit on the ministries' working groups, or members of the businessmen's forum who declare that hitherto there has been too much concern about equality of outcomes when it is equality of opportunity that is important.

Power distribution

The egalitarian characteristics of the Japanese system – the compressed reward differentials, the strong redistributive element in the welfare system and the health service, the emphasis on universal schooling – have all rested, not only on the benevolent sentiments of the élite, but also on the power to make trouble possessed by union and opposition parties. At a recent symposium on governments and markets, the point was made that Japanese industrial policy had not been solely growth policy, but also distribution policy with an egalitarian bias. The civil service head of MITI agreed. Hitherto, he said, with a Socialist Party able to get something like a third of the votes, a system of 'proportionate consensus' had developed. The Socialist Party was able to get 80% of what it wanted by negotiated compromise. Now, with the Socialist Party practically disintegrated, it was difficult to predict what would happen (particularly after the rump of the party ceased to be a member of the government coalition).

As for the unions, the steady decline in strike activity tells its own story about the ability of unions to make trouble for managers who might choose to take firms in an Anglo-Saxon, 'shareholder sovereignty' direction complete with downsizing, fabulous stock options and all the rest. What it does not tell, however, is exactly why and how. A full account would have to include:

(1) The driving force of earlier militancy. The leaders of the spring struggle, from the formation of the system in the mid-1950s to the mid-1970s, worked with a straightforward Marxist model of capitalism as a system in which capitalists extract surplus value from workers. Yearly wage negotiations were about wresting as much as possible of that surplus back. However, especially when the oil shock produced a national sense of crisis, the perception grew that capitalists were not getting much out of the system, and that the managers with whom they negotiated were as much concerned with workers' welfare as with that of their shareholders. (One can still get a laugh of embarrassed recognition from telling a Japanese audience that the difference between a Japanese firm and an American firm is epitomized in the outcome of wage negotiations. An American manager who manages to

screw down wages is likely to get a bigger bonus; a Japanese manager who does the same knows that the lower salary increase will probably apply across the board – including his/her own pay packet.)

That reality perception gradually took the fire out of the belly of union organizers as it reduced their capacity to inspire indignation against the bosses in their members. What that perception has not done, however, is to create a new and adequate rationale for the unions' existence. They clearly have one. They still can perform, and often do perform, a very real function as watchdogs of the managers' concern for the interests of their workforce, able to block or delay decisions taken without due consideration of their effects on the work and non-work lives of the lower ranks of the hierarchy. But they are still frozen in the rhetoric of the earlier era. Wage negotiations are still described by union leaders in the now-empty terms of 'struggle', 'victory' and 'defect'. And that is one reason why neither the industrial nor the national federations seem at all disposed to see the present structure of the typical corporation as something that operates to the workers' benefit, nor to react to the effort to restore 'shareholder sovereignty' as a threat.

(2) The other reason lies in the change in union leadership. The post-war generation included a large number of highly able shop-floor workers who had left school at 14. With the rapid and nationwide expansion of higher education, men and women of comparable ability levels were, by the 1960s, almost without fail entering the labour market as graduates from 'good' universities. In the 1960s some of these with a history of student activism became union leaders and injected new blood into traditional militancy. (The closed-ship enterprise union 'encompasses' graduate future managers until they reach positions of line responsibility—usually in their early-to-mid-thirties.) More recently, however, a position in an enterprise union has come to be seen, rather, as a mean of demonstrating the leadership qualities which get a manager early promotion. A bright young person might even find the personnel manager enquiring over a drink, 'Have you ever thought of standing in the union elections?' It will not be held against them that they might take a tough line in wage negotiations or in defence of members who have been unfairly treated—provided the consensus within the firm is that the line they take is 'reasonable'.

And, of course, what they and the managerial consensus deem reasonable is highly coloured by their prospective career track. The major union federation, Rengo, is on record as supporting many of the reformers' plans for a revamping of the Japanese employment system: for example, drastic modification of the seniority system to give more rapid promotion to the most able. That is why business federations are frequently heard to praise Rengo for its 'realism'.

(3) So where else might one look for an organized defence of the Japanese model? There remains a party of protest – The Japan Communist Party (JCP) – which can be sure of at least 10% of the vote in a general election and in a recent governorship contest scored almost as much as the main conservative opposition party. It, too, has an affiliated union federation, which is still very much wedded to traditional Marxist militancy, but almost wholly confined to the public sector where the capitalists against whom its literature rages are not very much in evidence.

It was characteristic of the JCP's position as an 'anti-system party', that through all the endless shuffling which produced the most improbable succession of coalition alignments in the first half of the 1990s there was never any suggestion that the JCP might become a member of a governing coalition. But that may change. The party's media prominence has certainly changed. The party political debates on the main national TV channel now regularly include a JCP spokesperson, who is usually able to run rings around the poor unhappy socialist appearing as a member of the governing coalition and defender of government policy.

The party's relevance to attempts to preserve a characteristically Japanese form of capitalism is, however, in doubt. It is still dedicated to the battle against capitalism in general and the local manifestation thereof in particular. In spite of the fact that it has recently published an analysis of the Japanese economy[14] which makes graphic and telling use of national income statistics to show the different 'reproduction cycles' of the UK, the US, the Swedish and the Japanese economies, and the resultant 'who gets what', there is no disposition to draw from these calculations the conclusion that Japan might have a more benign form of capitalism which the JCP might make its business to defend. Among its academic sympathizers, in fact, there is rather a disposition to welcome the reassertion of shareholder rights. Facts are easier to deal with when they conform to your theory.

Eventually, one would guess, generation change within the party and the need to win elections will put the JCP through the same sort of transition as its Italian counterpart began 20 years ago. But there are few signs of it yet. And whether, when it does so, it will transform itself into a defender of 'employee sovereignty' and the egalitarianism of the

Japanese model remains to be seen – as it remains to be seen whether, by then, there is any longer a 'Japanese model' to be defended.

Conclusion

The 'Japanese model' may well not preserve its distinctiveness in the general picture of global capitalism for many more decades. Those factors mentioned earlier as giving the system its coherence can also be mobilized for its dismantling. The high degree of 'institutional interlock' means that (as we suggested earlier *à propos* the relation between the bureaucratic employment structure and corporate governance) change in one institutional form has repercussions for many others. 'Psychological consonance' can work both ways. As people are seduced into bottom-line-oriented behaviour as savers, or as managers of their companies, so it becomes easier for them to adopt behaviour patterns based on similar values as employees.

However, if and when change comes, it will have very little to do with the current problems of Japanese banks or with the current economic downturn, much less with the panic crises which have afflicted four Asian economies. It will result partly from the long-term pressures stemming from global financial markets, partly from the worldwide effects of American cultural hegemony, and partly from the working through of profound social structural changes stemming from the society's arrival at the age of affluence.

Notes

* Much of the argument of this paper also appears in Dore (2000).

1. *International Herald Tribune*, Tokyo edition, 19 January 1998.
2. *The Economist*, 7 March 1998, Survey, p. 5.
3. See Wade (1998), quoting Mathews (1998).
4. There is disagreement about this. One journalist claims, somewhat implausibly, that the much publicized press conference by Ohga, the Sony President, at which he claimed that the Japanese economy was on the brink of disaster, was contrived by the activist faction within the government in order to increase *gaiatsu* on Japan at the London Asia–Europe summit and *therefore* make action more likely (Joanna Pitman, 'Letter from Japan', *Prospect*, May 1998).
5. For these and subsequent magnitude figures I am indebted to Fukukawa (1998).
6. Chihaya Noburi, interviewed in *Nihon keizai shimbun*, 14 January 1998. Perhaps he had good grounds for his confidence. In May his company and Posco announced plans for an equity swap (*Financial Times*, 20 May 1998).

7. A Japan Development Bank (JDB) calculation shows a trend decline of capital productivity in manufacturing (gross value added divided by the average of year-beginning and year-end fixed capital assets) from peak to peak of the business cycles from 148% in 1967 to 115% in 1988, with the corresponding figures for value added net of depreciation running in parallel from 126% to 98%. (The trend did slightly reverse from 1973 to the 1979 peak, from about 136% to 139%.) Intersectoral differences were marked, however, with the raw material industries showing no clear trends around the 80% mark and the 'transforming and assembling' industries climbing with every boom from 94% in 1965 to 160% in 1979 and then falling consistently to 110% in 1991 (where the series stops: these last figures all for gross value added. Nihon Kaihatsu Ginko, *Chosa: Dai-173-go: Seizogyo ni okeru shihon-shueki kozo*, May 1993, p. 23). A similar calculation in the 1994 Economic White Paper shows that the decline in capital productivity was accelerating in the 1987–91 upturn (the marginal productivity of capital – calculated without time lags, i.e., year *t*'s capital increase over year *t*'s added value increase – rose only by 3%, compared with 15% and 5% in the two previous cycles). However, the decline in overall ROA is more to be explained by declining profit margins on sales (partly associated with a rise in the labour share, for which see the JDB analysis, p. 25) than with a decline in capital productivity. The report blames 'soft-headed (*amai*) investment decisions'. The report, however (an indication of the way American business school economics has colonized the Economic Planning Agency?), considers only total assets and makes no attempt to calculate separately the productivity of fixed and financial assets, nor to separate decision-making on plant investment from that on financial investment (and this *à propos* of the period when *zaitekku* – financial technology': using spare cash for speculative short-term investment – was all the buzz). The report also takes the 'stick to your knitting' doctrine as so axiomatic that it treats the number of subsidiaries thrown off by major firms as an index of diversification leading to poor investment (*Keizai Hakusho*, June 1994).
8. Keizai Kikakucho (Economic Planning Agency), *Keizai yoran*, 1997, p. 64.
9. See, e.g., *Financial Times*, 13 May 1998.
10. Two notable recent ones are Miyamoto (1997) and Yambe (1997).
11. *Nihon keizai shimbun*, 17 July 1997.
12. *Nihon keizai shimbun*, 17 April 1998.
13. See, e.g., Kamiyama, 1995.
14. Nihon Kyosanto Keizai seisaku iinkai, *Nihon keizai e no teigen* (Proposals for the management of the Japanese economy), Tokyo, Shin Nihon Shuppansha, 1994 (9th printing, 1998).

References

Dore, R. (2000) *Shareholder Capitalism; Welfare Capitalisms: Japan and Germany versus the Anglo-Saxons*, Oxford, OUP.

Fukukawa, S. (1998) 'Asian Dynamism: Sustainable or Not?' Paper for 2000 Group Meeting, RIIA March.

Kamiyama, N. (1995) 'Nempo-sei donyu to nihongata koyo-kanko' (The introduction of the annual salary system and Japanese employment practices), Paper for the 1995 meeting of the Japan Industrial Relations Association (Roshi-kankei kenkyukaigi).
Mathews, J. (1998) 'Fashioning a new Korean model out of the crisis', Japan Policy Institute Paper 46, Cardiff, CA, May.
Miyamoto, M. (1997) *Nihongata shisutemu no shinso* (The deep structure of the Japanese model), Tokyo, Toyo Keizai.
Nye, Jr., J. S. (1991) *Bound to Lead: The Changing Nature of American Power*, New York, Basic Books.
Pitman, J. (1998) Letter from Japan, *Prospect*, May.
Wade, R. (1998) 'The Asian Crisis and Capitalist Triumphalism', April, mimeo.
Yambe, Y. (1997) *Itsuwari no kiki: hommono no kiki* (False crisis and true crisis), Tokyo, Toyo Keizai.

14
The Economic Impact of the Asian Crisis on India and China

A. S. Bhalla and D. M. Nachane

Introduction

Ever since the outbreak of the South-east Asian financial crisis, speculation has been rife about the likelihood of the 'contagion' spreading, and the extent of its possible spread. Policy-makers in different countries have also been preoccupied with examining what measures could be taken to forestall a similar fate befalling their respective economies. This chapter addresses these issues with respect to the two Asian giants, India and China. The two countries share certain common features such as size and geographical proximity to the crisis region, but differ widely in other respects. Apart from the well-known differences in their political systems and the role of markets, at least two other divergent features stand out. Firstly, attitudes to foreign investment in the recent past have differed sharply. Whereas India has been extremely cautious about foreign direct investment (FDI) but relatively open to foreign portfolio investment (FPI), the opposite seems to have been the case in China. Secondly, the Indian banking and financial system has evolved to a stage of maturity and sophistication that does not seem evident in China.

The aim of this chapter is to assess the vulnerability of these two countries to the Crisis. It is now generally agreed that the South-east Asian collapse was the logical culmination of an inappropriate financial liberalization strategy, with volatile capital flows acting as a triggering factor (see Radelet and Sachs, 1998). Thus a careful scrutiny of the domestic financial system and the international capital account in both countries is a first step in our analysis. But there is also the possibility of a transmission of the Crisis (from South-east Asia to either India or China) via the following two channels: (i) the direct and indirect impact on exports due to the Crisis, and (ii) the impact on the inflows of FDI and FPI. Finally, it is necessary to consider the possibility that contractionary domestic policies initiated in response to the Crisis, if not carefully designed, might bring about the very consequences that they were intended to avert.

There are a number of differences between the impacts on India and China, although in both cases the impact to date has been limited. While the Indian currency has declined appreciably, the Chinese yuan remains robust and has actually appreciated somewhat, thanks to massive inflows of capital and a large trade surplus in world markets. Despite cheapened exports following devaluation in the affected economies, China remains more export competitive than India and has introduced measures to expand exports into new sectors and destinations. China may have benefited from its 1994 devaluation of the yuan, making it relatively more competitive then than the South-east Asian economies. But the adverse effect on the latter's exports must have been much weaker than is often claimed, considering that the market exchange rate at which the bulk of Chinese exports were already being traded did not change (*The Economist*, 13 December 1997). The Crisis has also provoked a different response to liberalization from each country. The Chinese government decided to accelerate reform of the financial sector, banking industry and state enterprises, whereas in India, where financial sector reforms were undertaken during 1992–6, a certain deceleration of pace has set in. The two countries, however, have shown a common response in one aspect, namely, attempts to stimulate domestic demands through expenditure on infrastructure.

The plan of this chapter is as follows. Section 1 is devoted to an assessment of the vulnerability indicators in the two countries in respect of the domestic financial system and the international capital account. Section 2 discusses trade impacts, while Section 3 focuses on the impact of the crisis on capital flows. The effect of domestic contractionary measures is discussed in Section 4 and the future of economic reforms in Section 5. Finally, conclusions are drawn in Section 6.

Vulnerability indicators

In both India and China, growth slowed down in the wake of the Crisis (see Table 14.1). The Indian economy, which had achieved unusually high rates of growth (by past Indian standards) of around 7% during 1994–7, suffered a sharp reversal in 1997–8 when growth is

Table 14.1 Selected macroeconomic indicators for India and China

India	*1994–5*	*1995–6*	*1996–7*	*1997–8*	*1998–9*	*1999–2000*
Real GDP growth (%)	7.0	7.3	7.5	5.0	6.8	5.9
Export growth (US $ bn) (%)	26.9	17.5	5.6	4.5	–3.9	7.8*
Inflation (%) (consumer prices)	10.2	10.2	9.0	3.7	13.1	3.4
Government budget balance (% of GDP)	–6.0	–6.0	–5.2	–6.1	–6.4	n.a
Gross investment–GDP ratio (%)	26.9	27.1	27.3	n.a	25.1	n.a
FOREX reserves (US $ bn)	19.69	17.92	25.7	29.4	32.5	38.0
Total external debt (US$ bn)	101.95	92.98	93.43	94.40	97.7	98.4
External debt/GDP ratio	32.3	28.3	26.2	24.4	23.5	22.0
External debt service ratio (% of exports)	26.2	24.3	21.2	19.5	18.0	16.0
External debt service (% of GDP)	2.16	2.38	2.57	2.5	2.6	n.a
Short-term external debt (% of total external debt)	3.9	4.3	5.4	7.2	5.4	4.5
China	1994	1995	1996	1997	1998	1999
Real GDP growth (%)	12.6	10.5	9.7	8.8	7.8	7.1
Export growth (%)	11.5[a]	15.8[b]	1.5	2.1	0.5	6.0
Inflation (%) (consumer prices)	24.1	17.1	8.3	2.8	–0.8	–1.4
Government budget balance (% of GDP)	–1.2	–1.0	–0.8	–0.8	–1.2	–2.1
Forex reserves (US $ billion)	51.6	73.6	105.0	140.0	144.9	154.7
Total external debt (US$ billion)	n.a.	n.a.	150.5	161.8	175.1	
External debt/GDP ratio (%)	18.0	17.2	17.0	17.0	17.0	
External debt service (% of exports)	n.a.	9.9	n.a.	n.a.	n.a.	
External debt service (% of GDP)	n.a.	n.a.	n.a.	3.6	n.a.	
Short-term external debt (% of total external debt)	n.a.	n.a.	23.4	25.8	27.6	

* *April to September.*
[a] 1980–90.
[b] 1990–97.
Sources: IMF (1998); World Bank, *World Development Report 1998*; RBI, *Annual Reports and Handbook of Statistics on Indian Economy 2000*; Government of India, *Economic Surveys 1999–2000*, Goldman Sachs (Hong Kong); *China Stastical Yearbook 2000*.

estimated to have slipped to 5.1%. China's GDP growth is reported to have slowed from nearly 9% in 1997 to lower than the targeted 7% in the first six months of 1998. However, the sharp pick-up in exports experienced since July 1998 has led the Chinese State Statistical Bureau (SSB) to believe that the official target may actually be exceeded by 1% (*China Daily*, 10 October 1998).

In India, even though fiscal profligacy seems to have reasserted itself (the gross fiscal deficit in 1997–8 being placed at 6.1% of GDP), care seems to have been exercised to prevent a repetition of the 1991 scenario, when the fiscal deficit spilled over into a current account deficit via external commercial borrowings. The ratio of the current account deficit to GDP remains at a modest level of 1.7% (*Reserve Bank of India Annual Report* 1997–8). The situation in China is broadly similar, with the current account deficit of 3% of GDP in 1993, turning into a small surplus in 1997–8, thanks to massive FDI inflows and foreign exchange reserves (currently estimated at $140 billion).

In India, the external liabilities of banks at 2.8% of GDP in 1996–7 were of a magnitude comparable to the domestic liabilities at 3.6% of GDP. Thus bank borrowing abroad, while well below the South-east Asian levels, are not insignificant. At $10.1 billion, these external borrowings now constitute 37.2% of the FOREX reserves (as of June 1998). We do not have a breakdown of the external liabilities by state-owned banks and private banks, but it is likely that the former would account for nearly 85% of the total. The foreign liabilities of state-owned banks have a strong element of sovereign guarantee (since a government will rarely allow a state-owned bank to fail). In China, also, commercial borrowing (bank loans and bonds) represents the bulk (over 69%) of all foreign debt (*Beijing Review*, 29 December–4 January 1998).

The external liabilities of the Indian non-bank private sector are much higher, at 8.5% of GDP; the bulk of this would be from finance companies, which were finding it increasingly attractive to source funds from abroad. The external liabilities of finance companies are technically not guaranteed sovereign debt. Nevertheless, given that the financial health of banks is intimately connected to that of finance companies, widespread failures among the latter can and do affect bank portfolios adversely.

In China, also, parallel to state banks, non-bank finance institutions such as rural and urban credit cooperatives and trust and investment companies (TICs) have grown, but not as rapidly as in India. Financing by rural cooperatives at the local level has continued to suffer from abuses (diversion of agricultural procurement funds and speculative investment of rural deposits in the coastal areas) (Holmes, 1997). These non-banking institutions have not been functioning well and most TICs are known to suffer from 'triangular debt' (involving state-owned enterprises whose debt is shifted to third-party creditors who in turn are also financed by the Chinese government) which implicates state banks and various government agencies and disrupts normal institutional credit. The operations of these institutions are overgrown and they are unlikely to survive without speculative investments.

Indeed, in June 1998 China closed a powerful trust company, Venturetech Corporation, and in October 1998, Guangdong International Trust and Investment Corporation, after it went into bankruptcy, leaving an estimated $2 billion of foreign debt. Earlier, in June 1998, the collapse and closure of Hainan Development Bank after only three years of existence was also explained largely by the merger with it of 33 powerful but defaulting credit unions (*Far Eastern Economic Review*, 16 July 1998). These failures raise risk premia for fund-raising by other state-owned companies and their subsidiaries listed in Hong Kong (so-called 'red chips'). Other symptoms of financial crisis include: a high ratio of non-performing loans to total loans (about 20% to 30%), low equity-to-asset ratios, ineffective supervision of the banking industry, and a high ratio of short-term debt to total reserves. Heavy lending to state-owned enterprises, property lending and bad loans are features China has in common with the affected South-east Asian economies. There is also a lack of national legal standards of security and bankruptcy legislation.

Trade impacts

The direct impact of the Crisis on India's exports is likely to be limited since the six Crisis economies including Hong Kong account for between 10% to 15% of India's total exports. Nearly half of this figure is attributable to Hong Kong, which has been relatively moderately affected by the Crisis. India exports mainly to the industrial countries, with the US and Japan being its two top trading partners. In contrast, China's trade with the other Asian economies (including Japan) is significant and is much higher than that of India. Continued slow growth and recession in these economies has led to a decline in China's export growth, from nearly 26% in July 1997 to 3.4% in June 1998 (HKTDC, 1998). However, while Chinese exports to Korea and Japan fell by 30.3% and 4.3% respectively during the first seven months of 1998, its exports to Australia, Russia, the European Union and the US continued to grow appreciably (by 20.2%, 39.2%, 25.6% and 18.2% respectively). However, export growth slowed in 1997 and became negative in 1998 and 1999 (see Table 14.1).

If we take the sectoral composition, exports of resource-based primary products were particularly hard hit. For example, in the first five months of 1998, exports of mineral fuel dropped by 32%, iron and steel by 25% and cotton by 17%. While growth of manufactured exports also declined, it was less affected. Exports of such goods as garments, toys, footwear and electrical machinery continued to grow in the first half of 1998, particularly to the European Union and the United States (HKTDC, 1998). This suggests that China's exports remain price competitive despite the depreciation and realignment of Asian currencies.

In response to the possible negative impact of the Crisis, the Chinese government has introduced a series of special measures to maintain and expand exports: promotion of the export of high value-added high-tech goods; simplification of the export tax-refund system; raising export tax credits for textiles, machinery and electronics; the increase in June 1998 in the export tax rebate on coal, steel, cement and shipping; permission to private firms to export and import directly (from 1 January 1999) without having to go through the state-owned foreign trade companies; relaxation of export licences on some commodities; exploration of new markets in Africa, Latin America and the Commonwealth of Independent States; and diversification of the commodity composition of exports (*Beijing Review*, 30 March–5 April 1998; *Business Week*, 1 June 1998). China has not considered devaluation as an option for expanding exports. A devaluation of the yuan would be likely to result in competitive devaluations by the neighbouring economies, thus prolonging the Asian Crisis. It would also erode the international support and goodwill that China has built up by not devaluing (*Crédit Suisse*, 1998).[1]

In addition, responses to the Crisis by the South-east Asian economies are unlikely, at least in the short run, to drive Indian and Chinese goods out of export markets, for three reasons: (i) the tight monetary policies and restructuring of the financial systems of the affected Asian economies, which have hurt their exports; (ii) the import-intensive nature of exports from the Crisis-ridden economies (currency depreciation then cuts both ways); and (iii) the difficulties faced by exporters in the Crisis economies, not only in securing letters of credit through local banks, but also in securing containers to ship their exports.

The impact on capital flows

The impact of the Crisis on capital inflows has been rather mixed. In India, liberalization in 1991 led to a steady inflow of foreign investment, although such inflows were quite modest compared with those to China and the East and South-east Asian countries (see Table 14.2). Following the steep downward movements in the Indian stock markets in the second half of 1996, FPI flows dropped sharply in 1997–8, registering net outflows in 1998–9. Provisional estimates for FDI flows for 1998–9 also show considerable slackening. In the wake of the Crisis, too, FDI into India from the South-east Asian economies themselves declined, but as this constituted a meagre 6.5% of total FDI into India, the damage was not excessive.[2] Portfolio investment constituted a significant proportion of total external financing in the case of India.

In China, the situation with respect to composition of capital inflows is the reverse: portfolio investment is insignificant whereas FDI forms the bulk of inflows. FDI inflows into China remained high around the time of the Crisis, and the level attained in 1997 was much higher than in 1996, according to official statistics (see Table 14.2). However, in the first half of 1998 actual FDI fell by 1.3%, although contract foreign investment grew by 5.5% (*International Herald Tribune*, 18–19 July 1998). Besides Japan, Chinese investors from Hong Kong, Malaysia, Singapore and Taiwan were the major sources of FDI in China prior to the Crisis, accounting for 80% of FDI (see Bhalla, 1998). Hong Kong's share shrank from 55–60% in 1996 to 46% in 1997 and 48% in the first quarter of 1998. However, according to Professor Wang Zhenzheng, Deputy Director of the Institute of CASS (Beijing), FDI from Taiwan has actually increased (personal interview, October 1998).

Factors other than the Crisis also explain the slowdown in FDI inflows into China: the elimination of preferential treatment for foreign enterprises in the second quarter of 1996; and greater selectivity in accepting foreign projects, with emphasis on quality rather than quantity. From 1 January 1998, preference was given to FDI projects in agriculture, environmental protection, new technology and projects in the non-coastal provinces (World Bank, 1998b).

China made special efforts to restore foreign investors' confidence by offering them preferences. Thus, from 1 January 1999, foreign investors received the same tax rebate for exports as did local businesses; in Fujian, Jiangsu and Zhejiang, powers have been delegated to city officials and trade and development zones to approve certain

Table 14.2 Foreign inflows: India and China (US$ billion)

India	*1990–1*	*1993–4*	*1994–5*	*1995–6*	*1996–7*	*1997–8*	*1998–9*
Foreign direct investment (official estimates)	0.10	0.60	1.30	2.14	2.82	3.55	2.46
IMF/UNCTAD estimates	n.a	n.a	0.97	2.1	2.42	3.6	2.6
Foreign portfolio investment	0.09	3.60	3.58	2.74	3.30	1.83	–0.06
External assistance	2.2	1.9	1.52	1.01	1.12	0.9	1.13
External commercial borrowings	2.25	0.61	1.02	1.37	2.82	3.87	4.11
Non-resident deposits	1.54	1.2	0.17	1.15	3.35	1.15	1.78
Total inflows	7.18	9.69	9.16	4.68	11.29	10.98	n.a
Proportion of non-debt creating flows to debt creating flows (%)	1.7	223.5	224.3	179.28	78.57	97.17	n.a
Foreign direct investment as percentage of gross capital formation	0.3	1.7	1.4	2.4	2.6	3.8	2.9

China	*1990*	*1994*	*1995*	*1996*	*1997*	*1998*
Foreign direct investment						
UNCTAD estimates	4.4*	33.8	35.8	40.8	45.3	n.a.
IMF estimates	3.5	33.8	35.8	40.2	44.2	n.a.
Official estimates	3.5	33.8	37.5	41.7	52.4	34.0
FDI as % of gross fixed capital formation	3.3*	17.3	14.7	14.3	14.6	12.9
FDI as % of GDP	n.a.	7.0	6.3	5.8	5.6	n.a.
Foreign portfolio investment	0.6	3.9	0.7	2.4	7.8	0.09
External borrowing	6.5	9.3	10.3	12.7	12.0	n.a.

* 1991.

Sources: UNCTAD (1997, 1998); World Bank, *World Development Report (1998; 2000–2001)*; IMF, *International Financial Statistics and Balance of Payments Statistics; China Statistical Yearbook (1997; 2000)*; RBI, *Annual Report 1997–98; RBI Bulletin*, September 1999.

projects of up to $30 million; in Shanghai, procedures have been simplified for foreign investors registering and seeking approval of licences to run trading companies in the Waigaoqiao Free Trade Zone. Purchase by foreign investors of state-owned companies is also being encouraged, except in such strategic industries as telecommunications and banking.[3]

Portfolio capital flows to China tend to be limited, partly because of the limited size of an incipient stock market (which has, however, been growing very rapidly). Indirect investments in China's capital market via the Hong Kong stock market have been rising rapidly. The ratio of capitalization to GDP rose from 0.5% in 1991 to 14% in 1996, whereas for India these ratios were 12.9% in 1990 and 35.1% in 1996. In China, domestic companies listed on the stock market increased dramatically from a very small number in 1990, while the increase in the number of listed companies in India has been less dramatic. The future functioning of the stock markets is likely to be affected by the precise nature of the reform of local and central state enterprises. In China, securities firms are expected to be unlinked from state banks, and the government plans to allow mergers and acquisitions (M&A) of these firms. A beginning has been made by including M&A in the activities of the China International Capital Corporation, a new Chinese foreign investment bank. However, there is still an absence of clear guidleines on M&A of enterprises.

In India, the medium and long-term impacts of the crisis on FPI are far more difficult to assess. India might benefit from a substitution effect if global investors were to switch their portfolios away from the Asian economies into other emerging economies. The crucial imponderable here is stock market volatility. Examining the share prices in dollars from December 1997 to June 1998, Indian stock indices lost out to several other clear winners among the emerging markets (for example, China, Greece and Portugal). There is of course, a vicious circle here – FPI will not be forthcoming unless stock markets revive, but such a revival itself depends (to some degree) on the sustained inflow of FPI. With a view to reviving the flagging stock markets and encouraging FPI, takeovers were introduced by the Indian government in 1996, but it was widely felt that they did not go far enough to allow full-scale market-driven M&As, which is what foreign investors are really looking for. Much dissatisfaction was created by a clause which stipulated that those acquiring over 10% of a company's shares must make a public offer of another 20%, and in October 1998 the threshold was raised to 15%. Another source of difficulty was that company directors could ward off predators by issuing cheap shares to large shareholders via preferential allotments. Takeovers by foreign companies still face several obstacles.

As far as FDI is concerned, the crucial factor is the perceived official attitude to foreign investment. The Dabhol fiasco[4] drove home the strong message to foreign investors that India was a market where formal contracts made with state governments might not be honoured. Recent signals from the Indian coalition government similarly offer little encouragement to foreign investors. The 1998–9 Budget was widely interpreted abroad as a roll-back of the liberalization process. No explicit measures to attract FDI were announced except an assurance that the approval process would be speeded up. FDI will probably continue at its current modest level, if not fall off altogether to its pre-1991 trickle. But if this happens, it will be due to the Indian government's policies rather than to the Crisis. Foreign investor dissatisfaction with recent Indian policies is reflected in the international credit agency, Moodys, pushing India into the speculative grade category by lowering its rating by two notches to Ba2 in June 1998; similarly Standard & Poor lowered India's sovereign rating from BB+ to BB in October 1998.

China has traditionally given more credible signals to foreign investors than has India, where official ambivalence continues owing partly to a weak coalition government and political instability. Recent deals with Kodak and Citibank (see note 3, p. 252) re-confirm China's commitment to FDI inflows. FDI liberalization measures in China include special tax concessions, liberalized leasing of land to foreign enterprises in coastal cities, provision for increased foreign participation in property and port development, power generation and retailing. As a result of guidelines issued in 1995, such sectors as transportation and communications, insurance and other service industries have also been opened up. Foreign-funded law and consultancy agencies are now being allowed to operate. An FDI Confidence Index Survey undertaken in February–April 1998 by a US-based management consulting firm ranked China as the third most favoured FDI destination after the US and Brazil (World Bank, 1998b).

The impact on domestic macroeconomic policies

Attempts to ward off possible contagion from the South-east Asian Crisis have usually assumed the form of currency depreciation and a tightening of the macroeconomic screw by squeezing liquidity. The latter places steep upward pressure on interest rates, which may result in economic slowdown. A choice has to be made between a heavy currency depreciation and a rise in interest rates. Currency depreciation cannot continue indefinitely; at some stage, contractionary policies have to be introduced. The sooner they are, the lower is the adjustment cost to the economy. If these policies are introduced early (that is, before the currency has lost substantial ground), they can help restore investor confidence to some degree. The contractionary policy can be slowly eased as foreign inflows return to normal levels. Judging from its actions in the first half of 1998, the Reserve Bank of India (RBI) leaned towards (what seems to us) the lesser of the two evils by shoring up market interest rates rather than allowing very steep currency depreciation.[5] Since 1993, China has pursued a contractionary policy and an austerity programme of credit squeeze to control inflation and curb speculation in property and stock markets. In 1998, this austerity programme gave way to one of expansion and spending in an effort to accelerate growth. Interest rates have been lowered and the credit squeeze lifted. Thus, in contrast to India's tight monetary policy, China has followed a policy of monetary expansion to counter the Crisis.[6]

Impact on the future of reforms

To put the following discussion in perspective, it is perhaps best to spell out explicitly our own attitudes to liberalization. We believe that there are benefits in liberalization in economies like India and China, but we do not equate this with a move to a *laissez faire* regime. Content, pace and sequencing of reforms are crucial. Following the conventional taxonomy, we may divide reforms into those bearing on: (i) the domestic real sector (privatization, industrial delicensing and deregulation, subsidy removal and so on); (ii) the domestic financial sector (banking sector deregulation and capital market reforms); (iii) international real sector (liberalization of trade and FDI); and (iv) the international financial sector (liberalization of FPI, capital account and FOREX markets). The different aspects of the reform process are likely to meet varying degrees of political resistance in previously heavily regulated economies such as India and China. Hence progress in reform implementation is likely to be uneven and sometimes haphazard, while 'balance' and sequencing are necessary.

In our opinion, the early stages of reform should be characterized by an emphasis on the real sector (domestic and international) with particular attention to subsidy pruning, privatization, tariff reduction and liberalization of FDI. This should be accompanied by deregulation of interest rates and a move towards a market-determined exchange rate. Important domestic financial-sector reforms must follow on the heels of this development. In particular, financial institutions must be opened up to foreign competition and be freed from excessive government regulations. However, deregulation should be gradual and should not be equated with *laissez faire*. It is necessary to put a strong financial supervisory system in place, with the supervisor an autonomous body free of government control. Another key component of financial sector reforms is that of the capital market, where investor confidence needs to be built up through a credible supervisory authority and a general strengthening of shareholders' rights. Finally, our views on FPI and capital account liberalization are rather cautious. Recognizing that capital inflows can often be speculative and destabilizing, we feel that they should constitute the last stages of a liberalization strategy. A premature freeing of the capital account could abort an otherwise well-conceived reform package. In retrospect, the South-east Asian Crisis seems to vindicate this caution.

The most notable difficulty in assessing the Indian and Chinese governments' responses to the Crisis stems from the fact that it depends on what these governments perceive as the underlying key factors. In India, the 1998–9 budget has provided us with an inkling of what to expect in the future. The Budget has three major thrusts: (i) an explicit privatization programme (a maximum of 74% of government equity to be divested in non-strategic public-sector enterprises); (ii) a significant rise in import duties; and (iii) a massive programme of public borrowing to finance a steep increase in public investment outlay.

Although the budget intends privatization as a revenue-boosting fiscal measure (and its feasibility and ultimate implementation are also much in doubt), it still serves the useful purpose of sending signals that the reform agenda has not been completely abandoned. The raising of import duties on several items and the levy of a flat import surcharge could be explained either as an unequivocal assertion of the *swadeshi* (self-reliant) philosophy or as a temporary response to the Crisis. If the former interpretation is correct, it would mean rolling back much of the trade liberalization recorded in recent years. It could also presage several other import-substitution measures under the nationalist guise of self-reliance. But the alternative explanation (of a temporary response to the Crisis) cannot be ruled out altogether. After all, if

India's exporters are in danger of being squeezed by cheapened Southeast Asian products (though this has not happened so far), the government may well reason that Indian industries must have an assured domestic market to sustain their production levels.

On the other hand, if the Crisis is perceived as mainly a financial crisis, the appropriate remedies sought will be in the direction of strengthening financial supervision. The Chinese government has accelerated banking reforms since the Crisis. Such initiatives as the CHIBOR market (an interbank market initiated in 1996 to supplant formal and informal markets in bank deposits) and the People's Bank of China (PBC) open-market operations are steps in that direction. Other banking reforms include: recapitalizing banks; curbing the rampant growth of finance companies with irregular practices; reducing the number of branches of PBC to curb local fraud and speculation; tightening bank supervision and control; permitting bank branches to set interest rates for corporate loans based on risk, within a prescribed band; and lifting loan quotas so that banks can be more flexible in responding to demand. The closure in June 1998 of China Venturetech Corporation, Hainan Development Bank and Guangdong International Trust & Investment Corporation (noted above) are examples of China's determination and decisiveness in reforming its debt-ridden banking system. It is a clear signal to the banks and state enterprises that, in future, bail-outs and government guarantees cannot be counted on. China's Cabinet has approved new regulations on the closing-down of illegal financial institutions, which augurs well for a broader clean-up in future. As the restructuring programme for state enterprises makes progress, large amounts of bad loans ($200 billion) to these enterprises will have to be written off. In February 1998, the Finance Ministry planned a $32.5 billion special bond issue with a view to raising capital for state-owned commercial banks (*Far Eastern Economic Review*, 12 March 1998) which is a step in the right direction, although the amount is far below what is required for bank re-capitalization.

Financial liberalization without adequate safeguards is generally viewed as one of the factors responsible for the crisis in East and Southeast Asia. China exercises central control over its banks and corporations, which are not allowed to borrow or lend capital abroad without government approval. This makes the yuan much less vulnerable to changes in investor sentiment or speculative attacks. Indeed, capital liberalization is probably inadvisable until such time as the banking industry clears its bad debts and appropriate supervisory mechanisms are properly implemented.

In the Indian case, there is a tendency to slow-pedal reforms in such areas as privatization, trade and capital liberalization (judging by the recent significant increase in import duties and the levy of a flat import surcharge). China has also adjusted its import duties on equipment since 1 January 1998. But instead of raising them, it has exempted imports of equipment from import tax and value-added tax in order to encourage technological modernization (*Beijing Review*, 16–22 February 1998). However, some imported commodities continue to be subject to import tax in order to discourage the importing of low-technology machinery and equipment that can be manufactured at home.

China's response to the crisis is thus different from that of India. As noted above, China has in fact accelerated restructuring and reform of state banks and state enterprises. The Chinese Premier, Zhu Rongji, has given state enterprises and state banks only three years to restructure even at the cost of social hardship in terms of worker retrenchment. The number of government workers is to be reduced by half with the abolition of several ministries. Privatization of housing (formerly provided by the state) has been announced, to stimulate domestic demand to compensate for the fall in export demand resulting from the Crisis. Failure to reform and privatize state enterprises in China is likely to act as a drag on banking and financial reforms. These enterprises are making heavy losses and most of the non-performing loans by the state banks are to these enterprises; part of the losses by such enterprises are, of course, attributable to the various social services provided to the employees. In the absence of state enterprise reforms, commercial lending criteria cannot be introduced by state banks.

There are conflicting signals, however. In June 1998, the Central Bank appealed to commercial banks to provide more working capital to loss-making state enterprises. Further, in July 1998, the state economic and trade commission ordered local governments to slow down the sale of state-owned enterprises for fear of social unrest. In addition, the three policy banks (the State Development Bank, the Exports and Imports Bank and the Agricultural Development Bank) set up to relieve state banks of policy-directed lendings, have not been very successful owing to uncertainty of funding resources and lack of well-defined procedures (Holmes, 1997, p. 743). These add uncertainty to the process of reform in China.

Conclusion

So far, the impact of the Crisis on China and India has been limited. We noted that the Crisis can spread in several ways: through impacts on exports, foreign capital inflows and the effects of contractionary domestic policies in the wake of the Crisis. Both countries have escaped external shocks, possibly owing to capital controls – the two currencies are convertible on current account but not on capital account. However, in both countries symptoms of financial ailments do exist, which need to be addressed by reforms of the capital markets and the banking industry. A cautious approach is needed towards capital account convertibility. In recent years, the IMF has viewed capital account convertibility (CAC) as the natural follow-up to the establishment of current account convertibility, with free trade in goods and services to be succeeded logically by free movement of financial and physical assets. In this context, it is interesting to note that Keynes had always viewed capital mobility as incompatible with the preservation of reasonably free multilateral trade (see Minsky, 1975). The South-east Asian Crisis has amply demonstrated the perils of free capital flows, unchecked by any regulatory device. The Indian and Chinese governments should not make the fatal mistake of rushing into CAC without adequate preparation. This is one aspect of the reforms on which we can confidently recommend slow pedalling. In line with our diagnosis of the Asian Crisis as primarily a financial one, we also recommend capital market and banking sector reforms.

Capital market reforms call for the empowering of regulatory authorities, mainly to punish market violations and strengthen overall discipline. Strengthening of shareholders' rights will also go a long way towards restoring investor confidence in stock markets. In the risky environment of emerging markets, such as those of China and India, a capital adequacy ratio for the banks, in excess of the norm set by the Bank for International Settlements, may be desirable. Incentives need to be created to encourage banks to accumulate capital above the stipulated minimum. One such incentive (see Goldstein and Turner, 1996) is to make a bank's range of permitted activities and its regulatory obligations a function of the level of its capital. Finally, competition needs to be introduced in the banking sector by permitting the entry of private banks, foreign banks and money market mutual funds, which will encourage market-driven mergers among private banks. Undue procrastination on these measures could make a hitherto reasonably stable situation in India and China, a highly untenable one.

Notes

1. Other possible adverse effects of devaluation of yuan would be a possible decline in FDI and pressures on Hong Kong dollar. However, some observers believe that Hong Kong may actually benefit from a devaluation since an increase in mainland exports would pass through Hong Kong using its ports, airports, shipping agents, bankers and insurance firms.
2. There is one important difference between the way FDI is measured in India and China. The concept used in India does not include mergers and acquisitions (M&A) by foreign players, or allotment of preferences shares by them. The Chinese concept does. Making this adjustment would increase the total Indian FDI figure from $12 billion to $15 billion.
3. For example, Citibank was allowed to establish a joint venture with a Chinese air-conditioner-maker (government approval was granted in the remarkably short period of four months). The former will own 40% equity and the Guangdong Kelon Airconditioning Co., 60% (Saywell, 1988). In March 1998, Kodak Co. agreed on a $380 million deal to establish two companies, Kodak (China) and Kodak (Wuxi), which involved the taking over of three Chinese loss-making state enterprises. In 1998, Unilever purchased a leading Shanghai Soy Sauce manufacturer (Chai, 1998; Motoyama, 1998).
4. In which a change in government in the state of Maharashtra led to a cancellation and then renegotiation of a US$2.8 billion investment by Enron Development Corporation in the Dabhol Power Project.
5. This should not be construed as support of the contractionary IMF policies in the South-east Asian crisis, which we believe aggravated the situation. The crucial difference is that here we are talking of high interest rates as a *preventive* measure. Once a crisis sets in and the expectations of foreign investors turn averse, contraction can worsen matters. The latter seems to have been the case in post-crisis South-east Asia.
6. As a result of this policy, in September 1998 broad money supply M2 (total cash and all deposits) reached $202 billion, which reflects an increase of 16% over the same period in 1997. This figure is higher than those for the first and second quarters of 1998 by 1.7 percentage points and 1.4 percentage points, respectively. Narrow money supply M1 (total of cash and demand deposits) also grew, up 1.5 percentage points and 4.5 percentage points over the first and second quarters of 1998, respectively. At the end of September 1998, outstanding M1 values were $439.77 billion. Loan expansion had also occurred: loans of financial institutions were at a record high ($966 billion) in the third quarter of 1998, which is the highest level recorded during the first seven months of 1998.

References

Beijing Review (various dates).

Bhalla, A. S. (1998) 'Sino-Indian liberalisation: the role of trade and foreign investment', *Economics of Planning*, October.

Chai, J. (1998) '"One Careful Owner": China's SOEs up for sale', *China Direct Investor*, vol. 4, no. 1, September.

China Daily (various dates).
China Ministry of Foreign Trade and Economic Cooperation (MOFTEC) (1998) *Foreign Direct Investment in China*, Beijing, MOFTEC.
Crédit Suisse (1998) Special Feature: 'Will China Devalue?', *Equity Asia*, no. 7, September.
Economist, The (various dates).
Far Eastern Economic Review (various dates).
Financial Times (various dates).
Goldstein, M. and Turner, P. (1996) 'Banking Crises in Emerging Economies: Origins and Policy Options', Bank of International Settlements (BIS) Economic Papers no. 46, BIS, Basle.
Holmes, W. D. (1997) 'China's financial reforms in the global market', *Law and Policy in International Business*, vol. 28, no. 3, Spring, 715–76.
Hong Kong Trade Development Council (HKTDC) (1998) 'Outlook of China's exports for 1998', *Trade Watch*, Research Department, July.
Huang, G. (1998) 'The analysis of China's imports and exports during January to July 1998', *China Economic News*, no. 37, 28 September.
IMF (various dates) *Balance of Payments Statistics*, Washington, DC, International Monetary Fund.
IMF (various dates) *Direction of Trade Statistics Yearbook*, Washington, DC, International Monetary Fund.
IMF (various dates) *International Financial Statistics*, Washington, DC, International Monetary Fund.
IMF (1997a) *World Economic Outlook 1997, October*, Washington, DC, International Monetary Fund.
IMF (1997b) *Annual Report 1997*, Washington, DC, International Monetary Fund.
Khan, A. (1996) 'The Impact of Recent Macroeconomic and Sectoral Changes on the Poor and Women in China', ILO East Asia Multidisciplinary Advisory Team, Bangkok, unpublished paper.
Minsky, H. (1975) *John Maynard Keynes*, New York, Columbia University Press.
Morgan, J. P. (1998) *World Financial Markets*, Second Quarter.
Motoyama, Y. (1998) 'What the recent turmoil over Asian Currencies tells us', *Kyoto University Economic Review*, April–October.
Radelet, S. and Sachs, J. D. (1998) 'The East Asian financial crisis: diagnosis, remedies, prospects', *Brookings Papers on Economic Activity*, no. 1.
Reserve Bank of India (RBI) (various years) *Annual Reports*.
Reserve Bank of India (1998) *Bulletin*, October.
Reserve Bank of India (1999) *Bulletin*, September.
Saywell, T. (1998) 'Strategic trade-offs-China encourages mergers and acquisitions', *Far Eastern Economic Review*, 15 October.
UNCTAD (1997) *World Investment Report 1997*, Geneva, UNCTAD.
World Bank (1998a) *World Development Indicators*, Washington, DC, The World Bank.
World Bank (1998b) *Foreign Direct Investment in China*, Resident Mission in China, Note no. 1-FY99, 4 August.
World Bank (various dates) *World Development Report*, Washington, DC, The World Bank.

15

Three-and-a-half Cycles of 'Mania, Panic, and [Asymmetric] Crash': East Asia and Latin America Compared

*Gabriel Palma**

This paper argues that, despite some significant differences, the 1982 debt crisis, the 1994 Mexican crisis, and the 1997 East Asian crisis share the common characteristic that 'over-lending' and 'over-borrowing' are basically *endogenous* market failures of over-liquid and under-regulated financial markets – along the lines described by Kindleberger's *Manias, Panics, and Crashes* (although these crashes have tended to be 'asymmetric', as the largest international lenders have emerged relatively intact). The paper concludes with a discussion of Brazil's increasing vulnerability to a sudden collapse of confidence and withdrawal of finance, which indicates the probability of another impending crisis.

Introduction

In the last 15 years, the world economy has witnessed three major financial crises: the 1982 (mainly Latin American) debt crisis; the 1994 Mexican crisis, and its repercussions throughout Latin America (commonly known as the 'Tequila effect'); and the 1997 East Asian crisis. Furthermore, Brazil's growing financial vulnerability signals the probability of another major crisis in the not too distant future (see Postscript, p. 273). This paper argues that the last three financial crises share many common characteristics. Despite some significant differences, these crises show a clear pattern along the lines described by Kindleberger in his classic work *Manias, Panics, and Crashes* (1978) (although these crashes have tended to be 'asymmetric', or 'one-sided', as the largest international lenders have emerged relatively unscathed). The paper concludes with a discussion of Brazil's increasing vulnerability to a sudden collapse of confidence and withdrawal of finance.

The emergence of three financial 'manias': the four main ingredients

Perhaps the only issue on which almost everybody seems to agree regarding these crises is the prior appearance of at least two market failures: international financial institutions 'over-lent' to developing countries (LDCs), and the government, corporations, financial institutions and/or households of these countries 'over-borrowed'. This section discusses three related issues, which are among the most controversial topics in real-world economics today. First, are these market failures endogenous to financial markets or the result of particular exogenous factors? Second, were the 'over-lending' and 'over-borrowing' set in motion by relatively independent factors, or were they basically part of the same market failure, i.e., the result of a single interrelated process with a clear direction of causality? Third, what were the macro–micro dynamics that rendered lenders and borrowers unable to assess and price their risks properly?

In this essay I argue that, although exogenous factors were present (inexperienced financial players, misguided government policies, over-enthusiastic corporate governance, deceptive transparencies, and 'cronyism'), 'over-lending' and 'over-borrowing' are essentially *endogenous* market failures: under-regulated and over-liquid financial markets setting in motion Kindleberger's cycles of 'mania, panic and crash'.

With regard to the second issue, I argue that in the case of financial crises the 'chicken and egg' dilemma – that is, was it the propensity to 'over-lend' that induced the propensity to 'over-borrow', or was it the other way round – is a crucial one. Not only is there a clear interaction between excessive shifts in the supply and in the demand for funds, but (as far as it is analytically possible to separate the two sides of this interaction at any stage) a key similarity among these crises is that the supply schedule of funds leapt to the right, leading the demand schedule to do the same; as a result, both phenomena could basically be considered part of the *same* market failure. Finally, regarding the third issue, I argue that in these three financial crises the initial 'mania' dynamics were set in motion by excess international liquidity interacting with: (i) over-optimistic expectations of future performance in borrowing countries; (ii) distorted domestic incentives; and (iii) inadequate domestic regulation and supervision, particularly in respect of recently privatized and deregulated domestic financial institutions. I further argue that excess international liquidity was the crucial ingredient that led to 'manic' expectations, and a critical component in the process that led to the existence of distorted incentives and inadequate regulation.

Excess international liquidity leading to the first market failure: the propensity to 'over-lend'

As Kindleberger has argued (1978), we can always trace the start of a financial 'mania' to a sudden and significant increase in international liquidity. International financial markets seem to function reasonably effectively only when they are sellers' markets (especially when they can afford only to lend to those who do not need to borrow). However, when for differing historical reasons (which for limitations of space cannot be analysed here) international liquidity grows to such an extent that financial markets become buyers' markets, competitive pressures to recycle funds impair international financial operators' capacity to assess and price risks properly and to allocate resources effectively – i.e., they inexorably move to the other extreme, from lending to those who do not need to borrow to those who will be not be able to pay.[1] This market failure is the main reason why an effective regulatory system is particularly needed at such times, and why the trend in the last two decades of relaxing regulation at a time of rapidly growing liquidity has been associated with so many financial crises – not only the three studied here, but also others like the ERM crisis, several stock market collapses, the savings and loan débâcle in the US, and the more than 30 domestic banking crises since the early 1980s.[2]

One of the main reasons why free and competitive, but under-regulated, international financial markets often 'fail' (sometimes spectacularly) when they become buyers' markets is that their 'customer of last resort', i.e., developing countries, have a truly insatiable demand for funds. Moreover, when these countries have been allowed to borrow even to service their existing debt, their demand for funds has become infinitely elastic *at whatever interest rates and spreads are available*. LDCs have also provided investors with an ever-increasing range of (at least short-term) attractive investment opportunities. In other words, no matter how much liquidity international financial markets have on offer, their operators can always solve the problem of 'market clearing' by loosening their quantity restrictions to LDCs.[3] However, this process has proved to be an inefficient mechanism for allocating financial resources since it has led to the accumulation of risk at levels that are not privately efficient, let alone socially efficient.

This explains why, for example, bankers and financiers were happy to expand their lending to East Asia rapidly, and with declining spreads,[4] precisely at a time when the 'fundamentals' of these economies were deteriorating, the stock of short-term unhedged private debt mounting, gearing ratios rising, profit margins of the real sector declining, corruption and 'cronyism' worsening, and the level of investment in some economies (particularly in speculative real estate) was reaching heights which, even for this part of the world, should have produced feelings of vertigo.

In this respect, as Broughton has stated in an IMF working paper, one of the key issues is that '[f]inancial crises result from a specific market failure: financial markets at least occasionally – and sometimes spectacularly – initially misjudge and eventually aggravate bad news' (1997, p. 21). I would add to Broughton's argument that the three crises studied here show that the larger the amount of excess liquidity that under-regulated international financial markets needed to 'clear', the more likely (and more spectacularly) they, first, *exaggerate* good news and then, later, end up misjudging and eventually aggravating bad news.

Thus, the extraordinary growth in lending figures that preceded these three crises is on a par with the degree of misjudgement of the way in which the economic situation of the borrowing countries was deteriorating: more than US$600 billion (at 1998 prices) was disbursed to non-oil LDCs by private transnational banks between 1974 and 1982.[5] About US$100 billion entered Mexico in 1990–93; and over US$220 billion went into five East Asian countries in 1994–96.[6] Finally, Brazil's figure for 1995–97 is even higher than Mexico's in a similar period before 1994, and increased still further *after* the outbreak of the East Asian crisis, with inflows turned into serious flooding in January 1998.[7]

Appendix Tables 15.A2, 4 and 6 show the relative size of these capital inflows, and Appendix Tables 15.A1, 3 and 5 some of the 'bad news' that financial markets either were inclined to ignore, or simply misjudged (e.g., hugely overvalued exchange rates, runaway current account deficits, unsustainable consumption booms, etc., to be discussed in more detail below). In these tables the relative size of net inflows are measured in terms of 'net transfer of resources', a statistic that shows the funds actually made available to LDCs – i.e., net capital inflows (balance on financial and capital account plus errors and omissions and non-autonomous capital) minus net outflows due to interest payments on the foreign debt and profit repatriation (balance on the income account). In Chile, for example, between 1974–77 and 1978–81, the average 'net transfer' grew by an equivalent of 7.5% of GDP (to 8.3%); in Mexico the increase between 1984–90 and 1991–93 was of the order of 9.1% of GDP (from –4.1% to 5%), and in Korea between 1988–1995 and 1996 this figure grew by 4.1% of GDP (to 4.6%).[8] These inflows also became more short term in maturity – by June 1997, 62% of the debt in the five above-mentioned East Asian economies had a maturity of one year or less. Korea's total, at 68%, was the largest (US$70 billion by the official count, but more if all short-term debt is included). Worse still, about half this amount had a maturity of 90 days or less. In fact, before the crisis Korea's reserves were not enough even to cover the latter!

These figures make Alan Greenspan's oft-quoted post-East Asian crisis remarks something of an understatement: 'In retrospect, it is clear that more investment monies flowed into these economies than could be profitably employed at modest risks' (1997, p. 1).

Excess international liquidity leading to the second market failure: the propensity to 'over-borrow' due to fuelling domestic expectations

Kindleberger (1978) also shows that historically it has been the increase in lending *itself* which fuels expectations and entices the demand schedule for borrowing to leap towards the right. Sudden access to large amounts of external finance is an intrinsic part of the process that propels countries into the 'mania' part of the cycle, by making 'animal spirits' run wild. Alan Greenspan coined the phrase 'irrational exuberance' to refer to this phenomenon of exhilarating expectations. One of the main lessons of the crises studied here is that this phenomenon is particularly conspicuous in LDCs – the international financial market 'of last resort'. This can be viewed as a peculiar case of Say's Law, in which supply creates demand through fuelling expectations and optimism regarding the future prospects of the economy. This circle reinforces itself, becoming a self-fulfilling prophesy. Access to lending fuels expectations regarding the performance of the economy – performance which is improved, at least initially, by the additional expenditure brought about by the extra borrowing and availability of foreign exchange. That is, 'over-lending' and 'over-borrowing' were not set in motion by relatively independent sets of factors which happened to interact at these three specific points in time, but were the result of a closely interrelated process with a clear direction of causality: the propensity to 'over-lend' was a crucial factor that led to the propensity to 'over-borrow' (a well-known alternative view on 'over-borrowing' is McKinnon and Pill, 1997).

Also, as the increase in lending preceding these crises took place (especially in Latin America) within a context of radical market deregulation and economic liberalization, there was an additional stimulus to expectation and optimism. This was mainly the result of the massive 'spin' put on these reforms, making this the latest of many forms of 'populism' in LDCs. The new 'technocratic' populist spin-doctors advancing these reforms, particularly in their most radical versions, could be found not only among the many Chicago-trained Southern economists, but also among those working in the institutions that form the so-called 'Washington consensus' (and in the work of some academics who form part of their 'periphery').[9]

Another result of this over-optimistic view of the future was the lack of awareness of the need for interest-rate hedging before 1982 (even though almost all the debt was at a floating rate), and exchange-rate hedging before 1994 in Mexico and before 1997 in East Asia (despite worsening current-account deficits). If markets are not supposed to fail, the benefits of hedging are not immediately obvious.

Distorted domestic incentives reinforcing the likelihood of the first market failure: the propensity to 'over-lend'

US Under-Secretary of the Treasury Lawrence Summers, one of the most ardent proponents of financial liberalization, acknowledged recently 'the danger of opening the capital account when incentives are distorted' (1998). According to him:

> Inflows in search of fairly valued economic opportunities is one thing. Inflows in search of government guarantees or undertaken in the belief that they are immune from standard risks are quite another. (Quoted in Kregel, 1998b, p. 44)

Some of the worst distortions have emerged as a result of *policy-induced* artificially high interest and exchange rates (see Appendix Tables 15.A1, 3 and 5). These have produced spurious real interest-rate differentials that have attracted massive arbitrage flows. These, in turn, reinforce overvalued exchange rates and increase the need for high interest rates (partly due to the need to sterilize the expansionary effect of increasing reserves). Also, particularly in Latin America, as the dollar price of imported consumer goods has declined owing to substantial tariff reductions and overvalued exchange rates, dollar-denominated wages have increased, as wages but not exchange rates have been indexed to inflation (in Brazil, for example, the dollar value of wages increased 2.5 times during 1990–96), a huge artificial incentive to luxury consumption has emerged. This has been reinforced by 'short-sharp-shock'-style stabilization programmes, which not only have augmented relative price distortions, but have also proved very expansionary as the inflation tax on demand has practically disappeared overnight.[10] All these have provided financial markets with households artificially eager for credit.

Again mainly in Latin America, one-off capital gains due to privatization of often *under-priced* (sometime grossly so) public assets have been another important policy-determined source of (what Summers calls) 'unfairly valued' economic opportunities.[11] 'Thin' and extremely volatile stock markets have provided yet another form of short-term (and particularly pro-cyclical) distortion.[12] Another distortion that attracted foreign capital before these three crises was the guarantee, sometimes explicit, sometime implicit, that governments would bail out domestic banks in trouble. Despite numerous denials *ex ante* this was, in fact, exactly what happened in Latin America (with clear IMF blessing) *ex post* in the 1982 and 1994 crises (as well as with governments' guarantees on private debt).[13] The resulting moral hazard was an important component of the belief that, if a crisis situation developed in East Asia, the same would happen again. The rescue of several banks – particularly the controversial bail-out in 1996 of the Bangkok Bank of Commerce in Thailand – strongly reinforced the belief that governments in East Asia would also undertake a Latin American-style bail-out. Ironically, the World Bank seems to have unintentionally strengthened this belief when it lent US$307 million to the Indonesian government in 1992, to replenish the capital base of troubled state-run banks.[14]

Inadequate regulation and supervision of domestic financial markets reinforcing the likelihood of the second market failure: the propensity to 'over-borrow'

Few would argue that these crises were unrelated to market failure in domestic banking systems. The crucial issue, however, is to what extent these are directly related to the degree of inadequacy in the regulation and supervision of the domestic financial system, particularly when recently liberalized.

Starting with Chile in 1974, Latin American countries did not need much persuasion rapidly to deregulate and liberalize their domestic financial systems. East Asia needed more pressure from the IMF, the WTO and the US government to do so, but these countries were finally, and rapidly, converted in the early 1990s (implementing measures such as the reduction of reserve requirements, increased access to offshore borrowing, and the removal of restrictions on corporate debt financing; see Chang, Park and Yoo's chapter in this volume). But, as Stiglitz remarks,

> inadequate financial regulation allowed banks to make excessively risky loans without adequate monitoring. And part of that problem in turn was due to excessively rapid financial liberalisation without a commensurate strengthening of regulation and supervision ... While the advantage of these changes were lauded, the necessary increase in safeguards was not adequately emphasized. (1998, p. 11)

This combination of domestic financial markets with almost unlimited access to foreign borrowing, lax regulatory systems, and the existence of many inexperienced domestic players (with little initial knowledge of 'financial engineering', but high expectations of quick returns) was the recipe for financial crisis. Figures for the rapid increase in bank lending following deregulation are abundant. In Mexico, for example, the ratio of bank credit to GDP doubled between 1989 and 1994;[15] in Thailand, domestic bank lending increased 2.3-fold (in real terms) between 1990 and 1996 (and 4-fold between 1985 and 1996), and in the Philippines it did so 3.3-fold. In Indonesia, in turn, following an extreme form of financial deregulation in the mid-1980s, newly unregulated domestic private banks increased their lending (in real terms) nearly 9-fold between then and 1996 (see also the chapter by Ramli and Pincus in this volume). There was also a growing asymmetry in maturity structures: in Korea, for example, merchant banks ended up with 64% of their external liabilities short term, and 85% of assets long term (Chang, 1998).

There has been ample controversy regarding the related problems of transparency and information about domestic financial markets. One reason why these problems have become more difficult is the growing role of intermediaries. In this business it is increasingly the case that one needs three to tango: a lender, a borrower and an intermediary. There are many reasons for this phenomenon, almost all connected to increased international liquidity and deregulation. The rapid development of new financial instruments is just one notable case (see Kregel's chapter in this volume).[16] However, particularly for those who wanted to know, a large amount of information was available at the time. And warnings could be found in such influential publications as the BIS *Annual Reports* and were made by (some) credit-rating agencies. With regard to information, perhaps the worst 'informational imperfection' was the lack of monitoring of corporations and financial institutions to ascertain whether their managers were acting in the interests of shareholders and creditors. The problem is that this type of information is a public good, and, like any other, it tends to be undersupplied by the market. This type of imperfection is a market failure that especially distorts the working of capital markets; it encourages firms both to take excessive risks in the case of debt financing, and to enrich management at the expense of shareholders in the case of equity finance.

A key additional problem was one of *evaluating* the information that was available: as in most periods of 'mania', market operators were simply unwilling to focus on the down-side risks as the up-side was more seductive. Many governments were not too keen to encourage proper evaluations of their economies either. Also, the evaluation of information is obviously *relative*, i.e., normally made *vis-à-vis* specific alternatives. For example, the scramble to lend to East Asia was directly related to the Tequila hangover: between the year before and the year after the 1994 Mexican crisis, BIS-reporting banks increased the amount of assets held in the form of lending to Asia from US$15 billion to US$86 billion.

Finally, as in previous crises, in these financial 'manias' (together with overpowering greed and suicidal risk-propensities), corruption and lack of transparency developed into a new art-form (see Kindleberger, 1978; for an analysis of this issue applied to Chile before 1982, see Meller, 1984).

The outbreak of three financial 'panics' and the rapid reversal of capital flows

The 'panic stage' in Latin America was triggered by different mechanisms from those in East Asia. In both 1982 and 1994 Mexican reserve depletion and credit-rating collapse signalled the outbreak of the crisis; the first led to government default and the second to a devaluation. In East Asia the main detonators were the collapse of Thai banks and Korean corporations, followed by the Soros-led speculative attack on the Thai baht. However, the speed and the magnitude of the reversal of flows that followed in each case were relatively similar. In 1982, in Latin America, net inflow of foreign capital fell from US$70 billion in 1981 to less than US$5 billion in 1983 (figures expressed in 1998 prices). In terms of a 'net transfer of resources', the fall was from US$20 billion to less than –US$50 billion, respectively; this turnaround was equivalent to more than 40% of exports of the countries involved (from 10% to –31%, respectively).

In the case of 1994 Mexico, the autonomous net flows alone into Latin America fell from US$67 billion in 1993 to US$27 billion in 1995 (in 1998 prices). 'Net transfers' into Mexico, in turn, fell from US$22 billion in 1993 to –US$2 billion in 1994, and (as interest payments on the rescue package mounted) again fell to –US$13 billion in 1996 – another turnaround of about 40% of exports.

In Korea, Indonesia, Malaysia, the Philippines and Thailand, net external financing fell from US$93 billion in 1996 to an estimated US$15 billion in 1997. If one excludes official flows, they fell from US$93 billion to –US$12 billion – this turnaround was similar to these countries' reserves. The largest share of this fall was taken by commercial bank lending, which fell from US$56 billion to –US$21 billion, respectively (IIF, 1998, p. 2). The overall turnaround of net flows in East Asia, although lower than that in Latin America in terms of exports, was similar in terms of GDP: excluding official flows, both in East Asia and in 1994 Mexico, the turnaround in net flows exceeded 10% of GDP; and, including official flows, in East Asia and in 1982 Latin America they were roughly similar, at about two percentage points lower.

As Kindleberger said (1984), the one thing that international financial markets can do that is worse than lending excessive amounts to LDCs is to stop that lending abruptly. This phenomenon was common to the three crises studied here, and created supply shocks (mainly via shortages of foreign exchange and finance) with sharp contractionary effects on these economies. As has been quoted extensively, Stiglitz remarked in the *Financial Times* (25 March 1988) that '[w]ithout volatile international capital flows, the East Asian crisis of 1997 would probably have been no more memorable than the South Korean crisis of 1980 or the Thai one of 1983'. Kregel adds that without these volatile flows this crisis would have probably been no more than 'a local balance of payments crisis resolved with an exchange rate adjustment and a revision of internal policy' (1998b, p. 37). A similar point was made by Díaz-Alejandro (1984) regarding the Latin American 1982 crisis.

The main similarity and the main difference between these three financial 'crashes'

The main similarity: 'untouchable' international financial markets and asymmetric crashes

The most striking similarity between these crises is that, while all other participants have made substantial losses, international financial markets, particularly the largest international lenders, have emerged relatively unscathed. Each crisis gave international financial markets a considerable fright, and in the short term some players may have lost money and sleep. But as soon as these crises threatened to get out of control, as in an old Western, they could count on the cavalry arriving in the nick of time, in the form of a vast international rescue operation. Meanwhile, economic agents in countries directly affected (households, corporations, domestic financial institutions, and governments) had to pay dearly for their share of responsibility in the events that led to the crises, and other LDCs have also had to suffer the consequences of these crises, particularly in their terms of trade and finance.

The main characteristic of these costly international bail-outs is that they have provided whatever amount of foreign exchange liquidity is necessary to maintain capital account convertibility in the crisis-ridden economies, so that foreign capital can leave (sometimes immediately, at other times in stages) practically unharmed after the crisis. The size of the rescue packages, which in all three cases have contained record IMF lending, has increased at an incredible rate. While the initial package in Mexico reached US$40 billion, East Asia's stretched to about US$110 billion. In fact, in the case of the first two (mainly Latin American) crises (which have had more time to run their course), foreign capital not only did not pay its share of the losses, but actually made significant *gains* as a result of the financial packages eventually agreed with debtor countries.[17] Also, as mentioned above, in direct contradiction with the neo-liberal creed now being promoted all over the world, the strong arm of the IMF made sure that an important part of the international rescue operations in Latin America consisted of ensuring that governments gave *ex post* guarantees on private debt – even though both the lending and the borrowing had been done in free, competitive markets.[18] In fact, the IMF and the US government have become good at putting effective 'spins' on some components of their rescue operations when they happen not to go by the neo-liberal book.[19] Thus, international financial operators made profits while things went right, and made profits when things went wrong, making this the only market that operates with only carrots and no sticks.[20] That is, they have earned substantial amounts of profits and bonuses independently of whether or not they have been able to assess and price risks properly and allocate financial resources efficiently. This has also dramatically shortened (what Kindleberger calls) the financial markets' 'collective memory' of crises. This state of affairs provides an extraordinary moral hazard, that of being 'too big to fail', which does not augur well for the future performance of this crucial market.

Obviously the IMF and many OECD governments may have had little choice but to act quickly – it would have been far more expensive for them not to have done so.[21] However, although this may be perfectly true if one takes each crisis one at a time, it may not necessarily be so if one takes into consideration the moral hazard of making the next crisis more likely by so doing. Another issue is that conditionalities have been totally one-sided: only LDCs have had to accept adjustment and structural reforms which could, in theory, make them less crisis-prone. Firms which constitute the international financial markets, especially large ones, have received all the required help while having to accept hardly any institutional and regulatory reforms that would make it more likely that in the future they would assess and price risks properly and allocate financial resources efficiently. In fact, financial markets are quite happy to believe in systemic risk justifying *ex post* market intervention in the form of bail-outs, but not *ex ante* intervention in the form of prudent but effective regulations on exposure, gearing ratios, competition, taxation, bankruptcy, accounting practices, and standards in general. Even modest but imaginative reforms, such as the 'Tobin tax', have been rejected out of hand.

The main difference: while the two Latin American crises were mainly the result of wrong 'fundamentals', East Asia's was that of a sudden collapse of confidence and a withdrawal of finance

Appendix Tables 15.A1–6 show clearly the differences between the Latin American crises and the East Asian one in terms of 'fundamentals'. In Latin America, in 1981, for example, countries were running large public sector deficits (the median was equivalent to 5.4% of GDP), and massive deficits in their current accounts (the median was equivalent to 43% of exports, with the fastest growing item in the trade account being imports of consumer goods[22]). These tables also show that most countries had rapidly revaluing exchange rates; weak levels of investment; falling private savings; and economic growth which was clearly private consumption-led. In fact, in terms of median values, between 1979 and 1981 exports and investment made *no* contribution to GDP growth in Latin America, but private consumption contributed 2.3 percentage points (while, in terms of average values, exports made no contribution either, and investment only a small one). One case of note is Chile at the end of its first, more orthodox, cycle of trade and financial liberalization: between 1975 and 1981, its real exchange rate appreciated by a third while its current account was reaching a deficit equivalent to no less than *95%* of exports (*14.5%* of GDP). Household savings were *negative* and those of its corporate sector were so low that between 1978 and 1981 overall private sector savings were a meagre *1.4%* of GDP. Meanwhile, imports of consumer goods reached US$2 billion in 1981, a level equivalent to half the total goods exports (up from 9% in 1975; the average rate of growth between these low and high point in the cycle was 70% per annum). In fact, Chile was another peculiar case in Latin America of an 'export economy' where the contribution of private consumption to GDP growth was miles ahead of that of exports (five times larger).

Before 1994, Mexico's 'fundamentals' were not very different. Again, it was a case of 'export-led' growth in which exports made little contribution to GDP growth, in which the real rate of exchange was moving even more swiftly against exports and where the speed of the worsening of the current account defied belief.[23] Investment levels were weak and biased towards speculative real estate; comparing 1994 with 1981 (the previous peak), while in 1994 investment in machinery was only at half the 1981 level, and that in infrastructure at about a third, residential construction had increased 2.5-fold. Also, the share of private savings in GDP (current prices) fell *by half* during 1984–90 and 1991–93, and imports of consumer goods grew at 48% per year in the 7-year period between the beginning of trade and financial liberalization and the 1994 crisis – a 16-fold increase.

Appendix Tables 15.A1 and 2 show a significantly different picture for East Asia before 1997. These were export economies not just in name but where exports did actually make a significant contribution to GDP growth, at a rate (except for Indonesia – East Asia's honorary Latin American country) not too different from that of private consumption. In addition, imports of consumer goods, although growing fast by East Asian standards, were not part of a consumer boom which had actually undermined both the internal and the external macroeconomic equilibria. The public sector was in surplus; real rates of exchange were not moving against exports; and current-accounts deficits were still relatively small. Even the most famous deficit of all,

Thailand's, was 'only' equivalent to 21% of exports in 1997 – a figure that compares well with the deficits in Chile in 1981 (95%), Mexico in 1993 (38%), and Brazil in 1997 (57%). Finally, the share of investment and savings in GDP were not only very high, but growing. This does not mean, of course, that East Asia was a problem-free area: it had *voluntarily* switched to self-destructive forms of unhedged short-term external financing, there was misallocation of investment (particularly in speculative real estate), and, especially in Korea, it had accumulated dangerously high debt/equity ratios; but even then the macroeconomic 'fundamentals' were far superior to those found in Latin America prior to its crises.[24]

As a result, the crises in the two regions took different forms. In Latin America both crises ended up as relatively traditional balance-of-payments crises, brought about by reserve depletion and worsening credit ratings. In East Asia, however, the crisis took rather a 'Minsky debt deflation' path, brought about by the international capital market's sudden (and spectacular) loss of confidence in the region (see Kregel, 1998c). In the first case, hasty trade and (external and domestic) financial liberalization, at a time of high international liquidity, led to 'over-borrowing' to finance an excessive growth of imports, mounting debt servicing, and booming domestic lending, which eventually could not be financed by ever higher external borrowing. This led to a depletion of reserves and a plunge in credit rating, provoking an exchange rate crisis and then a fully-fledged foreign exchange crisis, which culminated in standard deflationary policies seeking to regain internal and external macroeconomic equilibria through expenditure reduction and expenditure switching mechanisms (and in a 'non-standard' policy of government taking over most of the domestic financial and corporate bad debt).

In the case of East Asia, hasty financial liberalization of the capital account and domestic economy, also at a time of high, and particularly volatile, international liquidity – a liquidity which, owing to factors such as the 'Tequila effect', the Japanese crisis, the slowing down of most OECD economies, and erratic commodity markets, was desperately seeking new low-risk/high-yield investment opportunities – led both the foreign and the domestic private sectors to take decisions that turned low-risk/high-growth economies into high-risk/low-return ones, increasingly vulnerable to a deterioration of external conditions or a sudden collapse of confidence. In this case the detonators were not reserve depletion and falling credit ratings leading to a government default or to a devaluation, but mainly bankruptcies in Thai banks and

Korean corporations, and an attack on the baht. In Thailand, the banking crisis quickly turned into an exchange rate crisis owing to the fact that the government used a large proportion of its reserves covering the dollar-exposure of its domestic banks. When it later had to defend its exchange rate it found itself without much left in its reserves; and what was left it managed to lose quickly in the forward markets for the baht. Without reserves, the government had no option but to allow its currency to float (2 July); this flotation immediately turned into an exchange rate crisis which led to a foreign exchange crisis. Three weeks later the IMF was called in. Suddenly, the (baht) penny dropped: at least five East Asian economies did not have enough reserves even to cover their very short-term unhedged debt, and what happened in Thailand could easily happen almost anywhere. This led to a generalized collapse in confidence, panic capital outflows, depreciating currencies and falling asset prices. In turn, these proved self-fulfilling because they aggravated the pressures on private sector balance sheets, restricted credit and undermined the real economy in general.

It has been widely argued that the failure of the IMF to understand the specific nature of this crisis and the extreme urgency for action led them to waste precious time and resources. The IMF first believed that it was a relatively traditional balance of payments-cum-domestic financial system crisis, and then that '[a] financial crisis calls for a similar response from the Fund as any other balance of payments problems except that the response must be quicker and possibly larger than in a more traditional case' (Broughton, 1997, p. 6). According to Kregel (1998c, p. 14), in Keynesian terms, the crucial thing that the IMF did not understand was that what was required was 'a shift in liquidity preference, not in spending propensities' (or, I would add, in expenditure levels). There are, of course, more differences between Latin America and East Asia, but for reasons of space they cannot be analysed here.[25] Some of these also help to explain why East Asia is finding it more difficult than Latin America (especially Mexico) 'to come out exporting'.[26]

Brazil's economy in the post-East Asian crisis era: another economic meltdown in the making?

As Stiglitz states: 'After the Mexican crisis many said that this was the last time anything like this would happen again. The East Asia crisis, just two years after the problems in Mexico, should serve to remind us that we will have more crises in the future' (1998, p. 21). Why Brazil? The short answer lies in Appendix Tables 15.A1 to 6. First, like East Asia in mid-1997, Brazil in mid-1998 is increasingly vulnerable to a sudden collapse of confidence and withdrawal of finance – in a world economy which is even more volatile, and with new economic problems expected in Russia and Venezuela, and political ones in the US. The key problem is the reliance since 1995 on massive inflows to close its balance of payments. In fact, Brazil's net inflows in the three-year period from 1995 to 1997, US$ 91 billion, are even larger than those into Korea (1994–96) and Mexico (1991–93).[27] However, in relative terms net inflows into Brazil in 1995–96 were equivalent to Korea's (4.3% of GDP), and lower than Malaysia's and Thailand's (9.1% and 11.2%); they were also lower than Mexico's in 1991–93 (8.6%) and Chile's extreme case in 1979–81 (13%). In terms of 'net transfers', Brazil's figure for 1995 and 1996, though large enough at US$40 billion (particularly if compared with the rest of Latin America, where in both years overall 'net transfers' were actually *negative*), is also lower in relative terms to Korea's (3.8% of GDP, versus 2.7% in Brazil) and Thailand's (8.8%); however, it was larger than Malaysia's and Indonesia's (1.7% and 1.4%, 1995 only). Brazil's figure is also lower than that of Mexico for 1991–93 (5%) and Chile for 1978–81 (8.3%).

High as these inflows were, after the initial mid-1997 shock – between August and November 1997 panic outflows brought Brazil's reserves down by US$11 billion – inflows increased again from December and turned into a flood in January. Over the first quarter of 1998, US$20 billion (mainly short term and exchange-rate unhedged) entered Brazil, a record amount that is roughly equivalent to inflows for the whole of 1997, and nearly twice the amount of exports of this quarter (and only 10% of this total was made up by foreign direct investment).

Second, drastic policies to stabilise the economy after July 1997 added distortions to an already distorted system of incentives; for example, towards the end of 1997 real deposit rates returned to the 1995 (40%!) level. At the same time, Brazil's domestic financial system has never been a model of transparency, regulation or supervision.[28] Third, there are also too many worrying similarities in terms of macroeconomic 'fundamentals' between Brazil since the beginning of its 'Real Plan' of stabilisation-cum-trade and financial liberalization in 1994 and Mexico in the years that preceded its December 1994 crisis. Some of them also apply to events in Chile and some other Latin American countries in the years before the 1982 crisis. Brazil's 'fundamentals' are also significantly worse than those in East Asia before July 1997 and, in many respects, also worse than those of Mexico before December 1994. Most importantly, Brazil had a large and growing deficit in the public accounts (3.8% of GDP in 1996 and 4.1% in 1997; first estimates for the first half of 1998 show a further deterioration).[29] Brazil also had a 'twin' deficit in the current account (4% of GDP in 1997, or more than half the value of exports),[30] and a real rate of exchange which revalued by nearly half in just three years.[31] That is, Brazil is today yet another Latin American economy in which swift trade and financial liberalizations, instead of producing an export and an investment drive, have led to a situation in which exports have made no contribution to GDP growth, and in which investment made a very small one. Meanwhile, private consumption has made all the running as far as GDP growth is concerned.

In turn, massive inflows have not only been associated with stagnant relative investment levels, but also with falling private-sector savings. The main reason for this is the already mentioned 'Diaz-Alejandro effect' of accommodating deregulation, restructuring and trade and financial liberalization with a private consumption boom. This Latin American tradition has been at its best (as in Brazil) when implemented together with drastic stabilization policies. As a result, imports of consumer goods nearly doubled to US$9 billion in just the first year of the reforms. In fact, in the six years after 1990 (i.e., since phased reductions in tariffs were first initiated by the 'Collor Plan') these imports increased 11-fold (although from a low beginning), or by 50% per year. Foreign debt reached US$188 billion in 1997. In 1996 the service of the long- and medium-term debt (principal and interest) reached US$27 billion, or 57% of exports. Moreover, according to IMF statistics, the maturity structure of the foreign debt deteriorated rapidly, from a share of about 20% of the total in 1994, to about 55% in 1997. This figure is even larger than Korea's before 1997 (50%).

As a result of turmoil in international financial markets after July 1997, policies were introduced to reduce the current-account deficit – mainly via decelerating the economy, extremely high interest rates, small devaluation of the real, and increased import restrictions. However, although they have had a significant impact on the trade account, so far they have only succeeded marginally as far as the current account is concerned: this deficit for the first two months of 1998 was only 7% below that of the same period in 1997, and recent forecasts for the whole year predict that at best it will be only 10%

below the 1997 level.[32] Also, in a year of presidential elections, in which the incumbent is running for re-election, in a country that probably invented populism, it is not the easiest of times to reduce public deficits.[33] As a result, at the time of finishing this paper, in July 1998, Brazil is not far from an alarming degree of vulnerability.

However, in some respects, Brazil's present situation is better than that of Chile (1982), Mexico (1994) and East Asia (1997). At least in relative terms, the current-account deficit is not as large as in the first two cases, and reserves are large (although as Great Britain found out, if trouble begins, they can never be large enough). Also, Brazil still has massive amounts of privatizable public assets, with strong magnetic effects for foreign capital; the misallocation of resources (particularly to speculative real estate) is not large; and the levels of debt/equity ratio of its corporate sector are still far from Korean levels (for an international comparison, see Singh, 1998).

In addition, and extremely importantly, since Brazil started its experiment with reforms in 1994, it has had the great advantage that first the Mexican and then the East Asian crises have had a healthy depressing effect on its emerging 'mania'. Unfortunately, judging by (among other things) precisely their recent behaviour towards Brazil, the same cannot be said for international financial markets; after rapidly converting to 'path-dependency', they are eager to believe that 'history matters' – i.e., that the IMF has no choice but to start already gathering a sufficiently large war chest to keep convertibility going if trouble begins in Brazil.

To summarize, I would argue that Brazil's problems are probably worse than those previously suggested by Dornbush: 'If Brazil does not shift to reform and savings, the *Real Plan* – in hindsight – will be nothing but another botched, populist plan' (1997, p. 16). Brazil certainly needs more savings and reforms, but, as East Asia has shown, an average level of private savings practically *twice* as large as in Brazil was not enough to avoid that crisis. And as the 'Díaz-Alejandro effect' shows, although *if properly implemented* deregulation, restructuring and trade and financial liberalization can have positive economic effects, so far Brazil has followed the Latin tradition of accommodating them with an expansion of private consumption – hardly the best incentive for private savings to grow. The solution would seem to come not via even more 'opening up' of trade and finance but *of the reform package itself*, in order to implement it more pragmatically. It is an open question whether in the end Brazil's policy-makers will show themselves to have the required flexibility to adapt, or whether, also after a promising start, they will show as disappointing a *'jogo de cintura'* as the performance of its football players in the final of the 1998 World Cup.

Conclusion

In this paper I have argued that although there were many exogenous factors in these three failures of international and domestic financial markets, 'over-lending' and 'over-borrowing' were basically *endogenous* market failures of over-liquid and under-regulated markets. Exogenous factors did play important reinforcing, but not primary, roles in them. The greatest irony of it all is that countries which embarked on investment-led 'over-borrowing', as in East Asia, have ended up (because of their huge corporate debt) with apparently worse crises than those in Latin America, such as Chile and Mexico, which engaged in consumption-led 'over-borrowing'.

The main avenues by which these LDCs have endogenized the crises (but by no means the only ones) are the 'over-borrowing' of risky finance, and the 'over-valuing' of real exchange rate and interest rates. I have argued that the first is associated with setting in motion the 'mania' dynamics via, among other things, exuberant expectations of future performance of the economy, and that this is fuelled by inadequate regulation and supervision of both the capital account and the domestic financial system. The second is associated with attracting foreign capital via distorted domestic incentives. The solution should come via 'opening up' the reform package, and its pragmatic implementation. So far, governments' withdrawal from prudent but effective regulation of the real and financial sides of the economy, in a highly liquid international and domestic environment, have not helped.

I would conclude, with Stiglitz, that

> deep, efficient, and robust financial systems are essential for growth and stability. But left to themselves, financial markets will not become deep, efficient, or robust. The government [should play] an essential role, both in directly overseeing and regulating the financial system and also in establishing the correct incentives to encourage prudential and productive behaviour. (1998, p. 2)

However, the long history of financial crises in LDCs makes it necessary to reinforce Stiglitz's argument with three additional points. The first is that particularly when in *an excess liquidity situation* financial markets have been 'left to themselves', that is precisely when they have 'not become deep, efficient, or robust'.[34] Second, excess liquidity has also tended to produce a strong 'diffusion of exuberance' pull on the domestic economy (to use Kindleberger's phrase), and this has led to a reinforcement of the lack of depth, efficiency and robustness of the financial markets. Third, regarding the issue of 'establishing the correct incentives to encourage prudential and productive behaviour', it has been in an excess liquidity environment that financial markets have needed the strongest *dis-incentives* to avoid the misallocation of financial resources; it is here that this market has most needed the 'discipline of the market'. Fortunately, financial market operators no longer need to jump out of windows; but we have moved to the other, absurd extreme, of having them sometimes magnificently recompensed for their *im*prudent and *un*productive behaviour – instead of committing suicide, now they are being allowed to get away with murder.[35]

Postscript

This paper was written during the first half of 1998, and the manuscript was delivered to the *Cambridge Journal of Economics* in July 1998; about a month before the Russian devaluation and default. As is now well-known, it was this crisis that exposed the vulnerability of the Brazilian economy, leading to a collapse in confidence and withdrawal of funds, and the January 1999 devaluation. Although it was dismissed by many observers at the time, particularly Brazilians, this paper was in fact one of the very few to identify the extent of the Brazilian economy's vulnerability to external shocks, and predict the likehood of an impending financial crisis. I have chosen not to re-write the paper for this publication, as I believe that much of its significance comes from its having been written at a particular point in time.

I have, however, written extensively on this subject since this paper was first published, in particular 'The magical realism of Brazilian economics: how to create a financial crisis by trying to avoid one', and 'The three routes to financial crises: the need for capital controls', in J. Eatwell and L. Taylor (eds), *International Capital Markets: Systems in Transition* (forthcoming, Oxford University Press, 2001); and 'A Brazilian-style Ponzi', in M. Baddeley and J. McCombie (eds), *What Financial Crisis?* (forthcoming, Palgrave, 2001). These three papers deal with the Brazilian crisis, but differ from this one in three ways. The first is that they were written with the benefit of hindsight; second, they tend to stress more the differences between the Mexican 1994 crisis and Brazil's 1999 one; and third, they place greater emphasis on the role of public finance in Brazil's crisis – the way the Brazilian economic authorities ended up walking into a public sector 'Ponzi' with their eyes wide open.

Appendix

Table 15.A1 Latin America and East Asia: some indicators of growth and macroeconomic performance before the East Asian crisis

	GDP growth % 1995–97	*Fiscal surplus % of GDP 1996*	*Current account % of exports 1996*[a]	*Real rate of exchange 1993 = 100*[e] *1996*[b]	*Contribution to GDP growth 1995–96*		
					Private consumption	*Investment*[b]	*Exports*
Latin America							
Argentina	2.2	(1.9)	(34.1)	120.3	(0.1)[c]	(1.1)	1.1
Brazil	***3.5***	***(3.8)***	***(57.3)***	***55.3***	***4.7***[c]	***1.3***	***0.2***
Chile	7.3	2.2	(15.4)	89.9	5.3	4.0	4.2
Colombia	3.7	(0.9)	(29.2)	81.6	3.0	1.4	1.1
Mexico	1.9	(0.5)	(5.4)	132.6	(3.1)	(2.1)	4.7
Peru	5.8	2.2	(40.8)	93.2	4.0	1.8	1.2
Average(6)	4.1	(0.5)	(30.4)	95.5	2.3	0.9	2.1
Average all LA (18)	3.7	(1.6)	(20.2)	96.0	3.3	0.6	2.3
Median all LA (18)	3.6	(1.9)	(15.1)	96.1	3.2	0.8	1.8
Asian NICs							
Indonesia	7.1	1.4	(15.3)	91.8	5.4	2.9	1.9
Korea	7.3	0.0	(14.9)	101.8	5.0	3.7	3.8
Malaysia	8.4	4.2	(8.8)[d]	97.1	n.a.	n.a.	n.a.
Thailand	5.2	1.6	(20.6)	106.2	4.3	4.0	3.5
Average (4)	***7.0***	***1.8***	***(14.5)***	***99.2***	***4.9***	***3.5***	***3.1***
Taiwan	6.1	0.2	6.1	103.6	n.a.	n.a.	n.a.
Singapore	7.7	8.4	9.2	104.9	2.2	3.7	n.a.
Average (6)	7.0	2.6	(7.1)	100.9	4.2	3.6	3.1

Notes: [a]1997 for Latin America; [b]1995 for Asian NICs; [c]includes public consumption; [d]1995; [e]1993 is used as base year because it is the year before the beginning of the 'REAL' Plan in Brazil.

Sources: See end of note 5.

Table 15.A2 Latin America and East Asia: net transfer of resources, private savings and investment before the East Asian crisis (as % of GDP, current prices)

	Net transfer of resources			*Investment*			*Private savings*			*Imports of consumer goods*
	1988–95 (1)	*1996 (2)*	*Change (2)–(1)*	*1988–95 (1)*	*1996 (2)*	*Change (2)–(1)*	*1988–95 (1)*	*1996–97 (2)*	*Change (2)–(1)*	*1992–96 (growth rate)*[e]
Latin America										
Argentina	(0.8)	1.4	2.2	19.5	23.4	3.9	18.7[a]	n.a.	n.a.	2.0
Brazil	***(1.0)***	***2.7***	***3.8***	***21.9***	***22.6***	***0.7***	***17.5***	***14.6***	***(2.9)***	***40.1***
Chile	0.2	2.8	2.6	24.4	28.9	4.6	19.4	17.7	(1.7)	17.0
Colombia	(2.1)	3.4	5.5	19.7	23.5	3.8	14.5	10.6	(3.9)	41.6
Mexico	0.9	(3.0)	(3.9)	18.2	15.3	(2.9)	13.5	16.1	2.6	3.9
Peru	3.2	6.2	3.0	23.2	27.6	4.4	19.7[b]	n.a.	n.a.	22.4
Average(6)	0.1	2.3	2.2	21.1	23.5	2.4	17.2	14.7	(2.5)	21.2
Average all LA (18)	1.8	1.6	(0.2)	19.0	20.3	1.3	14.2	13.6	(0.6)	15.5
Median all LA (18)	1.3	2.2	0.9	19.2	20.0	0.8	14.5	14.6	0.1	15.8
Asian NICs										
Indonesia	(1.0)	1.4	2.4	26.9	28.1	1.2	21.4	21.4	(0.0)	17.5
Malaysia	5.0	1.7	(3.3)	35.0	42.2	7.3	16.2	20.5	4.3	7.9
Korea	0.5	4.6	4.1	35.2	36.8	1.5	27.4	24.8	(2.5)	18.4
Thailand	8.6	6.4	(2.1)	38.4	40.8	2.4	22.3	21.4	(0.9)	13.0[c]
Average (4)	***3.3***	***3.5***	***0.2***	***33.9***	***37.0***	***3.1***	***21.8***	***22.0***	***0.2***	***14.2***
Singapore	0.8	(10.6)	(11.5)	34.2	36.5	2.3	33.2	37.3	4.2	10.0
Taiwan	(4.0)[d]	(3.2)	0.8	22.6	21.0	(1.6)	n.a.	n.a.	n.a.	n.a.
Average (6)	1.7	0.0	(1.6)	32.1	34.2	2.2	24.1	25.1	1.0	13.4

Notes: [a]1988–94; [b]1988–93; [c]1992–95; [d]refers to the financial account, 1989–95; [e]average annual rate of growth.

Sources: See end of note 5.

Table 15.A3 Latin America and East Asia: some indicators of growth and macroeconomic performance before the Mexican crisis

	GDP growth % 1991–93	*Fiscal surplus % of GDP 1993*	*Current account % of exports 1993*	*Real rate of exchange 1993[b] = 100 1993[a]*	*Contribution to GDP growth 1991–93* Private consumption	*Investment*	*Exports*
Latin America							
Argentina	9.0	1.4	(48.1)	60.8	7.9[a]	4.4	(0.2)
Brazil	1.1	(0.8)	0.0	71.0	1.4[a]	(0.3)	1.0
Chile	7.9	1.9	(17.6)	99.8	5.4	3.5	2.9
Colombia	3.8	0.3	(21.1)	97.8	1.8	4.8	2.0
Mexico	***3.3***	***0.3***	***(38.1)***	***58.3***	***3.0***	***1.8***	***1.0***
Peru	5.8	1.3	(48.5)	46.7	3.2	2.6	0.3
Average(6)	5.2	0.7	(28.9)	72.4	3.8	2.8	1.2
Average all LA (18)	3.9	(1.7)	(33.4)	98.6	3.8	2.2	2.1
Median all LA (18)	4.0	(0.7)	(19.7)	98.8	3.8	2.2	1.3
Asian NICs							
Indonesia	7.8	(0.7)	(5.2)	94.5	4.6	1.9	2.4
Malaysia	4.1	(2.6)	(5.7)	95.8	2.8	4.4	7.9
Rep. of Korea	6.7	(1.0)	1.1	120.5	3.5	2.3	1.8
Thailand	8.3	2.1	(13.4)	94.4	4.0	3.1	3.5
Average (4)	***6.7***	***(0.6)***	***(5.8)***	***101.3***	***3.7***	***2.9***	***3.9***
Singapore	8.0	14.3	4.6	116.1	3.3	3.3	n.a.
Taiwan	6.9	0.6	(13.4)	104.1	n.a.	n.a.	n.a.
Average (6)	7.0	2.1	(5.3)	104.2	3.6	3.0	3.9

Note:[a] Includes public consumption; [b]1987 is used as base year because it is the year before the beginning of the Mexican reforms.

Sources: See end of note 5.

Table 15.A4 *Latin America and East Asia: net transfer of resources, private savings and investment before the Mexican crisis (as % of GDP, current prices)*

	Net transfer of resources			Investment			Private savings			Imports of consumer goods
	1984–90 (1)	*1991–93 (2)*	*Change (2)–(1)*	*1984–90 (1)*	*1991–93 (2)*	*Change (2)–(1)*	*1984–90 (1)*	*1991–93 (2)*	*Change (2)–(1)*	*1987–94 (growth rate)*[e]
Latin America										
Argentina	(3.5)	1.8	5.3	17.3	19.8	2.5	22.8	15.3	(7.5)	38.1
Brazil	(3.2)	(0.8)	2.4	23.6	20.4	(3.2)	23.0	19.9	(3.1)	19.8
Chile	(1.8)	0.6	2.5	19.8	24.2	4.4	12.4	19.0	6.5	20.3
Colombia	(3.0)	(2.8)	0.2	18.8	17.8	(1.0)	14.8	15.7	0.9	19.2
Mexico	***(4.1)***	***5.0***	***9.1***	***16.7***	***19.6***	***3.0***	***26.1***	***13.8***	***(12.3)***	***48.3***
Peru	(0.4)	3.3	3.7	21.1	22.1	1.0	21.7	15.1	(6.6)	18.0
Average (6)	(2.7)	1.2	3.9	19.5	20.7	1.1	20.1	16.5	(3.7)	27.3
Average all LA (18)	0.7	2.6	1.9	18.0	18.9	0.9	13.5	12.0	(1.5)	17.1
Median all LA (18)	(0.2)	2.0	2.2	18.5	19.6	1.1	12.8	13.4	0.6	16.1
Asian NICs										
Indonesia	(1.5)	(0.7)	0.7	25.1	26.3	1.3	25.1[a]	29.1	4.0	12.6
Malaysia	(3.9)	11.4	15.2	28.1	36.9	8.8	18.3	14.2	(4.1)	16.6
Rep. of Korea	(3.6)	1.6	5.2	30.5	37.0	6.5	27.0	27.4	0.4	14.9
Thailand	4.6	8.4	3.8	30.7	40.1	9.4	20.7	23.2	2.6	20.6
Average (4)	***(1.1)***	***5.2***	***6.2***	***28.6***	***35.1***	***6.5***	***22.8***	***23.5***	***0.7***	***16.2***
Singapore	6.5	3.4	(3.1)	37.9	34.6	(3.3)	29.8	33.4	3.5	15.9
Taiwan	0.2	(2.2)	(2.4)	20.4	23.0	2.6	n.a.	n.a.	n.a.	n.a.
Average (6)	0.4	3.7	3.3	28.8	33.0	4.2	24.2	25.5	1.3	16.1

Note: [a]Includes public savings; [b]average annual rate of growth.

Sources: See end of note 5.

Table 15.A5 Latin America and East Asia: some indicators of growth and macroeconomic performance before the 1982 debt crisis

	GDP growth % 1979–81	*Fiscal surplus % of GDP 1981*	*Current account % of exports 1981*	*Real rate of exchange 1975 = 100 1981*	*Contribution to GDP growth 1979–81*		
					Private consumption	*Investment*	*Exports*
Latin America							
Argentina	(2.8)	(4.7)	(43.4)	59.7	(0.2)[a]	(1.5)	0.2
Brazil	3.0	(6.0)	(46.1)	103.4	1.5[a]	(0.2)	2.2
Chile	***6.8***	***(1.2)***	***(94.5)***	***65.4***	***5.5***	***2.4***	***1.1***
Colombia	3.2	(0.1)	(45.5)	79.0	1.3	1.7	(0.2)
Mexico	8.2	(6.8)	(57.4)	86.0	4.3	3.5	0.8
Peru	3.9	(4.9)	(43.0)	n.a.	3.0	3.1	(0.9)
Average(6)	3.7	(4.0)	(55.0)	78.7	2.6	1.5	0.5
Average all LA (18)	2.9	(5.1)	(45.4)	83.7	2.0	1.0	0.0
Median all LA (18)	3.1	(5.4)	(43.2)	78.9	2.3	0.1	(0.1)
Asian NICs							
Indonesia	6.8	(2.0)	(2.3)	112.1	5.3	5.9	n.a.
Malaysia	8.1	(14.9)	(17.9)	120.1	5.6	4.4	n.a.
Korea	7.1	(3.3)	(17.0)	84.0	4.9	1.6	n.a.
Thailand	5.6	(3.4)	(27.8)	99.5	3.0	(1.9)	n.a.
Average (4)	***6.9***	***(5.9)***	***(16.2)***	***103.9***	***4.7***	***2.5***	***n.a.***
Singapore	n.a.	0.7	(5.0)	124.2	n.a.	n.a.	n.a.
Taiwan	n.a.	n.a.	n.a.	n.a.	n.a.	n.a.	n.a.
Average (6)	6.9	(4.6)	(14.0)	108.0	4.7	2.5	n.a.

Note: [a]Includes public consumption.

Sources: See end of note 5.

Table 15.A6 Latin America and East Asia: net transfer of resources, private savings and investment before the 1982 debt crisis (as % of GDP, current prices)

	Net transfer of resources			*Investment*			*Private savings*			*Imports of consumer goods*
	1974–77 (1)	*1978–81 (2)*	*Change (2)–(1)*	*1974–77 (1)*	*1978–81 (2)*	*Change (2)–(1)*	*1974–77 (1)*	*1978–81 (2)*	*Change (2)–(1)*	*1976–81 (growth rate)*[c]
Latin America										
Argentina	(0.3)	0.6	0.8	24.8	23.8	(1.0)	n.a.	n.a.	(2.1)[a]	64.5
Brazil	3.5	1.6	(1.8)	22.8	23.1	0.4	19.1	16.2	(2.9)	(3.1)
Chile	***0.8***	***8.3***	***7.5***	***15.6***	***17.7***	***2.1***	***1.3***	***1.4***	***0.1***	***57.2***
Colombia	0.1	2.3	2.3	15.5	16.3	0.8	14.6	15.0	0.4	16.9
Mexico	1.5	1.9	0.4	20.5	24.0	3.5	12.2	17.5	5.3	34.8
Peru	5.3	(1.5)	(6.7)	22.9	25.0	2.1	n.a.	n.a.	8.8[a]	22.7
Average (6)	1.8	2.2	0.4	20.4	21.7	1.3	11.8	12.5	0.7	32.2
Average all LA (18)	3.5	3.2	(0.3)	20.6	21.8	1.2	14.9	14.8	(0.1)	18.1
Median all LA (18)	3.1	2.5	(0.6)	21.1	23.1	2.0	16.3	14.3	(2.0)	10.9
Asian NICs										
Indonesia	n.a.	(3.1)	n.a.	n.a.	24.2	n.a.	n.a.	n.a.	n.a.	0.0
Korea	3.4[d]	4.3	0.9	25.3	30.9	5.6	20.4	21.2	0.8	14.0
Malaysia	(0.1)	(0.7)	(0.6)	25.3	29.6	4.3	(1.5)	15.4	16.9	10.5
Thailand	4.1[b]	6.0	1.9	23.8	26.7	2.9	15.6	14.0	(1.5)	8.3
Average (4)	***2.5***	***1.6***	***(0.9)***	***24.8***	***27.8***	***3.0***	***11.5***	***16.9***	***5.4***	***8.2***
Singapore	15.6	13.8	(1.8)	n.a.	n.a.	n.a.	16.8	21.3	4.5	12.3
Average (6)	5.8	4.1	(1.7)	24.8	27.8	3.0	12.8	18.0	5.2	9.0

Notes: [a]Refers to notional savings; [b]1975–77; [c]average annual rate of growth; [d]1976–77.

Sources: See end of note 5.

Notes

* I should like to thank Daniel Hahn, Jan Kregel, Julie McKay, Jonathan Pincus, James Putzel, Ignês Sodré and especially Edna Armendáriz for their stimulating cooperation; two anonymous referees also made helpful comments. The title comes, of course, from Charles Kindleberger, whose writings have always been crucial to my thinking on international financial matters. Lastly, I am very grateful to Carlos Díaz-Alejandro, with whom I had frequent discussions on the 1982 crisis shortly before his sudden death. The usual caveats apply.

1. In a BBC television documentary in 1984 ('A Matter of Life and Debt'), a Latin American ex-finance minister explained in a graphic way the difference between a sellers' and a buyers' market in international finance. At the annual meetings of the IMF in the mid-1970s he often found himself queuing with other finance ministers outside the rooms of banks' executives; in the late 1970s it was the bankers who were doing the queuing outside his room.
2. See Demirguc-Kunt and Detragiache, 1997. What is also extraordinary is the increase in the amounts of funds involved; as Stiglitz remarks: 'Even after adjusting for inflation, the losses from the notorious savings and loan debacle in the US were several times larger than the losses experienced in the Great Depression. Yet when measured relative to GDP, this debacle would not make the list of the top 25 international banking crises since the early 1980s' (1998, p. 8).
3. One example of how 'elastic' the demand for funds in LDCs can be is that of CRAV, a Chilean sugar refinery, before 1982. This company enjoyed four-digit levels of effective protection until trade liberalization brought this crashing down to around 20%. As the production of sugar cane is not feasible in Chile, the company could only compete with imported refined sugar with high protection, as the cost of producing sugar from alternative inputs is much higher. In its need for new business, it 'diversified' into speculating in the futures markets of sugar, a particularly risky operation, especially for an inexperienced player. When the company inevitably went bust, it did so with foreign debts of about US$350 million (at 1998 prices). This was one of the many debts for which the Chilean government gave *ex post* guarantees, and later paid for. Episodes like this significantly exacerbate the 'adverse selection' problem of debt markets because entrepreneurs with excessively risky projects are encouraged to apply for loans in the knowledge that they will get all the up-side benefits but have limited down-side costs. In all, a hat-trick of failures: international financial markets, corporate governance and public policy.
4. As late as the first quarter of 1997 spreads were still being reduced even for loans to the two most vulnerable economies, Thailand and Indonesia; they reached a low of just 90 basis points (over US Treasury securities) in the former and 110 basis points in the latter.
5. In early 1982, BIS-reporting banks had an exposure/equity ratio to Latin America of 58%. In Britain, Lloyds' and Midland's ratios were 1.7 and 1.5, respectively. The average ratio for US banks was 1.2 (Manufacturers Hanover's was 2.3), while the nine leading US banks had an exposure-ratio

to Brazil and Mexico alone (both experienced moratoria countries) of 1.1. Shortly before this crisis Paul Volker, the then head of the FED, said: 'The impression I get from the data that I have reviewed is that the recycling process has not yet pushed exposure of either the borrowers or lenders to an unreasonable or unsustainable point in the aggregate, especially for [North] American banks ...' (quoted in Diaz-Alejandro, 1984, p. 21). Unless otherwise stated, the sources for all figures relating to the 1982 debt crisis are Palma (1995); for the 1994 Mexican crisis, Palma (1997); and for East Asia and Latin America since 1995, IMF (1997), BIS (1998), ECLAC (1998), O'Connell and Briozo (1998), and Palma (1998). Most figures for 1997 and 1998 are estimates.

6. These were Korea, Malaysia, Thailand, the Philippines and Indonesia. Between June 1994 and June 1997 (and not including important amounts of short-term debt) the foreign debt of these countries more than doubled (to US$275 billion). Recent estimates place Korea's total alone close to US$150 billion.
7. One peculiar aspect of lending to LDCs between 1990–96 is that, according to the IMF (1997), about half ended up accumulating reserves (US$575 billion). As most of these were recycled back to the international financial markets, they fed back into the same liquidity that made them possible in the first place. In the case of Brazil, by mid-1998 reserves had already reached US$75 billion, and should increase even further with the US$19 billion privatization of about 20% of Telebras' stock (it is expected that about a quarter of this amount will be made up of new capital inflows).
8. In East Asia, profit repatriation and debt servicing grew so quickly that in half of the countries of Appendix Table 15.A2 'net transfers' were already in decline *before* 1997 (Singapore, Malaysia and Thailand), and in two (Singapore and Taiwan) they were negative (but in Taiwan this was due to Taiwanese investment abroad).
9. A common theme in these works leading up to East Asia's 1997 crisis is how trade and financial liberalization are presented not only as necessary but sometimes even as sufficient condition for rapid and stable economic growth in LDCs. One illustration of the 'spin' put on the reform package is Deepak Lal's influential book (1984) where, among other things, Korea, of all countries, is presented as an example of 'virtual free trade', and Brazil in the 1970s (with a share of exports in GDP of only about 7%) as one of 'outward-looking' development. Stiglitz's move into the World Bank has brought much-needed fresh air into the thinking of the 'Washington consensus'; before his arrival the corridors of the international institutions of Washington were not used to statements like: 'Even with the buildup of vulnerability, it is unlikely that the [East Asian] crisis could have occurred without the *liberalization of the capital account*' (1988, p. 12); or that 'only an ideologue would claim that *but for their system of close government and business cooperation* [East Asian] countries would have grown even faster' (*ibid.*, p. 26; all italics in the original).
10. In Brazil, for example, when inflation was stopped dead in its tracks in 1994, consumption of refrigerators grew by 45%, that of TV sets by 43%, and video cassettes by 51% (Dornbush, 1997, p. 6; all figures refer to quan-

tities). For the extraordinary increase in imports of consumer goods, see Tables 15.A2, 4 and 6.

11. Studies of underpricing in privatization of public assets are abundant. See, for example, Marcel, 1998.
12. Venezuela is an extreme example of this 'thinness' and volatility. In the year starting in September 1996 just one stock (an electricity company) accounted for 39% of the amount traded, and two companies (electricity and telephone) were responsible for one-third of all capitalization; the top five stocks accounting for 60% of both accounts. In terms of volatility, in 1996 the stock-market index went up by 136% which, according to the *Financial Times* (21 October 1997), made it the top 'performer' in the world. In the following nine months, it went up again by 56%, to fall by nearly 60% in the next ten months (*Economist*, 25 July 1998). In turn, in Mexico the share index rose 10-fold between 1989 and early 1994, then moved erratically, to collapse spectacularly in December; and in Brazil, the most important stock, Telebras, went up (in dollar terms) by over 130% between November 1996 and July 1997, to fall by nearly half between then and mid-1998.
13. In Chile, Pinochet's bail-out operation took the form of re-nationalizing the recently privatized banks (and their massive bad debt); I suppose one could call this policy ('profits are private–losses are social') the 'Chicago Road to Socialism'.
14. These banks needed recapitalization because companies owned by Suharto's family and cronies had not paid back large loans; however, this being Suharto's Indonesia, much of the new money was then channelled back to the same companies that had drained the resources of these banks in the first place. As the then President of the Indonesian Central Bank famously said, 'countries like ours are not known for their strict bank supervision'.
15. Meanwhile, the amount of non-performing loans nearly doubled every year, to peak at a rate of growth of 170% in 1994, when they represented an amount equivalent to about 10% of GDP. See Kregel (1998b).
16. Neftci (1998) gives revealing examples of how the rapid development of derivatives has made the issue of transparency significantly more complicated, particularly by allowing banks to place an increasing amount of commitments 'off' balance sheets. One common form of intermediation by Asian financial institutions was the issue of bonds through their offshore operations; the issue of these bonds grew to US$25 billion in 1995 and US$43 billion in 1996. Offshore funds operated by Korean investment banks alone lost over US$1 billion in 1997.
17. According to IMF statistics, between 1982 and 1987 LDCs paid US$700 billion in debt servicing, US$260 billion in principal and $440 billion in interest; and despite these payments, and despite the fact that only a very small amount of 'new' money was lent during this period, LDCs' long-term debt almost doubled – from U$550 billion to US$1 trillion. In Mexico, the rescue package, by transforming risky *peso-denominated* private debt into secure *dollar-denominated* public debt, in just one year nearly doubled the relative size of the foreign debt (from 35% of GDP in 1994 to 65% in 1995). In turn, in East Asia, part of the conditionality of bail-outs was to allow

foreign capital to operate more freely within these economies; in Korea, for example, it can now have much-coveted full ownership of firms in the real sector and a substantial share in firms operating in the domestic financial market.

18. In a speech given in Chile before the 1982 crisis, Walter Robicheck, then Director of the Western Hemisphere Department of the IMF, praised the government for not meddling with the foreign debt of the private sector (Robicheck, 1981). In relative terms, this debt was already one of the highest in the Third World. Only months later, the private sector was falling into arrears, and they and the IMF (and also, presumably, Mr Robicheck) were telling the Chilean government that the only way forward was through *ex post* government guarantees. Chile's private sector telling international banks that the only way to get their money back was through the government is reminiscent of the tango *Mano a mano*: 'I believe I've already paid you for all those favours that I've received, but if any small debt has unintentionally been forgotten, why don't you charge it to the account of the fool you've got now'.
19. One such 'spin' is that on the 'Tesobonos' in Mexico. One of the conditions for the IMF/US bail-out was their convertibility. This bond was *peso-denominated*, but exchange-rate indexed, which is very different from being *dollar-denominated*. Instead, the 'Tesobono' holders were bailed out directly in dollars, while the Mexican government incurred a huge dollar-debt. As Taylor emphasized, '[t]he widely circulated assertion that Tesobonos were dollar-denominated was a follow-up public relations move by the US financial community to cover its players who had guessed badly wrong in increasing their Mexican exposure' (1998, p. 24).
20. Well after the discovery that a large proportion of Barings' profits was due to the falsified accounts of Nick Leeson, Barings' senior employees – including those responsible for the supervisory failure that brought the bank down – forced the bank's new owners to calculate their annual bonuses based on the fake profit accounts.
21. Keynes once said that if a customer owes (say) £1 million to a bank, it is the customer's problem. But if the debt is £100 million, it is the bank's problem. If he were alive today he would probably add that if the debt is US$200 billion (which is what Brazil and Russia owe today), then that would be *everybody's* problem!
22. In Argentina, for example, between 1976 and 1981 the dollar value of these imports grew at an average annual rate of 65%; that is, it grew 12-fold, with imports of durable consumer goods increasing 30-fold. In relative terms, these imports grew from a low of just 3% of exports of goods to 25%.
23. It changed from a surplus of US$4 billion in 1987, the year before the beginning of Salinas' reforms, to a deficit of US$21 billion in 1992; that is, a negative switch of US$25 billion, equivalent to 12% of GDP.
24. Although East Asian governments did eventually convert to the 'Lawson doctrine' in the early 1990s – the belief that governments should keep their own 'fundamentals' in order, but should not interfere with those of the private sector (i.e., the domestic and external private sectors should sort out their problems by themselves) – they did not take it so literally as did governments in Latin America.

25. The most important ones are different 'sequencing' in trade and financial liberalization, different types of capital inflow, and different types of borrower.
26. For example, owing to a much higher degree of export sophistication and of production integration, exports in East Asia are more import-intensive. Therefore, devaluations are not at all equal to net competitive gains. Also, East Asia is being much more affected by its own regional recession because of its large intra-regional trade (approximately half as opposed to Latin America's one-fifth). Also, among other factors, the much larger presence of subsidiaries of foreign multinationals in Mexico than, say Korea, means that in the former the corporate sector (particularly the large one) found it easier to obtain much needed finance for its operations after the crisis.
27. Net inflows had already increased before 1995, from a low –US$12 billion in 1989, to US$8 billion in 1994; then they jumped to US$30 billion *in just one year*, to increase again to US$33 billion in 1996. Even during the extraordinary year of 1997 they reached US$26 billion. The aggregate figure for these three years is equivalent to 61% of goods exports during this period, and the turnaround between 1989 and 1996 to 80% of 1996 exports.
28. For example, in 1997 the Banco Banmerindus, owned by the Minister for Commerce and Industry, went bust in an extremely 'untransparent' way, leaving a shortfall of about US$5 billion. Following the Latin American tradition, the government took over all this bad debt without ever doing a proper investigation; then, it sold what was left of the bank (the 'transparent' part) to the Hongkong & Shanghai Banking Corporation.
29. Between December 1994 and December 1997, the public accounts deteriorated by an amount equivalent to 5.4% of GDP. One self-propelling cause was the service of the public debt at such high interest rates (the latter grew by 37%, to US$241 billion in 1995–97).
30. The overall turnaround is from a surplus of US$6 billion in 1992 to a deficit of US$34 billion in 1997 (that of the trade account was of US$27 billion). Large as these deficits were, inflows have been so large that foreign reserves more than doubled (to US$75 billion) from December 1994 to mid-1998.
31. This figure refers to ECLAC's calculation. Dornbush (1997) provides alternative estimates (with similar results) and a discussion of whether this large appreciation of the real did in fact produce an overvalued currency
32. One of the problems is that increases in domestic interest rates doubled the net amount of foreign exchange leaving the country in the form of interest payments on foreign capital invested in Brazil in just the first two months of 1998 (from US$578 million to US$1.1 billion).
33. The problem of the public accounts is not just one of tax collection, or debt servicing, but also one of continuous refinancing, as most of the domestic public debt has a very short-term maturity structure: US$190 billion's worth of Treasury and Central Bank debt was due to mature in the first five months of 1998 alone!
34. Although, given the extraordinary real-world complexities, I do not believe that in economics there is such a thing as a necessary or sufficient condition, regarding financial crises, excess liquidity is probably as far as it gets.
35. It was widely reported in the financial press that, well after the outbreak of the East Asian crisis, those working from the City of London alone received annual bonuses of well over £1 billion.

References

BIS (1998) *The Transmission of Monetary Policy in Emerging Market Economies*, Basle, BIS.

Broughton, J. M. (1997) 'From Suez to Tequila: The IMF as Crisis Manager', IMF Working Paper, WP/97/90.

Chang, H.-J. (1998) 'The misunderstood crisis', *World Development*, vol. 26, no. 8.

Demirguc-Kunt, S. and Detragiache, R. (1997) 'The Determinants of Banking Crises: Evidence from Developing and Developed Countries', IMF Working Paper WP/97/106.

Díaz-Alejandro, C. F. (1984) 'Latin American debt: I don't think we are in Kansas any more', *Brookings Papers on Economic Activity*, 2.

Dornbush, R. (1997) 'Brazil's Incomplete Stabilization and Reform', mimeo.

ECLAC (1998) 'Impacto de la Crisis Asiática en América Latina', mimeo.

Greenspan, A. (1997) 'Statement before the US House of Representatives Committee on Banking and Financial Services', 13 November, Washington DC.

IIF (1998) *Capital Flows to Emerging Markets*, Washington, IIF.

IMF (1997) *World Economic Outlook: Interim Assessment*, December.

Kindleberger, C. P. (1978) *Manias, Panics, and Crashes: A History of Financial Crises*, New York, Basic Books.

Kindleberger, C. P. (1984) 'The 1929 Depression and Latin America – from the outside', in Thorp, R. (ed.), *Latin America in the 1930s*, London, Macmillan.

Kregel, J. A. (1998a) 'East Asia is not Mexico: The Difference between Balance of Payments Crises and Debt Deflations', mimeo.

Kregel, J. A. (1998b) 'The East Asian Financial Crisis and its Global Implications', UNCTAD, mimeo.

Kregel, J. A. (1998c) 'Yes, "It" Did Happen Again – A Minsky Crisis Happened in Asia', Jerome Levy Institute, NY, mimeo.

Lal, D. (1984) *The Poverty of 'Development Economics'*, London, Institute of Economics Affairs.

Marcel, M. (1998) 'Public Finance and the Privatisation of State-owned Enterprises: The Case of Chile 1985–89', Cambridge, mimeo.

Marcel, M. and Palma, J. G. (1988) 'Third World debt and its effects on the British economy: a Southern view on economic mismanagement in the North', *Cambridge Journal of Economics*, vol. 12, no. 3, and *El Trimestre Económico*, April 1990.

McKinnon, R. I. and Pill, H. (1997) 'Credible economic liberalizations and over-borrowing', *The American Economic Review*, May.

Meller, P. (1984) 'Elementos útiles e inútiles en la literatura económica sobre recesiones y depresiones', *Colección Estudios CIEPLAN*, no. 12, March.

Neftci, S. N. (1998) 'FX Short Positions, Balance Sheets, and Financial Turbulence: An Interpretation of the Asian Financial Crisis', Center for Economic Policy Analysis, New School for Social Research, mimeo.

O'Connell, A, and Briozo, S. (1998) 'Brasil: Informe de Coyuntura Económica', Buenos Aires, CEI, April.

Palma, J. G. (1995) 'UK lending to the Third World from the 1973 oil shock to the 1980s debt crisis', in Arestis, P. and Chick, V. (eds), *Finance, Development and Structural Change: a Post-Keynesian Perspective*, Aldershot, Edward Elgar Publishing.

Palma, J. G. (1997) 'On the economics of magical realism: is 'more savings and more transparency' really the main lesson of the 1994 Mexican crisis?', *Cambridge Journal of International Affairs*, vol. XI, no. 1, Summer.

Palma, J. G. (1998) 'An overview of Brazil's economy', in *Regional Surveys of the World: South America, Central America and the Caribbean*, London, Europa Publications.

Robichek, W. (1981) 'Alternativas de políticas financieras en economias pequeñas y abiertas al exterior', *Estudios Monetarios* VII, Banco Central de Chile.

Singh, A. (1998) 'Asian Capitalism and the Financial Crisis', Cambridge, mimeo.

Stiglitz J. E. (1994) 'The role of the state in financial markets', *Proceedings of the World Bank Annual Conference on Development Economics*, Washington DC.

Stiglitz, J. E. (1998) 'Sound Finance and Sustainable Development in Asia', Manila, mimeo.

Summers, L. (1998) US Government Press Release, 2286, 9 March.

Taylor, L. (1998) 'Lax Public Sector, Destabilizing Private Sector: Origins of Capital Market Crises', UNCATD, mimeo.

Index